Biblical Boundaries *of* Forgiveness

Biblical Boundaries *of* Forgiveness

A Biblical and Ethical Study of of Forgiveness as It Relates to Repentance, Reconciliation, and Justice

VEE CHANDLER

WIPF *&* STOCK · Eugene, Oregon

BIBLICAL BOUNDARIES OF FORGIVENESS
A Biblical and Ethical Study of Forgiveness as It Relates
to Repentance, Reconciliation, and Justice

Wipf & Stock
An Imprint of Wipf and Stock Publishers
199 W. 8th Ave., Suite 3
Eugene, OR 97401

www.wipfandstock.com

PAPERBACK ISBN: 978-1-6667-1469-2
HARDCOVER ISBN: 978-1-6667-1470-8
EBOOK ISBN: 978-1-6667-1471-5

NOVEMBER 10, 2021 11:20 AM

This book is dedicated to my remarkable friend Matthew Byrd.

Contents

Preface

THERE HAVE BEEN THREE periods of time in my life in which I desperately wanted to live: when my two daughters were young; when I was writing my dissertation on the subject of the atonement; and now, as I write on the subjects of repentance, forgiveness, and reconciliation. When my daughters were young I felt that I was the only one who could love, discipline, teach, and encourage them as needed. When I was writing my dissertation, I felt that I really had something to say that had not quite been said before. Now, with a broken relationship and a broken heart, I need to write—to be heard—to finish.

There is nothing in this book that has not been said before. It is based on Scripture, the work of philosophers who indeed think deeply, and my own desperate need to get it right. I am not claiming to have it all right, but I am claiming to have tried. I have searched the Scriptures, searched my soul, and researched the writings of both theologians and philosophers. This book is the result of that effort, and it is my hope that it will bring clarity, healing, and peace to many who also search.

As Alice MacLachlan says in her PhD dissertation, "The Nature and Limits of Forgiveness," "In our own lives, the question of forgiveness usually arises following some kind of injury from wrongdoing, be it an injury we ourselves have sustained or one that we have inflicted."[1] Those for whom this is the case know that easy assumptions about forgiveness should be challenged. They also know that those who speak of forgiveness should do so from the perspective of the wounded, or it is likely to do more harm than good.[2] My hope is that this book will help those who have already been harmed by "easy assumptions" and well-meaning Christian counsel. As stated in "Forgiveness in Challenging

---

1. MacLachlan, "Forgiveness," 1.
2. Burns, "Forgiveness," 147.

Circumstances" by Steven Burns, "An adequate theology of forgiveness will . . . steer clear of shallow celebrations of the merits of forgiveness which pay no regard to its complexities and costs, or which bypass the real difficulties encountered in various forms of abuse and their legacies."[3] Above all, what should not be bypassed is the biblical model.

This book is written for the wounded who struggle with the biblical concepts of repentance, forgiveness, and reconciliation after having been abandoned, betrayed, or worse.

---

3. Burns, "Forgiveness," 159.

Acknowledgements

THIS BOOK IS THE result of years of researching the writings of scholars, both theologians and philosophers, who write on the subject of forgiveness. Part of the book's uniqueness and value is that it is a compilation of the work of many as opposed to the thinking of one person.

Introduction

Thesis, Organization, and Contribution

THESIS

HISTORY CAN BE SEPARATED into three periods concerning the evolution of thought related to the practice of interpersonal forgiveness. (1) "The ancient world, whether Jewish or Gentile, gave little thought to the ethics of forgiveness. Plutarch and Seneca alone among pre-Christian writers discussed forgiveness and even Aristotle did not list forgiveness as a virtue."[1] In the Hebrew Scriptures God is forgiving, but he forgives those who repent of their sin and turn to him. No other basis for forgiveness is ever suggested, whether it be from God or between humans.

(2) Throughout the two millennia since Christ and until very recently, thought, discussion, and critical reflection about forgiveness principally took place within the context of Christian theology rather than the secular world.[2] The understanding of interpersonal forgiveness changed as a result of the influence of the Christian gospel. Christians believed forgiveness to be integral to the Christian gospel and an attribute of God that they ought to model in their relations with other people. Forgiveness thus became established as a moral virtue in spite of differences of opinion as to when it should be practiced.[3] (3) However, "the most significant contribution to recent understanding of forgiveness has come, not from Christian theologians, but from philosophers and psychologists who have

---

1. A. Bash, *Forgiveness and Christian Ethics*, 174.

2. A. Bash, *Forgiveness and Christian Ethics*, 174–75.

3. A. Bash, *Forgiveness and Christian Ethics*, 174.

generally sought to work from a nonreligious standpoint."[4] This fact has
resulted in new definitions for forgiveness from the fields of philosophy
and psychology, which often limit it to an internal and unilateral act. As
these new definitions gained influence in the church the result has been a
distortion of the biblical definition of forgiveness, as well as its insistence
upon repentance prior to forgiveness and its teaching that repentance
and forgiveness lead to reconciliation. Consequently in today's Christian
thought one finds a great deal of disagreement concerning how forgiveness is understood. In *Forgiveness and Truth* Alistair McFadyen says:

> Forgiveness is at the very heart of Christian faith and practice,
> centered as it is in God's gracious act of forgiveness and rec-
> onciliation. That much might be considered unarguable. But
> how forgiveness is to be understood—its precise relationship
> to reconciliation, judgment, justice, penitence, and confession;
> whether it is conditional or unconditional; whether an act or
> a process—on all of these matters, one finds a great deal of ar-
> gument. . . . [In other words] the interpretation of forgiveness
> within the Christian faith is neither unarguable nor uniform.
> Unsurprisingly, the range and subtlety of divergent Christian
> views of forgiveness do not inform media representations of
> Christian faith or the Church. Whether in serious journalism,
> the melodrama of soap opera, or the satire of column, cartoon
> or comedy show, one finds remarkable uniformity: Christianity
> obliges victims to instantaneous and unconditional forgiveness,
> where forgiveness is a kind of forgetting—acting as though no
> wrong had been done—which also involves a letting go of the
> truth of the situation. . . . It is this widespread popular view of
> Christianity . . . that makes this kind of Christianity unfit for
> handling the realities of a broken and damaged world. . . . This
> sense of forgiveness serves as a sign of Christianity's overly be-
> nign, and unrealistic . . . optimism; its moral offensiveness; or its
> lack of psychological, political, and interpersonal wisdom and
> insight. . . . Is forgiveness a synonym for forgetting or, worse,
> does it require pretense that nothing has happened? . . . [This
> kind of] forgiveness is impotent to bring about genuine recon-
> ciliation or healing . . . which seems to involve a more definite
> and more truthful accounting of the past.[5]

4. A. Bash, *Forgiveness and Christian Ethics*, 174–75.

5. McFadyen, "Introduction," 1, 2, 4.

Interestingly, it is the philosophical community that objects to this "impotent" distortion of Christian forgiveness rampant in the church today. As previously stated, until recently little has been written among moral philosophers about the subject of forgiveness. Joram Haber, in his book *Forgiveness*, points out that

> one reason [that little has been written until recently] is that forgiveness is part of a set of concerns on the role of feelings in the moral life. Traditionally, moral philosophy has placed great emphasis on such concepts as "right," "wrong," and "duty"—concepts applicable primarily to actions. . . . The idea that there is a duty to have feelings has always met with skepticism; for duties are generally taken to concern that which can be performed at will, while feelings are regarded as passions—states beyond the control of the will. . . . There is [still] a dearth of literature on the subject, . . . [probably because] forgiveness is often thought of as a *Christian* virtue and thus outside the purview of secular philosophy.[6]

This book attempts to correct the inadequacy, inaccuracy, and unbiblicalness of most current teaching/preaching in the church on the subject of forgiveness and to embrace the valuable contribution of Christian philosophers on the subject of the ethics of forgiveness. The background for this book is my personal study of the atonement that began because of moral, logical, and exegetical concerns about the penal substitution theory of the atonement. My dissertation, *Victorious Substitution: A Theory of the Atonement*, was completed in 2004. That effort in turn led to questions concerning interpersonal forgiveness and its relationship to repentance and reconciliation. Is reconciliation with God the model for reconciliation between persons? Should human forgiveness be different from God's forgiveness? In answering these questions it must be recognized that "a Christian theological system is . . . an integrated web of doctrine; and the ground for believing some doctrines to be true is often that they follow from others which in turn have their justification in considerations outside the theological system."[7] Conclusions therefore are developed partly from other theological doctrines (in this case atonement) and partly in consideration of moral theory. Each position is defended partly by adducing doctrinal claims and partly by adducing moral claims. I am aware that opinions may vary about many of the theological

---

6. Haber, *Forgiveness*, 1, 3.

7. Swinburne, *Responsibility and Atonement*, 121.

issues with which this book is concerned. Two or more rival positions exist within Christian tradition for each issue.[8] Therefore, the reader will need to *think*—to consider, to ponder, in order to *work* through these issues for himself.

ORGANIZATION

This book will examine the nature and value of forgiveness first from a biblical perspective, establishing biblical definitions and the biblical model for the practice. Forgiveness will then be considered from a moral point of view. Because forgiveness is an ethical subject a book written about it cannot help being a study of ethics,[9] and any so-called Christian teaching or practice that is not morally ethical should be questioned. Sermonizing will be avoided, for the purpose of this book is not to lead people into repentance, forgiveness, or reconciliation. That is the duty of the preacher or counselor. The author's hope is that a full examination of these subjects will inform the reader as to the *nature* of genuine repentance, genuine forgiveness, and genuine reconciliation. However, it is hoped that the reader may be relieved of unrealistic expectations and false guilt concerning the reluctance or inability to forgive in the absence of repentance and/or be challenged by the true nature of repentance.

This study is divided into three parts. Part I examines the question, When does God forgive? If God does not forgive everyone all of the time then other questions arise. When does God not forgive? Why does God forgive? Why does God not forgive? What are God's feelings when he forgives? What are God's feelings when he does not forgive? What is God's wrath? What is God's mercy? The study attempts to answer these questions by first defining terms according to their scriptural usage. The terms to be examined are *repentance, forgiveness, reconciliation*, and the *wrath of God*. Once terms are defined by their scriptural usage the relationship between repentance, forgiveness, and reconciliation is examined according to the biblical model.

Part II examines the question, When, according to Scripture, are God's people instructed to forgive and why? The harder but crucial questions follow concerning interpersonal forgiveness. Is forgiveness to be unconditional or should forgiveness wait on repentance? Is anger and

8. Swinburne, *Responsibility and Atonement*, 121.

9. Kolnai, "Forgiveness," 91.

resentment at injustice unacceptable, justifiable, or desirable? Should wrongs be forgotten or in the interest of truth remembered? If forgiveness is a free gift are reparations appropriate? Should repentance always lead to reconciliation? In attempting to answer these and other questions Part II examines exegetically all scriptural texts related to interpersonal forgiveness as well as passages concerning how God's people should relate to their enemies and to evil persons.

Part III examines the ethics of forgiveness from a moral and philosophical point of view. The same questions are considered from logical, ethical, and moral perspectives in an attempt to establish a model for forgiveness that is based on the biblical definitions of Part I and the exegetical conclusions of Part II, as well as the ethical considerations and explanations of Part III. In this process, contemporary definitions of forgiveness are compared to the biblical meaning. The place of resentment and anger over personal injury is examined from a logical and ethical perspective. The morality of retribution and the need for justice are related to the practice of forgiveness from both an ethical and biblical perspective. The place of remembering or non-remembering is also considered in the practice of forgiveness and reconciliation. A model for forgiveness and reconciliation is thus established based on the biblical pattern and defended from a logical and ethical perspective.

At the end of each chapter are several study questions (answers can be found in Appendix B). The concepts in this book are not difficult, but there are a lot of them, and grasping each concept requires both biblical knowledge and personal reflection. Study questions are intended to help the reader approach the book systematically, helping him or her reflect on each section before proceeding to the next. If this process is followed, the reader will not only comprehend the author's conclusions but will be well prepared to draw his or her own. Clarity is the goal.

CONTRIBUTION

The contribution of this book is that, with Scripture as its basis, it attempts to combine ethical and theological arguments concerning the practice of forgiveness and reconciliation. Philosophers do not cite scriptural passages in making their observations and arguments concerning morality and ethics. Although scriptural ideas may often be the foundation for their ethical thinking, philosophers do not present Scripture as authoritative. Therefore a Christian may find himself in agreement with a philosopher's point of view, but nevertheless find it somehow insufficient or not fully convincing. On the other hand, theologians who are scholars may accept Scripture as authoritative and base their beliefs on Scripture, but their writings often do not include scriptural exegesis. They largely talk to each other, and since they all know Scripture as well as the issues involved in the interpretation of each relevant passage, detailed scriptural references are unnecessary. So, as with the work of philosophers, the Christian may once again not be able to find the work of theologians sufficient or completely convincing. He may be plagued by thoughts such as, "But what about this verse or that verse that appears to contradict their viewpoint or even what seems practical, logical, or moral?"

This book is written, then, not to engage in the philosophical or theological discussions. It is intended for those who study the Bible believing it to be truth from God that serves as a "light to their path." Such persons have a strong need to search out Scripture, to decide for themselves what it teaches concerning how they should conduct their lives. Because this book is written for such persons each Scripture passage is examined before conclusions are reached. No other book in print (of which the author is aware) written on the subject of forgiveness considers in combination every Scripture passage, the arguments of theological scholars, and the arguments of philosophers. The author believes the inclusion of the work of exegetes, philosophers, and theologians presents a thorough and convincing model for the practice of forgiveness. May it serve those who "hunger and thirst for righteousness" (Matt 5:6), especially those who do so having been abandoned or betrayed.

1

Reconciliation

A Worthy, if Illusory, Goal

INTRODUCTORY COMMENTS

THIS BOOK WILL EMPHASIZE that, according to the biblical model of forgiveness, the purpose of which is reconciliation, forgiveness is preceded
by repentance and followed by reconciliation. Any model of forgiveness
that entails the restoration of relationship must insist that forgiveness
requires repentance. In such a model (in which reconciliation follows
forgiveness) a change of heart on the part of the wrongdoer is a prerequisite for reconciliation because relationships are by definition reciprocal.[1]
This model also requires that forgiveness entail the removal of the offense, because when a debt is forgiven nothing is then held against the
wrongdoer, and therefore no barrier exists to reconciliation. Forgiveness
is not the writing off of a debt but its elimination.[2] Forgiveness, when
reconciliation is expected, looks forward and not just backward at what
happened in the past; it is the beginning of something new.[3] Reconciliation means rebuilding and restructuring a broken relationship, but it
does not necessarily follow that the relationship will be the same as

---

1. Benn, "Forgiveness and Loyalty," 373.
2. Wilson, "Why Forgiveness Requires Repentance," 534.
3. MacLachlan, "Forgiveness," 85.

1

before it became damaged. Reconciliation, therefore, involves forgiveness following repentance coupled with a restored relationship appropriate to the situation of the parties after forgiveness.[4] The level of commitment to well-being and to future relationship will vary according to past relationship as well as according to the forgiver's sense of what is appropriate.[5] For example, a divorced couple may forgive and be reconciled but not necessarily marry each other again. They may simply part ways in peace.

Vincent Brümmer's book *What Are We Doing When We Pray?* distinguishes different kinds of relationships that can become broken: controlling relationships, contractual relationships, and relationships of love (see the discussion in chapter 6). Each broken relationship is healed in a different way. The discussion that follows is concerned with broken *love* relationships. Because the people with whom one is most intimate are the ones who cause the most hurt, intimate relationships are the ones for which reconciliation is both the most difficult and the most desirable. Reconciliation is especially difficult because in intimate relationships "moral injuries tend not to be just ordinary injustices but also *betrayals*."[6] Therefore "in love relationships anytime a wound is not addressed by repentance and forgiveness the quality of love in the relationship begins to deteriorate."[7] "To commit oneself to a lifetime relationship with another should surely involve a prior commitment to confront, repent, and forgive."[8]

In what follows, every effort is made to clarify and establish the fullest meaning of true repentance and true forgiveness. This chapter attempts to clarify the meaning of true reconciliation as the goal of repentance and forgiveness. What is the fullest meaning of this term and how and when is it achieved? Reconciliation can only be achieved if both repentance and forgiveness take place in the fullest sense. Then the stage is set for relationship to begin anew with the hope of the restoration of the fullness of love and trust that existed before the abandonment or betrayal.

---

4. A. Bash, *Forgiveness and Christian Ethics*, 25.

5. MacLachlan, "Forgiveness," 107.

6. Murphy and Hampton, *Forgiveness and Mercy*, 17.

7. Gulliford, "Healing of Relationships," 118.

8. Gulliford, "Healing of Relationships," 118.

LAMENTATION

One should not expect that this full restoration takes place quickly. The place or role of lament must be included in the process of reconciliation. As Christopher Wright says in *The God I Don't Understand*:

> Lament is not only allowed in the Bible; it is modeled for us in abundance. . . . It surely cannot be accidental that in the divinely inspired book of Psalms there are more psalms of lament and anguish than of joy and thanksgiving. . . . The language of lament is seriously neglected in the church. . . . There is an implicit pressure to stifle our real feelings because we are urged, by pious merchants of emotional denial, that we ought to have "faith" (as if the moaning psalmists didn't). . . . Lament is the voice of pain . . . the voice of faith struggling to live with . . . questions and . . . suffering.[9]

Before restoration can take place and the victim can actually hope for and believe in the possibility of reconciliation he must have time for lament, time to grieve, time to protest, and time to express his pain to God and perhaps others. Many have testified that in times of abandonment or betrayal they live in the psalms. The words of the psalms minister to the brokenhearted by voicing their pain and anger. Katongole and Rice in their book *Reconciling All Things* say, "Lament in Scripture teaches us that there is nothing romantic about reconciliation."[10] A victim must recognize the truth of the rupture of the relationship as well as the depth of his captivity in sorrow. There are no easy or fast ways out. "To lament is to become gripped by the truth of the rupture and the high cost of seeking reconciliation. To learn to lament is to be broken."[11] But it is also the only path toward healing.

> If lament is a way of dying, it is also a path to being raised into something new. To the extent that we do not experience a shattering, something new cannot break in. The relationship between lament and hope is crucial. . . . It is crucial to remember that lament is not despair or a cry into a void. Lament is a cry directed *to God*. . . . Through lament we come to that hard place of knowing that we cannot *achieve* reconciliation.[12]

9. C. Wright, *God I Don't Understand*, 51–53.
10. Katongole and Rice, *Reconciling All Things*, 87.
11. Katongole and Rice, *Reconciling All Things*, 87.
12. Katongole and Rice, *Reconciling All Things*, 88.

Victims must refuse the consolations of false hope.[13] Katongole and Rice also argue that "their hope [must be in] repentance and conversion," saying that, "Reconciliation is possible only through that gift the New Testament calls—*metanoia*—a turning the other way, a transformation."[14] Victims must refuse to embrace cheap hope but at the same time embrace the significance of small steps toward reconciliation, recognizing that the only way that broken love relationships can be transformed into new ways of life together is *slowly*.[15]

But the more difficult question is what can make victims *want* life together with those who have crushed them.[16] The answer is found in the renewal of love based on the sorrow and repentance of the once-loved (or perhaps still-loved) offender. To expect victims to want life together with those who have wounded them beyond what they could bear is reasonable only if they are fully convinced that the loved one is genuinely sorry and has really changed.

THE BIBLICAL MODEL

The model of repentance and forgiveness presented in this book attempts to adhere to the biblical pattern. The following comments summarize what must, according to this pattern, take place prior to reconciliation.

First there is the offense, a deep wound of abuse, abandonment, or betrayal by a close trusted loved one. Pain and grief follow, ensuring that the victim will never be the same.

The victim should then forswear retaliation but at the same time acknowledge to himself his own resentment and anger as he emerges from his pain. These emotions should be honestly expressed to God in lamentation and prayer. Generally, but depending on the circumstances, a statement of the wrongdoing should be made to the offender as a guard against condonation and as a first attempt to establish truth. The victim thereby refuses to condone the wrongdoing and takes a moral stand. In time, as he is able, the victim should seek and work to become willing to forgive and be reconciled should the loved one repent. As a general rule he should also let his willingness to forgive be known. During this

---

13. Katongole and Rice, *Reconciling All Things*, 95.

14. Katongole and Rice, *Reconciling All Things*, 101.

15. Katongole and Rice, *Reconciling All Things*, 101.

16. Katongole and Rice, *Reconciling All Things*, 102.

process the victim should accept the fact that reconciliation may not be possible in spite of his desire for it or his willingness to forgive. This is because it takes two to have a relationship. In time the victim should let go of the outcome and move on with his life. He should not dwell on the pain and injustice of what has happened. (This is easier said than done. Time is one's friend here.)

He must accept some level of pain (from the rejection), loss (from lost love), and injustice (false accusations that usually accompany abandonment or betrayal) common to broken relationships in a fallen world. The pain, loss, and injustice will likely not entirely disappear in his lifetime. The victim must also deal with/give up false guilt and shame. In time the victim will overcome the blow to his personhood inflicted by abandonment or betrayal, and his former sense of self and confidence will return. In addition, he should love his enemy in the biblical sense (i.e., desire his repentance/reform and salvation/deliverance and help him if his need requires it). Lastly, the victim must wait, hope, and pray. In summary, he is to be like God: *angry* at injustice and wrongdoing, *refusing* to condone the wrongdoing, *hurting* because of the rejection and/or betrayal, *desiring* vindication, *desiring* the salvation of the one loved, *calling* for repentance, *expressing* his willingness to forgive and be reconciled following repentance, and *helping* the wrongdoer if help is needed (enemy love). In other words, the victim should follow the biblical injunction, "Be ye holy; for I am holy" (1 Pet 1:16 KJV). As Scripture advocates, he should seek to have a pure heart even if it is a broken heart.

In order for reconciliation to occur the wrongdoer also has a role to play. His is, of course, easier than that of the brokenhearted one. First, he must recognize his wrongdoing and admit guilt to himself. He also needs to recognize the hurt inflicted and/or harm done to the victim and feel sorrow and regret for the pain he caused. Once the offense has become morally unacceptable he must determine to change and never to repeat it. Having repented he then needs to go to the victim and apologize, stating the wrong done and asking for forgiveness. In the apology his guilt should be admitted and he should accept responsibility for his actions. All of this should be done recognizing that he does not deserve or have a right to forgiveness. He requests it as a gift. He should also express his desire for relationship to begin again, offering and following through on any appropriate amends-making that demonstrates both his true repentance and his concern for the victim.

In the ideal scenario presented by the biblical pattern, the victim accepts the apology and amends-making efforts of the wrongdoer. He verbally gives the gift of forgiveness and thereafter acts with kindness and compassion toward the offender. He will begin to trust and be willing to relate to the offender while continuing to deal with any residual resentment/anger that could harm the reestablishment of a relationship of love. He commits to care for the other's well-being and acts accordingly. He must allow the sin of abandonment or betrayal to be wiped out completely according to the biblical pattern (i.e., it should not be "mentioned" again [KJV] or "remembered against him" [ASV]; Ezek 18:21–22; 33:16).

FULL RESTORATION

Both the OT and the NT give poignant stories to illustrate God's feelings when he is abandoned and betrayed by the people he loves (the parable of the prodigal son and Hos 1–2). In the book of Hosea he speaks of both abandonment and betrayal saying, "The land commits flagrant *harlotry*, *forsaking* the LORD" (Hos 1:2b NASB; emphasis added). God's longing for reconciliation is strong in spite of the abandonment and betrayal. He says, "How can I give you up, Ephraim? How can I hand you over, Israel?" (Hos 11:8). As the book of Hosea illustrates, God woos those who reject him and loves them even when they have abandoned and betrayed him. That is not to say that he takes pleasure in them or graces them with a sense of his presence and approval. In fact, he is not pleased and often removes his presence (2 Chr 30:6–9; Jer 52:3; Hos 5:15; Mic 3:4; Zech 1:3; 7:13; Mal 3:7). In spite of his hurt/anger/displeasure, he does not discard them but calls them to repentance (through prophets). As in the parable of the prodigal son (Luke 15:11–32), God, the rejected and abandoned father, sometimes simply waits, accepting that for the time being nothing can be done. In the parable, the fact that the father longs while he waits is demonstrated by his run to meet his returning son (Luke 15:20b). He does not condemn his son following the confession of unworthiness, but fully reinstates him by putting a ring on his finger. This action does not, however, reinstate the son's inheritance, for the father says to the elder brother, "Everything I have is yours" (Luke 15:31). The father then lays aside the shame and celebrates the return of the prodigal with a banquet.

The son does not presume upon the father. He hopes only to be a servant. Imagine the joy of the prodigal for this undeserved favor. But what is the relationship like thereafter? It is not the same as it was before, for they are each different now. He is now the son who left, but he is also the son who returned. The father is the father who waited and longed and suffered but who welcomed home and forgave freely. He is the father who is revealed as love. The father is and always will be a man wounded and now reconciled. The son is and always will be a man guilty and now forgiven. But the wounded/reconciled and the guilty/forgiven may be joined in love and trust again even though they are each never the same. One has known guilt, the other pain, but trust and love are restored.

Is this full restoration according to the biblical example given through allegory (Hosea) and parable (Luke) really possible? It is probably rare but surely possible, and if possible it should be hoped for and strived for by all those who strive to emulate their heavenly Father.

AMENDS-MAKING

Amends-making should be part of the process of reconciliation. As will be discussed later, in any way possible the offender should be prepared to make right the harm done as a demonstration of his repentance, out of his concern for the victim, and as a matter of simple justice by doing what is right and fair. "Repentance is genuine only if the wrongdoer is willing to restore to the victim that which wrongdoing took away."[17] Most often full restitution is impossible, but some form of restitution must take place to begin the process of restoring trust. "It is a fitting sign . . . that repentance is genuine."[18]

The wrongdoer often knows what needs to be done to make amends, but if it is not obvious he should be willing to ask the victim. In turn the victim should be prepared to inform the offender what is required to right the wrong and what changes in behavior he expects. Perhaps the victim should do this before granting the forgiveness. If this practice is followed the sincerity of the repentance will not be questioned, and the reconciliation that follows will be secure and meaningful. For example, if the offender has slandered someone, at a minimum he should go to each person who heard the slander and admit the lies and tell the truth.

Reconciliation is still a risk for the victim. It requires that he begin to trust the offender again while hoping that the repentance is sincere.

17. Volf, *Free of Charge*, 187.
18. Volf, *Free of Charge*, 187.

Without his taking this risk the relationship cannot be healed. Once again the victim deserves credit. He is the one who endures the pain; he is the one who forswears retaliation; he is the one who chooses to give up his destructive anger and even to love the one who wounded him so deeply; he is the one who gives the gift of forgiveness; he is the one who must lay aside even his justified anger when forgiveness takes place; and finally, he is the one who must become vulnerable and risk reconciliation in order for the relationship to be healed.

RECONCILIATION AND CONSEQUENCES

In certain cases, forgiveness and reconciliation are nonetheless not inconsistent with punishment. For example, forgiveness for someone who steals a car is not inconsistent with the requirement that the car be returned or that the legal penalty be paid. Neither is reconciliation inconsistent with consequences in a relationship. For example, trust may not be immediate but rather developed with time. In the example of embezzling, it might take time for the victim to trust the embezzler with his money.[19] Or a woman who discovers her fiancé is secretly seeing another woman may forgive him, but she may still choose not to marry him. This choice is not inconsistent with a willingness to reconcile, but the reconciliation may not always mean returning to the previous relationship. The reconciliation may even be closure. The wrongdoer is released from his moral debt, the victim forswears all resentment, and the two parties go their separate ways.[20]

If reconciliation does not require restoration to the *same* relationship, the victim should not dread giving the gift of forgiveness thinking he is being forced back into a relationship that he no longer desires. For example, should a pastor who sins grievously and repents be restored? In this case what sort of reconciliation is appropriate? Should he be restored to fellowship or to leadership? Love involves not just the pastor but also the congregation that has been betrayed. The question of what is best for them or for any victims must be considered.[21] In this case a return to leadership may not be what is right. In spite of forgiveness, consequences may still occur. This is another example of the fact that reconciliation

19. Murphy, *Forgiveness and Mercy*, 22.
20. MacLachlan, "Forgiveness," 113.
21. Carson, *Love in Hard Places*, 174.

may not duplicate the former relationship, but should be what is appropriate in the new situation.

There may even be some middle ground in which the wrongdoer has made a minimal or qualified admission of guilt that cannot be described as true and full repentance. This effort might result in an improvement in relations but not full reconciliation.[22] The new situation may evolve, for giving the gift of forgiveness may be a one-time event, but being reconciled is a process. For example, the beginning of the journey toward reconciliation may be the giving of a thoughtful gift or a simple meal shared together.[23]

IS RECONCILIATION ALWAYS POSSIBLE?

According to the Bible, God is not always reconciled and will not ultimately be reconciled to all, for persons must choose to be reconciled to God (thus the doctrine of eternal separation from God). For example, the prophet Isaiah says, "This is what the Sovereign LORD, the Holy One of Israel says: 'In repentance and rest is your salvation, in quietness and trust is your strength, but you would have none of it'" (Isa 30:15). Likewise, Jesus says, "Jerusalem, Jerusalem, you who kill the prophets and stone those sent to you, how often I have longed to gather your children together, as a hen gathers her chicks under her wings, and you were not willing" (Matt 23:37). It only takes the actions of one party for relationships to be broken, but it takes the actions of both for them to be restored. Therefore reconciliation is not always possible, even for God. If repentance is sometimes impossible (Heb 6:4–6), then reconciliation is not always possible. Knowing this truth, that reconciliation is not always possible even for God, is helpful to those who feel guilt, shame, or failure (albeit false guilt, shame, and failure) because of broken relationships in their lives. This truth should enable them to overcome the feelings of guilt, shame, and failure.

Acceptance of this truth, that restoration of relationship is not always possible, should not cause one to lose hope for reconciliation. Giving up or refusing to hope is often a way of protecting oneself from pain and disappointment. The negative side of that choice is that the loss of hope often makes a person cynical and bitter. Being realistic (by

22. MacLachlan, "Forgiveness," 129.

23. Volf, *Free of Charge*, 191.

accepting the truth of a broken relationship and the possibility that it may not be healed) and becoming cynical are two separate things. The former holds out hope, refusing to be cynical even if the hope keeps one in touch with his pain. Hope can be painful because it longs for its objective, and longing is painful when love is involved. But hope also keeps one in touch with his love.

Life without reconciliation or even reconciliation itself may involve accepting the fact that one has to "move . . . on into something new which will be tinged inevitably with a degree of pain and sadness."[24] Also, life without reconciliation or even reconciliation itself usually involves a loss that cannot be recovered. "This is the loss of the situation—both actual and psychological—which existed before the need for forgiveness arose."[25]

TRUTH AND RECONCILIATION

If reconciliation is to take place in a relationship, both parties must share the same account of reality.[26] "Reconciliation must ultimately be based on truth."[27] "In mercy and truth atonement [reconciliation] is provided for iniquity" (Prov 16:6a NKJV). Without truth concerning what happened, two parties *cannot* come to agreement concerning the wrong done, the forgiveness needed, the necessary amends, etc. In this case the relationship will remain broken in spite of love. Sometimes both parties would like to reconcile, but they truly cannot because they cannot come to this agreement. Each has his own version of truth that contradicts the other's version. As Miroslav Volf says in his book *Exclusion and Embrace*, "The embrace itself, full reconciliation, cannot take place until the truth has been said."[28] "The *will* to embrace is indiscriminate, the embrace itself is conditional."[29] Sometimes, then, even in situations in which both parties desire reconciliation, it must wait for the new creation when all truth will be made known (Rom 2:2).

24. Coate, "Capacity for Forgiveness," 134.
25. Coate, "Capacity for Forgiveness," 135.
26. McFadyen, "Introduction," 12.
27. Schreurs, "Truth and Reconciliation," 131.
28. Volf, *Exclusion and Embrace*, 29.
29. Volf, *Exclusion and Embrace*, 29.

A victim should also be truthful about his feelings and commitment to forgive. A victim who still harbors a great deal of hurt and anger may be able to sincerely say the words "I forgive you" but need to admit that he is not yet over his anger. The forgiveness is then given with the understanding and commitment on his part to work through and eliminate his anger.[30] He is in effect saying, "I forgive you, but bear with me. It may take me some time to get over this."[31] If he fails to do so, he is the one who is morally at fault because he has not followed through on his commitment.[32] If one doubts whether he can overcome his anger it would be better not to utter the words of forgiveness until or unless he is sure he is committed to that process and sure that he will succeed in his efforts.

A victim should also be truthful if he is unable or unwilling to be reconciled. If he is not able in some sense to be reconciled he should not utter the words "I forgive you." It would be better to admit that he cannot forgive at this time, but not rule out forgiveness and reconciliation in the future. Why would this be better? If there is no possibility of some level of reconciliation, then the words of forgiveness are not effective: they are not uttered sincerely. An unwillingness to be reconciled in some sense is in reality an unwillingness to forgive.

IS RECONCILIATION ALWAYS DESIRABLE?

If reconciliation is not always possible, is it always desirable? Scripture states that God desires that all would come to a knowledge of him and be saved (i.e., reconciled to him; 1 Tim 2:4). But it also states that there is an unforgivable sin. Scripture does not clarify whether the sin is unforgivable because God is unwilling to forgive it or because the one who commits it (willingly and knowingly according to the biblical example) is hardened to the point that he simply will never repent. The latter seems more likely based on 1 Tim 2:4. If this is the case, then reconciliation from God's point of view is always desirable but not always achievable. However, if the former is the case, that God is unwilling to forgive certain sin, then reconciliation in such situations is not even desirable due to the horrendous nature of the sin.

---

30. Haber, *Forgiveness*, 55.

31. MacLachlan, "Forgiveness," 88.

32. Haber, *Forgiveness*, 51.

REASONS RECONCILIATION MAY NOT OCCUR

Reconciliation, which is appropriate to the situation, is the natural and expected end of forgiveness. It should begin to take place and grow stronger with time following the repentance of the wrongdoer and the gift of forgiveness by the victim. However, for various reasons reconciliation may not occur. The most obvious is that one of the parties has died. The victim may have been murdered. Or the victim may have died before he could work his way through his pain and come to compassion. Or the victim may die before the offender realizes or repents of what he has done.[33]

Reconciliation may also be prevented by the possibility that too much pain exists for the victim to be able to consider reconciliation. In such cases perhaps some level of forgiveness may take place without reconciliation being insisted upon, despite the fact that this is not the biblical model. It may simply be all the victim can muster, "yet at its best forgiveness hopes for more."[34] In cases of extreme suffering the biblical pattern may have to wait for its fulfillment in the world to come.

Another reason that reconciliation may not occur is that, as previously stated, one party may not want it and refuses to repent or to forgive. In this case at least one of the parties is *unwilling* to be reconciled. In other situations, however, one or both parties may not *be able* to reconcile. The parties may not be able to agree concerning the truth of what happened, thereby prohibiting proper repentance and/or forgiveness. Other situations exist in which the horrendous nature of a crime of pure evil renders reconciliation impossible. In other words, in spite of the fact that reconciliation is the biblical pattern and the goal, there are cases in which it does not occur because the parties are unwilling, or unable, or it is inappropriate. The Bible confirms the conclusion that reconciliation, although the goal, is not always possible, saying, "If it is possible, *as far as it depends on you*, live at peace with everyone" (Rom 12:18; emphasis added).

In addition, reconciliation may not occur because time simply runs out. As Katongole and Rice say, "The vision of enemies and strangers becoming friends—and of all becoming God's companions takes time.

---

33. Biggar, "Forgiveness," 210.
34. Volf, *Free of Charge*, 188.

A long time. More time than we have. The work is never done in our lifetime. We never arrive. We never fix it all."[35]

THIRD PARTIES

In the process of reconciliation one should be wary of third parties who often want to smooth things over by calling for benevolence and good-will. They are usually not fully informed and therefore presumptuous in their advice. They may encourage premature reconciliation without the hard work of truth-telling, repentance, and forgiveness that is necessary to successful restoration of relationship. Often their interest, especially in families, derives from their own inconvenience, for broken relationships within families usually affect others as well. Third parties often advocate premature reconciliation because it is generally the case that people do not pay nearly as close attention to hurts that are not their own.[36] Bash cites the example of a Japanese prisoner of war who writes of those who told him that it was time to forgive and forget. The former prisoner says, "The majority of people who hand out advice about forgiveness have not gone through the sort of experience I had."[37] In contrast, the victim's deep-seated awareness of the impact of the wrongdoing is a natural moral corrective to this casual attitude of condonation that masquerades as reconciliation.[38]

In conclusion, reconciliation following deep wounds and painful betrayals is a process involving commitment and energy. In addition to repentance and forgiveness, the path to reconciliation includes lament, prayer, hope, courage, love, wisdom, and always time.[39] Each of these topics is discussed in more detail in the chapters that follow.

.

35. Katongole and Rice, *Reconciling All Things*, 145.

36. MacLachlan, "Forgiveness," 208.

37. A. Bash, *Forgiveness and Christian Ethics*, 61.

38. MacLachlan, "Forgiveness," 208.

39. Katongole and Rice, *Reconciling All Things*, 150.

CHAPTER 1 STUDY QUESTIONS

Introductory Comments

1. What is the purpose of forgiveness in the biblical model, and what precedes it?

2. What barrier to reconciliation is removed by forgiveness?

3. Why is reconciliation so difficult when it involves a love relationship?

Lamentation

1. What must the victim have had time to do before a relationship can be restored?

2. What does the Bible mean by lamentation, and what book often voices lamentation?

The Biblical Model

1. Summarize what must take place prior to repentance.

2. In what ways is the victim of abandonment or betrayal to be like God?

3. What actions does the wrongdoer need to take before a love relationship can be healed?

4. Ideally, how should the victim respond to the apology and amends-making actions of the offender?

Full Restoration

1. What OT book and what NT parable illustrate God's feelings when he is abandoned or betrayed?

2. How are victims and wrongdoers not the same following abandonment and betrayal?

Amends-Making

1. How and why should an offender demonstrate his repentance?

2. Why is reconciliation a risk for the victim?

3. For what reasons does the victim deserve credit for the restoration of a broken love relationship?

Reconciliation and Consequences

1. Are forgiveness and reconciliation inconsistent with punishment?

2. Does reconciliation always mean returning to the same relationship?

Is Reconciliation Always Possible?

1. Why is reconciliation not always possible, even for God?

2. How does this help those who feel guilt, shame, or failure because of broken relationships in their lives?

3. How is being realistic different from becoming cynical regarding broken relationships?

4. What loss can never be recovered, even following reconciliation?

Truth and Reconciliation

1. Why must both parties share the same account of what happened?

2. If both parties cannot agree, will there ever be a time when reconciliation can take place?

3. What should a victim do if he is too angry or hurt to genuinely offer forgiveness?

Reasons Reconciliation May Not Occur

1. What situations make reconciliation impossible?

2. Why, in cases of extreme suffering, may the biblical pattern of reconciliation have to wait for the world to come?

Third Parties

1. Why should one be wary of third parties who want to "smooth things over"?

2. Why do third parties often encourage premature reconciliation?

PART I

When Does God Forgive?

IN AN EFFORT TO understand when forgiveness should be given, Part I of this book examines the question, When does God forgive? For Christians this understanding should surely be the basis for any conclusions concerning the practice of forgiving one another.

Any effort to speak cogently, meaningfully, and scripturally about forgiveness must begin with definitions. This book therefore begins by defining the terms *wrath*, *repentance*, *forgiveness*, and *reconciliation* according to their biblical usages. Forgiveness in the modern usage of the word did not exist in classical antiquity or in the early Judeo-Christian tradition. The Judeo-Christian vision of divine absolution was predicated on repentance of the sinner and turning or returning to the ways of the Lord.[1] Modern and common use of the term forgiveness does not insist on this biblical pattern; therefore, the modern and common use of terms must be distinguished from biblical usage.

---

1. Konstan, *Before Forgiveness*, 164.

2

Repentance
The Call of Love

CHAPTER 1 EMPHASIZES THAT the reason for giving the gift of forgiveness is that two parties may be reconciled. Reconciliation, the restoration from alienation to a relationship of love, is the moral good that results. If this restoration of a loving relationship depends on one repenting and the other forgiving, then the call to repentance is the call of love. It represents God's call to his world that he might be reconciled to each person whom he loves. "God is love" (1 John 4:8), and all that he does proceeds from his love. The Bible is full of strong words concerning the necessity of repentance and God's actions to provoke it. One must remember that these words and actions, which sometimes appear harsh, are words and acts of uncompromising love. God actually pleads for repentance, so strong is his love and desire for reconciliation. Jesus endured unspeakable suffering in order to redeem humankind. How painful it must be when the call of repentance, the call of love, is ignored. The length of this chapter reveals the proper emphasis—the biblical emphasis—on God's call of love. Contemporary Christian preaching often emphasizes love, but too often it becomes a weaker version that compromises God's holiness. Christ died to free humans from the power of sin and death as its consequence. He gives his life to those who will receive him. Let us not ignore his sacrifice and his gift; let us not ignore his call of love, his call to repent, for it involves the offer of relationship with the creator God who blesses, guides, strengthens, and empowers. It is the call to be fully formed as the being you were created to be. To fail to call someone to repent is to fail to call someone out of shame and guilt and into love, strength, fulfillment, and peace—truly a failure to love.

This chapter examines the biblical call to repent by first defining the term and then examining its relationship to forgiveness.

THE TERM REPENTANCE

The biblical term *repentance* is relatively easy to understand but unfortunately is often watered down in contemporary thought. A correct understanding of the scriptural meaning of repentance is essential because of its close relationship to the concepts of forgiveness and reconciliation as presented in the Bible. In the Epistle to the Hebrews, repentance is referred to as the first foundational doctrine, followed by faith, baptisms, laying on of hands, resurrection, and judgment (Heb 6:1–2). In the NT the English word *repent* translates the Greek word *metanoein*. From classical Greek until the time of the NT this word meant to change one's mind. Emotions such as remorse, shame, or guilt may be involved in repentance, but its basic meaning involves not an emotion but a decision. If a person feels great remorse without that emotion resulting in a change of mind and behavior, he has not repented. Remorse is a present feeling related to past behavior, whereas repentance is a present decision related to future behavior.

In the OT, the English words most commonly used to translate the Hebrew word for repent are turn, return, or turn back. The Hebrew word denotes an outward action of turning back or in a new direction that is the result of an inner decision. To repent is to turn or return to God and his ways and involves a conscious moral and personal decision to forsake sin and obey God. Accordingly the call to repent is heard often from the OT prophets.[1]

That a change of mind and direction is the essential meaning of repentance is evident in that Scripture tells us that God also repents. When God is the subject of the verb repent, the word refers to decisions of God that prompt him to a different course of dealing with people. Most uses

---

1. Bromiley, *International Standard Bible Encyclopedia*, 135.

refer to God's change of mind concerning intended punishment. However, Jer 18 also refers to his change of mind concerning intended good: "And if that nation I warned repents of its evil, then I will relent ["repent" KJV] and not inflict on it the disaster I had planned. And if at another time I announce that a nation or kingdom is to be built up and planted, and if it does evil in my sight and does not obey me, then I will reconsider ["repent of" KJV] the good I had intended to do for it" (Jer 18:8–10). First Samuel 15:11 reports God's change of mind about making Saul king: "I regret ["It repenteth me" KJV] that I have made Saul king, because he has turned away from me and has not carried out my instructions." Yet in verse 29 Samuel says to Saul, "He who is the Glory of Israel does not lie or change his mind ["repent" KJV]; for he is not a human being, that he should change his mind ["repent" KJV]."[2] Samuel means that God is not capricious. He makes the right decision, which may involve a change of mind according to the change in the situation. A new course of action then only occurs in response to changing circumstances.

THE BIBLICAL CALL TO REPENTANCE

Because repentance precedes forgiveness of sins, the call to repentance is prominent throughout the Bible. This continuity between the OT and the NT is demonstrated at the beginning of the NT in Mark's Gospel when John the Baptist issues the call to repentance. Mark 1:1–4 says:

> The beginning of the good news about Jesus the Messiah, the Son of God, as it is written in Isaiah the prophet: "I will send my messenger ahead of you, who will prepare your way—a voice of one calling in the wilderness, 'Prepare the way for the Lord, make straight paths for him.'" And so John the Baptist appeared in the wilderness, preaching a baptism of repentance for the forgiveness of sins.

These verses make two points. First, the ministry of John the Baptist, the call to "repentance for the forgiveness of sins," continues that of the prophets. Second, repentance precedes the forgiveness of sins.

John prepares the way by calling people to repentance so that their sins may be forgiven. The initial message Christ preaches after John prepares the way is, "The kingdom of God has come near. Repent and believe the good news!" (Mark 1:15). This first recorded command of Jesus in the

2. Bromiley, *International Standard Bible Encyclopedia*, 135.

Gospel of Mark demonstrates the importance and priority of repentance. Just as repentance cannot be separated from forgiveness, it cannot be separated from faith. John calls the people to repent "for the forgiveness of sins" and Jesus calls the people to "repent and believe."

After his death and resurrection, Christ commissions his disciples to go to all nations with the gospel. He tells them, "This is what is written: The Messiah will suffer and rise from the dead on the third day, and repentance for the forgiveness of sins will be preached in his name to all nations, beginning at Jerusalem" (Luke 24:46–47). Here again forgiveness of sins is preceded by repentance, and forgiveness is not preached apart from repentance.

In the early apostolic teaching the connection between repentance and forgiveness is even more explicit.[3] On the day of Pentecost, in response to his listeners' question, "What should we do?" Peter says, "Repent and be baptized, every one of you, in the name of Jesus Christ for the forgiveness of your sins. And you will receive the gift of the Holy Spirit" (Acts 2:38). Later, in his words to the high priest after a night in prison, Peter says of Jesus, "God exalted him to his own right hand as Prince and Savior that he might bring Israel to repentance and forgive their sins" (Acts 5:31). At another time, in rebuking Simon, who had offered money for control of God's gift of the Spirit, Peter says, "Repent of this wickedness and pray to the Lord in the hope that he may forgive you for having such a thought in your heart" (Acts 8:22).

The same link between repentance and forgiveness is made by the voice that speaks to Saul of Tarsus and calls him to the Gentiles "to open their eyes and *turn* them from darkness [repent] to light, and from the power of Satan to God, so that they may receive forgiveness of sins and a place among those who are sanctified by faith in me" (Acts 26:18; emphasis added).

Repentance is also the message of Paul. In speaking to the elders in the church in Jerusalem, Paul outlines the gospel message he had been preaching, saying, "I have declared to both Jews and Greeks that they must *turn* to God in repentance and have faith in our Lord Jesus" (Acts 20:21; emphasis added). And to Timothy, who is ministering to the church in Ephesus combating false teachers, he writes, "Everyone who confesses the name of the Lord must *turn* away from wickedness" (2 Tim 2:19b; emphasis added). To King Agrippa Paul says, "First to those in

---

3. Shults and Sandage, *Faces of Forgiveness*, 135.

Damascus, then to those in Jerusalem and in all Judea, and then to the Gentiles, I preached that they should repent and *turn* to God and demonstrate their repentance by their deeds" (Acts 26:20; emphasis added).

So, from the words of the prophets, to John the Baptist, to Jesus, to the twelve Apostles, to Paul, the message emphasizing the necessity and priority of repentance is the same. The fact that the word "repent" occurs fifty-six times in the NT shows the importance of repentance.[4] Apart from repentance, faith is an empty profession. Thus unstable and unacceptable behavior is often seen in professing Christians because they profess faith without having repented of their sins. They procure neither the favor of God nor the respect of the world. The simplification of the gospel message has often distorted it. "Only believe" is not the gospel and is not the message of Christ or his apostles. Omitting the call to repentance misleads sinners and misrepresents God. As Wayne Grudem says in *Systematic Theology,* "When we realize that genuine saving faith must be accompanied by genuine repentance from sin, it helps us to understand why some preaching of the gospel has such inadequate results today."[5]

In summary, "the general edict of God to the entire human race is, 'All men everywhere must repent' (Acts 17:30), and 'Except you repent you shall all likewise perish' (Luke 13:3)."[6] As Isaiah says, "In repentance and rest is your salvation" (Isa 30:15b). It could not be stated more plainly. Verses like these, as well as the consistency and persistence of the call to repentance throughout the Bible, make it clear that in passages that mention only faith, repentance is presupposed. Such passages are considered in Part II. Although a few passages exist in which faith alone is named as the condition for coming to Christ for salvation, other passages exist in which only repentance is mentioned (e.g., Luke 24:46–47).[7]

REGRET VERSUS REPENTANCE

The NT idea of repentance is difficult to express in other languages. In Latin, the Greek *metanoeo* is rendered by "exercise penitence." But "penitence" etymologically signifies pain or distress rather than a change of mind and direction. Because of this translation problem, over time there

---

4. Bromiley, *International Standard Bible Encyclopedia,* 136.

5. Grudem, *Systematic Theology,* 716.

6. Prince, *Repent and Believe,* 15.

7. Norris, "Forgiving from the Heart," 86.

developed the tendency to think of repentance as grief over sin rather than a change of mind that results in abandonment of sin. However, the fundamental NT concept is a change of mind. Accompanying sorrow and change of life are the consequences of this change of mind. The most prominent psychological element in repentance is not emotion or even intellect but the will.[8] Recognition and admission of wrongdoing is possible without true repentance that leads one to turn from wrongdoing. A good example can be found in the words and actions of Pharaoh in the story of the exodus. Pharaoh says to Moses, "This time I have sinned . . . The LORD is in the right, and I and my people are in the wrong. Pray to the LORD, for we have had enough thunder and hail. I will let you go; you don't have to stay any longer" (Exod 9:27–28). Pharaoh admits guilt in an effort to avoid the consequent punishment, but he does not let the people go. Repentance has not taken place (see also Exod 10:16–17). Another example can be found in the life of king Saul, who admits sin but is denied pardon. Lack of repentance is obvious from Saul's actions following his confession (1 Sam 15:24–25, 30). This form of regret is motivated by little more than selfishness and a desire to avoid the consequences.[9] True repentance is neither the regret over wrongdoing because of the consequences, nor *even a change of behavior* motivated by a desire to avoid negative consequences. Repentance, by definition, is a change of mind resulting in a change of direction, but it is based on a deep feeling of shame for and abhorrence of sin (Ps 38:2–6; 51:1–17), which leads to a change of life.

A NT example of grief that did not result in repentance can be seen in the words and actions of Judas. Matthew 27:3–5 says, "When Judas, who had betrayed him, saw that Jesus was condemned, he was seized with remorse ["repented himself" KJV] and returned the thirty pieces of silver to the chief priests and the elders. 'I have sinned,' he said, 'for I have betrayed innocent blood.' . . . So Judas threw the money into the temple and left. Then he went away and hanged himself." In this case the Greek verb is not *metanoeo* (Matt 3:2, 8, 11; 11:20–21; 12:41; Acts 2:38; 17:30; 26:20) but rather *metamelein* (Matt 21:29, 32; 2 Cor 7:8; Heb 7:21),[10] which can be used to denote the emotion of remorse only.[11] The fact that Judas did

8. Bromiley, *International Standard Bible Encyclopedia*, 136.

9. Erickson, *Christian Theology*, 937.

10. Turner, *Matthew*, 649.

11. Erickson, *Christian Theology*, 936.

not repent can be seen in that he did not change his life. His suicide was only an extension of his remorse and guilt. Sorrow for sin and repentance from sin are not the same thing. As Scripture says, sorrow should lead to repentance: "Your sorrow led you to repentance. . . . Godly sorrow brings repentance that leads to salvation" (2 Cor 7:9–10). The clear implication is that sorrow *for* sin that does not lead to repentance *from* sin does not lead to salvation.

REPENTANCE IS THE CONDITION OF GOD'S FAVOR AND FORGIVENESS

The revelation of God's character as merciful means that God chooses to forgive those who repent rather than refusing to forgive them. Repentance is the condition of God's favor and forgiveness but not the condition of God's love. God's love exists apart from behavior and cannot be earned by any behavior. But his wrath, his hatred of injustice and evil, is a part of his love. His wrath prompts his disapproval/discipline/judgment. Without love for the sinner God would be indifferent to his or her behavior. Estrangement from God and judgment from him often constitute his call to repentance and holiness.

> For the LORD has rejected and abandoned this generation that is under his wrath. (Jer 7:29b)

> Yet they rebelled and grieved his Holy Spirit, so he turned and became their enemy and he himself fought against them. (Isa 63:10)

> We have sinned and rebelled and you have not forgiven. (Lam 3:42)

> So the people will be brought low and everyone humbled—do not forgive them. (Isa 2:9)

> The Ammonites also crossed the Jordan to fight against Judah, Benjamin and Ephraim; Israel was in great distress. Then the Israelites cried out to the LORD, "We have sinned against you, forsaking our God and serving the Baals." The LORD replied, "When the Egyptians, the Amorites, the Ammonites, the Philistines, the Sidonians, the Amalekites and the Maonites oppressed you and you cried to me for help, did I not save you from their hands? But you have forsaken me and served other gods, so I will no longer save you. Go and cry out to the gods you have

chosen. Let them save you when you are in trouble!" (Judg 10:9–14)

God is teaching the Israelites that, having abandoned him, they cannot presume upon his love. They cry out to him when they are in "great distress." His refusal to be used (mocked) by them is intended to teach them that they cannot commit idolatry and expect him to come when they are in need. They must take the steps necessary to reestablish a proper relationship with him. God's answer to their cry is severe but still based in his love for them. When their hearts are once again right with him, he delivers them (vv. 15–16).

Another example is found in the book of Zechariah. The prophet explains that the reason for the wrath of God that resulted in the judgment of the captivity is that the people "refused to pay attention; stubbornly they turned their backs and covered their ears" (7:11) to the Lord's call to holiness (7:9–10). As a result God says, "When I called, they did not listen; so when they called, I would not listen" (7:13; see also Jer 11:11; Mic 3:2, 4). If persons could experience the pleasure of God's presence, favor, mercy, and blessing while still engaging in willful disobedience, many would not repent and follow the Lord's way of holiness. This condition for fellowship is indicated by verses that say that God will not listen to the prayers of the willfully disobedient (Ps 66:18; Prov 15:29; Isa 1:15).

Another example is found in the book of Hosea. In announcing the judgment that would fall on Israel for their idolatry and corruption, Hosea says, "When they go . . . to seek the LORD, they will not find him; he has withdrawn himself from them" (Hos 5:6). In Hos 5:15 God says, "I will go away *and* return to My place until they acknowledge their guilt and seek My face; in their affliction they will earnestly seek Me" (NASB; emphasis added).

Throughout the Bible repentance is given as the necessary condition for God's forgiveness and for experiencing his presence, which brings peace and fellowship with him. Repentance as the condition for God's forgiveness is not an idea that is buried in Scripture; it is front and center, loud and clear, and is plainly revealed throughout the history of God's dealings with his people. By the time of the NT no Jew would need to be instructed concerning repentance as the condition for God's forgiveness. The following verses state the principle in an if/then framework (emphases and brackets added):

If you remain hostile toward me and refuse to listen to me, [*then*] I will multiply your afflictions seven times over, as your sins deserve. (Lev 26:21)

But *if* from there you seek the LORD your God, you will find him *if* you seek him with all your heart and with all your soul. When you are in distress and all these things have happened to you, *then* in later days you will *return* to the LORD your God and obey him. (Deut 4:29–30)

If my people, who are called by my name, will humble themselves and pray and seek my face and *turn* from their wicked ways, *then* I will hear from heaven, and I will forgive their sin and will heal their land. (2 Chr 7:14)

At the king's command, couriers went throughout Israel and Judah with letters from the king and from his officials, which read: "People of Israel, *return* to the LORD, the God of Abraham, Isaac and Israel, *that he may return* to you who are left, who have escaped from the hand of the kings of Assyria. Do not be like your parents and your fellow Israelites, who were unfaithful to the LORD, the God of their ancestors, so that he made them an object of horror, as you see. Do not be stiff-necked, as your ancestors were; submit to the LORD. Come to his sanctuary, which he has consecrated forever. Serve the LORD your God, *so that* his fierce anger will turn away from you. *If you return* to the LORD, then your fellow Israelites and your children will be shown compassion by their captors and will return to this land, for the LORD your God is gracious and compassionate. He will not turn his face from you *if you return to him*." (2 Chr 30:6–9)

Remember the instruction you gave your servant Moses, saying, "*If* you are unfaithful, [*then*] I will scatter you among the nations, but *if you return to me* and obey my commands, *then* even if your exiled people are at the farthest horizon, I will gather them from there and bring them to the place I have chosen as a dwelling for my Name." (Neh 1:8–9)

[*If you*] turn to my reproof, behold, I will pour out my spirit on you; I will make my words known to you. . . . Because I called and you refused . . . [*then*] [you] will call on me, but I will not answer. (Prov 1:23–28 NASB; wisdom personified speaking)

Let the wicked forsake their ways and the unrighteous their thoughts. Let them *turn* to the LORD, and [*then*] he will have mercy on them, and to our God, for he will freely pardon. (Isa 55:7)

If you really change your ways and your actions and deal with each other justly, *if* you do not oppress the foreigner, the fatherless or the widow and do not shed innocent blood in this place, and *if* you do not follow other gods to your own harm, *then* I will let you live in this place, in the land I gave your ancestors for ever and ever. (Jer 7:5–7)

And *if* that nation I warned *repents* of its evil, *then* I will relent and not inflict on it the disaster I had planned. (Jer 18:8)

Perhaps they will listen and each will *turn* from their evil ways. *Then* I will relent and not inflict on them the disaster I was planning because of the evil they have done. . . . *Now reform your ways and your actions and obey the* LORD *your God. Then the* LORD will relent and not bring the disaster he has pronounced against you. (Jer 26:3, 13)

Again and again I sent all my servants the prophets to you. They said, "Each of you must *turn* from your wicked ways and reform your actions; . . . *then* you will live in the land I have given to you and your ancestors." (Jer 35:15)

Perhaps when the people of Judah hear about every disaster I plan to inflict on them, they will each *turn* from their wicked ways; *then* I will forgive their wickedness and their sin. (Jer 36:3)

Then I will return to my lair *until they have borne their guilt* and seek my face—in their misery they will earnestly *seek me*. (Hos 5:15)

Therefore tell the people: This is what the LORD Almighty says: "*Return* to me," declares the LORD Almighty, "and [*then*] I will return to you," says the LORD Almighty. (Zech 1:3)

"Ever since the time of your ancestors you have turned away from my decrees and have not kept them. *Return* to me, and [*then*] I will return to you," says the LORD Almighty. (Mal 3:7)

Come near to God and he will come near to you. Wash your hands, you sinners, and purify your hearts, you double-minded. Grieve, mourn and wail. Change your laughter to mourning and your joy to gloom. Humble yourselves before the Lord, and [*then*] he will lift you up. (Jas 4:8–10)

If we confess our sins, [*then*] he is faithful and just and will forgive us our sins and purify us from all unrighteousness. (1 John
1:9)

These verses are only some of many that emphasize the priority of
repentance. In fact, the entire OT is a revelation of God's plan and provision for redemption, the revelation of the way to forgiveness and peace
with God through repentance and faith.

THE MINISTRY OF A PROPHET

Since God's forgiveness is conditioned upon repentance and his favor
upon obedience (Zech 7:9–13), the call to repentance is a prominent
feature of the ministry of a prophet. The following verses are only a few
examples that illustrate this (emphases added):

Return you Israelites, to the One you have so greatly revolted
against. (Isa 31:6)

The LORD said to me . . . "Go, proclaim this message . . . '*Return*
faithless Israel,' declares the LORD, . . . 'Only acknowledge your
guilt.'" (Jer 3:11–13)

But you must *return* to your God; maintain love and justice, and
wait for your God always. (Hos 12:6)

Return, Israel, to the LORD your God. Your sins have been your
downfall! (Hos 14:1)

"Even now," declares the LORD, "*Return* to me with all your
heart, with fasting and weeping and mourning." (Joel 2:12)

"I overthrew some of you as I overthrew Sodom and Gomorrah.
You were like a burning stick snatched from the fire, yet you
have not *returned* to me," declares the LORD. "Therefore this is
what I will do to you, Israel, and because I will do this to you,
Israel, prepare to meet your God." (Amos 4:11–12)

The prophet Micah says, "But as for me, I am filled with power, with
the Spirit of the LORD, and with justice and might, to declare to Jacob his
transgression, to Israel his sin" (Mic 3:8). Micah says this in contrast to
the false prophets who bring a false message of "peace" (3:5). Preaching
unconditional forgiveness is like preaching "peace." However, this call to
repentance should characterize the ministry of present-day preachers,

teachers, and indeed all Christians. They should not condone sin, but call for repentance that leads others into the blessing, presence, and approval of God. Condonation is a failure to love. It grants approval when approval is inappropriate and demonstrates a level of indifference that fails to consider the wrongdoer's well-being. Real love does not do that; God does not do that, and neither should Christians do that. The risk of modeling God's love by calling others to repent is rejection and animosity from others, both of which the prophets often experienced.

REPENTANCE AND FORGIVENESS LEAD TO RECONCILIATION

The Bible stresses that God will forgive the one who repents not because he is obligated to do so, but because he chooses to do so based on his love, which desires reconciliation. Sin is a cause of alienation and the barrier to reconciliation. As Isaiah says, "Your iniquities have separated you from your God" (59:2). According to Scripture, repentance followed by God's forgiveness results in the removal of sin (Ps 103:12; Isa 1:18; 44:22), therefore the barrier to reconciliation is eliminated. On the Day of Atonement (reconciliation) the complete removal of sin as the barrier to reconciliation is symbolized by confession of sins, laying on of hands, and sending the scapegoat, bearing the sins of the people, away into the desert never to be seen again. The result of this removal of sin is atonement/reconciliation (Lev 16:21).

　　The following passage from Deuteronomy shows God's desire to be reconciled when he is estranged from his people.

> When all these blessings and curses I have set before you come on you and you take them to heart wherever the LORD your God disperses you among the nations, and when you and your children return to the LORD your God and obey him with all your heart and with all your soul according to everything I command you today, then the LORD your God will restore your fortunes and have compassion on you and gather you again from all the nations where he scattered you. . . . He will bring you to the land that belonged to your ancestors, and you will take possession of it. He will make you more prosperous and numerous than your ancestors. The LORD your God will circumcise your hearts and the hearts of your descendants, so that you may love him with all your heart and with all your soul, and live. The LORD

your God will put all these curses on your enemies who hate and persecute you. You will again obey the LORD and follow all his commands I am giving you today. Then the LORD your God will make you most prosperous in all the work of your hands and in the fruit of your womb, . . . The LORD will again delight in you and make you prosperous, just as he delighted in your ancestors, if you obey the LORD your God and keep his commands and decrees that are written in this Book of the Law and turn to the LORD your God with all your heart and with all your soul. (Deut 30:1–10)

DEMONSTRATION OF REPENTANCE

True repentance involves a turning to the Lord with all one's heart and soul and results in full reconciliation and multiple blessings. A decision of the will and the appropriate change in behavior are essential. As the verses in Deuteronomy emphasize, this decision and change in behavior is based on a change of "heart and soul" (v. 10). If a change of ways is based on self-preservation but not on a real inward change of heart, true repentance has not taken place.

True repentance should be demonstrated initially by some form of outward reparation. The OT law provides the trespass offering for such a demonstration. The book of Leviticus says:

The LORD said to Moses: "If anyone sins and is unfaithful to the LORD by deceiving a neighbor about something entrusted to them or left in their care or about something stolen, or if they cheat their neighbor, or if they find lost property and lie about it, or if they swear falsely about any such sin that people may commit—when they sin in any of these ways and realize their guilt, they must return what they have stolen or taken by extortion, or what was entrusted to them, or the lost property they found, or whatever it was they swore falsely about. They must make restitution in full, add a fifth of the value to it and give it all to the owner on the day they present their guilt offering. And as a penalty they must bring to the priest, that is, to the LORD, their guilt offering, a ram from the flock, one without defect and of the proper value. In this way the priest will make atonement for them before the LORD, and they will be forgiven for any of the things they did that made them guilty." (Lev 6:1–7)

Confession should be made publicly, restitution given, and something more (20 percent, "a fifth of the value") offered to demonstrate repentance and the desire for forgiveness and reconciliation. Sometimes, however, no way exists to compensate the one sinned against, such as in the case of testifying falsely. One can imagine that in this case public confession, which attempts to undo the slander, is a necessity.

Demonstration of repentance is also presented as a necessity in the NT. John the Baptist refused to baptize the Pharisees and Sadducees who came to him until they would demonstrate repentance. Matthew 3:5–8 says:

> People went out to him from Jerusalem and all Judea and the whole region of the Jordan. Confessing their sins, they were baptized by him in the Jordan River. But when he saw many of the Pharisees and Sadducees coming to where he was baptizing, he said to them: "You brood of vipers! Who warned you to flee from the coming wrath? Produce fruit in keeping with repentance."

Echoing John the Baptist, Paul says to King Agrippa, "I preached that they should repent and turn to God and demonstrate their repentance by their deeds" (Acts 26:20).

Perhaps the best known NT example of true repentance is seen in the actions of Zacchaeus.

> Jesus entered Jericho and was passing through. A man was there by the name of Zacchaeus; he was a chief tax collector and was wealthy. He wanted to see who Jesus was, but because he was short he could not see over the crowd. So he ran ahead and climbed a sycamore-fig tree to see him, since Jesus was coming that way. When Jesus reached the spot, he looked up and said to him, "Zacchaeus, come down immediately. I must stay at your house today." So he came down at once and welcomed him gladly. All the people saw this and began to mutter, "He has gone to be the guest of a sinner." But Zacchaeus stood up and said to the Lord, "Look, Lord! Here and now I give half of my possessions to the poor, and if I have cheated anybody out of anything, I will pay back four times the amount." Jesus said to him, "Today salvation has come to this house." (Luke 19:1–9)

The actions of Zacchaeus demonstrate true repentance, which in this case involves recompense. The sincerity of Zacchaeus could not be questioned. When Zacchaeus carried through on these promises, would the people he had wronged have any trouble being reconciled to him? Surely not. If repentance is real, the offender wants to make up for the wrong he has done in whatever way possible, regardless of whether he is forgiven or not. In other words, making restitution is not an attempt to earn or deserve forgiveness, but rather an expression and demonstration of what has already taken place in the heart of the offender. The demonstration of true repentance by compensation enables forgiving to be less difficult and makes reconciliation joyful. If joyful reconciliation is rare, it is because true repentance is rarely demonstrated.

REPENTANCE, FORGIVENESS, AND JUDGMENT: A CASE STUDY

Ezekiel was a sixth-century-BC prophet (593–71) to the Israelites under God's judgment in exile in Babylon. Therefore he has much to say about God's justice and about repentance. The call to repent is an essential message of the book of Ezekiel: "This is what the Sovereign LORD says, Repent! Turn from your idols and renounce all your detestable practices" (Ezek 14:6). In order to convince the exiles to heed the call to repentance, Ezekiel first must convince them that they need to repent. To this end, in chapter 18, Ezekiel presents an ethical case study. The chapter begins by stating a point of contention between the exiles and God: "The word of the LORD came to me: 'What do you people mean by quoting this proverb about the land of Israel: "The parents eat sour grapes, and the children's teeth are set on edge?"'" (Ezek 18:1–2). The exiles complain that they suffer God's judgment because of the sins of past generations and therefore "the way of the Lord is not just" (18:25). As Wright says, "The complaint of the exiles encapsulates two fundamental human tendencies which have been apparent in fallen humanity ever since the garden of Eden— to blame somebody else and to blame God."[12] Ezekiel cannot possibly succeed in getting the people to repent unless they recognize and take responsibility for their own actions. Shifting the blame is a roadblock to repentance, and "without repentance there can be no forgiveness and salvation."[13] Ezekiel, here, does what Christians need to do for others to "attend to their deepest need and most urgent danger."[14] And that is to

---

12. C. Wright, *Message of Ezekiel*, 189.

13. C. Wright, *Message of Ezekiel*, 189.

14. C. Wright, *Message of Ezekiel*, 196.

refuse to "shore up their self-excusing defenses. [Instead they should] lead people to a restored relationship with God through the grace of forgiveness. But without repentance there can be no forgiveness. And without the acceptance of responsibility there can be no true repentance."[15]

What then is Ezekiel's understanding of repentance? To answer this question Ezekiel presents three case studies (18:5–18), the conclusion of which is found in verse 20: "The one who sins is the one who will die. The child will not share the guilt of the parent, nor will the parent share the guilt of the child. The righteousness of the righteous will be credited to them, and the wickedness of the wicked will be charged against them." This amounts to a statement of God's justice. The punishment of wickedness cannot be transferred; neither can the rewards of goodness be bequeathed.

This statement leads into what Ezekiel has to say about repentance:

> "*If* a righteous person *turns* from their righteousness and commits sin, [*then*] they will die for it; because of the sin they have committed they will die. But *if* a wicked person *turns* away from the wickedness they have committed and *does what is just and right*, [*then*] they will save their life. Because they consider all the offenses they have committed and *turn* away from them, that person will surely live; they will not die." (18:26–28; emphasis and brackets added)

Repentance is what makes the difference. These verses are a powerful affirmation of human freedom: one can choose to change. Ultimately a person decides for himself what kind of person he will be. Ezekiel echoes the words of Deuteronomy when he says the choice is a matter of life and death.

> See, I have set before you today life and prosperity, death and adversity. *If* you obey the commandments of the LORD your God that I am commanding you today, by loving the LORD your God, walking in his ways, and observing his commandments, decrees, and ordinances, *then* you shall live and become numerous, and the LORD your God will bless you in the land that you are entering to possess.
>
> But *if* your heart turns away and you do not hear, but are led astray to bow down to other gods and serve them, I declare to you today that you shall perish; you shall not live long in the land that you are crossing the Jordan to enter and possess. I call

---

15. C. Wright, *Message of Ezekiel*, 196.

heaven and earth to witness against you today that I have set before you life and death, blessings and curses. *Choose life* so that
you and your descendants may live, loving the LORD your God,
and obeying him, and holding fast to him; for that means life to
you and length of days, so that you may live in the land that the
LORD swore to give to your ancestors, to Abraham, to Isaac, and
to Jacob. (Deut 30:15–20 NRSV; emphasis added)

Ezekiel echoes the language of "life and death," urging the exiles
to "choose life,"[16] a blessed relationship with God at a personal level.
As these words in Deuteronomy say, life is "loving the LORD your God,
obeying him, and holding fast to him."[17] God is not a neutral party who
just waits to see what humans choose. He calls them to repentance and
reveals his heart to them: "Do I take any pleasure in the death of the
wicked? declares the Sovereign LORD. Rather, am I not pleased when they
turn from their ways and live?" (Ezek 18:23). This truth is repeated in
chapter 33 with even more urgency and emotion on the part of God.
"Say to them, 'As surely as I live, declares the Sovereign LORD, I take no
pleasure in the death of the wicked, but rather that they *turn* from their
ways and live. *Turn! Turn* from your evil ways! Why will you die, O house
of Israel?" (v. 11; emphasis added). Clearly God's will is that they would
turn/repent, but there is no suggestion that if they do not repent that
he will forgive and be reconciled to them. "The Bible gives examples of
those who, after a lifetime of wickedness, find mercy and grace through
repentance"[18] (e.g., Manasseh in 2 Chr 33:1–20), but does not suggest
that this grace is available apart from repentance. As Wright says, "The
offer is open only to those who truly repent."[19]

Ezekiel calls for repentance to be demonstrated both negatively and
positively.[20] Offenders must "turn away from all the sins they have committed" and must "keep [God's] decrees and do what is just and right"
(18:21). They must "give back what they took in pledge for a loan and
return what they have stolen" (33:15). Negatively, repentance means a
rejection of former ways, and positively, it means putting things right
even if it is costly.[21]

16. C. Wright, *Message of Ezekiel*, 198.

17. C. Wright, *Message of Ezekiel*, 199.

18. C. Wright, *Message of Ezekiel*, 201.

19. C. Wright, *Message of Ezekiel*, 203.

20. C. Wright, *Message of Ezekiel*, 204.

21. C. Wright, *Message of Ezekiel*, 206.

One should not think that the NT has a different definition of repentance or that it removes repentance as the condition for forgiveness.[22]
John the Baptist says:

> The ax is already at the root of the trees, and every tree that
> does not produce good fruit will be cut down and thrown into
> the fire. "What should we do then?" the crowd asked. John an-
> swered, "Anyone who has two shirts should share with the one
> who has none, and the one who has food should do the same."
> Even tax collectors came to be baptized. "Teacher," they asked,
> "What should we do?" "Don't collect any more than you are
> required to," he told them. Then some soldiers asked him, "And
> what should we do?" He replied, "Don't extort money and don't
> accuse people falsely—be content with your pay." (Luke 3:9–14)

John the Baptist's answers concerning what repentance involves are
in line with the OT. To the Pharisees who came to him to be baptized he
said, "Produce fruit in keeping with repentance" (Luke 3:8). The evidence
of radical change is what led Jesus to proclaim that salvation had come to
the house of Zacchaeus (Luke 19:1–10).[23]

The repentance of which Ezekiel speaks also cleanses. Of the one
who repents Ezekiel says, "None of the offenses they have committed will
be remembered against them. Because of the righteous things they have
done, they will live" (18:22; cf. 33:16). To say it will not be remembered
is a metaphorical way of emphasizing how thoroughly the wrongs are
removed. The slate is wiped clean. The debt is canceled. Reconciliation is
now possible. Wright says:

> This is the gospel that we as Christians know through the cross
> of our Lord Jesus Christ, the gospel so richly celebrated in many
> NT texts. But OT believers celebrated it in advance. Even if they
> did not yet know the means, they knew the character of Yah-
> weh their God: that he is "the compassionate and gracious God,
> slow to anger, abounding in love and faithfulness, maintaining
> love to thousands, and forgiving wickedness, rebellion, and sin."
> (Ezek 34:6–7)[24]

---

22. C. Wright, *Message of Ezekiel*, 206.

23. C. Wright, *Message of Ezekiel*, 206.

24. C. Wright, *Message of Ezekiel*, 208.

(These verses are good examples of ones in which forgiveness is proclaimed without mentioning repentance, but in which repentance is clearly presupposed.)

Ezekiel closes chapters 18 and 33 by proclaiming that repentance is the essential difference between life and death. God says, "Why will you die, people of Israel? For I take no pleasure in the death of anyone, declares the Sovereign LORD. Repent and live!" (Ezek 18:31–32; cf. 33:11). The same sentiment is expressed by Jesus in the NT. Jesus says of the heavenly reaction when the choice to repent and "live" is made, "There is rejoicing in the presence of the angels of God over one sinner who repents" (Luke 15:10).[25] God is distraught when his people refuse to repent and thereby "choose death," and he is joyful when they repent and thereby "choose life."

THE BIBLICAL MODEL

In both the OT and the NT, God's people are called to be like him ("Be holy because I, the LORD your God, am holy"; Lev 19:2). In the Jewish tradition the duty to forgive arises indirectly out of this duty to obey and emulate God. Since God will forgive all those who truly repent, his chosen people on earth should do the same. Although the duty of the offender to seek forgiveness is absolute, the duty to forgive is conditional upon the offender's repentance.[26]

The OT is replete with divine calls to the people of Israel and to other nations to repent of their sins against God (which includes crimes against humans), promising that, if they do, God will forgive them and not punish them as he otherwise would have done. In many verses God is described as merciful, compassionate, and forgiving in response to the repentant sinner who acknowledges his sins and makes an effort to change his behavior (1 Kgs 8:46–52; Ps 51:1–4; Jer 3:11–12; Ezek 18:21–23; Jonah 3:1–10). However, in none of these verses is God depicted as forgiving an unrepentant sinner. This unforgiveness is not a sign that he is antagonistic or unloving. In contrast, Jer 31 reveals that God is deeply pained by the suffering that Israel experiences as a result of her sins. God is not only willing to forgive in response to repentance, but also, like a loving parent, yearns for his child to return to him. He desires to forgive

---

25. C. Wright, *Message of Ezekiel*, 209.

26. MacLachlan, "Forgiveness," 35.

in order that the earlier relationship of love and companionship may be restored.[27] But in spite of his pain and his desire to be reconciled, the OT contains no indication that he will forgive apart from repentance.

However, a few passages exist that suggest that the remission of divine punishment may come apart from repentance if God's own historical purposes are at stake. The remission of punishment for God's purposes is not the same thing, however, as full forgiveness and restoration to fellowship. God may also remit punishment in response to intercession. An example is Moses' intercession for the people after the golden calf incident. The appeal of Moses is not on the basis of the people's repentance but on the basis of the preservation of God's own reputation among the nations (Exod 32:9–14). Yet the people are not depicted as forgiven or restored to fellowship in this case. The divine judgment is simply not carried out.

Certainly the Jewish concept of modeling God carries over into the NT. But does God's behavior change in any way in the NT, or are his people instructed to do differently than he does? In Matt 18:21 Peter comes to Jesus with a question saying, "Lord, how many times shall I forgive my brother or sister who sins against me? Up to seven times?" Jesus answers, "I tell you, not seven times, but seventy-seven times" (v. 22). The parallel passage in Luke is spoken to all of the disciples: "If your brother or sister sins against you, rebuke them; and if they repent, forgive them. Even if they sin against you seven times in a day and seven times come back to you saying 'I repent,' you must forgive them" (Luke 17:3–4). The verses in Matthew are the ones most often quoted, but the parallel passage in Luke demonstrates that repentance is presupposed in Matthew. In the parallel passage in Luke, Jesus makes it very clear that the forgiveness that the disciples are to offer is conditioned on repentance ("*if* they repent, forgive them").

The NT, then, parallels the OT understanding of the necessity of repentance, although that revelation is not the point of this passage. The disciples are being instructed to forgive as God does, without fail whenever the wrongdoer repents. They are to emulate God's mercy, which is endless. The OT text that is the background for Jesus' answer is Gen 4:15, 19–24. Here the criteria in question concerns vengeance that will be enacted sevenfold on anyone who harms Cain. Sevenfold is metaphorical for "completely." Lamech, who commits murder, boasts that if anyone comes after his life, vengeance will be enacted seventy-seven times,

---

27. Schimmel, "Interpersonal Forgiveness," 12.

meaning that Lamech's vengeance will be unlimited or unending.[28] Peter's question, "Should I forgive seven times?" is really asking what the complete number is. Is there a limit to how many times one must forgive? Jesus answers that "if they [the wrongdoer] repent" no limit exists. The disciples are to be like God, whose mercy is never ending. As Volf says, a distinction must be made between "the willingness to forgive and the act and specifics of forgiveness which itself waits on repentance."[29] (Other NT verses concerning God's instructions to his people concerning forgiveness are considered in Part II.)

MORAL AND ETHICAL CONSIDERATIONS RELATED TO REPENTANCE

Repentance Does Not Earn Forgiveness

Although repentance is a necessary condition for God's forgiveness, it does not earn his forgiveness. The choice to forgive and be reconciled is his free decision and is an act of mercy for which the wrongdoer should be grateful. Appropriately, the expressions of thankfulness for God's mercy and forgiveness by his people are numerous in Scripture, especially in the psalms. Similarly, in interpersonal relationships repentance does not entitle one to forgiveness. Forgiveness is a free gift of love and not a receipt for payment in full.[30] Reparations represent an attempt to put into practice the repudiation of the wrong done,[31] but they cannot bring about or earn forgiveness. One must avoid thinking in pride that he, through his repentance, is taking the initiative in the process of reconciliation or that he deserves forgiveness. Repentance does not set the terms for which forgiveness must be granted.[32] Expecting forgiveness as a right is presumptuous; one can only ask for it as a favor. In asking for forgiveness, one is acknowledging his dependence on the free decision of another for granting the request. Thus it takes the freewill decisions of two to repair a personal relationship, one choosing to repent and one

---

28. Howe, *Guilt*, 106–7.

29. Biggar, "Forgiveness," 204.

30. K. Carter, "Forgiveness Revisited," 202.

31. Brümmer, *When We Pray*, 99.

32. K. Carter, "Forgiveness Revisited," 202.

choosing to forgive, just as it takes two to establish it in the first place.[33] Although it requires the actions of both, the repentance of the wrongdoer is nevertheless primarily self-serving, whereas forgiveness is self-giving.[34]

Regret: Remorse

Sometimes in order to better understand a concept such as repentance it is helpful to understand what it is not. Repentance is not regret or remorse, but the change that is brought about by regret and remorse. Although by definition repentance is a decision not to repeat the offensive behavior, it does have an emotional component as its basis: repentance proceeds from feelings of regret and remorse. But several kinds of regret exist, not all of which lead to repentance. The kind of regret that leads to repentance is regret that serves as a motive for change. In contrast, intellectual regret comes from having misjudged the facts or miscalculated the future. Examples are regret over lending money to someone who misuses it, or regret that one did not finish a task. There is also moral regret that may follow recognition of wrongdoing. But even moral regret may not evoke change or may fail to acknowledge that the wrong has harmed other people. An example is cheating on one's income taxes. Other-oriented regret is the regret that leads to repentance, because forgiveness is essentially a personal response to moral injury and not just a response to the wrongdoing itself. In other words, the wronged party should expect a repentant wrongdoer to not only recognize and acknowledge the wrongful act but also the personal injury caused by the offense. True repentance acknowledges the wrongdoing and its injury to another person.[35]

Regret, then, may just be misgivings about actions that cause one's own discomfort, but remorse is a more significant emotion. It involves a keen awareness of moral wrong and sorrow for harm inflicted on another. Therefore it includes a deep kind of self-reproach.[36] This sorrow is what leads to repentance. As the Puritan preacher William Plumer says, "True repentance is sorrow for sin, ending in reformation. . . . Mere regret is not repentance. *Neither is mere outward reformation.* . . . He whose repentance is spurious, is chiefly concerned with consequences" (emphasis

---

33. Brümmer, *When We Pray*, 99.

34. Brümmer, *When We Pray*, 98.

35. Haber, *Forgiveness*, 91–92.

36. Konstan, *Before Forgiveness*, 9.

added).[37] Repentance involves rejecting the qualities of the self that led to the offensive behavior.[38]

Guilt

True repentance is actually even more than moral regret and a change of behavior. The moral principle needs not just to be recognized but internalized. Being moral involves having emotions such as guilt and shame. In other words, "morality . . . is not simply something to be believed: it is something to be *cared* about."[39] Guilt is healed only through a process that involves forthright admission, apology, amends-making by the wrongdoer, and forgiveness by the person who was wronged.[40] Apology and asking for forgiveness is not just about the relief from guilt for the offender: the motivation should be for the sake of the victim.[41] Concern for the victim shows deep moral regret.

One may be guilty of offenses that harmed another unintentionally. This kind of guilt is objective. One also may be guilty of doing something that he knows harms another person. This is subjective guilt. In this case the guilt is more serious, and more needs to be done to repair the damage. In addition, one may be guilty of an action whose very purpose is to harm another person. This guilt is of a qualitatively different kind. The guilt is even greater when an action is taken with the intent to harm a person who is related in some way, such as a friend or sibling. "Both objective guilt and subjective guilt are stains on a soul requiring action, but subjective guilt is embedded in the soul while objective guilt lies on the surface."[42] To recognize that one is guilty either objectively or subjectively is morally good, and for guilt to be accompanied by shame is also appropriate.[43] This is because guilt can only be removed by true repentance, which has this emotional component of shame.

---

37. Konstan, *Before Forgiveness*, 9.

38. Konstan, *Before Forgiveness*, 10.

39. Murphy and Hampton, *Forgiveness and Mercy*, 18.

40. Howe, *Guilt*, 86.

41. A. Bash, *Forgiveness and Christian Ethics*, 78.

42. Swinburne, *Responsibility and Atonement*, 75.

43. Swinburne, *Responsibility and Atonement*, 80.

Confession, Apology, and Reparations

One does not do a friend a kindness if he discourages his guilt. Rather, he should encourage repentance, apology, and amends-making, which relieve guilt feelings instead of burying them. This repentance should involve confession and disowning the act publicly by expressing to the victim the repentance that has taken place. Confession should be followed by apology that acknowledges the harm done to the victim. The apology should be followed by or include something beyond reparation to demonstrate sincerity and acknowledgement of the seriousness of the wrong done. It should be something costly in money, effort, or time. Thereby, not only is the wrongdoing admitted, but the wrongdoer distances himself from the act and shows respect for the victim. If one does not do what he can to remove the harm he did to another, he remains guilty for the harm. As in the trespass offering, reparation, as far as it lies in the power of the wrongdoer, is essential for the removal of the taint of guilt. To ask forgiveness is not to ask that those you have harmed forget the wrong you have done.[44] That would be presumption. From the trespass offering in the OT law to the words of John the Baptist and the actions of Zacchaeus in the NT, the Bible emphasizes the need for repentance to be demonstrated by reparations whenever possible.

Apology can often be very difficult. However, for some it seems to be easy. If this is the case, the apology is generally insincere.[45] Sometimes people are willing to say, "I am sorry you were hurt" or "I am sorry you were offended" without any confession of wrongdoing. They then claim to have done their part to make the relationship right. This is certainly not the biblical pattern or moral model for bringing about reconciliation or for seeking forgiveness. The steps in true repentance are regret and remorse, the decision to change, apology, asking for forgiveness in humility, making reparations, and a change in behavior. When these steps are followed, the wrongdoer has done all he can to bring about reconciliation.

The Limits of Amends-Making

In everyday situations, amends-making may fail if the compensation is insufficient for the particular offense. For example, if one loses an expensive

---

44. Park, *Hurt to Healing*, 98.

45. Swinburne, *Responsibility and Atonement*, 83.

piece of borrowed jewelry and buys in return a cheap copy, the amends are insufficient. Amends-making may also fail if the compensation is adequate in value but is not what the offended party wants. In these situations the offended party may recognize that little chance of real change (repentance) exists on the part of those who harmed or took advantage of him.[46] The offended party may accept the amends/apology but not want a restoration to the previous relationship. For example, a boyfriend may lie to his girlfriend. He may apologize, and she may choose to accept the apologies with no hard feelings, but not continue to go out with him.[47]

However, not all situations of wrongdoing are of an everyday character.[48] There are wrongs that no human being should inflict on another under any circumstances. Sometimes actions may bring about destructiveness in a victim's life that is beyond repair. There can be no amends-making—only repentance in the knowledge that it would be presumptuous to assume the restoration or establishment of relationship.[49] Grown children may accept their father's apology for abandoning them but not feel obligated to begin a relationship with him.[50]

Clearly, full reparation is often not possible.[51] As Howe says:

> There are situations . . . in which wrongdoing, whether deliberate or inadvertent, unleashes consequences that are too painful for apologies to salve and too destructive for amends to compensate. . . . Reconciliation is possible in such situations but not by making amends. When harm is irreparable, amends cannot suffice. Only forgiveness can.[52]

It is reasonable to think that some evildoing is so horrible that later repentance is simply irrelevant to the victim even if not to God.[53]

---

46. Howe, *Guilt*, 86.
47. Howe, *Guilt*, 86.
48. Howe, *Guilt*, 87.
49. Howe, *Guilt*, 88.
50. Howe, *Guilt*, 86.
51. Swinburne, *Responsibility and Atonement*, 82.
52. Howe, *Guilt*, 85.
53. A. Bash, *Forgiveness and Christian Ethics*, 237.

The Logic and Morality of Unforgiveness

The logic that forgiveness requires repentance is based on the understanding of forgiveness as entailing the restoration of a particular relationship.[54] The OT and the NT are united in regarding the purpose of forgiveness as a restoration to fellowship, and that forgiveness is conditional upon repentance and confession.[55] If there is no sign of a change of heart, then the reforming effect of a willingness to forgive or the reconciling effect of forgiveness itself is lost. Forgiveness without repentance encourages the sinner to persist in his line of wrongdoing. In these cases forgiveness is clearly open to practical and even moral objections.[56] Dietrich Bonhoeffer, in his book *The Cost of Discipleship*, says:

> The preaching of forgiveness must always go hand in hand with the preaching of repentance, the preaching of the gospel with the preaching of the law. Nor can the forgiveness of sin be unconditional—sometimes sin must be retained. It is the will of the Lord himself that the gospel not be given to dogs. He too held that the only way to safeguard the gospel of forgiveness was by preaching repentance. If the church refuses to face the stern reality of sin, it will gain no credence when it talks of forgiveness. Such a church sins against its sacred trust and walks unworthily of the gospel. It is an unholy church, squandering the precious treasure of the Lord's forgiveness.[57]

Christof Gestrich, in *The Return of Splendor in the World: The Christian Doctrine of Sin and Forgiveness*, follows Bonhoeffer in "attributing the decline of the Christian church in Western Europe in large measure to the preaching of forgiveness without discipleship."[58] The integrity of any reconciliation and the moral growth of the offender requires repentance.[59]

Love also requires repentance. Like a loving parent God does not forgive or overlook the child's wrongdoing as long as the behavior is ongoing. But God, again like a parent, is always "ready to meet the child's

54. Benn, "Forgiveness and Loyalty," 373.

55. Biggar, "Forgiveness," 204.

56. Kolnai, "Forgiveness," 103.

57. Bonhoeffer, *Discipleship*, 287–88.

58. Biggar, "Forgiveness," 204.

59. Biggar, "Forgiveness," 201.

first glimmer of regret with a loving embrace."[60] As shown in Scripture, prior to forgiveness God feels both wrath and love. After God forgives he feels love and joy. His love is constant. His wrath is a sign of his love in that he cares about both the wrongdoing and the well-being of the wrongdoer. His joy is a sign of his love in that it shows his goodwill toward the sinner. He desires that he repent and be forgiven, and when that happens it brings God joy.

Love wants the best for the one loved; therefore, forgiveness without repentance cannot be an act of love. In fact, as Bash says, "Forgiveness without repentance is morally irresponsible because it leaves the wrong-doer free not to accept that the action was wrong and so free to repeat the wrongdoing."[61] The Jewish thinker Emanuel Levinas writes, "There is no forgiveness that has not been requested by the guilty. The guilty must recognize his sin."[62] Otherwise forgiveness simply condones that which is morally wrong.[63] God cannot be morally wrong, therefore logically and morally he "cannot" forgive sin for which there is no sorrow.

God is depicted throughout Scripture as unwilling to forgive the unrepentant, but he is never depicted as unwilling to forgive the repentant. In other words, to say that God is forgiving is to say that he is willing to forgive and joyful in forgiveness, not that he automatically or always forgives. To be unforgiving, then, is the opposite of being forgiving. In the *New International Biblical Commentary: 1 and 2 Timothy, Titus*, Gordon Fee says that to be unforgiving means that one is "incapable of being reconciled to a fellow human being" (2 Tim 3:3).[64] To again quote Volf, "The *will* to embrace is indiscriminate, the embrace itself is conditional."[65] It is reasonable to assume that in this "will to embrace," or willingness to forgive, God's people are also called to emulate him, letting their willingness to forgive be known. Perhaps they should be active in wooing back the offender[66] just as God is active throughout the OT in calling his rebellious people back to himself.

---

60. Biggar, "Forgiveness," 183.

61. A. Bash, *Forgiveness and Ethics*, 63.

62. Konstan, *Before Forgiveness*, 8.

63. Konstan, *Before Forgiveness*, 8.

64. Fee, *1 and 2 Timothy, Titus*, 270.

65. Volf, *Exclusion and Embrace*, 29.

66. Biggar, "Forgiveness," 198.

SUMMARY: REPENTANCE

The meaning of the word repent, according to its biblical usage, is to change one's mind and turn in a new direction to God or back to God. Repentance involves a decision as well as outward change of life resulting from that decision. The call to repentance and the offer of forgiveness for the repentant person is a major biblical theme. The NT emphasizes the continuity with the OT concerning the necessity of repentance in that it quotes the OT prophets and repeatedly stresses repentance. The necessity of repentance is the essence of the ministry of John the Baptist and is also emphasized in Jesus' announcement of the kingdom, the Apostles' outreach to the world, and Paul's teaching. So the need for repentance is a biblical theme that is as prevalent in the NT as it is in the OT.

The Bible stresses that God's love is constant and that he longs for people to repent so that he may bless them with his presence and favor. God is merciful in that he chooses to forgive those who repent. There is no suggestion, however, that he will overlook sin or forgive sin apart from repentance. Neither does repentance obligate him to forgive: it is his free gift. God's wrath is his reaction to evil and is a sign of his holiness and his love. His judgments proceed from his righteousness. He does not have to judge, but he chooses to punish when it is the right thing to do. Indeed often he intends that punishment will help bring the wrongdoer back to himself. The Bible states that God is longsuffering, sometimes delaying punishment in order to allow increased time and opportunity for repentance.

The Bible also proclaims that God is just, meaning that he is always fair. The eighteenth chapter of Ezekiel speaks of God's justice, stating that each person will only have to answer to God for his own actions and not for those of others. Although God is always just, retribution and mercy (forgiveness) are acts of his free will based on his character. He does not always punish, and he does not always forgive. Repentance is the deciding factor.

Both the OT and the NT reveal God's deeply felt desire that people repent and come to him. Ezekiel also speaks of God's grief and pain when people refuse to repent and turn to him. God cries out, "Why will ye die, O house of Israel?" Their choice is a matter of life and death. Jesus expresses the same emotion as he looks at Jerusalem: "Jerusalem, Jerusalem, you who kill the prophets and stone those sent to you, how often I have longed to gather your children together, as a hen gathers her chicks under her wings, and you were not willing" (Luke 13:34).

Repentance on the part of the wrongdoer and forgiveness on the part of God result in the complete removal of the sin and therefore of any barrier to reconciliation. Reconciliation, which includes peace, fellowship, and a restored relationship, is the goal and the end of repentance and forgiveness. Relationships of love are God's heart desire, and therefore he is grieved whenever reconciliation is not possible because of an unwillingness to repent on the part of the wrongdoer.

Repentance may be motivated by remorse or guilt, but the word does not refer to those feelings. To repent of a sin means that a person (1) humbly takes responsibility for and confesses his sin (i.e., accepts guilt), (2) that he regrets his sin, (3) that he is ashamed of his sin, (4) that he recognizes the personal harm done to another person by his sin, (5) that if it were possible to go back in time he would choose not to commit the sin, (6) that he intends to forsake that sin in the future, (7) that he makes every possible effort to repair the damage done by his actions, and (8) that he does something beyond reparations to demonstrate goodwill and respect for his victim. All of these components are a part of true biblical repentance. These essential elements indicate that repentance is an act of the will that takes courage and is indeed powerful.

CHAPTER 2 STUDY QUESTIONS

The Term Repentance

1. What is the first foundational doctrine named in Hebrews?

2. What does *metanoein* mean? Does the basic meaning involve an emotion or a decision?

3. How does remorse differ from repentance?

4. When God is said to repent, to what does it usually refer?

The Biblical Call to Repentance

1. How does John the Baptist's preaching of repentance "prepare the way for the Lord"?

2. What is the first recorded command of Jesus in the Gospel of Mark?

3. What does Jesus commission his disciples to go into all the world and preach?

4. On the day of Pentecost how does Peter respond to the question, "What shall we do?"

5. What message was Paul called to preach to the Gentiles?

6. How does omitting repentance from the Gospel mislead sinners and misrepresent God?

Regret versus Repentance

1. How has the tendency to think about repentance changed over time?

2. Is recognition and admission of wrongdoing synonymous with repentance? Give biblical examples.

3. Does a change in behavior always indicate true repentance?

4. How are sorrow for sin and repentance from sin different?

Repentance Is the Condition of God's Favor and Forgiveness

1. Is repentance a condition of God's love?

2. Why is God's call to repentance often accompanied by judgment from him?

3. What is the "if/then" principle found throughout Scripture concerning repentance and forgiveness?

The Ministry of a Prophet

1. What OT role is characterized by the call to repentance? Should it also be a part of the ministry of present day Christians?

2. What does condonation of sin demonstrate?

Repentance and Forgiveness Lead to Reconciliation

1. Why does God forgive the one who repents?

2. What is symbolized by the scapegoat on the Day of Atonement?

Demonstration of Repentance

1. What OT offering demonstrates that true repentance should include outward reparation?

2. What did John the Baptist require of the Pharisees and Sadducees coming to him for baptism?

3. What actions of Zacchaeus demonstrated his repentance?

Repentance, Forgiveness, and Judgment: A Case Study

1. According to Ezekiel, the difference between life and death is based on what?

The Biblical Model

1. In the Jewish tradition, on what is the duty to forgive based?

2. Are there any biblical examples of God forgiving an *un*repentant sinner?

Moral and Ethical Considerations Related to Repentance

Repentance Does not Earn Forgiveness

1. Although it requires the actions of both parties, in what way is the repentance of the offender self-serving and the forgiveness of the victim self-giving?

Regret: Remorse

1. How does the decision to repent relate to feelings of regret and remorse?

Guilt

1. Repentance should be motivated by what in addition to relief from guilt?

Confession, Apology, and Reparations

1. Why is discouraging someone's guilt not an act of kindness?
2. How can one judge the sincerity of an apology?

The Limits of Amends-Making

1. Is amends-making always possible? Why or why not?

The Logic and Morality of Unforgiveness

1. Why is forgiveness apart from repentance morally objectionable?
2. According to Bonhoeffer, is forgiveness of sin unconditional?
3. What does God feel prior to the repentance of the wrongdoer? After?
4. Why is forgiveness apart from repentance not an act of love?
5. Does the fact that God is willing to forgive mean that he automatically or always forgives?

3

The Biblical Meaning of Forgiveness

HAVING COMPLETED THE EXAMINATION of the meaning of repentance in its biblical usage, the biblical meaning of the term *forgiveness* will now be examined. Modern definitions—and many exist—vary considerably from the biblical concept and often involve only the overcoming of resentment by the offended party. Forgiveness is then internal and may be unilateral (not based on repentance), and it does not necessarily lead to reconciliation. The biblical practice, however, always involves both parties (the sinner and the sinned-against), is an external act, and ends in reconciliation. In order to draw conclusions about the practice and purpose of forgiveness, the term must be clearly defined.

THE OLD TESTAMENT CONCEPT OF FORGIVENESS

Multiple Hebrew words are used to describe the OT concept of forgiveness. The principal meaning communicated has to do with sins being removed on behalf of the sinner so that there can be atonement. The etymological meaning of the word atonement can be readily discerned. It can be broken down into three words belonging together: at-one-ment.[1] It is, then, an Old English word signifying "setting at one," and hence the removal of enmity and the healing of estrangement. Originally it was a term of ordinary daily speech.[2] English Bibles of the sixteenth and

1. Peters, "Atonement and Final Scapegoat," 153.
2. Smith, *Atonement in Light of History*, 3.

seventeenth centuries began using atonement to translate the Hebrew *kaphar* and the Greek *hilasmos* and *katallage*, meaning expiation and reconciliation. In the developing theological vocabulary the term came to refer to the state of reconciliation between a gracious God and estranged humanity, the state of at-one-ment accomplished through the work of the savior, Jesus Christ.

In our modern speech the word atonement is not commonly used in secular contexts, but when it is used it generally implies compensation for wrong, rendered by the wrongdoer. That the words atone and atonement have changed their meaning in this way is largely due to the influence of Christian usage in a theory of atonement that views Christ's death as a satisfaction for sins, a payment of the debt incurred by man to God.[3] However, when the word atonement is used in its biblical application it refers only to at-one-ment (reconciliation) and not to payment for sins. Repentance and forgiveness result in atonement/reconciliation.

In the OT, the most commonly used verb that expresses forgiveness is *kaphar*, and it is found most often in the sacrificial rites. In common usage *kipper* means cover and hence its soteriological sense is to cover sin, meaning to make atonement for (forgive) sin. But cover is actually its derivative sense, the root idea of the verb being to wipe or smear. *Kipper*, then, is a picturesque synonym for *salach*, "forgive" or "be merciful." It signifies the removal of sin brought about by repentance and forgiveness, which results in the removal of wrath and in atonement (i.e., reconciliation). Sins are covered (removed—atoned for) by the blood of the animal that is offered as a sacrifice on behalf of the life of the sinner. The reference to covering as God's forgiveness of the offender is usually translated "atone" or "forgive" (Deut 21:8; Ps 78:38; Jer 18:23), and represents a divine act of dealing with human sins effecting atonement/reconciliation.[4]

A second Hebrew word translated "forgive," *salach*, simply means to send away or let go. The reference again is to the removal of sin. This verb is not used with forgiveness among people but exclusively with God granting forgiveness. It is used for the denial of forgiveness when God rejects a plea (Deut 29:20; Jer 5:7), the granting of forgiveness when God is willing (Num 14:20; 15:22–25; 30:6–12; 2 Chr 7:12–14; Neh 9:17; Ps 25:11; 86:5; 103:3; Isa 55:7; Jer 31:31–34; 33:8), and the plea for

---

3. Burnaby, *Christian Words*, 96.

4. Musekura, *Models of Forgiveness*, 27.

forgiveness itself (Exod 34:9; Num 14:19; 1 Kgs 8:30–50; 2 Kgs 5:18; 2 Chr 6:21–39; Amos 7:1–3).[5]

A third Hebrew word translated as forgiveness is *nasa*, which means to lift, lift up, take away, or carry away. The idea is that guilt is being taken away, atoned for, or borne, resulting in divine pardon and human forgiveness. This verb can be used figuratively to express the idea of God taking and carrying away the sin and guilt of his people. As a result of this action God is described as one who "[forgives] wickedness, rebellion and sin," and the one "who pardons sin and forgives the transgression of the remnant of his inheritance" (Exod 34:7; Mic 7:18). This image is also used in the NT when Jesus is called the "Lamb of God, who takes away the sin of the world" (John 1:29). This verse makes a statement concerning Jesus' character and work, and does not mean that all sin is automatically forgiven. The verb *nasa* is also used for bearing someone's sin and guilt, bearing injustice by taking the consequences of someone else's sin. The image presented by this verb is of God freeing the sinner of his sin and guilt by lifting it up, taking it away from him, and bearing the consequences himself.[6]

The fourth Hebrew verb used in the OT, *machah*, means to wipe, wipe out, erase, blot out, exterminate, and obliterate from the memory. This verb expresses forgiveness in the sense of wiping out sins and guilt, ensuring that the stain is removed and that the offender has a clean record and a new beginning. To forgive and forget does not literally mean the loss of memory, but rather that the offense has lost its significance in the mind of the forgiver. This verb is used in Moses' prayer to "blot out" his name from the divine book (Exod 32:33) and by David when he asks that his sins be "blotted out" and that he be washed clean (Ps 51:1–2).[7]

By definition, then, the OT words rendered "forgive" demonstrate that forgiveness involves the complete removal of sin. Psalm 25:18 says, "Look on my affliction and my distress and take away [*nasa*] all my sins." Psalm 103 says in reference to God that "he does not treat us as our sins deserve or repay us according to our iniquities. . . . as far as the east is from the west, so far has he removed our transgressions from us" (103:10, 12). To whom is this mercy and forgiveness extended? To "those who fear

---

5. Musekura, *Models of Forgiveness*, 27.

6. Musekura, *Models of Forgiveness*, 28.

7. Musekura, *Models of Forgiveness*, 29.

him" (vv. 11, 17). And what does this forgiveness involve? The complete removal of sins (v. 12).

THE NEW TESTAMENT CONCEPT OF FORGIVENESS

In the NT four major Greek words are used to speak of forgiveness. The first is the Greek verb *aphiemi*, which comes from two other words meaning "from" and "to put in motion" or "to send." In most cases the NT uses this verb with reference to trespasses (Matt 6:14, 15), sin (Luke 5:20), and debts (Matt 18:32). The idea conveyed is the removal of sin.[8]

The second, *aphesis*, (the Greek cognate noun of *aphiemi*) means freedom or liberation from something that confines, for example, from an obligation, guilt, or punishment. The common meaning of the verb is to leave or to abandon (e.g., Luke 4:39, "[the fever] left her"). In pre-Christian secular Greek, *aphesis* does not refer to forgiveness.[9] In its NT context it denotes pardon, forgiveness of sin, or the cancellation of the guilt of sin. Forgiving is a voluntary mental action whereby one cancels the debt due for the suffering, pain, disappointment, and injury caused by another. The noun, translated "forgiveness" (*aphesis*), denotes a dismissal or release and is used of the remission of sins (Mark 3:29; Eph 1:7; Col 1:14). When *aphesis* is translated "forgiveness," it usually refers to forgiveness that is granted by God.[10] The forgiving action by God has liberating results for the wrongdoer: the removal of sin or its consequences. Therefore forgiveness (*aphesis*) is not unilateral but involves both parties.

A third Greek word sometimes used to express the idea of forgiveness, *charizomai*, has a range of meanings: to give freely as a favor, to cancel a sum of money that is owed, and to show oneself gracious by forgiving wrongdoing. It can express either divine (Eph 4:32; Col 2:13; 3:13) or human forgiveness (Luke 7:42, 43; 2 Cor 2:7, 10; 12:13; Eph 4:32). The most common meaning is to pardon, to graciously remit a person's sin (Col 2:13). This forgiveness is expected in the community and is based on the model of Christ. "Be kind and compassionate to one another, forgiving each other, just as in Christ God forgave you" (Eph 4:32). The emphasis is on kindness and undeserved favor, and therefore the meaning is to forgive because one is gracious. Although this word can

---

8. Musekura, *Models of Forgiveness*, 29.

9. Bash and Bash, "Early Christian Thinking," 30.

10. Musekura, *Models of Forgiveness*, 29, 30.

legitimately be translated "forgive," this is not the normal rending of the word. *Charizomai* is essentially "saying or doing something agreeable, showing favor, kindness, pleasantness."[11]

The fourth NT word translated "forgive," *apoluo*, is formed from a combination of two words meaning "loose" and "from." This verb is generally used in the sense of release, to send away, dismiss, let go, send off, set free, forgive, and leave. In Luke 6:37 the phrase "forgive and you will be forgiven" is a reference to setting a person free in a quasi-judicial act. One is set free from sin because it is removed.[12]

By definition, then, the NT words that are translated "forgive," like the OT words, involve the removal of sin as the barrier to reconciliation. Romans 4:7 says, "Blessed are those whose transgressions are forgiven, whose sins are covered [*aphiemi*]" (quoting Ps 32:1–2). The NT speaks of both forgiveness of sins and forgiveness of sinners. If the direct object of the verb forgive is sins, then the reference is to the removal of sin. If the direct object is the sinner, then the reference is to setting the sinner free from sin's power or consequences. The core meaning of the concept of forgiveness in the NT indicated by these Greek words reveals a removal of sin, a release from a sin, and a pardon from sin. The NT concept is thus like the OT concept.

BIBLICAL METAPHORS FOR FORGIVENESS

By using these various words the Bible gives several different pictures of what forgiveness accomplishes: carrying (away) a burden, covering up or blotting out a stain, canceling a debt, and giving a gift. All involve the removal of sin; however, these different metaphors describe the meaning and significance of forgiveness from different points of view. For the wrongdoer there is release from the burden of sin (guilt feelings) as well as the remission of debt. For the forgiver, forgiveness is a gift given in spite of pain, a gift that eliminates the offense as a barrier to reconciliation. From the viewpoint of the moral community, the significance is the erasure of the stain of sin. Each of these metaphors speaks of a different aspect of forgiveness and brings out features of forgiveness that might otherwise be overlooked. An understanding of each image is essential to understand the practice of forgiveness. Any account of the Christian

11. Musekura, *Models of Forgiveness*, 30, 31.

12. Musekura, *Models of Forgiveness*, 31.

practice of forgiveness should accommodate all of the images presented in these metaphors.[13] Each of these metaphors will now be examined more closely.

Lifting a Burden and Bearing It Away

First, the biblical model of forgiveness involves lifting a burden and bearing it away (Hebrew *nasa*: to lift up or carry away, and *salach*: to let go or bear; Greek *aphiemi*: to remit, send away, or liberate). The wrongdoer is involved in the process and is definitely affected by the action of the forgiver. This imagery focuses on the effect of wrongdoing on those who do it. Sin is pictured as a burden that weighs the guilty one down, and forgiveness brings relief from the burden of guilt. For this understanding of forgiveness to be plausible, the wrongs must be burdensome. If the wrongdoer feels no guilt, then this metaphor does not hold up—therefore the biblical practice of forgiveness would not be applicable. Forgiveness given would not accomplish its end.

What makes wrongdoing harmful to the wrongdoer? Generally, the reference is to the burden of guilt. However, it can be the punitive consequences, perhaps retaliation or prosecution. So, in addition to relieving guilt feelings, the lifting of the burden can refer to the remission of punishment, relief from the threat of revenge, or the ending of alienation or estrangement. Yet forgiveness must be distinguished from the remission of punishment, although it may sometimes involve the remission of punishment.[14]

The Hebrew expression involved in this metaphor is "bearing sin." The guilty one bears responsibility for their wrongdoing and its consequences. People will bear their iniquity for doing anything forbidden by the Lord's commandments (Lev 5:17; for example Lev 5:1; 7:18; 17:16; 19:8; 20:17, 19; Num 5:31; Ezek 14:10; 18:19–20; 44:10–12).[15] But when forgiveness is involved, the sin is borne by the forgiver, with most references to God or to the priest bearing it on God's behalf. Thus Tim Carter in his book *The Forgiveness of Sins* says:

> After the golden calf incident, Moses asks God either to bear
> the sin of the people or to blot him out of the book of life (Exod

13. MacLachlan, "Forgiveness," 56.

14. MacLachlan, "Forgiveness," 37.

15. T. Carter, *Forgiveness of Sins*, 25.

32:32). God subsequently reveals himself to Moses as the one who bears iniquity, transgression and sin (Exod 34:7), and Moses reminds the Lord of this as he asks him to bear the iniquity of his people after they refuse to enter the Promised Land (Num 14:18–19): God's response is to say that they will bear their iniquity for forty years (14:34) . . . . When God tells the people that he will send an angel ahead of them to bring them into the place he has prepared for them, he warns them to be attentive and to listen to his voice without rebelling; he will not bear their transgression, because God's name is in him (Exod 23:21). Joshua warns the people at the end of his life that God is a jealous God who will not bear their transgressions or their sins (Josh 24:19). Job demands to know why God will not pardon his transgression or bear his iniquity (Job 7:21).

In Ps 25:18 we find a request that the Lord will bear all the psalmist's sins, while Ps 32:5 records a testimony that the Lord bore the iniquity of his people and covered their sin. Isaiah records God's promise that the iniquity of the people living in Zion will be borne, presumably by the Lord, since the import is that their iniquity is forgiven (33:24). Hosea urges Israel to return to the Lord and entreat him to bear all their iniquity (14:2), while Micah draws on God's revelation of his nature to Moses in Exod 34:7 as he concludes his prophecy with the declaration that God bears iniquity and will pass over the transgression of his people (7:18).[16]

In these examples the perpetrator is pictured as bearing responsibility and guilt. In forgiving, the victim chooses to lift the burden, thereby bearing the sin himself in the sense of lifting it.

Blotting Out Sin

Second, the biblical act of forgiveness involves blotting out (removing) sin from the view of the one sinned against. There are actually several different images that convey this idea. Sin is removed (Ps 103:12), blotted out (Ps 51:1, 9; Isa 43:25; 44:22), or washed away (Isa 4:4; Acts 22:16; 1 Cor 6:11). A strong image is presented in Mic 7:19: "You will tread our sins underfoot and hurl all our iniquities into the depths of the sea."

This removal of sin means that after the victim forgives, he, like God, no longer sees the offense when he looks upon the one who harmed him.

16. T. Carter, *Forgiveness of Sins*, 26.

The wrong done is no longer a part of his relationship with the offender. This is only possible and is even actually reasonable because the offender has repented. The offender has, through his apology and demonstrated repentance, rejected in himself that which caused the offense, therefore the one sinned against can now correctly view him in a different way. The barrier to restored relationship is truly removed. Having committed a crime, "it can never, being once true, cease to be true" that the crime was committed, but is the offender forever a liar or thief? No. Repentance effects an alteration in his essential self.[17] Therefore the sin may be reasonably and justly "blotted out" from view. Psalm 32:1–2 says, "Blessed is the one whose transgressions are forgiven, whose sins are covered. Blessed is the one whose sin the LORD does not count against them and in whose spirit is no deceit." The fact of the offense is not removed, rather, the offense is no longer counted against the guilty one because the offender has become one "in whose spirit is no deceit." He does not hide or deny his guilt and need for forgiveness, and as a result he is blessed (v. 1). Just as Ps 32:1 equates forgiveness with sins being covered or removed from view, the NT speaks of forgiveness in this same metaphorical way (1 Pet 4:8; Jas 5:20).

Remission of Debt

Third, biblical forgiveness is metaphorically pictured as the remission of a debt. When it comes to financial transactions, the meaning clear. The term forgiveness is used in such cases, for one is said to forgive a debt.[18] Scripture speaks in the same way. God does not "reckon sin" ("count against" NIV) wrote the apostle Paul (Rom 4:8), quoting the psalmist (Ps 32:2). One may incur debt, but God in forgiveness blots out the debt column of his life.[19]

In what way is the wrongdoer indebted to the victim of his actions? The victim is entitled to retribution as satisfaction (payback), which symbolically is a kind of currency against which the harm done is balanced. The forgiver makes a choice to waive this debt, this right to insist on retribution, the desire to even the score. The choice to forgive is based on the debtor's asking for debt cancellation. "If we confess our sins he is

---

17. Moberly, *Atonement and Personality*, 37.

18. Volf, *Free of Charge*, 169.

19. Volf, *Free of Charge*, 142–43.

faithful and just and will forgive us our sins" (1 John 1:9); "If your brother sins, rebuke him; and if he repents, forgive him" (Luke 17:3–4 NASB). His request for forgiveness clearly acknowledges a debt (as a metaphor for sin). Once again both the victim and the wrongdoer are involved in the practice of forgiveness as it is presented in this biblical metaphor. Forgiveness is not unilateral.

Giving a Gift

In the remission of debt metaphor, the offender receives a gift in that his debt is canceled. From the perspective of the forgiver, a gift is given. In the act of forgiving, the victim not only declines to exact what is owed, he actually extends something positive to the wrongdoer. This gift metaphor emphasizes the elective and gracious nature of forgiveness. Forgiveness is a gift because no obligation to forgive exists. Like forgiveness viewed as the remission of a debt, the gift metaphor demonstrates that both the forgiver and the offender are involved, for if a gift is to be given, the gift must be received.[20] The giver should forget what he has given, but the receiver should remember what he has received. "Thus the giver's pride is banished [and] the . . . recipient's gratitude is retained."[21] "To forgive is to give wrongdoers the gift of not counting the wrong against them," which presupposes that a wrong has been done and condemned.[22]

Again, recognition of wrongdoing and confession is essential for this to take place, for without repentance the wrongdoer does not even recognize forgiveness as a gift. Therefore this gift metaphor, involving canceling a debt (not counting a wrong) and lifting a burden (guilt feelings), does not hold up in the absence of repentance.

The gift metaphor emphasizes that when one forgives he is not primarily seeking his own good but the good of the wrongdoer who receives this gift. One does benefit from forgiving just as one benefits from giving, for it is more blessed to give than to receive (Acts 20:35). Forgiveness brings inner peace and freedom. But just as one gives for the benefit of another, one should forgive for the other's benefit and not for selfish reasons. Emotional healing is desirable, but it is not the main reason to forgive. To forgive means to forgo a rightful claim against someone who

---

20. MacLachlan, "Forgiveness," 73.

21. Volf, *Free of Charge*, 113.

22. Volf, *Free of Charge*, 129–30.

has done wrong. As the biblical metaphor emphasizes and as Miroslav Volf says in his book *Free of Charge*, "[Forgiveness] is a gift we give not so much to ourselves as to the one who has wronged us whether we are emotionally healed as a result or not."[23]

SUMMARY: THE BIBLICAL DEFINITION OF FORGIVENESS

In conclusion, by definition the biblical concept of forgiveness involves the removal of sin. In fact, each Hebrew and Greek word used has as its core meaning the elimination of sin as the barrier to reconciliation. This is not open to interpretation; reconciliation occurs only after the repentance of the sinner and the giving of forgiveness by the one sinned against. Then the sin, the cause of the problem and estrangement and the barrier to reconciliation, is removed. According to the biblical model, no justification exists for the removal of sin through forgiveness without repentance. Neither can there be reconciliation without the removal of the sin through forgiveness. NT forgiveness is in harmony with the OT concept in which God, through grace, forgives in response to repentance, which always precedes forgiveness. Forgiveness is a gift because God does not have to forgive.[24]

THE MEANING OF SACRIFICE

Forgiveness as a gift of God's grace is presented in the OT through the system of sacrifice. It has already been shown that sin is removed following repentance; therefore, reconciliation/atonement takes place. Sacrifice is the symbolic ceremonial provision that enacts the process (repentance and removal of sin) and the resulting atonement (restoration of fellowship demonstrated by the peace offering).

Sacrifice is the expression of a person's desire for friendship with God. It served the divine purpose of emphasizing the heinousness of all sin in the sight of a holy God. It provided the way of drawing near to God and was a promise and symbol of God's readiness to forgive and to accept those who followed the appointed means of restoring their covenant

---

23. Volf, *Free of Charge*, 168–69.
24. A. Bash, *Forgiveness and Christian Ethics*, 24.

relationship.[25] An offering, usually in the form of blood, is brought to God. The blood symbolizes the life or soul of the offerer that is presented to God. Sin is forgiven, the offerer is cleansed, and communion with God is restored. There were no provisions of sacrifice for willfully defiant sins that were punished by death or excommunication (Num 15:27–31).

Sacrifice was the means of reconciliation appointed by God himself in his grace. The significance of the sacrificial actions are summarized as follows. A person comes to make his offering and identifies himself with the animal by the laying on of hands. It is slain, symbolizing the surrender of his life to God. The priest takes the blood, which represents the life surrendered, into the Holy Place, signifying God's acceptance of it. The body of the animal is burned upon the altar, signifying the offerer's total giving of himself to God. There follows a meal indicating that peace and fellowship with God are restored. God and the worshiper are reconciled. "Life is offered, completely surrendered, accepted by God, transformed, and shared."[26] This summary forms a composite of the elements of the sacrificial ritual that are never found in this unity in any one type of sacrifice, yet all these actions are a part of one type of sacrifice or another. No vicarious punishment is suggested by the actions taken in making sacrifice. The essential element is the surrender of life, not its destruction.[27]

Appointed by God

The first point made is that sacrifice is the *result* of God's grace and not its cause.[28] It is given *by* God before it is given *to* him. God designed the ritual of the sin offering in his desire for reconciliation. Individuals may respond to the way appointed by God by bringing the offering, but God, in his mercy, takes the initiative in providing the means of reconciliation.[29] Therefore when one brings a sacrifice, it is not so much that he brings a gift to God as that he comes to appropriate God's gift: the institution of sacrifice itself.[30] The sacrificial ritual reveals God's heart, that he does not desire the death of a sinner but his restoration. (The NT also

25. Robinson, *How Jesus Christ Saves Men*, 25–26.

26. Robinson, *How Jesus Christ Saves Men*, 132.

27. Robinson, *How Jesus Christ Saves Men*, 132.

28. Forsyth, *Cruciality of the Cross*, 89.

29. Baillie, *God Was in Christ*, 187.

30. Forsyth, *Cruciality of the Cross*, 90.

stresses the activity of the Father in restoration: "But God demonstrates his own love for us in this: While we were still sinners, Christ died for us"; Rom 5:8; also Rom 3:21–25; Eph 1:6–7; Col 1:13, 20.)

God does not save, however, against the will of the sinner; he does not override the freedom he has granted to human beings.[31] Any Israelite was free to choose whether or not to repent and bring a sacrifice (just as any person is free to choose Jesus as God's provision for salvation). Sacrifice, then, is not something humans do for God but something that God does for humankind. Sacrifice is intended to heal broken lives here and now. It is an attack upon the defilement in human life and brings about expiation of sins.[32]

The Meaning of Blood

Why is the offering of blood necessary in the sacrificial rites? Scripture states that the sacrifice of the animal expiates sin or removes the guilt or uncleanness from the offerer. This necessity is confirmed in the NT: "Without the shedding of blood there is no forgiveness" (Heb 9:22). How does the blood accomplish this expiation? What is the meaning of the blood? This question is significant because the NT also refers to the blood (of Christ) as the redeeming or cleansing agent, as may be seen in the following:

> the new covenant in my blood (Luke 22:20; 11:25)

> he bought with his own blood (Acts 20:28)

> with your blood you purchased for God persons from every . . . nation (Rev 5:9)

> redemption through his blood (Eph 1:7; see also 1 Pet 1:19; Rev 1:5)

> sacrifice of atonement, through the shedding of his blood (Rom 3:25)

> justified by his blood (Rom 5:9)

> making peace through his blood (Col 1:20)

> [you] have been brought near by the blood of Christ (Eph 2:13)

31. Robinson, *How Jesus Christ Saves Men*, 140.

32. Fiddes, *Atonement*, 71.

the blood of Jesus, his Son, purifies us from all sin (1 John 1:7; cf. Heb 9:14)

sprinkled with his blood (1 Pet 1:2; cf. Heb 12:24)

to make the people holy through his own blood (Heb 13:12)

washed their robes . . . in the blood of the Lamb (Rev 7:14)

without the shedding of blood there is no forgiveness (Heb 9:22)

Although the exact statements vary, the NT emphasizes that the sacrificial blood of Christ is expiatory. The sacrifices of the OT are fulfilled and annulled by Christ's superior and more effectual sacrifice.

How does blood expiate sin and reconcile God and humans? Several passages in the OT reveal the significance and value of blood. Once the significance of this blood is understood, a meaningful interpretation may be given. Leviticus 17:11 gives the clearest statement of the meaning of blood. It says, "For the life of the flesh is in the blood: and I have given it to you upon the altar to make an atonement for your souls: for it is the blood that maketh an atonement for the soul" (KJV). Deuteronomy 12:23 also indicates that "the blood is the life" (cf. Gen 9:4). Attention may also be drawn to the prohibition of eating flesh with the blood in it (Gen 9:4; Lev 3:17; 7:26–27; 17:10, 12, 14) and the parallel statements that God will require "your blood of your lives" and "the life of man" (Gen 9:5 KJV), as well as the parallel use of "life" and "blood" in Ps 72:14 (NASB). These verses "represent a formidable body of evidence and indicate that among the Hebrews there was a recognized close connection between life and blood."[33] If blood symbolizes life, then the thing pleasing to God is not death but the offering of life. The blood is shed with the purpose of separating it from the body and presenting it to God.[34] It represents a life surrendered in repentance and self-sacrifice to God.[35] The blood is never to be consumed for it is too sacred.[36]

The material sacrifice is meant to be only the outward symbol of the real inner sacrifice of the offerer. It is the symbol of a life surrendered to God (i.e., of a submitted will). The thing that is pleasing to God is a person's humble surrender. The will is what persons cling to and give up

33. Morris, *Apostolic Preaching of the Cross*, 110.

34. Forsyth, *Cruciality of the Cross*, 89.

35. F. Young, *Sacrifice and Death of Christ*, 55.

36. Forsyth, *Cruciality of the Cross*, 90.

last. The blood as life means the whole will is submitted to God in love. Scripture consistently states that God values the heart of obedience more than any outward act (1 Sam 15:22), therefore a widow's mite could be more precious than the wealth of many (Mark 12:41–44).[37]

As expiation purifies the human soul, the blood sacrifice purifies or consecrates such sacred places and persons as the altar, the sanctuary, the priest, or an Israelite. The blood is effective in either the establishment (in the covenant-sacrifice) or restoration (in the sacrifice of expiation) of union between God and his people. When a person is separated from God by his sin, he may seek to be restored by bringing his sacrifice, offering his life to God. He is forgiven by God, his sins are expiated, his guilt is removed, and his conscience is cleansed. The sin that separated him from God is removed and he is reunited and at peace with God. Atonement has taken place.[38]

The immolation, which every sacrifice with blood necessarily presupposes, expresses a great truth: no reconciliation with God takes place unless man dies to his egotism or, to use the biblical term, to his flesh. He must surrender his life. The effectiveness of sacrifice, therefore, does not depend on any external ceremony, but on the internal act of the worshiper.[39]

THE MESSAGE OF THE PROPHETS

The vanity of the outward sacrifice without a corresponding inward change of heart is emphasized by the prophets who saw clearly that sacrifice was of no avail without emendment of life. They taught that sins were forgiven if a person turned to God in repentance (Isa 55:7; Ezek 18:21–22). They also proclaimed that it is the moral offenses (rather than ceremonial) that are important: injustice, dishonesty, bribery, perjury, oppression, violence, cruelty. So long as these sins go on, God cares not for offerings. In fact, he hates them and will not look with favor on any who offer them.[40]

> To what purpose is the multitude of your sacrifices unto me? . . .
> Bring no more vain oblations; incense is an abomination unto

---

37. Forsyth, *Cruciality of the Cross*, 91–92.

38. Lyonnet and Sabourin, *Sin, Redemption, and Sacrifice*, 180–81.

39. Lyonnet and Sabourin, *Sin, Redemption, and Sacrifice*, 169.

40. Baillie, *God Was in Christ*, 176.

me; . . . Your new moons and your appointed feasts my soul
hateth. . . . And when ye spread forth your hands, I will hide
mine eyes from you: yea, when ye make many prayers, I will not
hear: your hands are full of blood. (Isa 1:11–15 KJV)

The teaching of the prophets is beautifully expressed by Norman
Robinson in his book *How Jesus Christ Saves Men*. He says:

> When we turn to the writings of the great prophets of Israel and
> ask what is their contribution to the question of atonement or
> the reconciliation of sinful humanity to God, we are conscious
> of a very different religious emphasis from what we meet in the
> Levitical Law. The prophets have a far profounder and more
> searching view of sin. Whereas, sacrifice dealt largely with sin as
> ritual transgression, the prophet's sole concern is with spiritual
> disobedience, with moral iniquity, with failure to "do justly, to
> love mercy and to walk humbly with God." Sin to them is rebel-
> lion against God, disobedience to his righteous will, unfaithful-
> ness to the covenant-bond, and this is shown chiefly in social
> injustice and inhumanity. Upon such sin in the clearest and
> strongest terms the prophets pronounce God's sure judgment.
> Moral iniquity and God's inexorable judgment thereon, is that
> all the prophets have to declare?
>
> By no means. They have a gospel too, for they believe in
> God's gracious covenant with his people, and they abound in
> declarations of God's long-suffering and readiness to forgive his
> people, if they will but truly repent and return to him. "Let the
> wicked forsake his way, and the unrighteous man his thoughts,
> and let him return unto the LORD, and he will have mercy upon
> him, and to our God, for he will abundantly pardon" (Isa 55:7).
> "Come now, let us reason together, saith the LORD: though your
> sins be as scarlet, they shall be as white as snow: though they be
> red like crimson, they shall be as wool" (Isa 1:18). God will for-
> give and restore the penitent nation, yes, and the truly penitent
> individual too; such in brief is the prophetic gospel. Who can
> forget the cry of God's longsuffering love in Hosea, "How shall I
> give thee up Ephraim?" . . . or the wealth of gracious promises of
> pardon and restoration in Isaiah, Jeremiah and other prophets?[41]

The sacrificial system taught the rudiments of relationship with a
holy God, "the alphabet of sin and pardon," but the prophets deepened
the revelation by speaking the words of judgment and mercy directly,
and thus also preparing the way for him who was "the word made flesh"

---

41. Robinson, *How Jesus Christ Saves Men*, 26–27.

and "the Lamb who taketh away the sin of the world."[42] Although sacrifice had its part in the education of God's people and in preparation for the coming Christ as its fulfillment, the time would come when not one stone of the temple would be left upon another and offering the blood of bulls and goats would give way to another offering. In the new covenant, Christ's blood, the sacrifice of a completely surrendered will, would provide the way of atonement. The prophets saw that the true meaning of animal sacrifice was a spiritual offering of love and obedience, the only real sacrifice that was pleasing to God.[43] The sacrifices were all types of this pure and holy offering that would be fulfilled in Christ.

THE MESSAGE OF THE SCAPEGOAT: THE REMOVAL OF SIN

In addition to the routine provision for forgiveness and reconciliation in OT sacrifice, one special day is set aside for the people to "humble [their] souls" (Lev 23:27 NASB). This Day of Atonement was a day of fasting and repentance, a day for Israel to confess and to mourn over her sins. The seriousness of this requirement is emphasized by the words in Lev 23:29: "If there is any person who will not humble himself on this same day, he shall be cut off from his people" (NASB). On the Day of Atonement one animal is taken by the high priest for a sin offering, and its blood is offered to God at the Mercy Seat, the place of mercy and forgiveness (Lev 16:11–15). Then the high priest takes another animal, called the scapegoat (for "escape goat"), and lays his hands on its head, confessing over it the sins of Israel. This goat is then taken into the desert where it symbolically carries away the sins of the people (Lev 16:8, 10). These elements of the Day of Atonement emphasize that the forgiveness of God requires confession and repentance, and that in God's merciful forgiveness sins are completely removed. Thereby atonement/reconciliation is achieved.

As a side note, the interpretation of the sin offering *assumes* that the sins of the offerer are symbolically laid on the sacrificial animal by the laying on of hands in the same way as with the scapegoat on the Day of Atonement. However, there are differences between the scapegoat and the sin offering. The scapegoat is not killed and its blood is not shed. It is sent into the desert. The sin offering, however, is pure and is offered to God.

---

42. Robinson, *How Jesus Christ Saves Men*, 26–27.

43. Robinson, *How Jesus Christ Saves Men*, 26–27.

The scapegoat is impure and anyone who touches it is also considered impure, therefore the priest who carried out the ceremony had to purify himself afterward (Lev 16:26). In addition, both hands of the priest are laid on the scapegoat, whereas only one is placed on the sin offerings. Most revealing is the fact that not once in the NT, when the authors speak of the sacrifice of Christ, is the ceremony of the scapegoat mentioned.[44] The scapegoat, then, is not a type of Christ, for in the ceremonies of the Day of Atonement the two ideas of a sacrificial victim and sin-bearing are mutually exclusive. An animal could be sacrificed or offered to God only because it was thought *not* to be contaminated with the sins of the people. On the Day of Atonement one goat was designed to symbolize the means of atonement and the other the effect of atonement, in bearing away the sins of the people to the land of forgetfulness.[45]

THE REMOVAL OF SIN

In addition to the ritual of the scapegoat, there are many other verses that speak of the complete removal of sin that takes place following repentance and forgiveness:

> Then David said to Nathan, "I have sinned against the LORD." Nathan replied, "The LORD has taken away your sin." (2 Sam 12:13)

> Blessed is the one whose transgressions are forgiven, whose sins are covered. Blessed is the one whose sin the LORD does not count against them. (Ps 32:1–2)

> Hide your face from my sins and blot out all my iniquity. (Ps 51:9)

> You forgave the iniquity of your people and covered all their sins. (Ps 85:2)

> As far as the east is from the west, so far has he removed our transgressions from us. (Ps 103:12)

> Though your sins are like scarlet, they shall be white as snow; though they are red as crimson, they shall be like wool. (Isa 1:18)

44. Lyonnet and Sabourin, *Sin, Redemption, and Sacrifice*, 182–83.

45. Hodge, *Atonement*, 134.

> With [the coal] he touched my mouth and said, "See, this has touched your lips; your guilt is taken away and your sin atoned for." (Isa 6:7)

> You have put all my sins behind your back. (Isa 38:17)

> I, even I, am he who blots out your transgressions, for my own sake, and remembers your sins no more. (Isa 43:25)

> I have swept away your offenses like a cloud, your sins like the morning mist. (Isa 44:22)

> For I will forgive their wickedness and will remember their sins no more. (Jer 31:34)

When the sin is removed and forgotten (no longer a factor) through the merciful act of forgiveness, no reason for alienation and separation exists. Restoration of fellowship is then possible.

SUMMARY: SACRIFICE

The most prominent metaphor for forgiveness and atonement in Scripture is sacrifice. In the OT, atonement is pictured in the sacrificial ceremonies; in the NT the sacrifice of Christ fulfills those sacrificial rites. Each aspect of forgiveness is involved. The sacrificial system is a gift from God showing his willingness and readiness to forgive because of his love. The offering of blood, symbolizing a life surrendered, and the accompanying confession of sin indicates the repentance of the offerer. The sharing of a meal in fellowship in the peace offering is a picture of the reconciliation that takes place with the removal of the sin. The removal of sin is emphasized by the definition of words translated "forgive," as well as the ceremony of the sending away of the scapegoat. In sacrifice all elements of the biblical model for forgiveness are present: confession and repentance by the wrongdoer, forgiveness given by the one wronged (that by definition removes the sin), and the reconciliation that takes place by the actions of both parties.

HIGH-HANDED SIN

The sacrificial rites, then, were given by God to his people for the purpose of forgiveness and restoration of relationship with himself. However, sacrifice was not allowed for high-handed sin. Numbers 15:27–31 says (emphasis added):

> But if just one person sins *unintentionally*, that person must bring a year-old female goat for a sin offering. The priest is to make atonement before the LORD for the one who erred by sinning unintentionally, and when atonement has been made, that person will be forgiven. . . . But anyone who sins defiantly [with a high hand], whether native-born or foreigner, blasphemes the LORD and must be cut off from the people of Israel. Because they have despised the LORD's word and broken his commands, they must surely be cut off; their guilt remains on them.

The NIV's "unintentionally" ("ignorantly" KJV) translates the Hebrew *shegagah* (Lev 4:2, 22, 27; 5:15, 18; Num 15:24, 25, 26, 27, 28, 29). However, Young's Concordance gives the meaning of *shegagah* as "to wander, err, go astray" rather than a want of knowledge (in ignorance).[46] In Num 15:30 it is contrasted with sinning "with a high hand." "With a high hand" (literal translation to be interpreted figuratively) can be translated "defiantly" (NIV, NASB) or "presumptuously" (KJV; Young's meaning for "presumptuously" is "proudly"). The *NIV Quest Study Bible* notes that a high hand describes a fist raised in defiance of God.[47] The contrast in Num 15:27–31 is not between intentional and unintentional sin, but between sin as going astray (whether intentional or unintentional) and sin as willfully defiant. The words presumptuously, willfully, defiantly, as well as the fact that the sin is not expiable by sacrifice, lead to the conclusion that, as James Hamilton says in his book *God's Glory in Salvation through Judgment*, "In the Levitical system high-handed sin is unrepented sin."[48] For this sin no sacrificial rite exists and the sinner's guilt remains on him (Num 15:31).

According to Ashley in the *NIV Commentary on the Book of Numbers*, "This kind of rebellion differs from the intentional sin described in Lev 6:1–7 for which a reparation offering may be made, 'when the offender feels guilty' (6:4, 7). The one who sins with a high hand feels no guilt, therefore the offense is not sacrificially expiable."[49] He goes on to say of Num 15:30–31:

---

46. R. Young, *Analytical Concordance to the Bible*, 508.

47. *NIV Quest Study Bible* note on Num 15:30, 213.

48. Hamilton, *Salvation through Judgment*, 109.

49. Ashley, *Numbers*, 288.

> Three further clauses specify this type of sin. First, such a one "reviles Yahweh" (15:30). . . . Second, the sinner with a high hand "disdained the word of Yahweh" (15: 31). . . . The verb "to disdain, despise" means to regard with contempt. "The word of Yahweh" includes the legislation that Yahweh has given, but this legislation is the communication of God, designed to bring humans into a relationship with him. Treating that personal communication with contempt means rejecting the relationship with God as well.[50]

Since the purpose of forgiveness is the restoration of relationship, the forgiveness of unrepented sin is pointless. God does not forgive those who are unrepentant and contemptuous.

SUMMARY: THE BIBLICAL MEANING OF FORGIVENESS

Forgiveness in Scripture, by definition, refers to the removal of sin following repentance that together result in reconciliation. In the OT as well as the NT forgiveness is seen first of all as something God does, clearing everything out of the way that may separate a person from himself and leaving him with a clean slate and a new opportunity for communion with the Creator. Offering a sacrifice, symbolizing the offering of one's life accompanied by confession of sin, is the OT ritual whose purpose is restoration to fellowship/peace/reconciliation with God. The offerer comes with his sacrifice in the full knowledge that forgiveness cannot be bought. He is depending on God's undeserved mercy, on his choosing to accept his sacrifice, which alone makes it effectual for atonement. In the biblical record the receiving of forgiveness is always connected with genuine repentance. The law made ample opportunity for sacrifice with its sin and guilt offerings, but the prophets of Israel had to remind the people repeatedly that "it was inward repentance that really mattered" (Ps 51:16–17; Hos 6:6; Joel 2:12–13a; Amos 5:22–24; Mic 6:7–8).[51] However, for unrepented, defiant, "high-handed" sin no sacrifice could be made (Num 15:27–31).

In Scripture, God is called forgiving, merciful, and gracious in that he does not turn away the repentant offerer but removes the sin from

---

50. Ashley, *Numbers*, 289.

51. K. Carter, "Forgiveness Revisited," 201.

his sight (scapegoat) and is reconciled. God is joyful in forgiveness and grieved when the absence of repentance precludes forgiveness.

God makes available the system of sacrifice, but it is the individual who must offer it. It is quite contrary to the spirit of the Bible to suppose that men's sins are removed without their being involved in the process. This would be overlooking sin rather than taking it seriously. The sinner must identify, symbolized by laying hands on the sacrifice, with the sacrifice, which is typical of Christ (without blemish) who gives his life (blood). The sinner accepts the sufficiency of the sacrifice that is without blemish, but he also must repent and receive God's forgiveness.[52] God is then faithful and merciful to forgive and rejoices in the now-healed relationship with his beloved.

---

52. Swinburne, *Responsibility and Atonement*, 152.

CHAPTER 3 STUDY QUESTIONS

1. What do modern definitions of forgiveness say the offended party must overcome?

2. How does this concept of forgiveness differ from the biblical concept?

The Old Testament Concept of Forgiveness

1. What English word communicates the meaning of forgiveness in the OT?

2. How does the modern use of the word atonement differ from the biblical meaning?

3. The Hebrew word *kipper* signifies the removal of what two things from the sinner?

4. What is the meaning of *salach*, another Hebrew word translated forgive?

5. What does the Hebrew word *nasa* mean in relation to forgiveness?

6. What does the Hebrew word *machah* picture in depicting forgiveness?

The New Testament Concept of Forgiveness

1. What are the four primary Greek words translated "forgiveness" in the NT, and what is the meaning of each?

2. What do these four words indicate is removed by forgiveness? What is the result?

3. How does the meaning of forgiveness in the NT compare to that of the OT?

Biblical Metaphors for Forgiveness

1. What biblical metaphors are used to depict forgiveness?

2. How is forgiveness described from the viewpoints of the wrongdoer, the forgiver, and the community?

Lifting a Burden and Bearing It Away

1. Why would the biblical practice of forgiveness not be applicable if the wrongdoer does not recognize or acknowledge his guilt?

Blotting Out Sin

1. What does the biblical image of sin being blotted out mean from the perspective of the victim?

2. Why is this blotting out of a truth a reasonable and just thing to do?

Remission of Debt

1. What action is taken by the forgiver in the metaphor of forgiveness as the remission of debt?

2. What action does the wrongdoer need to take?

Giving a Gift

1. Why is forgiveness a gift to the wrongdoer?

2. What truth does the gift metaphor emphasize concerning the forgiver's motivation to forgive?

The Meaning of Sacrifice

1. What OT ceremonial practice depicts repentance, forgiveness, and reconciliation?

2. Summarize the elements of the sacrificial ritual and what each depicts.

Appointed by God

1. How can sacrifice be considered the result of God's grace and not its cause?

The Meaning of Blood

  1. What does blood symbolize when offered in sacrifice?

  2. What does a blood offering accomplish?

The Message of the Prophets

  1. In what situations do the prophets reveal that God "hates" and will not accept sacrifice?

The Message of the Scapegoat: The Removal of Sin

  1. In what two ways does the scapegoat ritual emphasize that God's forgiveness requires repentance?

High-Handed Sin

  1. What is "high-handed" sin, and why is sacrifice not allowed for it?

4

Eschatological Forgiveness
"The Forgiveness of Sins"

CHRIST FULFILLS THE OT sacrificial provision by dying as a sacrifice for sins. His own words show that he thought of his death in sacrificial terms (see previous verses on the blood). He offers his life, symbolized by his blood, as a ransom for all men (1 Tim 2:6) and in doing so "[reconciles] the world to himself" (2 Cor 5:19). In what sense is the world reconciled to God through Christ's sacrifice? Gregory Jones, in his book *Embodying Forgiveness*, answers well, saying, "The crisis of the human condition is not simply [individual] sins but rather the evil, suffering, and brokenness" of the world.[1] This is the situation, created by Satan, sin, and death, that Jesus comes to address. These he overcomes, delivering the whole world from bondage. It is in this context (the deliverance of the whole world) that atonement/reconciliation is effected without prior repentance. Through this offering Christ is victorious over sin (which separates), death (which follows), and Satan (their source). The consequence of this offering of Christ is sometimes in Scripture simply called forgiveness (*aphesis*/liberation). This messianic/eschatological forgiveness or liberation is proclaimed in Scripture as Christ's liberation or redemption of the whole world (Eph 1:7; Col 1:13–14). It does not represent

---

1. L. Jones, *Embodying Forgiveness*, 117.

the actual forgiveness of individuals that requires repentance, but rather the proclamation of what Christ comes to accomplish—the defeat of evil and all that would separate people from God (except their own choice of separation through refusing to repent and believe).

Both John the Baptist and Jesus proclaim this forgiveness, this coming of the kingdom of God that involves liberation or release from the powers of evil (sin, Satan, and death). As stated earlier in reference to the definition of *aphesis*, in pre-Christian secular Greek, *aphesis* does not refer to forgiveness. It denotes a dismissal, release, or liberation and is rendered forgiveness only when it refers to the dismissal of sins and the consequent liberating effects of that release. At two key points in Luke's Gospel, concerning the ministry and message of John the Baptist and the ministry of Jesus, the word forgiveness (*aphesis*) is used in this way. The first of these two key passages is Luke 3:3–6. John calls the people to "repentance for [in preparation for, with a view to] the forgiveness [*aphesis*/liberation from] of sins" that is to come with the coming of the Lord and his salvation. The second is at the beginning of Jesus' ministry when he proclaims the fulfillment of Isa 61:1–2. The good news of the coming kingdom is that liberty (*aphesis*) is promised to those who are captives (Luke 4:18). The kingdom of God is a new order that Jesus ushers in and that for a time will coexist with the present world. Forgiveness (*aphesis*, liberation/redemption) is what God will come to accomplish at the *eschaton* when the kingdom of God is fully present. Forgiveness, as is seen elsewhere in the gospel, can be personally and individually experienced in the present, as can healing and salvation. Such experiences anticipate and are foretastes of the eschatological forgiveness (liberation from the power of sin) that is both present and yet to come.[2] The forgiveness of sin, as an eschatological proclamation, refers to what God will do at the end of the age when he transforms the world into a place in which all sin is removed (which is the meaning of the word forgive). This forgiveness "refers to release from the present evil age into the age to come."[3]

N. T. Wright speaks of this proclamation of eschatological forgiveness in many of his writings as the message of Jesus regarding the coming of the promised kingdom. Jesus declares, after the manner of someone issuing a public proclamation, that Israel's God is finally becoming king. "The time is fulfilled!" he says. "God's kingdom is arriving! Turn back,

---

2. A. Bash, *Forgiveness and Christian Ethics*, 90.

3. Bash and Bash, "Early Christian Thinking," 31.

and believe the good news!" (Mark 1:15). "If it is by God's finger that I cast out demons," he declares, "then God's kingdom has come upon you" (Luke 11:20 NTE).[4] What exactly did the announcement of God's kingdom (Matt 28:18; Rev 11:15) mean? There was already a kingdom in power. ("He has rescued us from the dominion of darkness and brought us into the kingdom of the Son he loves, in whom we have redemption, the forgiveness of sins"; Col 1:13–14.) What sort of campaign would there be to bring this kingdom in fully? Jesus does not initially reveal the answer, but he demonstrates what it means by his healings, which are part of the meaning of God becoming king. Part of putting the world right is the healing of broken people: paralytics, epileptics, demoniacs, people with horrible skin diseases, a servant at the point of death, an old woman with a high fever, blind men, deaf and mute men, a little girl who is already dead, and an old woman with a persistent hemorrhage.[5]

Closely connected with the healings as a sign of the kingdom is the theme of people being forgiven. Forgiveness is a kind of healing that removes a debilitating burden. This close relationship can be seen in the story of the healing of the paralytic (Mark 2:1–12). Jesus says to him, "Son, your sins are forgiven." But was not forgiveness what one normally received in the temple by sacrifice? That was how it normally happened, but Jesus is saying that something new is taking place.[6] When challenged (v. 8) he says, "Which is easier: to say, 'Your sins are forgiven,' or to say, 'Get up and walk'?" (Matt 9:5; cf. Mark 2:9) In other words, in either case one is set free. Healing and forgiveness are interrelated here in the sense that they both are demonstrations of the truth that God's kingdom has come.

To recognize this new movement of God, the history of God's people must be understood. Jesus was not announcing the arrival of God's kingdom in a vacuum.[7] He knew the stories of God's people and was aware how they expected the story to end. He also knew, as did all teachers of the law, that what Israel had to do for God to come with his new exodus (deliverance) was to turn, to repent from evil ways and turn to God in repentance and faith. Moses made this clear in Deut 30, and Jeremiah and Ezekiel said the same with reference to the exile of God's people to

---

4. N. T. Wright, *Simply Jesus*, 67.

5. N. T. Wright, *Simply Jesus*, 69–70.

6. N. T. Wright, *Simply Jesus*, 72.

7. N. T. Wright, *Simply Jesus*, 69.

Babylon.[8] The prophets declared that the people were exiled because of wickedness and idolatry. "Instead of being a light to the nations Israel had become a byword for a god-forsaken people. . . . [Joel 2:17b; Ezek 36:20] [Therefore] most Jews of Jesus' day saw the Babylonian exile as the beginning of what became a much longer period of history in which God's people remain unredeemed, unrescued, and unforgiven."[9]

The expectation of Israel is expressed in classic kingdom passages such as Isa 52:7–12.[10] As N. T. Wright says in his book *Simply Jesus*, "Throughout Isa 40–55, this 'forgiveness' means, quite explicitly, return from exile; exile had been the punishment for the people's sins, and their return is their embodiment of their forgiveness."[11]

Christopher Wright, in his book *Salvation Belongs to Our God*, also recognizes this expectation of Israel saying:

> The post-exilic period brought an even greater longing for a final solution to the problem of sin, and recognition that only God could provide it. But that day would come, "On that day a fountain will be opened to the house of David and the inhabitants of Jerusalem, to cleanse them from sin and impurity" (Zech 13:1). That would be a day when the one anointed by God would "finish transgression, . . . put an end to sin, . . . atone for wickedness, and . . . bring in everlasting righteousness" (Dan 9:24).[12]

Thus the eschatological meaning of the phrase "the forgiveness of sins" is a final solution to the problem of bondage to sin. As Christopher Wright says, "In Jesus, they realized, God was bringing in the promised new era of salvation, for his Old Testament people Israel and for the world. . . . Through Jesus God would deal finally and fully with sin"[13] (as in Rom 3:25–26).

This act of liberation and redemption is the purpose of Jesus' coming, and he announces it in the proclamation of forgiveness and healing as God's intention. He backs up this proclamation with demonstrations of healing and forgiveness. God's kingdom creates a new state of affairs in which the power of evil is decisively defeated (John 12:31), and Jesus'

---

8. N. T. Wright, *Simply Jesus*, 71.

9. N. T. Wright, *Simply Jesus*, 73.

10. N. T. Wright, *Surprised by Hope*, 201–202.

11. N. T. Wright, *Simply Jesus*, 155.

12. C. Wright, *Salvation Belongs to Our God*, 27.

13. C. Wright, *Salvation Belongs to Our God*, 28.

followers are commissioned to put that victory and that inaugurated new world into practice.[14] When Jesus announces forgiveness both on the personal level and more widely, this understanding is what the Jews would have had. Just as physical healing is the personal part of what it means when God mends the whole world, so individual forgiveness is the personal part of what it looks like when God does what he promised to do and restores his exiled people.[15] It was commonly thought that this forgiveness/restoration would be a messianic forgiveness in that it would be brought about by a messiah. First-century Jews longed for this messianic forgiveness, hoping for the restoration of the corporate identity of Israel as God's people (see Isa 65:17–25; Jer 31:31–34),[16] which would demonstrate their forgiveness for their failure and idolatry.

Messianic/eschatological forgiveness also recalls the original call of Abraham and Israel to be a blessing to all the world and a light to the Gentiles (Gen 12:2–3; Isa 42:6). God's desire is to rescue his whole creation. As mentioned previously, the most formal of Jesus' proclamations of messianic/eschatological forgiveness is in Luke's Gospel (4:16–30) at the beginning of his ministry,[17] in which the worldwide dimension of this rescue is revealed. In the synagogue on the Sabbath, in his home town of Nazareth, Jesus reads a passage from the prophet Isaiah (61:1–2) about the coming new age, the release from slavery, the new exodus and restoration from exile, all of which form the hope of the Jewish people of his day. He reads:

> "The Spirit of the Lord is on me,
>   because he has anointed me
>   to proclaim good news to the poor.
> He has sent me to proclaim freedom for the prisoners
>   and recovery of sight for the blind,
> to set the oppressed free,
>   to proclaim the year of the Lord's favor."

> Then he rolled up the scroll, gave it back to the attendant and sat down. The eyes of everyone in the synagogue were fastened on him. He began by saying to them, "Today this scripture is fulfilled in your hearing." (Luke 4:18–21)

---

14. N. T. Wright, *Surprised by Hope*, 204.

15. N. T. Wright, *Simply Jesus*, 73.

16. L. Jones, *Embodying Forgiveness*, 109.

17. N. T. Wright, *Simply Jesus*, 73.

His message is forgiveness, but not just for individuals. "This forgiveness is a kind of corporate forgiveness, tapping into the ancient Jewish hope of the jubilee, the year when all debts would be forgiven and when slaves would be set free" (Lev 25).[18] Jesus is announcing a time of great celebration of release, forgiveness, and rescue from all that ruins human life. Jesus' listeners would understand the passage in this new beginning corporate sense. They would want to know how these great prophecies would be fulfilled. Jesus' next words indicate that they are being fulfilled, but not in the way the people expected. He claims that the people who benefit from this great act of God are not just the people of Israel.

> Everyone remarked at him; they were astonished at the words coming out of his mouth—words of sheer grace. "Isn't this Joseph's son?" they said. "I know what you're going to say," Jesus said. "You're going to tell me the old riddle: 'Heal yourself, doctor!' 'We heard of great happenings in Capernaum; do things like that here, in your own country!' Let me tell you the truth," he went on. "Prophets never get accepted in their own country. This is the solemn truth: there were plenty of widows in Israel in the time of Elijah, when heaven was shut up for three years and six months, and there was a great famine over all the land. Elijah was sent to none of them, only to a widow in the Sidonian town of Zarephath. And there were plenty of people with virulent skin diseases in Israel in the time of Elisha the prophet, and none of them was healed—only Naaman, the Syrian." When they heard this, everyone in the synagogue flew into a rage. (Luke 4:22–28 NTE)[19]

Jesus is saying that not only the Jews but also the Gentiles will benefit from the fulfillment, from the coming of the kingdom, perhaps even the commander of the enemy army like Naaman (2 Kgs 5).[20] His jubilee expectations are not just about God forgiving Israel its debts and punishing its enemies. Rather, this message is good news for all, even the enemies of Israel. This inclusive message is not well received in Jesus' local synagogue. He is run out of town and just escapes with his life. The proclamation of forgiveness that Jesus announces does not reassure God's people that they will be all right; in fact, the message does not really say

---

18. N. T. Wright, *Simply Jesus*, 74.

19. N. T. Wright, *Simply Jesus*, 75–76.

20. N. T. Wright, *Simply Jesus*, 76.

that at all. Their God is not coming to endorse their national agenda. He is doing what the prophet said he would, but not in the way they think.[21]

The Greek word used for forgiveness in this passage in Luke is *aphesis* (translated "freedom" in v. 18). As stated earlier, its meaning is release and freedom from what constrains people, whether from sin and its effects, or from physical sickness, or captivity, or from the consequences of not having the salvation of God (Luke 3:6) or the Lord's favor (Luke 4:19). In order to avoid misinterpretation, understanding this broader meaning of *aphesis* (as the salvation that comes with Jesus' inauguration of the kingdom of God) is essential. The following verses (with emphases added) refer to this eschatological forgiveness that constitutes the primary meaning of the coming kingdom of God:

> No one living in Zion will say, "I am ill"; and the sins of those who dwell there will be *forgiven*. (Isa 33:24)

> No longer will they teach their neighbor, or say to one another, "Know the LORD," because they will all know me. . . . For I will *forgive* their wickedness and will remember their sins no more. (Jer 31:34)

> When Jesus saw their faith, he said to the man, "Take heart, son; your *sins are forgiven*." . . . Which is easier: to say, "Your sins are forgiven," or to say, "Get up and walk"? (Matt 9:2, 5)

> God exalted him to his own right hand as Prince and Savior that he might bring Israel to repentance and *forgive* their sins. (Acts 5:31)

> Then Peter began to speak: "I now realize how true it is that God does not show favoritism but accepts from every nation the one who fears him and does what is right" (Acts 10:34–35). (Clearly God's acceptance is conditional. The conditions are fearing God and doing what is right. More is involved than just believing.)

> [Jesus] commanded us to preach to the people (Acts 10:42). (What did Jesus command that they preach? In Luke 24:46–47 Jesus teaches his disciples, "This is what is written: the Messiah will suffer and rise from the dead on the third day, and repentance and forgiveness of sins will be preached in his name to all nations, beginning at Jerusalem." Peter is fulfilling this commission, therefore the preaching of repentance, although not mentioned here in the Acts passage, is presupposed.)

---

21. N. T. Wright, *Simply Jesus*, 77.

All the prophets testify about him that everyone who believes in him receives *forgiveness of sins* through his name (Acts 10:43). (The prophets spoke of the forgiveness of sins as a future event equated with the coming of God to rescue his people. Peter refers to this forgiveness of sins as a historical event that one can now choose to *receive* through faith in Christ.)

Therefore, my friends, I want you to know that through Jesus *the forgiveness of sins* is proclaimed to you. (Acts 13:38)

I will rescue you from your own people and from the Gentiles. I am sending you to them to open their eyes and *turn* them from darkness to light, and from the power of Satan to God, so that they may receive *forgiveness of sins* and a place among those who are sanctified by faith in me (Acts 26:17–18). (The context here is Paul's commission of *turning* the Gentiles from darkness to light. The passage indicates that repentance, turning, is necessary.)

In him we have redemption through his blood, *the forgiveness of sins*, in accordance with the riches of God's grace. (Eph 1:7)

For he has rescued us from the dominion of darkness and brought us into the kingdom of the Son he loves, in whom we have redemption, *the forgiveness of sins* (Col 1:13–14). (In the previous two verses, rescue "from the dominion of darkness" unto "the kingdom of the Son" is equated with "redemption," which is equated with "the forgiveness of sins." Each refers to the atonement as a completed work of Christ [a historical event] and not to individual forgiveness and reconciliation with God.)

None of these verses indicate that some kind of general forgiveness takes place apart from repentance or prior to repentance. These verses refer to the work of Jesus, who comes to redeem the captives and therefore be the means of forgiveness of which the sacrifices are a type. "While we were still sinners, Christ died for us" (Rom 5:8). He redeems his world, his creation, from the power of Satan, sin, and death. This confrontation with evil, which brings restoration, healing, and forgiveness is God's victory. It would surely be a distortion of scriptural revelation to interpret any of the verses above to mean that God, through Jesus, forgives all people of all sins apart from individual repentance and faith. Rather, these verses refer to messianic/eschatological forgiveness, the coming forgiveness, or redemption, of humankind for which Jesus gives his life. John the Baptist refers to Jesus as the one who would "take away the sin of the world" (John 1:29). "The sin of the world" is a reference to the fall, humankind's own choice to rebel against God and his authority, which results in humankind's bondage to sin. Jesus comes to deal finally and fully with this situation, giving himself as a ransom to free humankind from the consequences of its own "sin." Individual repentance and faith, which brings individual salvation, should follow as a result of God's initiative, his sacrifice, and his love.

In summary, messianic/eschatological forgiveness is the forgiveness of sin (a historical event, the coming of God that brings liberation/redemption/salvation/rescue/release) that Christ announces and enacts, foretold by the prophets (Isa 33:24; 53:4–6; Jer 31:34; Ezek 36:25–27; Zech 13:1). In Scripture, individual forgiveness and messianic/eschatological forgiveness must be distinguished according to the context of the passage. *Thus, misinterpretation, such as a claim that God has forgiven all sin and sinners prior to and apart from repentance, can be avoided.*

In Scripture the word reconciliation is also used in this messianic/eschatological sense and is also not to be confused with individual, personal reconciliation with God (salvation) that flows from repentance and faith.

> For if, while we were God's enemies, we were reconciled to him through the death of his Son, how much more, having been reconciled, shall we be saved through his life! Not only is this so, but we also boast in God through our Lord Jesus Christ, through whom we have now received reconciliation. (Rom 5:10–11)

> All this is from God, who reconciled us to himself through Christ and gave us the ministry of reconciliation: that God was reconciling the world to himself in Christ, not counting people's sins against them. And he has committed to us the message of reconciliation. (2 Cor 5:18–19)

These verses indicate that a finished work of Christ precedes Christian experience. The English verb *reconcile* does not mean exactly the same as the Greek verb. The English indicates that both parties are reconciled, implying that humans have already entered into a state of peace with God apart from any response on their part to the work of Christ. But the Greek does not go this far, and this idea would clearly contradict even the immediate context. If reconciliation is complete there is no need to "receive reconciliation" (Rom 5:11) or for "the ministry of reconciliation" (2 Cor 5:18). These verses do indicate, however, that Christ finishes the work of reconciliation/atonement, in some sense even before the preaching of the gospel. God acts apart from humanity and in spite of human sin.

When Scripture says "not counting people's sins against them" (2 Cor 5:19) it does not refer to what happened after Christ came and died as if he no longer counts anyone's sins against them. *Rather it refers to the fact that their sinfulness did not prevent him from acting on their behalf.* Before he came he decided not "to count their sins against them," meaning that he chose to redeem them in spite of their unworthiness. At that time they were still "enemies" (Rom 5:10) in the sense of being alienated from him. In other words, human sinfulness did not stop God from intervening to rescue humankind.

The human situation changes because of God's initiative and Christ's victory.[22] Jesus pays the price for all humankind, providing for the liberation of all people ("from the dominion of darkness" Col 1:13). (Even the false prophets are said to have been "bought" by Christ in 2 Pet 2:1.) Individual personal forgiveness is waiting for every sinner who repents.

SUMMARY

Individual forgiveness is not to be confused with the OT expectation of messianic/eschatological forgiveness (liberation) which the NT proclaims. This proclamation of the coming of God's kingdom as a historical event (the incarnation) bringing redemption (the release of humankind from the kingdom of darkness, paid for by the blood of Christ) is also called "the forgiveness of sins" (as in Eph 1:7 and Col 1:13–14). The phrase "the forgiveness of sins" when equated with redemption refers to this OT expectation which is now a past historical event. It does not refer to the actual forgiveness of individual sins. This OT expectation of messianic/eschatological forgiveness is provided for the world in a corporate sense through Jesus' sacrificial death, paying the ransom and thereby defeating evil.

---

22. Chandler, *Victorious Substitution*, 146.

CHAPTER 4 STUDY QUESTIONS

1. How does the sacrifice of Christ reconcile the world to God? Was repentance involved?

2. Does the liberation brought about by this messianic or eschatological forgiveness represent forgiveness of sins for individuals?

3. To what does this "forgiveness of sins" refer in relation to the end of the age (the eschaton)?

4. What actions of Jesus indicate that the kingdom of God is breaking into the world?

5. How does eschatological forgiveness recall God's promise to Abraham?

6. In what way does eschatological forgiveness bring to mind the year of jubilee?

7. Why is understanding the broader meaning of *aphesis* necessary to avoid misunderstanding the Bible's teaching concerning God's forgiveness of individuals?

8. Does reconciliation spoken of in an eschatological sense refer to individual salvation?

5

The Justice of God

THE CONCEPT OF JUSTICE

ANOTHER TERM OR CONCEPT that must be examined in seeking to understand the biblical relationship of repentance, forgiveness, and reconciliation is *justice*. Biblical justice includes not only judgment, but mercy, forbearance, and wrath. Before asking how a Christian should apply these concepts to his relationships, one should ask how God's mercy, forbearance, wrath, and judgment apply in God's desire for justice and reconciliation.

One understanding of the atonement (the penal substitution theory) relies on a concept of God's justice that is morally and theologically problematic (see author's book *Victorious Substitution: A Theory of the Atonement*, chapter 3). According to this theory, to say that God is just is to say that he must not allow sin to go unpunished. Justice means that sin must be punished, and since justice is an innate attribute of God, he has no alternative but to punish sin. In other words, he cannot forgive sin based on repentance, apart from punishment, without violating justice. The so-called solution to this problem is the theory that Christ's substitutionary death was meant to propitiate (appease) God's wrath and to satisfy (pay back) his justice. This conclusion, however, is based on a deficient understanding of God's justice as well as his character. That God is just, righteous, is a truth clearly and repeatedly revealed in Scripture. That God judges sin is also found throughout the Bible. But the concept that God *must* judge sin to be just, righteous, is nowhere to be found. Indeed, the opposite is true: God is longsuffering with his people, calling them to turn away from their sin and return to him so that he might forgive and bless them (Exod 34:6; Ps 86:15; 2 Pet 3:9). God desires to bless his people, and he does so for all who repent. As long as he sees a chance for repentance, he delays judgment. God's desire to avoid judgment and show mercy is indicated by the many passages in which God is said to be "slow to anger" (anger being a metonym for judgment; Exod 34:6; Num 14:18; Neh 9:17; Ps 86:15; 103:8; 145:8; Jer 15:15; Joel 2:13; Jonah 4:2; Nah 1:3). Only when people refuse to heed his commands and refuse to repent will he judge them (Exod 34:7; Num 14:18; Ezek 18:30).

The purpose of God's judgment of his people, however, is not retribution but discipline (Heb 12:5–11). It serves for instruction and is often the means of continuing the call to repent and be reconciled with God (as in the book of Judges). His judgment for disciplinary purposes is then a part of his love and even of his mercy. "Also unto thee, O Lord, belongeth mercy: for thou renderest to every man according to his work" (Ps 62:12 KJV). God may exercise his judgment as he wills. If and when he makes this choice is his prerogative as the God of the universe. It is not within his character, however, to be unfair or unjust (Ezek 18:25–29). Therefore, retributive judgment will indeed be exercised in the absence of repentance (Exod 34:7; Num 14:18; Ezek 18:30–32).

Because God is just, humans are capable of recognizing justice, and the idea of justice is deeply embedded in us.[1] In order to understand what justice is, it is helpful to establish what it is not. The concept of justice cannot be confined to the administration of law. Even if the law is good and thoroughly administered, it does not necessarily follow that justice is done. If someone is crippled as the result of a crime, the wrong cannot be made right even when the wrongdoer is punished. Punishment may be beneficial for the one who has done wrong, but punishment is not the same thing as justice. Neither does punishing the wrongdoer necessarily bring about reconciliation. Only repentance and forgiveness reconciles. Even when reconciliation occurs, the offended party may not receive justice, because nothing can undo, for example, permanent physical injury. To say that justice means punishing sin and that mercy means letting sin go unpunished is an incomplete and therefore inadequate view of justice.[2]

What is divine justice, the sort of justice that God gives? If true justice is merely punishing sin, then any cruel judge could, by punishing

---

1. MacDonald, *Character of God*, 245.

2. MacDonald, *Character of God*, 246–247.

every offender, be called just. But the justice of God is much more: God gives every man, woman, and child fair play. He simply does nothing that is unfair. "Will not the Judge of all the earth do right?" (Gen 18:25). Punishment of the guilty is a part of the justice of God, but not the whole of it.[3] Justice is more than retribution. There can be justice even if retribution is forgone. The guilty party is surely not deprived of his rights or oppressed by injustice if the wronged party forgives him. If he were, then wrongs could never be justly forgiven.[4] Perhaps rulers and judges commit injustice when they fail to punish the guilty; in doing so they undermine the law's authority, which is not their authority but the authority of God himself. However, God as the source of all authority is not himself subject to a law that demands retribution.[5] For God to forgive sins without receiving satisfaction (payback) or inflicting punishment is simply to forgo his own right to punish.[6]

Any view that claims a law of retribution that has ultimate authority, even when the law is said to be God's own law, confines God to legal restraints. Law ceases to be a practical guideline to God's purpose for his creatures and becomes a supreme principle. It does not allow God to employ a justice of another kind, a justice that certainly requires a penalty to fall upon rebellious creatures while they are in the state of rebellion, but is satisfied when they repent and return to him.[7] God must not be regarded as a judge whose actions are based on some external legal authority and who cannot deviate from the letter of the law. Rather, God is the sovereign Lord of the universe; his will alone is law, a law that is exercised in accord with his righteous nature.[8] God is always just or fair, but that is not to say that he always insists on retribution. *Punitive* justice cannot be an attribute residing in God, but is rather an effect of the divine will inflicted in judgment according to God's wisdom and love. Punitive justice is a term that is more properly designated in Scripture as "severity" or "vengeance," and is in no way an attribute of God. It is merely

3. MacDonald, *Character of God*, 249.

4. Gomes, "Faustus Socinus," 73.

5. Gomes, "Faustus Socinus," 74–75.

6. Gomes, "Faustus Socinus," 61.

7. Fiddes, *Atonement*, 101.

8. Gomes, "Satisfaction of Christ," 215–16.

God's decision to punish sin. God is just, but, as an innate characteristic, this is the opposite of injustice, not mercy.[9]

GOD IS FREE TO REMIT SINS

Why should God not be free to dispense with punishment altogether? In fact, he is and he does, as Scripture illustrates time and again (based on sacrifice: Lev 4:20, 26, 31, 35; 5:10, 13, 16, 18; 6:7; 19:22; Num 15:25, 26, 28; based on confession: 1 John 1:9). God forgives sins freely, that is, apart from satisfaction (payback), and he is free to dispense with satisfaction altogether.[10] Not only is God able to forgive sins, he is also willing to do so. Consider the following scriptural examples, which are but a few among many:

> But they, our ancestors, became arrogant and stiff-necked, and they did not obey your commands. They refused to listen and failed to remember the miracles you performed among them. They became stiff-necked and in their rebellion appointed a leader in order to return to their slavery. But you are a forgiving God, gracious and compassionate, slow to anger and abounding in love. Therefore you did not desert them. (Neh 9:16–17)

This prayer speaks plainly of both punishment and pardon, yet emphasizes God's mercy. The following passage also mixes punishment with pardon and culminates in God's merciful deliverance:

> Nevertheless they were disobedient, and rebelled against thee, and cast thy law behind their backs, and slew thy prophets which testified against thee to turn them to thee, and they wrought great provocations. Therefore thou deliveredst them into the hand of their enemies, who vexed them: and in the time of their trouble, when they cried unto thee, thou heardest them from heaven; and according to thy manifold mercies thou gavest them saviours, who saved them out of the hand of their enemies. But after they had rest, they did evil again before thee: therefore leftest thou them in the hand of their enemies, so that they had the dominion over them: yet when they returned, and cried unto thee, thou heardest them from heaven; and many times didst thou deliver them according to thy mercies. (Neh 9:26–28 KJV)

9. Gomes, "Satisfaction of Christ," 219.

10. Fiddes, *Atonement*, 102.

These verses state clearly that God desires to forgive the penitent of their sins and will do so.[11] Psalm 32 also declares this same truth:

> Blessed is he whose transgression is forgiven, whose sin is covered. Blessed is the man unto whom the LORD imputeth not iniquity, and in whose spirit there is no guile. . . . I acknowledged my sin unto thee, and mine iniquity have I not hid. I said, I will confess my transgressions unto the LORD; and thou forgavest the iniquity of my sin. (vv. 1–2, 5 KJV)

Not only does God give plain examples of his ready mercy, but he also reveals clearly that he always will forgive in such cases. God says, "I shall speak concerning a nation, and concerning a kingdom, to pluck up, and to pull down, and to destroy it; if that nation, against whom I have pronounced, turn from their evil, I will repent of the evil that I thought to do unto them" (Jer 18:7–8 KJV). Furthermore, God says, "When I say unto the wicked, Thou shalt surely die; if he turn from his sin, and do that which is lawful and right, . . . he shall surely live, he shall not die" (Ezek 33:14–15 KJV).

God does not change in situations in which he revokes sentences; rather, the people themselves change. Although God judges those who persist in sin and do not humble themselves before him, he graciously forgives those who repent and rely on his power to help them live righteously.[12]

REPENTANCE: THE DETERMINING FACTOR

What, then, is the determining factor in God's choice between forgiveness and punishment? It is the state of the sinner's heart, which God sees and knows. Justice demands not payment but repentance; it is not satisfied by any penalty, rather by a change of heart that leads to a changed life. "I have no pleasure in the death of the wicked; but that the wicked turn from his way and live: turn ye, turn ye from your evil ways; for why will ye die, O house of Israel?" (Ezek 33:11 KJV). The Father wants nothing more than his children to return to him.[13] God is ever ready to forgive when one repents (Deut 4:30–31; 30:2–3; 2 Chr 7:14; Ezek 18:21–22; 1 John 1:9).

11. Gomes, "Faustus Socinus," 87–88.
12. Gomes, "Faustus Socinus," 93–94.
13. Gomes, "Faustus Socinus," 104–5.

This is the message of John the Baptist. He prepares the Lord's path by preaching "a baptism of repentance for the forgiveness of sins" (Mark 1:4; Luke 3:3). His message is the same as that of the law and the prophets: God is merciful and faithful to forgive those who repent. Peter's message also restates the OT truth that God delays judgment because he desires to forgive the repentant (2 Pet 3:7–9). He says, "The Lord is not slow in keeping his promise, as some understand slowness. Instead he is patient with you, not wanting anyone to perish, but everyone to come to repentance" (v. 9).

Does free forgiveness undermine morality?[14] Although God forgives freely, he requires true repentance, which always involves emendation of life by those whom God has pardoned (Ezek 33:15). Righteousness in God's sight demands a change in conduct as well as in heart (Matt 3:8).[15]

MERCY

The fact that God says "Vengeance is mine" (Rom 12:19 KJV) shows that vengeance (exacting proper retribution) is just.[16] However, justice does not require retributive punishment in order to be fair.[17] The essence of mercy is waiving a right that in justice could be asserted.[18]

God is characterized throughout the Bible as merciful in that he forgives the repentant. The repentant sinner has no right to forgiveness by virtue of his repentance. In asking for forgiveness one acknowledges dependence on God's free decision to grant the request. Therefore, one can never demand forgiveness, for it is not a right. God has revealed that, "If we confess our sins, he is faithful and just and will forgive us our sins" (1 John 1:9). Showing mercy in forgiveness does not deny justice. One may hope that God will forgive, or even count on God to forgive, but since repentance does not entitle a person to forgiveness, one cannot presume upon God's mercy. Although repentance is *necessary* for forgiveness, it is not a *sufficient* condition. The one who forgives shows mercy by choice, not because the score is even. "Forgiveness of sins means that sins are remitted (that is, canceled or covered), not that the penalty for

14. Robinson, *How Jesus Christ Saves Men*, 178.

15. Gomes, "Satisfaction of Christ," 223.

16. Murphy and Hampton, *Forgiveness and Mercy*, 163.

17. Swinburne, *Responsibility and Atonement*, 99.

18. Haber, *Forgiveness*, 64.

sins is paid."[19] Whether God chooses to forgive the sinner and to accept him in fellowship depends on free decision. It is an act of mercy. One's attempts to make good the injury he has caused cannot be more than a token of repentance or an attempt to repudiate the wrong. He can neither bring about nor earn forgiveness, as this remains up to God to decide.[20] Scripture says, "Let the wicked forsake their ways and the unrighteous their thoughts. Let them turn to the LORD, and he will have mercy on them, and to our God, for he will freely pardon" (Isa 55:7). Forgiveness is always an act of mercy in that it is free. But to say that forgiveness is free does not mean it is unconditional. *Forgiveness is freely given in that it is not earned by satisfaction (payback), but it is conditional in that it requires repentance.*[21]

THE WRATH OF GOD

Another term that must be understood in the scriptural study of forgiveness is the *wrath of God*. What is God's wrath and how is it removed? In *Following Jesus*, N. T. Wright says, "The wrath of the Lamb of which Revelation speaks from time to time is the anger of love against all that hurts and damages the beloved."[22] What Scripture describes as the wrath of God is his personal reaction to sin, a holy displeasure that results in estrangement and immutability of judgment. Care should be taken with such a concept. Just as God's love exhibits none of the fickleness or weakness of humanity, neither does his wrath. In fact, God's "wrath with regard to Israel is the reverse side of his love for them; closely bound up with it is the conception of his jealousy" (Deut 32:20–21; Ps 78:58).[23] Because God loves his children he may feel wrath at their behavior. His wrath can be exhibited against his own people or against the enemies of his people. Seen from this perspective, God's wrath arises from his love. An absence of wrath would reveal apathy.

19. Bash and Bash, "Early Christian Thinking," 37.

20. Brümmer, *When We Pray*, 99.

21. The meaning of "unconditional" must be clarified. When I refer to forgiveness as unconditional I mean forgiveness apart from repentance. However, some use the term unconditional to refer to the absence of satisfaction (payback). With this meaning someone can be said to forgive unconditionally even if repentance is a condition.

22. N. T. Wright, *Following Jesus*, 61.

23. Kleinknecht et al., "Ὀργή," 50.

God's wrath is exhibited in two senses in Scripture: one is disciplinary judgment, which is restorative; the other is retributive judgment, which is just. Disciplinary suffering may "educate one towards penitence."[24] Suffering inflicted upon a person to make him better in the future is not so much punitive as disciplinary.[25] Punishment begins as discipline, but this purpose or process may be thwarted because the one judged is not responsive. When punishment fails its purpose as discipline, it may remain as retributive justice.[26] Scripture uses the word judgment in both these senses. The two senses of judgment are very different in result but not in origin, for the source is love and goodness.[27]

Many times in the OT, because of his love, God withholds judgment, awaiting repentance (Exod 34:6–7; Num 14:18; Isa 48:9; Ps 103:8; Nah 1:3). By individual judgments he warns his people and exhorts them to repent before he proceeds to more severe action (Isa 9:12–15; Amos 6:4–10). The people of Israel are denied the propitiatory means of averting God's judgment that their neighbors practiced toward their gods. Instead, their prayers of intercession are directed to God's mercy. Thus Moses prays for the people (Exod 32:11–13; Deut 9:19; Ps 106:23) or for guilty individuals (Num 12:13; Deut 9:20); Amos prays for Israel (7:2, 5); Jeremiah prays for Judah (14:7–9; 18:20); and Job prays for his friends (42:7–10). God accepts the intercession and reduces the effects of his judgment (Num 14; Deut 9; 2 Sam 24) or averts it entirely (Num 11). Nonetheless, the OT warns that a time may come when God no longer responds to intercession (Amos 7:8; 8:2; Ezek 14:14) and even forbids its offering (Jer 7:16). Before this time the prophets announced that God's wrath could be averted by repentance (Jer 4:4, 8; Dan 9:16).

Like the OT, the NT declares the wrath of God as well as his grace and mercy (Rom 1:18; John 3:36; Rev 14:10), but "God is not provoked to anger arbitrarily; wrath is not a trait of the divine nature."[28] The phrase "the wrath of God" is used most often as a metonym for God's judgment. It is in this sense that John the Baptist says to the Pharisees, "Who warned you to flee from the coming wrath?" (Matt 3:7; see also Luke 21:23; Rom 1:18; 2:5; 4:15; 5:9; 13:4; Eph 5:6; Col 3:6; 1 Thess 1:10; 2:16; Rev 6:17;

---

24. Moberly, *Atonement and Personality*, 13.
25. Moberly, *Atonement and Personality*, 4.
26. Moberly, *Atonement and Personality*, 14.
27. Moberly, *Atonement and Personality*, 13.
28. Kleinknecht et al., "Ὀργή," 116.

11:18). Thus, that God is "slow to anger" (Neh 9:17; Ps 103:8; 145:8; Joel 2:13; Jonah 4:2; Nah 1:3) means that he is slow to execute judgment. Romans 2:4–5 says:

> Or do you show contempt for the riches of his kindness, forbearance and patience, not realizing that God's kindness is intended to lead you to repentance? But because of your stubbornness and your unrepentant heart, you are storing up wrath against yourself for the day of God's wrath, when his righteous judgment will be revealed.

These verses show that God is patient with the sinner and gives ample time to come to repentance and thereby avoid judgment (Rom 2:4). Again, like the OT, the NT speaks of God's forbearance (Rom 2:4; Rev 2:21; 2 Pet 3:9) as giving the sinner time for repentance and therefore acting as an aid to salvation (2 Pet 3:15; 1 Tim 1:16). John the Baptist tells us how to be spared the wrath (judgment) to come: "Repent, for the kingdom of heaven has come near" (Matt 3:2) and "Produce fruit in keeping with repentance" (Matt 3:8). For the unrepentant, however, God's wrath is not compromised; it will result in judgment (Rom 2:5, 8).

FORBEARANCE

God demonstrates his love through his forbearance. "Should not a loving God be patient and keep luring the perpetrator into goodness? This is exactly what God does: God suffers the evildoers through history as God has suffered them on the cross."[29] God desires that his people come to him in repentance and faith so that he can forgive and accept in his love (Ezek 18:30–32; 1 Tim 2:4). "God is love" (1 John 4:8), therefore he is longsuffering.

What does the term *longsuffering* mean? Scripture tells us that "God cannot be mocked" (Gal 6:7). This means that God will not be made a fool or be taken for granted. Eventually the unrepentant offender will pay the consequences for his choices. Meanwhile, God is patient. In other words, he will suffer a long time in hopes that there will be a turning to him. During this time of waiting and wooing, he is suffering. In Jer 3:19 God says concerning his wayward people:

> How gladly would I treat you like my children

---

29. Volf, *Exclusion and Embrace*, 299.

and give you a pleasant land,
    the most beautiful inheritance of any nation.
I thought you would call me "Father"
    and not turn away from following me.

Walter Brueggemann, in his *Commentary on Jeremiah*, says of this verse:

> Verse 19 is among the most poignant in Jeremiah. The poet has taken the anguish of a parent as his medium. The poet portrays for us a parent who has labored and dreamed for the glorious day when the child will be old enough and responsible enough to receive all that has been saved for the child from the beginning. The father wants to give the child this inheritance . . . but the moment of gift never comes. . . . The wounded father is left with the shambles of hard work and broken dreams and knows the bitter combination of deep hurt and heavy resentment.[30]

But how patient should God be? The day of reckoning must come, not because God is eager to punish, but because every day of patience in a world of violence and every postponement of vindication means letting insult accompany injury. "How long will it be before you judge and avenge our blood?" cry out the souls under the altar to the Sovereign Lord (Rev 6:10 NRSV). The response calls the souls "to rest a little longer, until the number would be complete both of their fellow servants and of their brothers and sisters, who were soon to be killed as they themselves had been killed" (v. 11 NRSV). "But the response underlines that God's patience is costly, not simply for God but for the innocent. Waiting for the evildoers to reform means letting suffering continue."[31]

JUDGMENT

Suffering will not continue forever. Because God hates evil and suffering, he is a God of wrath. Because God is a God of wrath, evil has been defeated in Christ and will one day be eliminated altogether. As Miroslav Volf says, "There can be no new creation without judgment, without the expulsion of the devil and the beast and the false prophet (Rev 20:10), without the swallowing up of the night by the light and of death by life

---

30. Brueggemann, *Jeremiah*, 46.
31. Volf, *Exclusion and Embrace*, 299.

(Rev 21:4; 22:5)."[32] If God were *not angry* at injustice and violence and *did not* make the final end to evil, God would not be worthy of our worship.[33] "God inflicts violence against the stubbornly violent to restore creation's original peace. Hence in the Apocalypse, the creative word at the dawn of creation becomes the double-edged sword at the sunset before creation's new and unending day."[34]

"The Anabaptist tradition, consistently the most pacifist in the history of the Christian church, has historically had no hesitation about speaking of God's wrath and judgment,"[35] and with good reasons. No trace of a nonindignant God exists in the biblical texts, be it OT or NT, be it Jesus of Nazareth or John of Patmos. The evildoers who "eat up my people as they eat bread," says the psalmist in God's name, will be put in "great terror" (Ps 14:4–5 NRSV). Why terror? Why not simply reproach? Even better, why not reasoning together? Why not just display suffering love? Because the evildoers are "corrupt" and "they do abominable deeds" (v. 1); they have "gone astray," they are "perverse" (v. 3). "God will judge, not because God gives people what they deserve, but because some people refuse to receive what no one deserves; if evildoers experience God's 'terror,' it will not be because they have done evil, but because they have resisted to the end the powerful lure of the open arms of the crucified Messiah."[36] "The violence of the Rider on the white horse . . . is *the symbolic portrayal of the final exclusion of everything that refuses to be redeemed by God's suffering love.* For the sake of the peace of God's good creation, we can and must affirm *this* divine anger and *this* divine violence. . . ."[37] "Underlying the theology of judgment in the Apocalypse is the assumption that *nothing* is potent enough to change those who insist on remaining beasts and false prophets."[38] Therefore, as Volf says:

> The violence of the Rider is the righteous judgment against [those who oppose] the system of the one called "Faithful and True" (Rev 19:11). Without such judgment there can be no world of peace, of truth, and of justice: terror (the "beast" that devours) and propaganda (the "false prophet" that deceives)

32. Volf, *Exclusion and Embrace*, 52.

33. Volf, *Exclusion and Embrace*, 303.

34. Volf, *Exclusion and Embrace*, 300.

35. Volf, *Exclusion and Embrace*, 298.

36. Volf, *Exclusion and Embrace*, 298.

37. Volf, *Exclusion and Embrace*, 298.

38. Volf, *Exclusion and Embrace*, 297.

must be overcome. Evil must be separated from good, and darkness from light. These are the causes of violence and they must be removed if a world of peace is to be established.[39]

So the concept of the wrath of God and its resulting judgment is essential to a proper understanding of God's nature and plan of redemption. Sin lies under the wrath of God causing estrangement between God and his creatures (Rom 5:10 calls humankind God's "enemies"). If the sinner is to be reconciled to God, then God's wrath must be removed. According to Scripture, God's wrath is removed not by propitiation (appeasement) or satisfaction (payback), but by the expiation (wiping out) of sin. God's wrath cannot be removed by a propitiatory sacrifice as in pagan religions. When repentance and God's gracious pardon eliminate the source of a person's alienation, rebellion, and sin, he or she can be reconciled to God. Verses 2 and 3 of Ps 85 indicate this connection between forgiveness and the removal of wrath: "You forgave the iniquity of your people and covered all their sins. You set aside all your wrath and turned from your fierce anger." In no way does removal of divine wrath through repentance and pardon deny the reality of the wrath of God or compromise the fact that God is hostile to everything that is evil. No NT text states that the sacrifice of Christ is intended to appease God's wrath or that Christ is himself the object of that wrath in the place of sinners.[40] Rather, Scripture indicates consistently from beginning to end that God's wrath is removed by repentance and his gift of forgiveness.

SUMMARY

In chapter 5 the concept of God's justice has been examined along with the subsidiary concepts of his mercy, his wrath, his forbearance, his judgment, and his forgiveness. Important conclusions are that God is always just in that he is always fair, and that he is always merciful in that he is always willing to forgive a repentant sinner. But, that conclusion does not mean that God always judges (punishes) or, conversely, always forgives (pardons). Justice and mercy cannot be juxtaposed, but judgment and forgiveness must be juxtaposed. God is always just and merciful, but he chooses whether to punish or to forgive. That choice is determined by the sinner's repentance or absence thereof. In spite of his wrath, his hatred

39. Volf, *Exclusion and Embrace*, 296.

40. Chandler, *Victorious Substitution*, 70–71.

of evil, God is often longsuffering, forbearing with sin while he waits for the sinner to repent in hopes that he may forgive rather than punish. In the meantime, fellowship and reconciliation are hindered and sometimes even made impossible due to the absence of repentance and the persistence of sin. But God forbears because he loves, and in his love he longs for reconciliation and fellowship.

What can be determined about God's mercy, his wrath, his justice, and even his love by the fact that repentance is the condition for his forgiveness? (1) Repentance brings forth God's mercy, his willingness and desire to forgive and be reconciled to all. (2) Repentance eliminates his wrath and the barrier to reconciliation. (3) His justice does not insist on punishment but is free to respond to repentance in forgiveness. (4) The purity of his love is demonstrated in that he wants nothing less than cleansing and holiness for his beloved. These conclusions are important if God's people are to correctly model his behavior. They lay the foundation for Part II, which examines the question, When are God's people to forgive?

CHAPTER 5 STUDY QUESTIONS

The Concept of Justice

1. What conclusion of the penal substitution theory is based on the faulty concept that justice is denied by the absence of punishment?

2. What is the purpose of God's judgment of his people?

3. What does it mean to say that God is just?

4. What right does God forgo when he forgives sins without receiving satisfaction (payback) or inflicting punishment?

5. If God is always just or fair, does that mean he always insists on punishment?

6. God's innate characteristic of justice is the opposite of what? What is sometimes wrongly considered the opposite of justice?

God Is Free to Remit Sins

1. What does it mean to say that God forgives sins freely?

Repentance: The Determining Factor

1. What factor determines God's choice between forgiveness and punishment?

2. According to Scripture, does God take pleasure in punishing the guilty?

3. If God's forgiveness is given freely, is it given unconditionally?

Mercy

1. Why is forgiveness always an act of mercy?

The Wrath of God

1. What is the wrath of God, and why would its absence reveal a lack of love?

2. In what two senses is God's judgment exhibited in Scripture?

3. Why is God "slow" to execute judgment (or "slow to anger")?

Forbearance

1. How does God's longsuffering, or forbearance, relate to Gal 6:7, "God cannot be mocked"?

Judgment

1. What must God do before there can be a new creation?

2. Why must the wrath of God be removed for reconciliation to take place? How is it removed?

6

Restoration of Relationship

IN ADDITION TO REPENTANCE, forgiveness, and justice, another term that must be defined according to its scriptural usage is *reconciliation*, or atonement. As indicated in chapter 3, the doctrine of the atonement refers to the state of reconciliation between a gracious God and estranged humanity accomplished through the work of the savior, Jesus Christ. What sort of reconciliation or relationship is envisioned in Scripture for persons who repent and are forgiven by God?

THE HEBREW ORIGINAL

The Hebrew verb *kipper* means to atone, to reconcile. In common usage it means to cover, hence its soteriological sense is to cover sin, meaning to make atonement for sin. But "cover" is actually its derivative sense, the root idea of the verb being to wipe or smear. This is the meaning it bears in the Syriac; it also occurs in Hebrew, for instance, in the command to Noah that he should "coat [the ark] with pitch" (Gen 6:14). From this root meaning come the various uses of the verb in the Hebrew Scriptures. Thus, when a covenant is annulled, it is said to be smeared over or wiped away (Isa 28:18). So also is sin smeared over or wiped away when it is pardoned (Ps 65:3). *Kipper* is a picturesque synonym for *salach*, meaning to forgive or be merciful.[1] It signifies the removal of sin brought about by repentance and forgiveness, which results in the removal of wrath, or

1. Smith, *Atonement in Light of History*, 157.

atonement, that is, reconciliation. The purpose of forgiveness, then, is atonement/reconciliation. *In fact, forgiveness and atonement are almost synonymous in Scripture, indicating that Scripture does not envision forgiveness without reconciliation.*

THE NATURE OF RECONCILIATION

In addition to involving both a historical event and an event in the lives of individual Christians, atonement also involves a continuous process of reconciliation, of becoming one with God (John 17). What is the nature of this reconciliation?

The answer depends on the nature of the divine/human relationship. Different theories of the atonement perceive this relationship in different ways. In an article titled "Atonement and Reconciliation," Vincent Brümmer analyzes three basic models of relationship with God and their implications for understanding the nature of reconciliation.[2] This outstanding analysis clarifies the nature of the relationship that God desires and that Jesus died to make possible.

MODELS OF RELATIONSHIP

Relationship with God is often understood in terms of relationships that people have with each other. Three distinct kinds of relationship can be distinguished among people: controlling, contractual, and fellowship. In reality, humans are almost always in a combination of all three.[3]

Controlling relationships are those in which one person dominates another person. These relationships are asymmetrical because one person is the object of another's control. The controlling person is able to establish, change, or prevent the relationship. The relationship is impersonal because only one in the relationship is functioning as a person—the other is treated as an object.[4]

Contractual relationships are those in which persons relate to each other in terms of social agreements. Each party accepts certain rights and duties toward the other. People enter into such relationships looking to benefit from the terms. Such relationships are quite different from those

2. Brümmer, "Atonement and Reconciliation," 435–52.
3. Brümmer, "Atonement and Reconciliation," 435.
4. Brümmer, "Atonement and Reconciliation," 436.

of mutual fellowship in which each partner chooses to serve the interests of the other and not primarily his own, or in which one identifies with the other so completely that he considers the interests of the other to be his own. In contractual relationships goodwill toward another is conditional and limited. Each person keeps his part of the bargain provided the other person keeps theirs. A person's value is determined by their usefulness, and the good one does for the other is proportional to this usefulness. Another who could provide the same services would do just as well. There are no commitments to a person beyond the limits of the agreement.[5]

In relationships of fellowship, however, a person is inherently valuable, and the relationship has intrinsic value irrespective of usefulness. Neither another person nor another relationship can substitute, because one cannot have *that* relationship with anybody else. That irreplaceability gives people in such relationships personal value and identity.[6]

BREAKING AND RESTORING RELATIONSHIPS

All three types of relationships can be damaged; however, the way in which each of these relationships must be restored is different. In controlling relationships, it is up to the controlling partner to manage and repair the relationship. He therefore receives the credit for restoring the relationship or the blame if there is no improvement.[7]

In a contractual arrangement, the relationship breaks down when one party fails in his duties or responsibilities to the other. The other is then no longer obligated to fulfill his part of the arrangement. There are three ways this kind of relationship can be restored. The offending party could try again to do that which he failed to do, or render some kind of equivalent service. The other party's rights would be satisfied and the offender would be restored to a position in which he could expect to receive his rights. If the offending party is unwilling or unable to make satisfaction, the offended party could restore the balance by punishing the other, or by withholding the services that would have been due. If punishment is borne, then the debt is paid and the balance of rights and duties is restored to the relationship. Providing satisfaction or bearing

---

5. Brümmer, "Atonement and Reconciliation," 437.

6. Brümmer, "Atonement and Reconciliation," 437–38.

7. Brümmer, "Atonement and Reconciliation," 439.

punishment are therefore two ways that the guilty party could earn restoration. A final way in which a contractual relationship could be restored
is for the offended party to condone the wrong done him by not requiring
any reparation.[8] In this case the action becomes an accepted part of the
relationship or of the contract.

Relationships of fellowship are those in which persons relate to each
other in such a way that they treat the interests of the other as their own.
Their communion and union is such that one loves the other as himself.
Humans are not able to sustain this level of fellowship consistently. Because of selfishness they put their own interests above those of the other
and therefore act in ways that cause the other injury. When this occurs,
the relationship has been damaged and the offended party has grounds
for resentment.[9]

There are two conditions that must be met for the relationship to
be healed. The wronged party must be willing to forgive and refuse to be
resentful afterward. They must consider the breach in the relationship a
greater evil than the wrong done to them, and therefore continue to treat
the interests of the other as their own. This attitude, which is an essential
element for healing the relationship, is characterized by suffering. The
one who is hurt is the one who suffers. He is the one who pays the price
for healing the relationship. This attitude is not the same as condonation;
the offense remains offensive. It does not become an acceptable element
of the relationship.[10] If maintaining this attitude of love is easy, it probably
involves indifference. This sort of condonation is easy if one does not care
deeply about the one who has wronged him. However, if one is betrayed
by a family member it is more difficult and painful.[11]

The second element essential for restored fellowship is repentance
on the part of the offending partner. Love, which is willing to forgive, is
one's willingness to identify with the other in spite of their offense. If,
however, the offending party refuses to acknowledge his wrong and does
not repent of his actions, continued identification entails acquiescence
or condonation. Therefore the offending party must seek forgiveness, acknowledge his wrong, and have a change of heart for the relationship to
be restored. Forgiveness from one party and repentance from the other

---

8. Brümmer, "Atonement and Reconciliation," 440–41.

9. Brümmer, "Atonement and Reconciliation," 440.

10. Brümmer, "Atonement and Reconciliation," 440.

11. Cave, Work of Christ, 280.

are both required for true restoration of relationship.[12] Although repentance is necessary, it cannot demand or earn forgiveness. Forgiveness cannot be demanded as a right; it can only be sought. In asking for forgiveness, one acknowledges his or her dependence on the free decision of the other. Both parties must be involved in restoring the relationship just as both parties were involved in establishing it in the first place. Neither repentance nor forgiveness can be forced or earned. Bearing punishment or making satisfaction earns reinstatement in a contractual relationship, and what is earned the other party is required to give. Punishment or satisfaction makes forgiveness unnecessary.[13]

If there is both confession and forgiveness, a relationship can not only be restored, it may be strengthened, as suggested by John Burnaby in his book *Christian Words and Christian Meanings*:

> We shall be to one another what we were before, save for one important difference. I know now that you are a person who can forgive, that you prefer to have suffered rather than to resent, and that to keep me as a friend, or to avoid becoming my enemy, is more important to you than to maintain your own rights.
>
> And you know that I am a person who is not too proud to acknowledge his fault, and that your good will is worth more to me than the maintenance of my own cause. . . . Forgiveness does not only forestall or remove enmity: it strengthens love.[14]

RECONCILIATION WITH GOD

What are the implications of these three types of relationships for reconciliation between God and humankind? In a theology that describes the divine/human relationship in terms of a controlling model, salvation is brought about exclusively by the action of an omnipotent God. Salvation is generally viewed in terms of deliverance from the consequences of sin rather than the healing of relationship. God is the only active party in the reconciliation of this type of relationship. Thus John Calvin in his "Articles Concerning Predestination" says:

> Before the first man was created, God in his eternal counsel had determined what he willed to be done with the whole human

12. Brümmer, "Atonement and Reconciliation," 441.

13. Brümmer, "Atonement and Reconciliation," 441.

14. Burnaby, *Christian Words*, 87.

race. In the hidden counsel of God it was determined that Adam should fall from the unimpaired condition of his nature, and by his defection should involve all his posterity in sentence of eternal death. Upon the same decree depends the distinction between elect and reprobate: as he adopted some for himself for salvation, he destined others for eternal ruin.[15]

The theological benefit of this model is that it excludes any chance of salvation by merit. All glory belongs to God. However, there are serious disadvantages to this model. This view does not consider Christ to have died for the salvation of all persons, it compromises human free will, and it even circumvents the need for the death of Christ.[16]

These disadvantages vanish when the divine/human relationship is described in terms of a contractual relationship. According to this view, God commits himself to provide humans with eternal happiness if they obey his will. However, humankind fails to keep its end of the agreement by not giving to God the obedience that is his right under the covenant. Humans disturb the balance of rights and duties—therefore they forfeit eternal life. As previously mentioned, there are three ways in which this balance may be restored: punishment, satisfaction, or condonation. H. A. Hodges, in *The Pattern of Atonement*, summarizes the contractual view:

> Our relation to God as sinners is this: we must pay a penalty appropriate and adequate to our wrongdoing, we must undergo punishment adequate to our guilt, we must make satisfaction adequate to the affront which we administer to God's honor, and by these means or by direct appeal to his mercy we must propitiate him.[17]

God cannot condone human sin. God can restore balance to the relationship by punishment, denying humans the eternal happiness that would have been theirs had they not broken the contract. This fate could be avoided if humans could make satisfaction by good works that *earn* a restoration of balance and merit eternal life. Sinners, however, do not have the ability to make adequate satisfaction. Christ's work is to make adequate satisfaction in the place of humankind. All credit for salvation goes to him, but it is still a salvation that is *earned*. Salvation is earned by

---

15. Calvin, "Predestination," 179.

16. Brümmer, "Atonement and Reconciliation," 444.

17. Hodges, *Pattern of Atonement*, 45.

Christ rather than by humans (Anselm's satisfaction theory of the atonement employs this argument).[18]

There are many weakness in this view of the atonement (see chapter 3 of the author's book, *Victorious Substitution: A Theory of the Atonement*), including the relationship it assumes between God and humankind. In this type of relationship each party is valued for the services they can provide for the other rather than for who they are as persons. God is not valued for himself alone, but for the eternal happiness he is able to provide. God loves an individual only for the obedience that brings him honor. In other words, God values his own honor more than he does the individual person. This view of the divine/human relationship presents a defective picture of the nature of God's love as well as the worth of man.[19] Rather, individual worth should be derived from God's love for the individual person. This love, and the resulting relationship, is what gives a person dignity and life meaning.

In a relationship of fellowship (love) each partner makes the other's interests his own. When applied to the divine/human relationship, God makes individual human salvation and eternal happiness his own concern. Individuals identify with God by making his will their own. Neither partner is compelled to consider the interests of the other. Each is free to give love. Individuals are not obliged to love God; neither is God obliged to love persons who do his will. Salvation is entirely by grace. Any possibility of a merit-based theology is excluded from this relationship of fellowship. God desires for humans to love him based on who he is and not on what he can provide them. Individuals who seek their own interests in their relationship with God fail to identify themselves with his interests and his will. According to this understanding of divine/human relationship, sin is not a mere rule that has been broken, but the cause of alienation, and it requires reconciliation. The essential conditions for reconciliation are repentance and forgiveness.[20] Scripture reveals that God will always forgive the repentant: "If we confess our sins, he is faithful and just and will forgive us our sins and purify us from all unrighteousness" (1 John 1:9). But this assurance does not mean one can presume upon God's love and forgiveness; neither does it contradict the fact that it is

18. Brümmer, "Atonement and Reconciliation," 445–46.

19. Brümmer, "Atonement and Reconciliation," 446–47.

20. Brümmer, "Atonement and Reconciliation," 448.

free and unearned.[21] Nor does the fact that God knows each human heart mean that one need not confess before God. As C. S. Lewis says, "By unveiling, by confessing our sins and making known our requests, we assume the high rank of persons before [God]."[22]

This concept of the method of reconciliation does not compromise the reality of the wrath of God. One is not obliged to choose between a God of judgment and a God of love, for wrath is the other side of love. Even in human love there is an analogy. The more a father loves a son, the more he hates the son's hypocrisy or lying or immorality. In this sense there can be great wrath and great love at the same time.[23] God's love never varies and its consistency should not be doubted, but God's wrath is removed in reconciliation.

In this analysis, broken relationships are restored with two essential elements—repentance and forgiveness. It cannot be a unilateral affair; both parties must take action of their own free will. This is the biblical model and the reason that God does not (cannot) always forgive. In Part II it will be shown from Scripture that God's love and his desire to forgive are ever-present. In addition, the offer of forgiveness is ever-present prior to repentance, and his forgiveness is limitless following repentance. He suffers, he hopes, he longs, he forbears, he woos. Finally he gives: he gives forgiveness when the time is right, following repentance.

APPLICATIONS FOR MODELS OF RELATIONSHIP

Human relationships are not as clear-cut as these distinctive models, but the models are nevertheless helpful for considering when forgiveness is appropriate.[24] For Brümmer, forgiveness is only applicable with mutual fellowship, and then it still requires repentance. Other relationships are restored by satisfaction (restitution, as in the trespass offering, where it is required), punishment, and/or condonation. If the context of the relationship is not clear, an apology may be accepted as sufficient when what is needed is restoration of balance through punishment, satisfaction (payback), or both. Condonation has taken place. In other words, apology (and even repentance) without restitution is insufficient in the

---

21. Brümmer, "Atonement and Reconciliation," 449.

22. Lewis, *Letters to Malcolm*, 21.

23. Morris, *Apostolic Preaching of the Cross*, 197.

24. Burns, "Forgiveness," 157.

restoration of contractual relationships. The relationship has not been restored, but rather changed by the condonation of the offense, which then becomes an accepted amendment of the contract.

Understanding the nature of the relationship is important when considering proper means of restoration. There can be no restoration of fellowship in relationships where no fellowship has previously existed. For example, relationships of manipulation (such as the abuse of children by adults) are not in the arena of reconciliation.[25] Forgiveness in interpersonal relationships will be considered in detail in Part II.

SUMMARY

Atonement/reconciliation is what Christ comes to accomplish. What is the nature of this atonement that he dies to make possible? He gives his life that the world might be redeemed from the powers of evil, and that whosoever will may become reconciled to God and be free from sin as a power that enslaves and from death as its result. The relationship he desires with each person is one of mutual love and fellowship, not one of control. This desire is revealed in that God gives us free will. When one's relationship with God is damaged it cannot be restored through satisfaction (payback), punishment, or condonation, as it can in contractual relationships. Rather, it must be healed through the actions of both parties: the repentance of the wrongdoer, the forgiveness of God, and their mutual commitment of love for one another.

25. Burns, "Forgiveness," 158.

CHAPTER 6 STUDY QUESTIONS

The Hebrew Original

    1. How are forgiveness and atonement almost synonymous?

Models of Relationship

    1. What are the three basic types of relationships, and what is a distinguishing feature of each?

Breaking and Restoring Relationships

    1. How is a controlling relationship repaired?

    2. How is a contractual relationship repaired?

    3. How is a fellowship, or love, relationship restored?

Reconciliation with God

    1. If the divine/human relationship were controlling, how would it be repaired?

    2. If the divine/human relationship were contractual, how would it be repaired?

    3. As the divine/human relationship is one of fellowship, how is it repaired?

Applications for Models of Relationship

    1. Why is understanding the nature of a relationship important when considering the means of restoration?

PART II

When Are God's People to Forgive?

PART I CONSIDERED THE following questions: When does God forgive, and when does God not forgive? Why does God forgive, and why does God not forgive? What are God's feelings when he forgives, and what are God's feelings when he does not forgive?

Scripture reveals that God forgives when a sinner repents, and that he does not forgive when a sinner refuses to repent. God forgives because he loves and desires reconciliation with those alienated from himself. His love is also the reason he does not forgive, for his love for the sinner, as well as his righteousness, means he will not condone sin. The desire of God's love is fulfilled when people choose to repent, receive his forgiveness, and be reconciled, entering into a relationship of fellowship with him. When people refuse his offer of forgiveness and relationship, his longing goes unfulfilled and he is grieved. Love, then, is the answer to all the questions surrounding God's practice of forgiveness—love of persons that requires their repentance, love of persons that endures hurt and offers forgiveness in spite of it, and love of persons that desires a relationship of fellowship and intimacy.

In order to answer the questions in Part I, the biblical concepts of repentance, forgiveness, reconciliation, and the justice of God were examined. Part II now addresses the question, When are Christians to forgive? Broken relationships are a part of this present age; God has them and people have them. Therefore people who desire to follow the Lord should seek to learn and to obey his instructions concerning their personal relationships both within and without the Christian community. What does Scripture reveal about interpersonal forgiveness? Is God's forgiveness the model for interpersonal forgiveness? In Part II we examine the scriptural texts concerning interpersonal forgiveness.

7

When and Why Does Scripture Instruct God's People to Forgive?

INTERPERSONAL FORGIVENESS IN THE OT

VERY LITTLE IS SAID in the OT about interpersonal repentance, forgiveness, and the restoration of broken relationships. Yet the few OT texts that speak to these issues lay the foundation for the NT instructions concerning interpersonal relationships within the community and are often quoted in this regard. A few OT narratives describe repentance and reconciliation, such as the stories of Jacob and Esau and of Joseph and his brothers. David also forgoes revenge and controls his anger in the narratives of Saul, Nabal, Absalom, and Shimei. However, no OT law commands the forgiveness of someone who has done another harm. In fact, the psalms are full of prayers for the punishment of enemies or of thanksgiving for vindication against them.

Leviticus 19:17–18 states, "Do not hate a fellow Israelite in your heart. Rebuke your neighbor frankly so you will not share in their guilt. Do not seek revenge or bear a grudge against anyone among your people, but love your neighbor as yourself. I am the LORD." God's people are instructed to verbally confront the wrongdoing of a brother, but not to take vengeance (personally get even by doing another harm) on anyone. They are also warned against hatred "in their heart" of a brother. This admonition, then, prohibits concealed hatred and revenge. It does not prohibit, but commands, that confrontation be expressed openly. This prohibition and command is given with respect to a "brother" and a "neighbor." Love of a neighbor involves a willingness to confront and correct. To love is to act correctly; it is not necessarily to forgive injuries.[1] (Jesus broadened the term neighbor with the ushering in of the eschatological kingdom.)

The OT law also instructs a wrongdoer to confess his sin and to make a sacrifice to God so that his sin may be forgiven (Lev 5:5). In addition, he is to make restitution to the one harmed by his actions (Lev 5:16; 6:5). Finally, certain sins are punished by exclusion from the assembly (Num 15:31).

JUDAISM VERSUS CHRISTIANITY

A rift exists between Judaism and Christianity concerning the subject of forgiveness. Solomon Schimmel, in his book *Wounds Not Healed by Time*, acknowledges "a range of opinions within both Judaism and Christianity as to how and when to temper justice with mercy, and when and whom to forgive, and under what circumstances to do so." However, he also says that "Judaism overall is more concerned with guaranteeing justice than with forgiving incorrigible sinners, whereas Christianity, . . . if not in its actions, talks more of forgiveness as an act of grace, given even to the undeserving and not-yet-repentant, than of justice."[2] This statement is undoubtedly true, but should it be so? Should there be a rift between Judaism and Christianity concerning the practice of forgiveness? Does the NT change the conditions of God's grace? Part I demonstrated that a rift exists between the OT and the NT only if there is a faulty understanding. Contrary to what is often assumed, the OT contains no shortage of God's grace, and the NT is not without the same condition of repentance that is established in the OT.

Schimmel also says that many Christians glibly preach forgiveness of unrepentant enemies, yet in their own lives are no less prone to anger and resentment than are non-Christians.[3] This, too, is undoubtedly true. In contrast, Judaism avoids this hypocrisy. Jews often see forgiveness of the unrepentant as a violation of justice and as "narcissistic self-help at the expense of moral indignation and pain at evil."[4] Many argue that Christians who think they must utter the words "I forgive you" even when it

---

1. Schimmel, "Interpersonal Forgiveness," 15.

2. Schimmel, *Wounds Not Healed*, 64.

3. Schimmel, *Wounds Not Healed*, 65.

4. Schimmel, *Wounds Not Healed*, 66.

is untrue are in "an emotionally and morally compromising position of saying one thing while feeling another—an absence of inner integrity."[5] Jews believe the notion that forgiveness encourages repentance "doesn't seem to be confirmed by *most* human experience with evil." At least, they argue, this theory should be studied empirically before it can be asserted.[6] The Jewish belief is that one should "imitate God, and God, for the most part, punishes unrepentant sinners and forgives repentant ones. . . . Repentance is emphasized as the precondition for forgiveness, in both human/divine relationship and in interpersonal relationships."[7]

The ethical issues surrounding forgiveness that have historically separated Jews and Christians will be examined in Part III. In Part II, interpersonal forgiveness in the NT is examined to see if this rift can be reconciled scripturally. This book contends that the Jewish/Christian rift can be reconciled scripturally, because the rift is caused by a mishandling of the NT subject of interpersonal forgiveness, specifically by the claim that Christians must forgive in the absence of repentance.

INTERPERSONAL FORGIVENESS IN THE NT

The NT says more about interpersonal forgiveness than the OT, and it states explicitly that the forgiveness of God offered in Christ is the model (Eph 4:32; Col 3:13). To reveal what this model involves, Part I established the pattern of God's forgiveness in both the OT and NT. Part II determines whether Christians are instructed *by Scripture* to forgive in the absence of repentance. The question is not what one's mother says or what one's preacher says or what one's well-meaning friends say. The question is, Can a text be found in Scripture that instructs Christians to do what God does not do, that is, forgive in the absence of repentance?

CONFRONTATION

> Do not hate a fellow Israelite in your heart. Rebuke your neighbor frankly so you will not share in their guilt. (Lev 19:17)

---

5. Schimmel, *Wounds Not Healed*, 67.

6. Schimmel, *Wounds Not Healed*, 68.

7. Schimmel, *Wounds Not Healed*, 69.

If your brother or sister sins, go and point out their fault, just between the two of you. If they listen to you, you have won them over. But if they will not listen, take one or two others along, so that "every matter may be established by the testimony of two or three witnesses" [Deut 19:15]. If they still refuse to listen, tell it to the church; and if they refuse to listen even to the church, treat them as you would a pagan or a tax collector. Truly I tell you, whatever you bind on earth will be bound in heaven, and whatever you loose on earth will be loosed in heaven. Again, truly I tell you that if two of you on earth agree about anything they ask for, it will be done for them by my Father in heaven. For where two or three gather in my name, there I am with them. (Matt 18:15–20)

If another disciple sins, you must rebuke the offender, and if there is repentance, you must forgive (Luke 17:3b NRSV). ("In 17:3b some manuscripts add 'against you.' [The] *Greek New Testament* rejects this edition with an {A} decision, indicating that the text is certain."[8])

Warn a divisive person once, and then warn them a second time. After that, have nothing to do with them. (Titus 3:10)

As MacLachlan says, "Forgiveness always presupposes moral confrontation of some kind, . . . [for] the sphere of forgiveness is the sphere of blame."[9] In these verses both the OT and the NT speak of confrontation concerning sin within the community of believers. The words "against you" are found in some translations of Matt 18:15. They are omitted in the NIV (2011) because they are not found in many early manuscripts.[10] Also, the shorter reading is in agreement with the parallel passage in Luke 17:3b. Although an argument can be made for either addition or deletion,[11] the shorter version is preferred. The addition of "against you" changes an altruistic concern about a brother's spiritual danger into a personal matter as well.[12] A personal situation is in view beginning in verse 21 (and in Luke 17:4) with Peter's question concerning the number of times to extend forgiveness, but it is premature here. The issue is how a disciple is to act when he perceives a fellow disciple's spiritual danger.

8. Blight, *Luke 12–24*, 203.

9. MacLachlan, "Forgiveness," 39.

10. Turner, *Matthew*, 444.

11. Turner, *Matthew*, 447.

12. France, *Matthew*, 689.

A grave and recognized sin is involved, and this, as well as the severe consequences for a disciple who does not repent, adds to the argument that it is not a personal matter. The passage assumes that the person raising the issue is right and that the behavior is wrong.[13] Of course, personal matters may also involve obvious and serious sins. In any case, the process, which culminates in the whole church taking action, is certainly not appropriate for small offenses or matters of dispute in which culpability is not clear-cut. Perhaps the process of confrontation can sometimes be applied to personal matters, but that is not in view here. Therefore, a universal ruling of confrontation in personal matters is not warranted from this passage.

If the whole church is in agreement, the offender should accept the united testimony. A refusal to do so renders a person no longer fit to be a member of the community.[14] The final instruction in this passage is to treat the offender as a Gentile or a tax collector if he refuses to repent.

An essential element in understanding the passage is coming to grips with what this admonition means. R. T. France, in *The Gospel of Matthew*, says:

> The terms "Gentile" and "tax collector" (used in 5:46–47) represent those of whom a high standard is not expected. . . . The terms thus seem to stand for a person who has no place among the holy people of God, and who is to be shunned, in particular by refusing table fellowship. That would be the natural meaning if spoken by most Jews, but could Jesus (or Matthew) have used the terms in this way since this gospel has emphasized . . . Jesus' sympathy for outsiders and his willingness to break conventional taboos in order to reach them . . . (Matt 8:10–13; 9:9–13)? Would it not be more natural to take "treat as a Gentile or a tax collector" as an invitation to extend friendship and understanding to the offender? [In fact, this interpretation would be appropriate if it involved someone outside the church.] But that would make nonsense of the sequence of these verses, where every effort has been made to restore fellowship with the offender up to this point, but now their final repudiation of the consensus of the community has made further accommodation impossible. [Therefore, it must be concluded that] the terms ["Gentile" and "tax collector"] are being used here in their conventional Jewish sense, and that the disciple is being

---

13. France, *Matthew*, 692.
14. France, *Matthew*, 693.

instructed to suspend normal fellowship with the offender. [However, the passage does not include language that calls for] formal "excommunication."[15]

When the condition of repentance is met, however, forgiveness should be granted.[16]

What is the procedure for confrontation? The passages in Matthew and Luke are both based on Leviticus, demonstrating harmony between the OT and the NT. Leviticus makes it clear that if a brother is not reproved, the one who fails to do so is guilty. This is because he violates the law of love. Confrontation is the loving thing to do because its purpose is to call forth repentance and effect reconciliation. Confrontation is the act of one who cares—one who cares about wrongdoing, about the well-being of the offender, and about being reconciled with the offender.

Matthew presents three steps in a process intended to regain a lost brother and perhaps a relationship.

The first step is private admonishment. The privacy, with no witnesses, preserves the honor of the offender. It shows that the one who confronts cares about and respects the other. Without this care and respect, the wrongdoer is less likely to respond to the confrontation.

If private confrontation fails, witnesses are arranged. (Deut 19:15 is cited as support for this procedure.[17]) Witnesses protect both parties. The witnesses are not those in authority in the church, but fellow believers, ensuring an encounter of equals.

If this second confrontation fails, the whole church is called to be involved. If the offender will not listen to the whole church (which is tantamount to a rejection of God[18]) he is to be treated as a pagan or tax collector.

Confrontation of a brother demonstrates a readiness to forgive (Luke 17:3b, "if they repent") and a desire for reconciliation. In other words, confrontation demonstrates mercy and love. Note again that repentance, as the condition for forgiveness and reconciliation, is clearly stated in Luke and therefore presupposed in the parallel passage in Matthew. Note also that this passage involves the sin of a "brother," a fellow

15. France, *Matthew*, 693–94.
16. Marshall, *Luke*, 643.
17. Turner, *Matthew*, 445.
18. Turner, *Matthew*, 445.

Christian. Nothing is said about how to handle offenses from those outside the church.

In verses 18–19 the "you" is plural, referring to the whole church. These verses speak of "binding" and "loosing" by those who come together to confront the sinning brother. (Remember from chapter 3 that the definition of *aphesis* [forgiveness] is liberation or release. Therefore, loosing is another way of referring to forgiveness because one is loosed from his sin.) In verses 15–17 the church is authorized to determine whether a sinning disciple continues with the community or is excluded. His fate is determined by the outcome of the process laid out in verses 15–17. "Repentance leads to loosing, or forgiveness, and continued fellowship. The lack of repentance leads to binding, or retention of sin, and exclusion from the community."[19] As Bonhoeffer says, "The Gospel is protected by the preaching of repentance which calls sin sin and declares the sinner guilty. The key to loose is protected by the key to bind. The preaching of grace can only be protected by the preaching of repentance."[20]

"In [Matt] 18:18 the consequences of the process are shown to be extremely serious, involving the eternal destiny of the offending party."[21] Regarding the consequences, David Turner, in his commentary on the Gospel of Matthew, says:

> The process and promises of Matt 18:15–20 seem mechanical and harsh when these verses are isolated from their setting. But the passage is "embedded in a section filled with kindness." Jesus has been speaking tenderly of his disciples as humble children (18:5), little ones (18:6), lost sheep (18:12–13), and brothers (or sisters; 18:15, 21, 35). He has emphasized the necessity of proper care of these little ones (18:6–14). He will go on to stress the necessity of forgiveness (18:21–35). Even the discipline process allows three chances for repentance. Those who are involved in it should view themselves as agents of the Father/Shepherd seeking straying little ones/sheep. The goal is reconciliation and return to the fold, not severance from the flock.[22]

Turner also says, "Another comment is warranted by the flippant way in which 18:19–20 is often cited to assure small meetings of Christians that God is with them. This is disturbing because it twists a

19. Turner, *Matthew*, 436.

20. Metaxas, *Bonhoeffer*, 293.

21. Turner, *Matthew*, 446.

22. Turner, *Matthew*, 446–47.

solemn passage into a humorous cliché. Indeed, God is present with any legitimate meeting of his people, whatever its size, yet one should not mishandle Scripture to prove this."[23] This solemn passage promises the presence of Jesus in the difficult process of discipline. Taking it out of context makes light of the seriousness of the duty of the church to call forth repentance and to maintain its holiness.

Different situations are in view and different motives are involved in the confrontation depending on the inclusion or rejection of "against you" in this passage. If these words are excluded based on the manuscript evidence against them, then neither the OT nor the NT give any specific instruction concerning confrontation in handling personal grievances. If the words "against you" are accepted, they counsel breaking off relationships in which every effort has been made to no avail to bring forth repentance on the part of the offender. In either case, these instructions do not apply to relationships outside the Christian community. Nor can these words be applied to personal grievances that do not involve obvious and serious sin. Therefore no formula is given in these verses for handling personal issues that have resulted in broken or strained personal relationships within or outside the Christian community. Without such a formula, Christians must seek God's wisdom through prayer in each personal relationship or situation.

One example exists in Scripture, in which Paul rebukes Peter publicly:

> When Cephas came to Antioch, I opposed him to his face, because he stood condemned. For before certain men came from James, he used to eat with the Gentiles. But when they arrived, he began to draw back and separate himself from the Gentiles because he was afraid of those who belonged to the circumcision group. The other Jews joined him in his hypocrisy, so that by their hypocrisy even Barnabas was led astray. When I saw that they were not acting in line with the truth of the gospel, I said to Cephas in front of them all, "You are a Jew, yet you live like a Gentile and not like a Jew. How is it, then, that you force Gentiles to follow Jewish customs?" (Gal 2:11–14)

Peter and Paul clearly reconciled (if there was ever a breakdown in their relationship) as indicated by Peter's words about Paul in 2 Pet 3:15.[24] All that can be concluded from this example is that a time may exist when

---

23. Turner, *Matthew*, 447.

24. Carson, *Love in Hard Places*, 161.

confrontation must take place, risking the relationship, even at the expense of unity. This confrontation between Peter and Paul involved an extremely important issue—the very nature of the gospel—and all ended well. However, the outcome of Paul's instructions to Titus to warn the false teachers in Crete is not known (Titus 3:10).

SEVENTY TIMES SEVEN

> So watch yourselves. If your brother or sister sins against you, rebuke them; and if they repent, forgive them. Even if they sin against you seven times in a day and seven times come back to you saying "I repent," you must forgive them. (Luke 17:3–4)

> Then Peter came to Jesus and asked, "Lord, how many times shall I forgive my brother or sister who sins against me? Up to seven times?" Jesus answered, "I tell you, not seven times, but seventy-seven times." [25] (Matt 18:21–22)

The context of Matt 18:21–22 and Luke 17:4 is a situation in which a "brother or sister," i.e., a fellow disciple, has wronged another. The question concerns forgiveness within the community.[26] Luke's version clearly states that repentance is the condition for forgiveness.[27] In Matthew, repentance is presupposed in that Matthew's version has a second part to Jesus' answer to Peter's question—the parable of the unmerciful servant—in which repentance is evident.[28] Luke does not record this parable, thus the need to state plainly the condition of repentance. So the question put to Jesus concerns how often forgiveness should follow repentance.[29]

At the time of Christ some rabbis suggested that a person should forgive three times, thus the question to Jesus. The number seven

25. Turner, *Matthew*, 449. Turner argues that the number should probably be translated seventy-seven times (as it is in NIV, NRSV, BDAG 269; cf. Gen 4:15, 24); not "seventy times seven" (as it is in KJV, NASB, NLT, RSV); France, *Matthew*, 701. France says, "The KJV rendering of seventy times seven (i.e., 490 times), still represented in some English versions, is a literal reproduction of [an] idiom which is better understood as an idiomatic way of expressing the adverbial form of the compound number seventy-seven in Greek. Its meaning here is determined by the clear allusion to Gen 4:24, where the same phrase in the LXX is translated 'seventy-seven.'"

26. Turner, *Matthew*, 448.

27. Beale and Carson, *New Testament Use of Old Testament*, 57.

28. Norris, "Forgiving from the Heart," 86.

29. Bock, *Luke*, 439.

mentioned by Peter suggests the upper limit, symbolically indicating completion or perfection.[30] But Jesus' reply is startling. He says that no matter how many times the victim is sinned against he should forgive a repentant fellow disciple. Why should this be so? The scriptural answer is that Christians are to forgive each other in the same way that God forgives them (Luke 6:37–38; Eph 4:32; Col 3:13). God's grace has no limits, and therefore no reason exists for keeping a count of forgivenesses. The phrase "seven times a day" in Luke is hyperbolic,[31] for in reality the sincerity of the repentance should be questioned if the offense is repeated seven times in one day.

THE PARABLE OF THE UNFORGIVING SERVANT

> Therefore the kingdom of heaven is like a king who wanted to settle accounts with his servants. As he began the settlement, a man who owed him ten thousand bags of gold was brought to him. Since he was not able to pay, the master ordered that he and his wife and his children and all that he had be sold to repay the debt. At this the servant fell on his knees before him. "Be patient with me," he begged, "and I will pay back everything." The servant's master took pity on him, canceled the debt and let him go. But when that servant went out, he found one of his fellow servants who owed him a hundred silver coins. He grabbed him and began to choke him. "Pay back what you owe me!" he demanded. His fellow servant fell to his knees and begged him, "Be patient with me, and I will pay it back." But he refused. Instead, he went off and had the man thrown into prison until he could pay the debt. When the other servants saw what had happened, they were outraged and went and told their master everything that had happened. Then the master called the servant in. "You wicked servant," he said, "I canceled all that debt of yours because you begged me to. Shouldn't you have had mercy on your fellow servant just as I had on you?" In anger his master handed him over to the jailers to be tortured, until he should pay back all he owed. This is how my heavenly Father will treat each of you unless you forgive your brother or sister from your heart. (Matt 18:23–35)

---

30. France, *Matthew*, 700.

31. France, *Matthew*, 705.

The parable of the unforgiving servant immediately follows Jesus' initial answer ("seventy-seven times") to Peter's question concerning how many times one should forgive. The parable is joined to what precedes by the word "therefore" and should not be separated from it. In the parable Jesus gives an example of how receiving God's gracious and unlimited mercy should affect disciples in their relationships with each other. The main point of the parable is plainly stated, "Shouldn't you have had mercy on your fellow servant just as I had on you?" God's forgiveness is the pattern to be emulated. Peter is asking how many times must this pattern be repeated.[32]

As previously discussed, one of the metaphors for the practice of forgiveness in Scripture is canceling a debt. The debt owed represents the sin that needs to be forgiven.[33] The aspect of forgiveness that this metaphor emphasizes is forgiveness as a free gift. In this parable the servant asks forgiveness for a debt that he cannot pay. (The amount is hyperbolic and suggests the English translation "zillions."[34]) The debtor is not denying the debt, and he is aware that he cannot repay it. This acknowledgment of debt and humble request for relief from that debt is the equivalent of repentance when wrongdoing is involved. The parable is therefore not an example of forgiveness preceding repentance. On the contrary, the servant's debt is forgiven only after he comes to his master, acknowledges his debt, and asks for forgiveness. Also, the context of the parable is the instruction to forgive a *repentant* (based on the parallel passage in Luke 17:3–4) brother seventy-seven times. Debt itself does not involve wrongdoing, but debt as a metaphor for sin makes repentance relevant.

The debt metaphor emphasizes that forgiveness is a free gift, but this is not the point of the parable. Rather, the parable's message is that a clear link exists between receiving God's forgiveness and forgiving other disciples. In God's actions Christians have been given a moral virtue to practice and an ideal to follow. This parable gives two motives for forgiving: the fear of punishment (vv. 34–35, the reversal of one's own forgiveness) and the more basic motive of gratitude and imitation of the grace of God.[35] Christians should attempt to model God's forgiveness even if

32. Turner, *Matthew*, 449.

33. France, *Matthew*, 703.

34. Turner, *Matthew*, 450.

35. France, *Matthew*, 702, 703.

they may not be fully able. Perhaps the failure of the man whose debt of ten thousand bags of gold was remitted is not so much that he failed to forgive, but that he made no effort to forgive. This unmerciful servant apparently does not even aspire to do for others what was done for him. His actions are both violent (v. 28) and implacable (v. 30), revealing a heart condition that lacks the humility characteristic of the repentant.[36] This servant's behavior shows that his own forgiveness is obtained under false pretenses of sorrow. His forgiveness is revoked based on his true heart condition that is revealed by his treatment of his fellow servant.[37] R. C. Moberly, in his book *Atonement and Personality*, says, "The most obvious teaching of [this] parable is that the fullest forgiveness of God towards man, in the conditions of this present life, is provisional, and may be revoked and reversed. This is one characteristic of forgiveness upon which it is well to lay stress."[38] This aspect of the parable, that in the present life forgiveness is provisional and can be "forfeited and reversed," is rarely mentioned, much less taught or stressed.[39]

The statement concerning the loss of forgiveness is unqualified, but does this mean that refusal to forgive is an unpardonable sin? France points out that in Matt 12:31–32 the unforgivable sin is not a refusal to forgive. Therefore,

> to set the present passage against the wider spread of Jesus' teaching may suggest some qualification of its absolute language; even the unforgiving may not be beyond redemption. The language concerning God's condemnation may be hyperbolic in that God's mercy is not granted based on performance, in this case the performance being the forgiving of others. But such considerations . . . must not be allowed to weaken the impact of this sobering parable and of the solemn words [which follow the Lord's Prayer] in Matt 6:14–15 which it illustrates. Those who will not forgive must not expect to be forgiven; the measure they give will be the measure they get back (Matt 7:1–2).[40]

In summary, the message of the seventy-seven times saying of Jesus (Matt 18:22) is that forgiveness within the church following repentance is to be unlimited. The point of the parable that follows (Matt 18:23–35)

---

36. France, *Matthew*, 707.
37. Turner, *Matthew*, 451–52.
38. Moberly, *Atonement and Personality*, 60.
39. Moberly, *Atonement and Personality*, 60–61.
40. France, *Matthew*, 708.

provides motivation for this unlimited forgiveness: the Father's judgment and example. "Human forgiveness is to find its inspiration in man's experience of the forgiveness of God. God's forgiveness must find an expression of itself in man's forgiveness of man."[41]

Matthew 18:5–35 should be viewed as a unit, the controlling motif being the proper treatment of brothers and sisters. In verses 15–20 a sinning member of the family must be treated with love, which means confrontation in hopes of bringing about repentance. Ultimately, if repentance does not take place the member is to be excluded. If he repents at a later time he should of course be welcomed back into the community. The situation in Matt 18:21–22 concerns personal offenses between members of the community. In this situation, when one brother wrongs another, the extent of forgiveness is unlimited if he repents. Thus the family is protected both from sinful offenses and from personal quarrels. Turner summarizes the unit by saying, "The controlling motif of the chapter is the proper treatment of little ones [v. 5], brothers and sisters, children of the heavenly Father. . . . Disciples must receive each other as they would a child (18:5–10), shepherd each other as they would a lost sheep (18:12–14), deal patiently but decisively with unrepentant sinners in their midst (18:15–20), and genuinely forgive those who sin against them as many times as necessary (18:21–35). These values will strengthen the community's relationships and enable it to withstand the rigors that are ahead in Jerusalem and beyond."[42]

Without accepting repentance as the condition for forgiveness in the seventy-seven times saying, it would be very difficult to reconcile the discipline process of Matt 18:15–20 with the obligation of unlimited forgiveness in Matt 18:21–25. Matthew would be contradicting himself within the same teaching unit. Yet if the condition of repentance is accepted in the seventy-seven times saying (based on the parallel passage in Luke, the parable which follows, and the teaching in the rest of Scripture concerning repentance), then the passage in Matthew is consistent and clear.

---

41. Moberly, *Atonement and Personality*, 63.

42. Turner, *Matthew*, 452.

THE LORD'S PRAYER

> Forgive us our debts, as [Greek: *hos*] we also have forgiven our
> debtors. . . . For if you forgive other people when they sin against
> you, your heavenly Father will also forgive you. But if you do not
> forgive others their sins, your Father will not forgive your sins.
> (Matt 6:12, 14–15)

> Forgive us our sins, for we also forgive everyone who sins against
> us. (Luke 11:4)

The same link between the experience of God's forgiveness and forgiving
others is made in the Lord's Prayer. In this prayer Jesus instructs his disciples to pray for ongoing personal forgiveness (Matt 6:12). Repentance on
the part of the disciple who prays is indicated by the context of prayer in
which the disciple, by asking for forgiveness, acknowledges wrongdoing.

What does the word "as" (*hos*: like, in the same manner[43]) mean in
these verses? Can it mean that if, and only if, one forgives others God will,
in some sort of quid pro quo arrangement, forgive? Surely not, as this
would make the bestowal of divine grace something rightfully earned
by behavior. According to this view, divine forgiveness is rationed out
as payment. But human forgiveness cannot force divine forgiveness,
nor limit the extent of divine forgiveness to a reciprocal action. A better
understanding in this context is that *hos* (which means "like") *implies*
"since" (NIV translates it "for"). This means that since one forgives others, demonstrating what it means to be thankful for God's forgiveness, he
asks God to continue to forgive him.[44] The request for forgiveness in the
Lord's Prayer on the basis of forgiving others is simply a way of saying
that in asking God for forgiveness one understands the parable of the
unforgiving servant. The request for forgiveness (v. 12), which is itself
an admission of guilt, indicates that the disciple knows that repentance
is required. The statement that he has forgiven others "as," or like, he is
asking God to forgive him indicates the disciple knows he must be willing
to do for others what God has done for him, that is, be *willing* to show
mercy and forgive the repentant one who likewise asks for forgiveness.[45]

What is the relationship between the Lord's Prayer in Matt 6 and the
parable of the unmerciful servant in Matt 18? The Lord's Prayer reverses

43. Zodhiates, *Complete Word Study Dictionary*, 1501.

44. A. Bash, *Forgiveness and Christian Ethics*, 95.

45. Turner, *Matthew*, 190.

the "forgiving as" found in the parable of the unforgiving servant. In the parable, the king expects the servant to forgive others *as* he has forgiven him. The actions of the servant, humbly acknowledging his debt and asking for mercy, come prior to the forgiveness. God's forgiveness is a free gift, but it is not unconditional. The condition is repentance. God does not wait to see if one will forgive others before he forgives those who come to him asking for mercy. The servant in the parable is expected to forgive others "as" God first forgave him. That the servant's act of unforgiveness follows the king's act of lavish forgiveness makes the servant's act especially morally offensive.

In light of the parable of the unmerciful servant, the conditional statements of the Lord's Prayer presuppose the prior divine act of forgiveness explicit in the parable. The instructions in Matthew are given to those who are already disciples, forgiven and redeemed. In the Lord's Prayer, Jesus instructs these disciples to pray that God would "forgive [their] debts *as* [they] also have forgiven [their] debtors" (Matt 6:12). They are to pray that God will continue to do for them what they have done for others in response to the warning in the parable. The parable of the unmerciful servant shows that God's gift of forgiveness cannot be presumed upon. The forgiveness received can be forfeited by unwillingness to forgive others (following their repentance).[46] The servant's act of unforgiveness is a manifestation of a heart that scorns God's grace. In such a case the sinner has chosen to step out of the sphere of God's grace and forgiveness into which God initially brought him. Clearly Paul's instruction in Eph 4:32 and Col 3:13, to forgive "as" the Lord forgives, is based on this parable. Matthew 6, then, does not claim that human acts of forgiveness condition God's forgiveness of a repentant sinner. An interpretation that would make a person's ultimate acceptance by God depend on whether he was able to forgive perfectly every time is clearly unacceptable.[47] Logically, if forgiving apart from repentance is something that God does not do, God's forgiveness must be correlated not with a person's *actual* forgiveness of others, but with his *willingness* to forgive others when it is right to do so.[48] Otherwise God's readiness to forgive would be based not on forgiving *as* (like, in the same manner) he forgives,

---

46. France, *Matthew*, 703.

47. Schreurs, "Truth and Reconciliation," 171.

48. A. Bash, *Forgiveness and Christian Ethics*, 95.

but on misguided forgiveness of those who have not repented—a moral wrong that he himself does not commit.

The Lord's Prayer and the parable of the unforgiving servant raise a question: How does this conditional forgiveness relate to the gospel's free and unmerited grace? The same question arises from the parable of the sheep and the goats (Matt 25:31–46) and from the parable of the wedding feast (Matt 22:1–14). In the parable of the sheep and goats, salvation is conditioned upon one's treatment of others. Also, like the parable of the unforgiving servant, in the parable of the wedding feast, one of the recipients of grace does not meet the expectations on which the continuation of that salvation depends. "Salvation according to that parable [the wedding feast] may be undeserved and unexpected, but it is not without conditions."[49] So also in these verses following the Lord's Prayer, forgiveness cannot be presumed upon.[50] One can ask for God's forgiveness on the basis of repentance and a willingness to forgive others. When one prays in this way, *stating* the fact that he has forgiven others, he is acknowledging that he cannot expect God to do for him what he refuses to do for others. He is stating his understanding of the prerequisite for his prayer to be heard.[51]

VERSES IN WHICH REPENTANCE IS PRESUPPOSED

Forgive *as* God Forgives

> Be kind and compassionate to one another, forgiving each other, just as in Christ God forgave you. (Eph 4:32)

> Bear with each other and forgive one another if any of you has a grievance against someone. Forgive as the Lord forgave you. (Col 3:13)

Both of these verses emphasize that forgiveness should characterize the corporate life of Christian communities. Christians are instructed to forgive "as in Christ God forgave you." In other words, they are to forgive others in the same way that God forgave them, that is, freely and following repentance. Christians should consciously model the forgiveness that

---

49. France, *Matthew*, 253.
50. France, *Matthew*, 253.
51. Marshall, *Luke*, 461.

they themselves have experienced and received from God. Just as God is merciful, willing to forgive the repentant sinner, so they should be also. The link between the Lord's forgiveness and interpersonal forgiveness would not be parallel unless repentance is presupposed. Also, it would not be logical for the Lord to ask his people to forgive in the absence of repentance when he himself does not. These verses are surely a conscious allusion to the Lord's Prayer and the parable of the unmerciful servant.

Forgiveness in these verses can refer to forgiving sins that are moral wrongs, in which case repentance is presupposed, but forgiveness here may also refer to one of several virtues (along with kindness and compassion) that have to do with getting along in a community. In this case forgiveness is not about reconciliation after a serious offense has been committed, but about interpersonal difficulty. Colossians 3:13 mentions a "grievance." As Bash says, "Probably, forgiveness here (and in Eph 4:32) refers not to a person's virtuous response after having been morally wronged but to how one responds with grace to someone in a community who can be irritating, difficult, or awkward."[52] The Greek word translated forgive in these verses is *charizomai*, which in classical and NT Greek means "to give" or "to grant." *Charizomai* is related to the word *charis*, which means grace or gift, and its NT usage implies undeserved kindness given freely. The verb is used of God's gracious and generous actions in general and can be properly translated "to give something by grace."[53] For kindness and compassion (Eph 4:32) to be shown in response to irritations or grievances, repentance would not be involved.

Forgive and You Will Be Forgiven

> Do not judge, and you will not be judged. Do not condemn, and you will not be condemned. Forgive, and you will be forgiven. Give, and it will be given to you. A good measure, pressed down, shaken together and running over, will be poured into your lap. For with the measure you use, it will be measured to you. (Luke 6:37–38)

The injunction, "Forgive, and you will be forgiven," found in these verses does not mention repentance. It would surely be a distortion of Scripture, however, to say that all one need do to be forgiven is to forgive others. The

52. A. Bash, *Just Forgiveness*, 48.
53. A. Bash, *Just Forgiveness*, 43.

first part of the verse says, "Do not judge, and you will not be judged." It would equally be a distortion of Scripture to say that all one need do to avoid God's judgment is to refuse to judge others. This distortion would suggest that in order to be forgiven one only need not hold others accountable in any way. Therefore in these verses repentance should be presupposed as a condition for forgiveness (based on Luke 17:3–4 and the teaching of the rest of Scripture concerning repentance) as well as for avoiding God's judgment.

The injunction not to judge does not forbid one from making a judgment in the sense of discriminating between good and evil, right and wrong. Neither does the statement imply indifference to the moral condition of others nor does it forbid a serious appraisal of those with whom one has to live. Rather, evaluations should be made with awareness of one's own faults and the fact that God will judge all. The disciple should be compassionate just as he desires that God be merciful to him. The second command forbidding condemnation (v. 37b) elucidates the first injunction not to judge. It forbids an attitude of superiority and harshness. Rather, a disciple should be merciful, ready to forgive, just as he expects God to be with him.[54] Repentance may be presupposed as the condition for forgiveness based on its emphasis in so many other Scripture verses. The necessity of repentance simply does not need to be restated every time forgiveness is mentioned. The verse means that if one refuses to forgive *under circumstances in which he should forgive* (based on the repentance of the offender), then God will also withhold forgiveness. These verses are simply saying the same thing as the parable of the unmerciful servant, that one should not expect to be treated with mercy and generosity by God if he or she is unwilling to treat others with mercy and generosity.

Just as in the Lord's Prayer (Matt 6:15) the notion that God's forgiveness is contingent on human forgiveness of others cannot, however, be pushed too far. If it is pushed too far the idea that unforgiving people will not be forgiven would contain a contradiction. If God's forgiveness is a gift to the undeserving, how can it be made contingent on the degree to which one person forgives another? Perhaps it simply means that if people strive to forgive as best they can, responding to their own experience of God's forgiveness, then God will forgive them with all the mercy and understanding that he offers. However, if they take what God gives

---

54. Marshall, *Luke*, 266–67.

and reject its transformative power, then God will limit their experience of his forgiveness (as in the parable of the unmerciful servant). Christians should strive to follow God's example even if they sometimes fail to do so perfectly.[55]

If one took Luke 6:37 out of the context of the rest of Scripture, he could interpret it to mean that all interpersonal sins should be forgiven regardless of whether the offender has repented or not. But this would be an argument from silence, for this verse is silent concerning repentance. However, the rest of Scripture is not silent, and the rest of Scripture must always be taken into account in the practice of sound hermeneutics. The broader context of repentance is self-evident.[56] As Richard Swinburne, in his book *Responsibility and Atonement*, says, "There are places in the NT where it speaks of God 'forgiving men' without there being any explicit mention of the need for prior repentance. But it must be assumed from other passages where this need is explicit."[57]

Your Sins Have Been Forgiven

> I am writing to you, dear children, because your sins have been forgiven on account of his name. (1 John 2:12)

Another example of a verse in which repentance is presupposed is 1 John 2:12. This verse is addressed to "children" of God—those who know him as Father, having been born into his family through repentance and faith. The forgiveness here simply refers to the forgiveness of sins that they experienced when they became God's children. Their repentance and faith is therefore presupposed.

The Woman Who Anoints Jesus' Feet

> "Therefore I say to you, her sins, which are many, are forgiven, for [meaning 'therefore'] she loved much. But to whom little is forgiven, the same loves little." Then He said to her, "Your sins are forgiven." . . . "Your faith has saved you. Go in peace." (Luke 7:47–50 NKJV)

55. A. Bash, *Forgiveness and Ethics*, 94.
56. A. Bash, *Forgiveness and Ethics*, 99.
57. Swinburne, *Responsibility and Atonement*, 153.

Commentators have taken Luke 7:47 in two ways: (1) Because of the woman's conduct her sins, which are many, have been forgiven, namely because she loved much. But the NT does not support the view that love atones for sin. (2) A second view is that since she loved *much* it follows that *many* sins have been forgiven her. In this second view, the Greek word translated "for" should be understood to mean "as is evidenced by the fact that" she loved much. The first view runs contrary to the context.[58] The parable of the two debtors (which Jesus tells in verses 40–43) states clearly that great love is the consequence of having been forgiven much. He to whom little is forgiven loves little; he to whom much is forgiven loves much.[59] Therefore, according to the context, the better translation of verse 47 would be, "Her sins, which are many, have been forgiven, therefore she loved much." Her actions are those of a person who has been forgiven much.[60] (The NIV reflects this view by translating Luke 7:47, "Therefore, I tell you, her many sins have been forgiven—as her great love has shown. But whoever has been forgiven little loves little.")

In either case, the passage ultimately suggests that those who have little love for Jesus have not realized the magnitude of their sin and their need for forgiveness.[61] The passage ends with Jesus pronouncing her forgiveness and citing her faith as the reason for her salvation. There is no mention of repentance, but whether one views her love as the result or as the cause of her forgiveness, repentance is presupposed. In the former view the woman's love is given as the evidence of the transformation of her heart.[62]

Imagine how awkward it would be to add, perhaps parenthetically here, "By the way she did repent of her sins." This addition is simply not necessary because of the clarity of the rest of Scripture concerning the necessity of repentance. Jesus says to this woman, "Go in peace." "Peace" means peace with God, that is, reconciliation, which is not offered to the unrepentant.

---

58. Marshall, *Luke*, 313.

59. Creed, *Luke*, 110.

60. Craddock, *Luke*, 106.

61. Marshall, *Luke*, 313.

62. Norris, "Forgiving from the Heart," 86.

Prayer and Forgiveness

> And when you stand praying, if you hold anything against anyone, forgive them, so that your Father in heaven may forgive you your sins. (Mark 11:25)

The implication of Mark 11:25 is that one should not pray expecting God to hear and answer when he will not do for others what God has done for him. One expects God to forgive his sins if he repents, not because he has a right to God's forgiveness, but because God has revealed that his desire is to do so. To refuse to treat another in the same way that you expect God to treat you is to presume upon God's mercy and forgiveness. This verse makes clear that this presumption is unacceptable. If one is to continue to experience fellowship with God and a clear conscience, based on repentance and God's grace, then he must forgive as God forgives. Otherwise, fellowship with God is broken by this disobedience.

Repentance is presupposed as necessary for forgiveness. Note also that faith, although occasionally not mentioned, is presupposed as necessary for salvation. For example, Titus 3:7 says, "Having been justified by his grace, we might become heirs having the hope of eternal life." Gordon Fee points out that, in reference to the fact that God "saved us" (Titus 3:5), Paul "*always* means 'by grace through faith' as in Eph 2:8–9."[63] In other words, although not mentioned in Titus 3:7, faith is presupposed as a condition for God's saving grace. This presupposition is made definite by verse 8, which uses the phrase "those who have trusted in God."[64] First Corinthians 6:11 presents another example in which faith is presupposed.[65] It says, "You were washed, you were sanctified, you were justified in the name of the Lord Jesus Christ and by the Spirit of our God." Faith is not mentioned, but is the condition for being justified as set forth in the rest of Scripture.

Thus, in the previous five instances (Eph 4:32 and Col 3:13; Luke 6:37–38; 1 John 2:12; Luke 7:47; Mark 11:25), just as faith is not always stated as the condition for salvation, so repentance is not always stated as the condition for forgiveness. In both cases, the condition may be presupposed because it is made abundantly clear in the rest of Scripture.

---

63. Fee, *1 and 2 Timothy, Titus*, 206.

64. Fee, *1 and 2 Timothy, Titus*, 207.

65. Fee, *1 and 2 Timothy, Titus*, 209.

CONFESSION OF SIN

Confession, so foreign to much of the church today, characterizes ancient Israel. Israel had both public confession through the sacrificial ritual as well as procedures for restitution (Num 5:5–10). The injunction found in the NT concerning confession is not new, but carries forth the OT practice of admitting one's guilt before God and others. This same practice should characterize the new community of God's people.[66]

> I [God] will go away and return to My place until they acknowledge their guilt and seek My face; in their affliction they will earnestly seek Me. (Hos 5:15 NASB)

> If we confess our sins, he is faithful and just and will forgive us our sins and purify us from all unrighteousness. If we claim we have not sinned, we make him out to be a liar and his word is not in us. (1 John 1:9–10)

This verse in 1 John is a straightforward statement of the necessity of admitting one's sin as a condition for forgiveness. To not do so is to not allow God's "word" to be "in us" (have no place in our lives). First John 1:9 also contains the great promise that God always welcomes and forgives those who come to him in this way. Confession and repentance are to be ongoing practices of Christian life so that fellowship with God is not hindered. Confession of sin is a life practice of those who "walk humbly with [their] God" (Mic 6:8) and is the basis for forgiveness in the NT just as in the OT.[67] "Without confession [one remains] unforgiven . . . because a refusal to confess is a rejection of forgiveness."[68]

> And the prayer offered in faith will make the sick person well; the Lord will raise them up. If they have sinned, they will be forgiven. Therefore confess your sins to each other and pray for each other so that you may be healed. (Jas 5:15–16a)

In this verse, confession brings forth not just forgiveness but also healing. Confession is a part of the healing process. One should not presume upon God's gifts of forgiveness or of healing; if one is unwilling to confess and repent, he should not expect forgiveness and healing from God.

---

66. McKnight, *James*, 445–46.

67. Painter, *1, 2, and 3 John*, 155.

68. Volf, *Free of Charge*, 154.

As Luther says, "There are two kinds of sin: one is confessed, and this no one should leave unforgiven; the other kind is defended, and this no one can forgive, for it refuses either to be counted as sin or to accept forgiveness."[69] If Christians are to model their forgiveness of others after God's practice, then confession by the wrongdoer is clearly an essential element.

THE UNFORGIVABLE SIN

> And everyone who speaks a word against the Son of Man will be forgiven, but anyone who blasphemes against the Holy Spirit will not be forgiven. (Luke 12:10)

In both Matthew (12:31) and Mark (3:28–29), the sin of blasphemy against the Holy Spirit is found in the context of the controversy in which the Pharisees accuse Jesus of being in league with Satan. Apparently this unforgivable sin is attributing the miraculous work of the Holy Spirit to Satan. Charging the Spirit of God with evil is blasphemy against the Holy Spirit.[70] This sin, which involves rejecting God's messenger (as in Exod 23:20–21), cannot be forgiven (also as in Exod 23:20–21 in the context of the exodus) because it is, in effect, rejecting God himself and making God one's enemy (see Isa 63:10). Since Jesus is inaugurating God's eschatological salvation, those who utterly reject it can find no forgiveness. They have refused to take part in God's new exodus.[71]

This verse and the nature of sin against the Holy Spirit could certainly involve a more lengthy discussion. But that is not necessary here because this book's point is that all sin is not forgiven.

FORGIVE VERSUS RETAIN

> Again Jesus said, "Peace be with you! As the Father has sent me, I am sending you." And with that he breathed on them and said, "Receive the Holy Spirit. If you forgive anyone's sins, their sins are forgiven; if you do not forgive them, they are not forgiven." (John 20:21–23)

69. Volf, *Free of Charge*, 153–54.
70. Craddock, *Luke*, 161.
71. R. Watts, "Mark," 150.

These verses do not mean that whenever a person wants to forgive someone—or not forgive them—God will do likewise.[72] The context forbids
this interpretation. Jesus speaks these words to his disciples when he appears to them on resurrection evening. He commissions them to go into
the world and proclaim the gospel in the power of the Holy Spirit. In
so doing Jesus gives his disciples (and all believers after them; see John
17:20–21) authority to forgive or retain sins—that is, to proclaim the
forgiveness or retention of sin. The saying reveals the central content of
the disciples' mission: they are to proclaim with authority, as represen-
tatives of the exalted Lord, the remission of sins. They have known his
love, forgiveness, and peace, and they are to go and proclaim it to others.
However, the proclamation of the gospel must also involve the possibility
of the retention of sin.[73]

Although these verses do not elaborate on the conditions for the
remission or retention of sins, the rest of John's Gospel does. Both the
forgiveness and permanent retention of sins come in many images: "The
Lamb of God who takes away the sin of the world" (1:29); redemption
from being a "slave to sin" (8:34–36); movement from "darkness" to
"light" (3:19–21); not perishing but having "eternal life" (3:16); having
"the right to become children of God" (1:12)—as opposed to remaining
under God's wrath (3:36); dying in sin (8:24); and sin remaining (9:41).
This authority to forgive or retain people's sins consists of placing before
people the choice to repent and accept in faith the forgiveness of God
or to remain in sin and fall under divine judgment (cf. 3:18, 19).[74] As
Bonhoeffer says, "Christ has given his church power to forgive and to
retain sins on earth with divine authority (Matt 16:19; 18:18; John 20:23).
Eternal salvation and eternal damnation are decided by its word. Anyone
who turns from his sinful way at the word of proclamation and repents,
receives forgiveness. Anyone who perseveres in his sin receives judgment. The church cannot loose the penitent from sin without arresting
and binding the impenitent in sin."[75]

"This may well be what Jesus had in mind when he promised that
the disciples would do works 'greater' than his own (14:12)."[76] Elsewhere,

---

72. K. Carter, "Forgiveness Revisited," 203.

73. Ridderbos, *John*, 644.

74. Ridderbos, *John*, 645.

75. Metaxas, *Bonhoeffer*, 292.

76. Michaels, *John*, 1013.

Jesus claims for himself "authority on earth to forgive sins" (Matt 9:6), yet in John's Gospel he never displays that authority, at least not explicitly. When he speaks of sin it is to retain and not forgive (see 8:21, 24, "You will die in your sin[s]"; 9:41, "Your guilt remains"; 15:22, "They have no excuse for their sin"). In the Gospel of John, the ministry of Jesus is characterized positively as giving life rather than negatively as forgiving sin. The promise that Jesus is "the Lamb of God who takes away the sin of the world" (1:29) only comes to realization after the resurrection. The Gospel of John views sin as not truly taken away (whether in forgiveness or judgment) until the work of atonement is "finished" (19:30). When Jesus is risen he commissions his disciples as his agents to carry out the "greater" works of forgiving sin and pronouncing judgment.[77]

Although these verses require interpretation based on the context, one point is clear: all sin is not forgiven by God and therefore is not to be forgiven by the disciples as his agents. Unrepented sin is unforgiven and therefore retained by the sinner. The disciples declare this forgiveness or retention; to do otherwise would misrepresent God. To claim that God forgives all sin would be a blatant and obvious contradiction of this verse.

"FATHER FORGIVE THEM . . ."

> Jesus said, "Father, forgive them, for they do not know what they are doing." (Luke 23:34)

In this verse Jesus prays for those who crucify him and cast lots for his garments, that they might be forgiven on the basis of their ignorance. Jesus' words could be interpreted as saying that one is not held accountable for sins of ignorance. In Acts 3:17, however, Peter says, "Now, fellow Israelites, I know that you acted in ignorance, as did your leaders."[78] This is said in reference to crucifying Jesus (v. 13). Peter then goes on to say, "Repent, then, and turn to God, so that your sins may be wiped out, that times of refreshing may come from the Lord" (v. 19). Clearly both a recognition of truth and repentance are necessary for sin to be wiped out. It would be greatly out of harmony with the rest of Scripture to take Luke 23:34 to mean that forgiveness (which according to its biblical meaning involves the wiping out of sin) should be granted apart from repentance.

77. Michaels, *John*, 1013.
78. Konstan, *Before Forgiveness*, 121.

The biblical pattern for sins committed in ignorance is that wrongdoers should be brought to truth, feel convicted of their sin, and repent "so that [the] sins may be wiped out" (Acts 3:19).

Anthony Bash makes the point that this verse actually supports the conclusion that repentance must precede God's forgiveness because, contrary to what is often said, Jesus did not forgive from the cross precisely because his crucifiers had not repented. His words do not *offer* forgiveness but are a *prayer* to the Father.

> For those who in ignorance kill the Messiah there is forgiveness, so long as they adhere to the biblical pattern of repentance first. What Jesus is asking is for God to hold true to his promises, as of course God truly will. So, if you wrong me, I might say to you, "May God forgive you," or I might pray to God, "Forgive him," and that prayer is made within the framework of what I believe the biblical pattern to be, namely divine forgiveness out of grace for those who repent.[79]

In other words, Jesus is asking, should his crucifiers come to repentance, that the Father be willing to forgive them. An argument for assuming this presupposition would be that had Jesus thought they should be forgiven at that time, prior to repentance, he could have simply pronounced them forgiven himself. And, of course, he did not. Rather, the prayer indicates "that he thought they could be forgiven if they repented. In other words, they had not taken themselves outside the possibility of forgiveness, as with those who blaspheme against the Holy Spirit. . . . As they sinned in ignorance, they were 'eligible' for forgiveness."[80] The prayer is, then, an expression of Jesus' mercy and compassion toward his enemies who kill him, but not a statement of their forgiveness.

This verse is further complicated because of its textual problems. Tim Carter points out that "among the earliest manuscripts of Luke's gospel, Codex Sinaiticus stands alone in including this prayer from the cross. . . . The verse is missing from P75 ℵ1 B D* W Θ 070 579 597* 1241 itad syrs copsa,bo, Cyril. On the other hand, later attestation for the verse is widespread."[81] All translations of the Bible note that this verse is not in the earliest manuscripts. Concordances will therefore include it only in parentheses. The Nestle-Aland 27th edition of the NT (published by

---

79. A. Bash, correspondence with author, April 2017.

80. A. Bash, correspondence with author, April 2017.

81. T. Carter, *Forgiveness of Sins*, 249.

the Institute for New Testament Textual Research) maintains that this verse is an interpolation (a later insertion not original to Luke).[82] *The New International Greek Testament Commentary* by I. Howard Marshall says, "Against its genuineness it can be argued: The combination of early manuscript evidence against its inclusion is particularly impressive. . . . If the saying is a genuine part of Luke it is impossible to account for its willful excision. . . . The saying could have been modeled on Acts 7:60 [Stephen's words at his martyrdom]." Marshall's commentary also says that the "weight of the textual evidence" is against the saying, and it breaks the connection between 23:33 and 23:34b.[83] The omission of the saying does not impede the flow of the narrative.[84] (For a more comprehensive discussion, see Appendix A: Luke 23:34a.)

A truth seeker should be willing to abandon a well-loved verse if the evidence indicates that the verse is an interpolation. Based on the manuscript evidence, there is reason to believe that this verse may be such an interpolation. This verse is consistently used to make the point that forgiveness should be granted in the absence of repentance, a point the verse does not make. If one wants to make this argument, it would clearly be better to use other Scripture verses because of the textual questions concerning the authenticity of this saying. The problem arises in that no other verses exist that make this point. That is why this verse is quoted so often by those who advocate unconditional forgiveness.

Many say that the defining characteristic of Christianity is forgiveness. If asked whether they are commanded to forgive the unrepentant, Christians would often answer "yes." Most would quote Jesus on the cross, not realizing that these words indicate that Jesus did not, in fact, forgive, and being unaware that these words are not found in the oldest manuscripts. Any application of this verse that suggests a person automatically forgive all sins committed against him would be inaccurate and in spite of the textual evidence against it.

REDEMPTION/THE FORGIVENESS OF SINS

For the sake of thoroughness, with the intention of mentioning every NT verse that uses the word forgive, the verses that refer to forgiveness in an

---

82. Konstan, *Before Forgiveness*, 121.
83. Marshall, *Luke*, 868.
84. T. Carter, *Forgiveness of Sins*, 250.

eschatological context are here listed again (see chapter 4, Eschatological Forgiveness—"The Forgiveness of Sins"). It should be clear that these verses do not speak of God's forgiveness of individuals who come to him in repentance or of interpersonal forgiveness. They speak rather of God's redemption of the world, and are a proclamation of his forgiveness in the sense of dealing with the curse of sin and the coming of the kingdom of God.

> Some men brought to him a paralyzed man, lying on a mat. When Jesus saw their faith, he said to the man, "Take heart, son; your sins are forgiven. . . . Which is easier: to say, 'Your sins are forgiven,' or to say, 'Get up and walk'?" (Matt 9:2, 5). (That this verse should probably be taken in a messianic/eschatological sense is discussed in the following section.)

> He is the one whom God exalted to His right hand as a Prince and Savior, to grant repentance to Israel, and forgiveness of sins. (Acts 5:31 NASB)

> All the prophets testify about him that everyone who believes in him receives forgiveness of sins through his name. (Acts 10:43)

> Therefore, my friends, I want you to know that through Jesus the forgiveness of sins is proclaimed to you. (Acts 13:38)

> I will rescue you from your own people and from the Gentiles. I am sending you to them to open their eyes and turn them from darkness to light, and from the power of Satan to God, so that they may receive forgiveness of sins and a place among those who are sanctified by faith in me. (Acts 26:17–18)

> In him we have redemption through his blood, the forgiveness of sins, in accordance with the riches of God's grace (Eph 1:7). (Here, forgiveness is equated with the redemption of the world.)

> [He] brought us into the kingdom of the Son he loves, in whom we have redemption, the forgiveness of sins (Col 1:14). (Again, forgiveness is equated with the redemption of the world.)

THE HEALING OF THE PARALYTIC

> Some men brought to him a paralyzed man, lying on a mat. When Jesus saw their faith, he said to the man, "Take heart, son; your sins are forgiven. . . . Which is easier: to say, 'Your sins are

forgiven,' or to say 'Get up and walk'? But I want you to know
that the Son of Man has authority on earth to forgive sins." (Matt
9:1–8; cf. Luke 5:17–26)

Like the case of the woman who anointed Jesus' feet, in these verses there
is a pronouncement of forgiveness with no mention of repentance. It is
argued earlier that in the case of the woman, repentance is presupposed
and indicated by her love. The case of the paralytic is a difficult one and
may be somewhat different. In the OT, forgiving sin and healing are
found together at the time of God's reign through his messianic king (Isa
33:24, and specifically of a lame man, v. 23b).[85] For Jesus to wipe away
sins apart from sacrifice is a sign that the world to come is breaking in.
Since announcing forgiveness and healing the sick were both signs of the
inbreaking of the kingdom of God, Jesus put them in the same category
saying, "Which is easier?" Jesus heals the man, demonstrating his authority to forgive sins (9:6–7). Such authority is related to Jesus' mission to
save his people from their sins (Matt 1:21) by giving his life as a ransom
for them (Matt 20:28) and thereby inaugurating the new covenant (Matt
26:28; cf. Jer 31:31). Both the pronouncement of the forgiveness of sins
and the healings demonstrate that Jesus is the Messiah and is inaugurating the eschatological kingdom of God. In other words, Jesus' healing
ministry signifies that the ultimate defeat of sin and Satan has begun.[86]
The healing itself is brought into the service of this overriding theme of
the kingdom come (the forgiveness of sin), demonstrating its truth.[87]

A close connection between sin and physical illness or disability
would have been made by many people at this time (cf. 1 Cor 11:28–30).
This connection is made by Jesus in only one other situation, and in that
case to dismiss the idea of sin as the cause of blindness (John 9:1–3).
In the story of the paralytic the connection is left unexplained; it is not
stated that the paralysis is caused by sin. No other gospel story indicates
that forgiveness is a means to physical healing. Faith is the usual requi-
site, and faith is not mentioned here. One can only speculate concerning
the possibility that this is a case of a psychosomatic problem (no sin involved), a spiritual problem (sin involved), or neither.[88] The speculation
should probably be avoided. The point of the story is clearly stated that

85. R. Watts, "Mark," 133.

86. Turner, *Matthew*, 248–49.

87. France, *Matthew*, 343.

88. France, *Matthew*, 345.

the curing of this disability is to be taken as proof of Jesus' authority to deal with sin. Sin and sickness are connected here in that both are characteristics of the fallen world that Jesus comes to redeem. Jesus could claim the authority to forgive sins, but the claim could not be verified and could be denied. However, the healing cannot be denied and therefore verifies his claim to be able to forgive sins.[89]

THE WOMAN CAUGHT IN ADULTERY

> "Has no one condemned you?" "No one, sir," she said. "Then neither do I condemn you," Jesus declared. "Go now and leave your life of sin." (John 8:10b–11)

The NIV inserts a note between John 7:52 and 7:53: "The earliest manuscripts and many other ancient witnesses do not have John 7:53—8:11. A few manuscripts include these verses, wholly or in part, after John 7:36, John 21:25, Luke 21:38, or Luke 24:53." For this reason *The New International Commentary on the Gospel of John* by Leon Morris adds these verses with commentary in the Appendix only. This commentary begins,

> The textual evidence makes it impossible to hold that this section is an authentic part of the Gospel. It is not attested in the oldest manuscripts, and when it does make its appearance it is sometimes found in other positions, either after verse 36, or after verse 44 or at the end of this Gospel, or after Luke 21:38. It seems clear enough that those scribes who felt it too important to be lost were not at all sure where to attach it. And if they could not agree on the right place for it, they could not agree on the true text for it either. The manuscripts that have it do not agree closely. The very large number of variants indicates that the textual history of this passage is different from that of the fourth Gospel. . . . There is also the fact that the passage does not fit well into the context, whereas 8:12 follows naturally after 7:52.[90]

Obviously, if this passage is not authentic it should not be used to argue any position concerning forgiveness. Nevertheless it should be pointed out that the words "neither do I condemn you" (v. 10) are used in the legal sense of passing sentence. Jesus sends the woman away without the death sentence. He does, however, condemn her actions when he calls

---

89. France, *Matthew*, 346.
90. Morris, *John*, 778–79.

her to repentance, saying, "Go now, and leave your life of sin."[91] How the woman responds is not revealed.

THE PRODIGAL SON

> The son said to him, "Father, I have sinned against heaven and against you. I am no longer worthy to be called your son." But the father said to his servants, "Quick! Bring the best robe and put it on him. Put a ring on his finger and sandals on his feet. Bring the fattened calf and kill it. Let's have a feast and celebrate. For this son of mine was dead and is alive again; he was lost and is found." So they began to celebrate. (Luke 15:21–24)

Although neither the word repentance nor the word forgiveness appears in the parable of the prodigal son, the story involves both. Luke 15:10 says, "There is rejoicing in the presence of the angels of God over one sinner who repents." The story of the prodigal son follows with the introductory words "Jesus continued" (v. 11). This son refuses to be presumptuous and asks to be taken back only as one of his father's hired servants (v. 19). It can be seen from this request and from Luke's transition sentence in verse 10 that he repents. He acts in humility after he sees himself as he is, in the pig pen, and he turns back to his father.[92] Miroslav Volf, in his book *Exclusion and Embrace*, says of this parable:

> The son's "strategy of return" had events arranged in a different sequence: going up to the father—confession—acceptance into service (vv. 18–19). The father's welcome, however, interrupted the sequence ("but," v. 20). Confession followed acceptance (v. 21). But it did follow, without interruption. . . . After the son's departure the relationship was infected by a transgression and therefore had to be healed by a confession. For the embrace to be complete—for the celebration to begin—confession of wrongdoing had to be made.[93]

The open arms of the father show that the "will to embrace" (to use Volf's phrase), to be reconciled, was always in the heart of the father, just as God's arms are always open. Open arms are a call to come home. God is always ready to receive a person who returns to him, but the embrace is

---

91. Ridderbos, *John*, 291.

92. L. Jones, *Embodying Forgiveness*, 58.

93. Volf, *Exclusion and Embrace*, 160.

not unconditional. Certain conditions must be fulfilled—not before the invitation is issued, but before the reconciliation signified by the banquet can take place.[94] Note that "the father has not reinstated the younger son exactly into all his former privileges."[95] Clearly, if the father can tell the older son, "Everything I have is yours" (v. 31), the younger son will get no second inheritance; the ring he receives is a sign of the father's love, not of the son's disposition over all property.[96]

The parable of the prodigal son is often interpreted as presenting unconditional acceptance of one who has betrayed love. But clearly the son who is returning has seen truth and repented. The father's joyful running to meet his returning son with open arms reveals his heart of love and willingness to forgive. The actions of the father are to be emulated in the lives of those who would follow God, but the actions of the father do not teach reconciliation apart from the "return"—that is, repentance.

SUMMARY: WHEN AND WHY DOES SCRIPTURE INSTRUCT GOD'S PEOPLE TO FORGIVE?

Chapter 7 seeks to answer the question, When are God's people to forgive? Specifically, are they to forgive in the absence of repentance? Neither John 8:10b–11 ("neither do I condemn you . . .") nor Luke 23:34 ("Father, forgive them . . .") should be cited to make any point concerning forgiveness because of textual problems.

Ephesians and Colossians both instruct Christians to forgive as the Lord forgives. To follow this model means that a Christian is always willing to forgive a repentant wrongdoer just as God is always willing to do so. When the disciples ask Jesus how many times they should forgive, Jesus' answer is seventy-seven times—understood to mean without limit. Why should this be so? Surely it is because they model the Lord whose grace knows no bounds. However, Jesus does not instruct them to forgive in the absence of repentance. Surely this, too, is because their Lord does not do so.

An example of this principle is found in the Kairos Document, which contributed significantly to the South African debate on apartheid. It states:

94. Volf, *Exclusion and Embrace*, 142.

95. Volf, *Exclusion and Embrace*, 163.

96. Nolland, *Luke 9:21–18:34*, 785.

> No reconciliation, no forgiveness and no negotiations are possible *without repentance.* The biblical teaching on reconciliation and forgiveness makes it quite clear that nobody can be forgiven and reconciled with God unless he or she repents of their sins. Nor are *we* expected to forgive the unrepentant sinner. When he or she repents we must be willing to forgive seventy times seven but before that, we are expected to preach repentance to those who sin against us or against anyone else.[97]

Christians are also instructed to forgive as the Lord forgives because they should be willing to do for others what God does for them. To refuse to forgive a repentant wrongdoer is not acceptable for a follower of God. On the other hand, if a Christian models his Lord and forgives repentant wrongdoers graciously, then God responds with mercy and grace to his confessions.

Repentance is not mentioned in every act of forgiveness in Scripture, but can be presupposed based on the emphasis on repentance throughout the OT and the NT. One such example is Jesus' pronouncement of forgiveness for the woman who anointed his feet.

Also listed in this chapter are verses that speak of messianic/eschatological forgiveness—the pronouncement of the coming of the kingdom of God and God's redemption of the world. None of these verses should be taken out of their messianic/eschatological context and applied to individual forgiveness by God or to interpersonal forgiveness. The healing of the paralytic, although spoken to an individual, is probably an example of such a proclamation. In this case, the forgiveness offered is equated with the healing offered—both of which signify the breaking in of the kingdom and God's ultimate purpose in redemption.

The parable of the prodigal son serves as an example of God's love and forgiveness. The parable cannot be used to advocate forgiveness in

---

97. Brümmer, *Atonement*, 47–48. Brümmer says in response to this statement: "This statement is correct on two points. First, as we have already argued in the previous section, there can be no reconciliation without repentance by the perpetrator. Without repentance, forgiveness cannot be effective in bringing about reconciliation. Secondly, since forgiveness is aimed at bringing about reconciliation, the one who forgives should also desire the repentance of the perpetrator and should therefore 'preach repentance to those who sin against us or anyone else.' However, the Kairos document is wrong in claiming that repentance is a condition not only for reconciliation but also for forgiveness. It remains possible for the victim to *forswear all resentment* and to forgive even though this does not by itself suffice to bring about reconciliation" (emphasis added). Clearly Brümmer's objection is based on his definition of forgiveness, which is to "forswear all resentment."

the absence of repentance, because the prodigal clearly sees himself as he is, realizes his error, returns to his father, and humbly confesses. This parable reveals the heart of a father who longs for his son's return. Christians should model not only the willingness of the father to receive his son, but also his longing for this repentance to take place.

CHAPTER 7 STUDY QUESTIONS

Interpersonal Forgiveness in the OT

1. Summarize the commands concerning interpersonal forgiveness in the OT.

Judaism versus Christianity

1. What rift exists between Jewish and Christian teaching concerning forgiveness? What does the author contend is the cause of this rift?

Interpersonal Forgiveness in the NT

1. What does the NT state is the model for interpersonal forgiveness?

Confrontation

1. Does Matt 18:15 teach a universal requirement for confrontation in personal matters?

2. Why are Christians told to "treat as a Gentile or a tax-collector" one who refuses discipline?

3. What is the procedure for confrontation given in Matt 18? What is the motivation?

4. To what do "loosing" and "binding" refer in this passage, and how is repentance involved?

5. In context, how should God's presence "where two or three gather" be understood?

Seventy Times Seven

1. What is the context of Matt 18:21–22 and Luke 17:4? Is "seventy-seven" to be taken literally?

2. How do Matthew and Luke each demonstrate that repentance is presupposed?

The Parable of the Unforgiving Servant

1. What is the context and the plainly stated point of the parable of the unforgiving servant?

2. What does the debt represent in the parable? How does the debtor show repentance?

3. What two motives for forgiving a repentant offender does this parable give?

4. How does the unmerciful servant's fate demonstrate the provisional nature of forgiveness?

The Lord's Prayer

1. How is repentance on the part of the disciple who prays indicated in the Lord's Prayer?

2. How does the request for forgiveness in the Lord's Prayer reveal an understanding of the parable of the unmerciful servant, who should have "forgiven as" he was forgiven?

Verses in Which Repentance Is Presupposed

Forgive as God Forgives

1. How are Christians instructed to forgive in Eph 4:32 and Col 3:13? Why?

Forgive and You Will Be Forgiven

1. Why would it be a distortion of Scripture to say that "forgive, and you will be forgiven" in Luke 6:37–38 means that all one need do to be forgiven is to forgive others?

The Woman Who Anoints Jesus' Feet

1. How can repentance be presupposed in Luke 6:37–38, 1 John 2:12, and Luke 7:47?

Prayer and Forgiveness

1. Give two examples of faith being presupposed based on the rest of Scripture.

Confession of Sin

1. What is the if/then principle stated in 1 John 1:9? Why must confession precede forgiveness?

2. James 5:15–16 states that confession of sins is essential for what, in addition to forgiveness?

The Unforgivable Sin

1. According to Luke 12:10 are all sins forgivable?

Forgive versus Retain

1. What is the context of forgiving and retaining sin in John 20:21–23?

2. Why does the proclamation of the gospel, which includes remission of sin, also involve the possibility of retention of sin? How is this related to "loosing" and "binding" in Matt 18?

"Father Forgive Them . . ."

1. On what basis does Jesus ask God to forgive in Luke 23:34? Is repentance in view?

2. Does Luke 23:34 teach that one should automatically forgive all sins committed against him?

3. Why should no conclusions concerning forgiveness be drawn from this verse?

4. Why is this verse quoted so often in recommending forgiveness apart from repentance?

The Healing of the Paralytic

1. How are sin and sickness connected in the story of the healing of the paralytic (Matt 9:1–8)?

2. What claim of Jesus is verified by healing the paralytic?

The Woman Caught in Adultery

1. What textual evidence makes it impossible to regard this story as authentic to John's Gospel?

2. What is the meaning of Jesus' words, "Neither do I condemn you"?

The Prodigal Son

1. What words immediately precede the story of the prodigal son?

2. What words and actions in the story indicate that the prodigal son repented?

3. What does the story reveal about the Father?

8

What Does Scripture Say about How Christians Are to Relate to Evil Persons and Enemies?

HAVING COMPLETED AN EXAMINATION of all NT Scripture verses concerning forgiveness, a related topic will be considered in this chapter. The discussion of the issue of forgiveness and unforgiveness involves human relationships and the question of whether to become alienated or reconciled after serious harm inflicted by wrongdoing. A similar question involves how Christians should react to evil done to them and how they should relate to personal enemies or evil persons in general. Scripture speaks to this issue specifically in the following verses.

RESISTING EVIL

> You have heard that it was said, "Eye for eye, and tooth for tooth." But I tell you, do not resist an evil person. If anyone slaps you on the right cheek, turn to them the other cheek also. And if anyone wants to sue you and take your shirt, hand over your coat as well. If anyone forces you to go one mile, go with them two miles. Give to the one who asks you, and do not turn away from the one who wants to borrow from you. (Matt 5:38–42)

> The very fact that you have lawsuits among you means you have been completely defeated already. Why not rather be wronged? Why not rather be cheated? (1 Cor 6:7)

In order to understand Jesus' words concerning resisting evil, the OT background must be examined. In Matt 5:38–42, Jesus contrasts his teaching with that of the scribes and Pharisees regarding the OT *lex talionis* ("an eye for an eye"). In the OT, lex talionis is the guiding principle for justice, to be implemented on a societal and governmental level in the judicial process of the nation of Israel. Jesus' words do not change the fact that in courts of law the punishment should fit the crime. But he does say, just as the OT does, that lex talionis does not apply in personal situations (because God says, "Vengeance is mine"). This is apparently in contrast to the teaching of the scribes and Pharisees. The examples he gives are personal situations in which an individual is offended or wronged. A personal sacrifice is required on the part of the offended one, which diffuses the situation and does not resort to personal retaliation.[1]

First is the general command not to resist "evil." Three major options exist for understanding the meaning of "evil": (1) Satan (Matt 13:19), (2) evil in general (Mark 7:23), or (3) an evil person (Matt 12:35). When Jesus says, "do not resist evil," he could not mean do not resist Satan. James and Peter use the same verb urging believers to resist him (Jas 4:7, "Resist the devil, and he will flee from you"; 1 Pet 5:9). Their teaching would not directly contradict that of Jesus. In addition, Eph 6:13–18 specifically instructs believers in the resistance of evil and Satan. Evil in general also could not be in Jesus' mind here. The OT allows for resistance in the case of self-defense (Exod 22:2), and in the NT believers are instructed to abstain from evil (1 Thess 5:22). It is absolutely impossible that Jesus is saying that Christians should not stand against injustice, violence, and evil in the world. That idea would contradict all that God is and all that Christians are called to be. An evil person is what Jesus has in mind, as can be seen from the examples that he gives following the general exhortation (e.g., Matt 12:35).[2] (Thus the NIV translates, "Do not resist an evil person.")

The OT law "eye for eye, tooth for tooth" (Exod 21:24; Lev 24:20; Deut 19:21) is sometimes cited as an example of the harshness of the OT. This assertion is untrue. In the tribal environment of early Israel, this law

---

1. Davis, *Lex Talionis*, 138.
2. Davis, *Lex Talionis*, 141.

existed for institutions of justice, which had been recently established. A law of strict reciprocity could be recognized by all as fair and was intended to bring payback to an end. Jesus, however, recommends a readiness to disarm violence by accepting double what the enemy demands. He gives specific renunciations of violence that are feasible for individuals, but are not realistic or applicable for society as a whole or for institutions of justice where evil and evildoers must be restrained.[3] In interpersonal situations, godly kindness should transcend retaliation.[4] Like the OT (Exod 23:4–5; Job 31:29–30; Prov 24:17–18), Jesus advocates a personal ethic that does not contradict the legitimate role of the state in protecting its citizens from lawlessness and violence.[5]

Jesus gives six hypothetical situations to illustrate his teaching on non-retaliation. The first pictures a personal dispute that leads to an insulting backhanded slap by a right-handed person to the right cheek of another person (Job 16:10; Ps 3:7; Isa 50:6; Lam 3:30; Matt 26:67; Acts 23:2–3; 2 Cor 11:20). In the OT a slap on the cheek is seen as a humiliating insult (1 Kgs 22:24; 2 Chr 18:23; Job 16:10), and a backhanded slap is even more insulting. This passage can be applied in many situations involving personal insult. Two OT passages refer to the Messiah as one who would voluntarily give his cheek to the smiter (Isa 50:6; Lam 3:30).[6]

The second situation refers to a legal dispute in which one has to forfeit his shirt as collateral for a debt (Exod 22:25–27; Deut 24:10–13, 17) or to satisfy a claim for damages. From the context (an example of not resisting evil), it can be assumed that the lawsuit being brought is unjustified. Not to resist evil or injustice in this case is a personal choice and not how the state should handle disputes. Historically Israel is rebuked severely for garments being improperly kept or taken in violation of the Torah's regulations (Amos 2:8).[7] Jewish literature also expresses concern for justice for the lender who should be paid back.[8]

The third situation involves an occupying Roman soldier conscripting a Jewish person to carry his equipment (cf. Matt 27:32; Mark 15:21). Biblical examples of commandeering are rare, but the OT strongly

3. Byrne, *Lifting the Burden*, 61.
4. Turner, *Matthew*, 174.
5. Turner, *Matthew*, 174.
6. Davis, *Lex Talionis*, 134.
7. Davis, *Lex Talionis*, 134.
8. Davis, *Lex Talionis*, 135.

condemns forced labor. In fact, the practice split the nation of Israel after Solomon's death.[9]

These first three examples are diverse, but each presents a situation in which the disciples of Jesus are not to take part in furthering the cycle of evil action and escalating evil reaction, but are to submit to injustice and even go beyond the required response. A disciple should be willing to suffer personal loss with the faith that his loving heavenly Father will meet his needs and deal with injustice in his own time.[10] *The knowledge of God's provision and justice are key to maintaining an attitude of submission to injustice and to being able to allow oneself to be wronged.* As Peter quotes King David, "The eyes of the Lord are on the righteous, and his ears are attentive to their cry; but the face of the Lord is against those who do evil" (Ps 34:15–16; 1 Pet 3:12).

The fourth and fifth examples display the more positive actions of giving and lending. Not only should the disciple avoid evil by non-retaliatory reaction when oppressed by a more powerful person, but he should also promote good by a generous, benevolent response to those who are less powerful (cf. Luke 6:34–35). Regarding lending, the primary OT background passage is Deut 15:7–11, which requires lending to the poor among fellow Israelites. Lending to the poor is regarded as a righteous act (Ps 37:21, 26; 112:5–10; Prov 28:27) resulting in the blessing of the Lord (Deut 23:20). Interest could be charged to foreigners but not to fellow Israelites (Lev 25:35–37; Deut 23:20). Loans are to be forgiven in Sabbatical years (the seventh year; Deut 15:1), and refusing to lend during the years leading up to the Sabbatical year is forbidden (Deut 15:9).[11] The exhortation to lend to one who asks thus involves accepting the possibility of not being repaid.

A sixth and final example of Jesus' teaching "resist not evil" refers to loving enemies.

LOVING ENEMIES

> If you come across your enemy's ox or donkey wandering off,
> be sure to return it. If you see the donkey of someone who hates

---

9. Davis, *Lex Talionis*, 135.

10. France, *Matthew*, 175.

11. Davis, *Lex Talionis*, 135.

you fallen down under its load, do not leave it there; be sure you help them with it. (Exod 23:4–5)

Do not seek revenge or bear a grudge against anyone among your people, but love your neighbor as yourself. I am the LORD. (Lev 19:18)

Do not gloat when your enemy falls; when they stumble, do not let your heart rejoice. . . . Do not say, "I'll do to them as they have done to me; I'll pay them back for what they did." (Prov 24:17, 29)

If your enemy is hungry, give him food to eat; if he is thirsty, give him water to drink. In doing this, you will heap burning coals on his head, and the LORD will reward you. (Prov 25:21–22)

You have heard that it was said, "Love your neighbor and hate your enemy." But I tell you, love your enemies and pray for those who persecute you, that you may be children of your Father in heaven. He causes his sun to rise on the evil and the good, and sends rain on the righteous and the unrighteous. If you love those who love you, what reward will you get? Are not even the tax collectors doing that? And if you greet only your own people, what are you doing more than others? Do not even pagans do that? Be perfect, therefore, as your heavenly Father is perfect. (Matt 5:43–46)

But to you who are listening I say: Love your enemies, do good to those who hate you, bless those who curse you, pray for those who mistreat you. If someone slaps you on one cheek, turn to them the other also. If someone takes your coat, do not withhold your shirt from them. Give to everyone who asks you, and if anyone takes what belongs to you, do not demand it back. Do to others as you would have them do to you. If you love those who love you, what credit is that to you? Even sinners love those who love them. And if you do good to those who are good to you, what credit is that to you? Even sinners do that. And if you lend to those from whom you expect repayment, what credit is that to you? Even sinners lend to sinners, expecting to be repaid in full. But love your enemies, do good to them, and lend to them without expecting to get anything back. Then your reward will be great, and you will be children of the Most High, because he is kind to the ungrateful and wicked. Be merciful, just as your Father is merciful. (Luke 6:27–36)

LOVE AND HATE

Many assume that the NT command to love one's enemies mandates unconditional forgiveness for all. Is this the proper interpretation? To answer, one must determine what love of enemy means in Scripture. We will examine the OT background of the concept, what this love involves, and in what situations it applies.

The meaning of the words love and hate should not be rigidly interpreted in Scripture, for context is all-important in determining the meaning or the level of feeling. Hate may mean "not love" and sometimes even "love less."[12] An example is Jacob's hate of Leah (Gen 29:31–34). Concerning the laws of divorce in Deut 24:1–3, hate means the wife finds no favor in the eyes of her husband. By contrast hate can also mean extreme distaste (2 Sam 13:15) or a strong desire for someone's total destruction (Ps 139:19–22).[13] NT examples of hate meaning to love less are the words concerning "hate" of mother and father (Luke 14:26) and the statement, "Esau have I hated" (Rom 9:13).

Like the concept of hate, the meaning of the word love also varies according to context. D. A. Carson, in his book *Love in Hard Places*, says that the Bible speaks of God's love in different ways, and these various ways need to be analyzed to avoid incorrect clichés about love that are commonly used by Christians. He maintains that an incorrect understanding of the concept of love has resulted in Christians often having an overly sentimental view of God.

> The sentimental view breeds expectations of transcendental niceness. Whatever else Christians should be, they should be *nice*, where "niceness" means smiling a lot and never hinting that anyone may be wrong about anything (because that isn't *nice*). In the local churches it means abandoning church discipline (it isn't *nice*), and in many contexts it means restoring adulterers (for instance) to pastoral office at the mere hint of repentance. After all, isn't the church about forgiveness? Aren't we supposed to love one another? And doesn't that mean that, above all, we must be, well, *nice*?[14]

---

12. France, *Matthew*, 225.

13. Piper, *Love Your Enemies*, 28.

14. Carson, *Love in Hard Places*, 12.

Carson also points out that it is not easy to "think clearly with exegetical evenhandedness when you are being told that . . . you are not nice, you are not displaying Christian love."[15]

A cliché concerning the biblical concept of love is that God's love is always unconditional. The Bible speaks of some ways that God displays unconditional love. His providential love is unconditional in that it is poured out on the just and the unjust (Matt 5:45). But is God's love in the sense of his favor always unconditional? Is God willing to fellowship with humans regardless of their behavior? The relationship of love with God spoken of in John 15 (vv. 1–17, the vine and the branches) and Jude 21 ("keep yourselves in God's love") is explicitly conditional. John 15 speaks of the conditional nature of God's favor no less than eight times. The providential love of God is certainly not the same as his love for one of his faithful children.

What kind of love, then, is meant when Scripture says "love your enemies"? What does the Bible mean when it commands love of neighbor? The command to "love your neighbor" found in the Sermon on the Mount comes from Lev 19:18. In each case presented in Matt 5–7, Jesus reveals the true meaning of the OT text, which had been distorted. The context of Lev 19 speaks of loving one's neighbor in reference to fellow Israelites, including Israelites who are personal enemies. (Exod 12:49 indicates that non-Israelites who have become part of the Israelite community are likewise included.) But non-Israelite national enemies are not in view in this context. Therefore, to the Israelite, the OT love command was thought to be limited.[16] But apparently there is debate, as the Pharisees asked Jesus, "Who is my neighbor?" (Luke 10:29). Is the meaning of neighbor limited by nationality? No. As the parable of the good Samaritan (Luke 10:25–37) shows, Jesus does not accept a restrictive interpretation. Evidently the conventional view of the OT command mistakenly restricted the scope of neighbor to legitimize hatred of national enemies. But many OT texts speak of humane treatment of non-Israelites (Lev 19:33–34; Deut 10:18–19; cf. Exod 22:21; 23:9; Deut 1:16; 27:19; Ps 94:6; 146:9; Jer 7:5–6; 22:3; Ezek 22:7, 29; 47:22–23)[17] and even "love" of enemies (Gen 45:1–6; Exod 23:4–5; 1 Sam 24:7; 2 Kgs 6:22; Prov 25:21–22; etc.).[18]

15. Carson, *Love in Hard Places*, 12.

16. Piper, *Love Your Enemies*, 30.

17. Turner, *Matthew*, 176.

18. Bonhoeffer, *Discipleship*, 147.

The parallel passage in Luke commands prayer for one's persecutors, a striking demonstration of enemy love (6:27). The content of the prayer is not specified, but presumably it would include the petition that the enemy might see truth and repent.[19] Prayer for enemies is also an OT concept (Gen 20:17; Num 12:13; 21:7; 1 Sam 24:17–19; 1 Kgs 3:11; Job 31:29; Ps 7:3–5; Jer 29:7; Jonah 4:10–11).[20]

Matthew 5 speaks of love of neighbor and hate of enemy, but no OT text exists that says "hate your enemy." Leviticus 19:18 commands love for neighbors, not hatred for enemies. From where, then, did this idea come? There are OT texts that authorize a certain kind of hatred—a judicial hatred of those who oppose the Lord or his people. One example is found in 2 Chr 19:2, when Jehoshaphat returns from battle with the Syrians: "Jehu the seer, . . . went out to meet him and said to the king, 'Should you help the wicked and love those who hate the LORD? Because of this, the wrath of the LORD is on you.'" The obvious meaning is that love and alliance are completely wrong responses concerning the enemies of God's people, "those who hate the LORD" (v. 2).[21] Another example is found in Ps 139:21–22, in which David says, "Do I not hate those who hate you, LORD, and abhor those who are in rebellion against you? I have nothing but hatred for them; I count them my enemies." David is careful not to seek vengeance (Ps 139:19) but nevertheless prays to God for it. This psalm contains a clear statement of hatred, but the object of the hate is not nations but individuals, and the cause is not national allegiance. He pronounces them his enemies because they are already God's enemies. He is seeking to align his thoughts with God's, and the declaration of this hate is proof of his love for God and his hatred of evil. He is seeking to emulate God himself, who hates evil and injustice.

God's judicial hatred and his love are not mutually exclusive. God is the God of both mercy (because he loves) and judgment (because he hates evil). The NT makes it clear that on the last day, when the time for repentance is exhausted, God will take vengeance on his enemies (Matt 13:30; 25:46; Rom 2:8; 12:19; Rev 14:9–11; 20:9, 15). Therefore Jesus does not correct the OT balance between judgment and mercy, but exposes the false interpretation of the OT used to justify personal hatred. His words about loving enemies must not be taught to the exclusion of his

19. France, *Matthew*, 226.

20. Turner, *Matthew*, 176.

21. Piper, *Love Your Enemies*, 32.

words about wrath and judgment,[22] such as his pronouncement against the scribes and Pharisees, "Woe to you, teachers of the law and Pharisees. . . . You snakes! You brood of vipers! How will you escape being condemned to hell?" (Matt 23:29, 33).

Matthew 5 gives a specific reason for Christians to love their enemies. They are told to love their enemies "that [they] may be children of [their] Father in heaven" (Matt 5:45). Loving in this way means imitating the Father, because in that time most sons did (for a living) what their fathers did. The example given to clarify the meaning of this enemy love is God's unconditional providential love, for "he causes his sun to rise on the evil and the good" (Matt 5:45). How would one imitate this unconditional providential love? One would do his enemies no harm and would welcome their repentance. So, although it is important not to diminish what is being said, it is equally important not to expand its meaning simply because the word love is used in these verses.[23]

ENEMIES

As with love, we must determine the meaning of enemy based on the context of Matt 5 for a correct interpretation of Jesus' command to love enemies. To whom did this command apply—national enemies, personal enemies, or both? Let us examine the OT background.

Statements about enemies in the OT are diverse. In Exod 23:4–5 the Israelites are instructed to help their enemies: "If you come across your enemy's ox or donkey wandering off, be sure to return it. If you see the donkey of someone who hates you fallen down under its load, do not leave it there; be sure you help them with it." In this case the enemy is a fellow Israelite. In 1 Kgs 3:10–14 Solomon is commended because he asks for wisdom rather than for the life of his enemies. Proverbs 24:29 denounces taking revenge on one's neighbors: "Do not say, 'I'll do to them as they have done to me; I'll pay them back for what they did.'" Here again a "neighbor" (v. 28), the enemy, is a fellow Israelite. Proverbs 24:17–18 says not to rejoice at the fall of an enemy: "Do not gloat when your enemy falls; when they stumble, do not let your heart rejoice, or the LORD will see and disapprove and turn his wrath away from them." This biblical injunction not to rejoice when your enemy falls speaks of a personal enemy,

---

22. Carson, *Love in Hard Places*, 44.
23. Carson, *Love in Hard Places*, 45.

not of the fall of evil, for Nah 3:19b says, "All who hear the news about you [the King of Assyria, representing imperial evil] clap their hands at your fall, for who has not felt your endless cruelty?" Volf agrees, saying, "Does not heaven rejoice at the sight of the destruction of Babylon? (Rev 18:20). Do not the saints gleefully cheer from the sides, 'Render to her as she herself has rendered, and repay her double [meaning full] for her deeds; mix a double drought for her in the cup she mixed' (Rev 18:20)."[24] In addition, Nehemiah prays against his enemies, who are God's enemies attempting to stop God's work (Neh 4:5; 6:14; 13:29). Proverbs 25:21 says, "If your enemy is hungry, give him food to eat; if he is thirsty, give him water to drink." In each of these cases the enemy is personal rather than national. The meaning of love in this personal context is defined by the examples: declining vengeance, refusing to gloat over misfortune, and showing kindness to one in need. *To love one's enemy, then, refers to one's personal enemy and simply means showing human kindness and maintaining a pure heart.*

Love of enemy nations is not emphasized in the OT. In fact, many OT texts show the enemy as the object of hate or destruction. To begin with, there is the conquest of Canaan. According to Deuteronomy, when the Israelites defeated seven nations they were to utterly destroy them (Exod 34:12; Deut 7:1–2; 25:17–19). In spite of this, the word hate does not occur in Deuteronomy or Joshua with reference to national enemies. Two reasons are given in Deuteronomy for the complete destruction of enemies: (1) "Otherwise, they will teach you to follow all the detestable things they do in worshiping their gods" (Deut 20:18), and (2) "Because of these same detestable practices the LORD your God will drive out those nations before you" (Deut 18:12). Thus, the command to destroy the enemy is a command to fulfill God's will directed against evil. The destruction is both a judgment of the nations for sin as well as a means of preventing Israel from future sin.[25]

In light of verses that refer to national enemies, it is easy to understand how it was said in Jesus' day, "Hate your enemies." But the true meaning was a hatred of all that was opposed to God, to evil itself. Israel is called to be a light to the world by revealing a God who is near and whose laws are just (Deut 4:5–8). This calling, which can be interpreted as enemy love, seems to have been largely lost in Jesus' day. The proper

---

24. Volf, *Exclusion and Embrace*, 295.
25. Piper, *Love Your Enemies*, 32.

hatred of evil, of all that which is opposed to God, had become hatred for nations, especially for the Romans.

Jesus' teaching on enemy love, then, is not at odds with the OT. In fact, the OT is the basis of the command to love one's enemy, both in the call of Israel to be a light to the nations and in the commands concerning treatment of personal enemies. Neither is the command of enemy love in the NT a weakening of a proper abhorrence of evil (Rom 12:9). The next section shows that when personal enemies are in view in the NT, the OT is quoted for guidance. Even when the NT context indicates that the command is to love national enemies, the background is the OT. For instance, the book of Jonah demonstrates that God's mercy is not limited to the Israelites, but is extended to repentant enemies. Jesus' teaching on enemy love is not a new revelation concerning God's character or will; rather, his words guide his disciples in the proper understanding of the OT teaching.[26]

CONTEXT

However, the teaching of Jesus is unique because of the new eschatological context of enemy love.[27] This context is clear because the mission of Jesus is the inauguration of the kingdom of God, a kingdom in which the people of God will no longer be one nation taking up arms against their national enemies. When rabbis ask Jesus, "Who is my neighbor?" (Luke 10:29) and nationalistic feelings run high, the command to love enemies includes the refusal to take up arms in rebellion. Jesus tells them that defeating enemy nations is not the eschatological calling of the people of God: love of neighbor is love of all people regardless of nationality. He does not mean love for all regardless of behavior. This context, then, is important for a proper understanding of Matt 5:43–47. Jesus speaks in the context of Roman oppression and the expectation of God's intervention and the overthrow of Rome. So, the context is not just personal but also political, and it applies to Israel in the first century. "The words did not mean, 'Lie down and let people walk all over you.' They meant, 'Don't join the normal resistance movements.'"[28] John the Baptist had already said that the kingdom of God was coming. Jesus reveals that this

---

26. Piper, *Love Your Enemies*, 35.

27. Piper, *Love Your Enemies*, 34.

28. N. T. Wright, *Simply Jesus*, 147.

kingdom will not involve a military overthrow of Rome. Israel is to follow a different path. They are to spread the news of God's kingdom to all the world, resulting in a new Israel—a spiritual Israel. God's people will not just be Israelites, but Gentiles also, for Israel's military history against the Gentiles is coming to an end.[29] Jesus' exhortation to love enemies in this context is therefore not just personal but also political and redefines the Jewish expectation of the kingdom of God.

REASONS FOR LOVING ENEMIES

Matthew 5:46–48 not only gives the injunction to love your enemies, but also the reasons for doing so. Verse 48 says, "Be perfect, therefore, as your heavenly Father is perfect." Christians are to emulate the character of their Father. Once again, this is an OT concept: "Be holy because I, the LORD your God, am holy" (Lev 19:2).[30] Other NT texts stress how Christians' love for others, especially enemies, marks them as members of God's family (Eph 4:31—5:2; 1 Pet 1:14–25; 1 John 4:7–12). God's children are to reflect his character. The term *perfect* is broad, signifying spiritual maturity rather than moral flawlessness (1 Cor 2:6; 14:20; Phil 3:15; frequently in Hebrews).[31] A second reason for loving enemies is that a reward awaits those who live with this high standard (Luke 6:35).[32]

In summary, the six examples in Matthew contrast Jesus' teaching of the OT with the traditional understanding of the OT. The righteousness he proposes is greater than that of the scribes and Pharisees (5:20) and reflects the benevolent character of the Father.[33] The challenge is to live on a level above that of merely decent people.[34] However, any realistic account of what loving enemies looks like in practice must take into account the way Jesus reacted to the opposition of the scribes and Pharisees in Matt 23. He is clearly angry and unforgiving when he says to them, "You snakes! You brood of vipers! How will you escape being condemned to hell?" (v. 33). Jesus' concept of enemy love includes not

---

29. N. T. Wright, *Simply Christian*, 101.

30. Turner, *Matthew*, 117.

31. France, *Matthew*, 228.

32. France, *Matthew*, 227.

33. Turner, *Matthew*, 118.

34. France, *Matthew*, 224.

just being nice, but also confrontation and rebuke, refusing to let error or evil go unchallenged.[35]

THE TEACHING OF THE EARLY CHURCH ON ENEMY LOVE

> Bless those who persecute you; bless and do not curse. . . . Do not repay anyone evil for evil. Be careful to do what is right in the eyes of everyone. If it is possible, as far as it depends on you, live at peace with everyone. Do not take revenge, my dear friends, but leave room for God's wrath, for it is written: "It is mine to avenge; I will repay," says the Lord. On the contrary: "If your enemy is hungry, feed him; if he is thirsty, give him something to drink. In doing this, you will heap burning coals on his head." Do not be overcome by evil, but overcome evil with good. (Rom 12:14, 17–21)

> Make sure that nobody pays back wrong for wrong, but always strive to do what is good for each other and for everyone else. (1 Thess 5:15)

> Do not repay evil with evil or insult with insult. On the contrary, repay evil with blessing, because to this you were called so that you may inherit a blessing. For, "Whoever would love life and see good days must keep their tongue from evil and their lips from deceitful speech. They must turn from evil and do good; they must seek peace and pursue it. For the eyes of the Lord are on the righteous, and his ears are attentive to their prayer, but the face of the Lord is against those who do evil" (1 Pet 3:9–12). (Peter quotes Ps 34:12–16a in order to elucidate and support the command of enemy love.)

The NT passages listed above relate to the idea of loving enemies. The essence of all the passages is non-retaliation. Each relates an OT concept in which the expected behavior for Christians is no different than what is expected in personal relationships in the OT. Both the Romans passage and the 1 Peter passage make this point by directly quoting the OT. The passage in 1 Thessalonians simply paraphrases the OT command against taking vengeance.

---

35. France, *Matthew*, 226.

The fact that Jesus' command to love enemies is not specifically re-peated in writing anywhere in the early church (i.e., the rest of the NT) shows that the concern of the early church was not with national enemies but with personal relationships. The situation in the early church was different from that of Jesus' day in that neither nationalistic allegiance nor rabbinic exegesis forms the context of the love command. Rather, the question the early church addresses is how to behave toward unbeliev-ers, hostile people, or ridiculing friends. The NT specifically describes enemies as slanderers (1 Cor 4:13; 1 Pet 3:16), persecutors (Rom 12:14), and those who do evil to you (Rom 12:17; 1 Thess 5:15; 1 Pet 3:9). Loving your enemies in this context would not include a nationalistic perspec-tive. This fact may well be why the exact words "love your enemies" are never repeated. In fact, the NT texts of the early church choose to quote and apply OT texts that involve *personal* enemies or relationships rather than the words of Jesus that also apply to the Jewish national situation. Far from modifying God's commands concerning love, these passages repeat rather than expand the OT concept of loving enemies.

Examining each of the three NT passages will demonstrate that they reiterate rather than expand the OT concept of loving enemies.

Romans 12:17–20

The first passage outside of the Gospels concerning enemy love is Rom 12:17–20. In Rom 12:1—13:7, OT quotations occur only in the section on treatment of enemies; there are several different OT references in only a few verses:

> Rom 12:17b, "Be careful to do what is right in the eyes of ev-eryone," echoes Prov 3:4, "Then you will win favor and a good name in the sight of God and man."

> Rom 12:18, "If it is possible, as far as it depends on you, live at peace with everyone," reflects Ps 34:14, "Turn from evil and do good; seek peace and pursue it."

> Rom 12:19a, "Do not take revenge, my dear friends, but leave room for God's wrath," quotes Lev 19:18, "Do not seek revenge."

> Rom 12:19b, "For it is written, 'It is mine to avenge; I will repay,'" quotes Deut 32:35, "It is mine to avenge; I will repay. In due time their foot will slip; their day of disaster is near and their doom rushes upon them."

Rom 12:20, "If your enemy is hungry, feed him; if he is thirsty, give him something to drink. In doing this, you will heap burning coals on his head," quotes Prov 25:21–22, "If your enemy is hungry, give him food to eat; if he is thirsty, give him water to drink. In doing this, you will heap burning coals on his head, and the LORD will reward you.[36]

Why does Paul quote the OT so often with reference to enemies? For Paul, following Jesus means establishing the OT, not abolishing it. He says, "Do we, then, nullify the law by this faith? Not at all! Rather, we uphold the law" (Rom 3:31). According to Paul, Christ lifts the veil from the reading of Moses (2 Cor 3:14) so that the OT is seen to be "written for our instruction." Therefore, to lend weight to this hardest of all commands and to deflect criticism that might be brought against it from the OT, it is verified by OT citations. Indeed, the love command is the essence of the OT itself—love of God and love of neighbor.[37] Jesus expands the Jewish understanding of neighbor in the parable of the good Samaritan (Luke 10:29–37), making clear that the meaning of neighbor should not be limited to friends and countrymen. God's kingdom and God's love are offered to all, and "whosoever will" may come (John 3:16). Jesus lays the groundwork for the "dissolution of the Jewish distinction" that will occur in the church in which there is "neither Jew nor Gentile" (Gal 3:28; 1 Cor 12:13).[38]

When specifying *how* the Christian should behave toward his enemies, *how* he should love them, the NT only repeats the OT: do not repay evil for evil; bless those who revile you, and do not curse them; do good to them; seek peace; do not avenge yourselves; give food and water to your needy enemies. In other words, enemy love is ready and willing to meet the physical needs of the enemy: it desires and seeks the spiritual well-being of the enemy; enemy love nonetheless maintains that evil is abhorrent (Rom 12:9). This love is the same kind that is offered in the OT—help for one in need (Rom 12:20 and Prov 25:21–22). The command to pray for one's enemy (Matt 5:44) is to seek his well-being. It is a command to be like God in that he desires good for all humans. If one prays for his enemy, he aligns himself with God's will and maintains a pure heart (of course, the prayer can be for the enemy to repent and

---

36. Piper, *Love Your Enemies*, 111–12.

37. Piper, *Love Your Enemies*, 114.

38. Piper, *Love Your Enemies*, 92.

turn to God). The love command also includes greeting people (Matt 5:47) and is an admonition for good conduct and manners to be seen by everyone.

Such behavior is pleasing to God because it emulates him, and it also leads to "inheriting a blessing" (Matt 5; 1 Pet 3:9). Being blessed is to have God's presence and activity in one's life.[39] The early church emphasizes the imitation of God's love for enemies, as well as the fact that God's vengeance is *not* to be imitated. Vengeance is specifically forbidden in the NT (Rom 12:19) as it is in the OT (Deut 32:35), not because it is wrong (for God will ultimately execute vengeance), but because it is solely God's prerogative. Romans 12:19–20 emphasizes this fact:

> 19a) Do not take revenge, my dear friends,
>
> 19b) but leave room for God's wrath;
>
> 19c) for it is written: "It is mine to avenge; I will repay," says the Lord.
>
> 20a) If your enemy is hungry, feed him;
>
> 20b) if he is thirsty, give him something to drink.
>
> 20c) In doing this, you will heap burning coals on his head.

The parallel structure shows that "heaping burning coals on his head" (v. 20c) refers to the same eschatological judgment (vengeance) as verse 19c. In the OT, live coals in reference to God are a symbol of divine anger (2 Sam 22:9; Ps 18:8), or of punishment for the wicked (Ps 140:10). Also, the word *fire* in Paul's vocabulary always refers to eschatological judgment (1 Cor 3:13, 15; 2 Thess 1:7–8). Therefore, in spite of the context of enemy love, the phrase "heap coals of fire" should not be interpreted in a favorable sense (although some commentators interpret it as referring to burning pangs of shame and contrition). The parallel structure clearly indicates a meaning of judgment. The first set of three lines gives the negative injunction, what Christians should not do. The second set of three lines gives the positive command, what Christians should do. In both sets, the third line provides the same motivating reason: it is God's prerogative to punish, and he will do it in due time.[40]

Because the parallel structure and the biblical meaning of "coals of fire" indicate that judgment is in view, an interpretation of "heap burning

---

39. N. T. Wright, *After You Believe*, 104.

40. Carson, *Love in Hard Places*, 50.

coals" as judgment should be sought that is compatible with the context of enemy love. How can "heap burning coals" and enemy love be compatible ideas within the same context? Verse 19b gives a clue. "Give place to wrath means . . . give the wrath of God a chance to work its purpose."[41] The initial command is to "bless" (v. 14), therefore any interpretation of "give place to wrath" that would call for the destruction of an enemy is excluded. C. H. Dodd says, "To bless is to wish well and to turn a wish into a prayer."[42] In the OT narratives God sometimes causes his people to experience his wrath to draw them back to himself. The loss of his favor, and therefore his protection, results in famine and/or domination by foreign enemies (as in the book of Judges). Under these circumstances his people often repent and turn back to him, seeking his help and deliverance. Therefore, experiencing God's wrath is not always negative, but may have positive reformative results (Zech 13:9; Mal 3:2–3). The Bible simultaneously affirms God's wrath toward people and his love for them. God's love and his judicial hatred are not mutually exclusive. The same may be true of Christians.

Romans 12:19–20 also suggests that Christians can love their enemies, knowing that if their kindness is scorned and their enemies do not repent, then God will ultimately and certainly take vengeance on them. Christians need not worry about justice, for God will take care of that. The knowledge that God is just is a comfort for those who follow his lead in blessing enemies. The Christian's love for his enemies is like Christ's love for his enemies: either it brings about their conversion or it multiplies their guilt as they become hardened in their sin.[43] Christ died for his "enemies" (Rom 5:10), yet God will still ultimately wipe out all evil, including those who choose to remain God's enemies (Luke 20:43) despite his sacrifice and offer of love. If God never brings vengeance on those who persist in disobeying the truth, or destruction of the "enemies of the cross of Christ" (Phil 3:18), but rather continues to see his people suffer (Phil 1:29) while their enemies prosper and are blessed (Rom 12:14), then he is an unfaithful and unrighteous God whose covenant is worthless. The Christian's charitable actions toward his enemies are founded on his faith in God's righteousness. On the one hand, there is no indication that the good deeds offered are intended to have any reforming or

41. Piper, *Love Your Enemies*, 116.

42. Piper, *Love Your Enemies*, 116.

43. Carson, *Love in Hard Places*, 50–51.

reconciling effect, although this is certainly possible. On the other hand, one could assume in this passage an unexpressed conditional clause, "If the enemy is not moved to repentance by your love." Romans 12:19, then, reminds the Christian that if the enemy spurns his love, the enemy's guilt will be compounded. Like the command to forgive as God forgives, the command is to love as God loves, for the same is said of God's own love, which is "intended to lead you to repentance" (Rom 2:4). But if this does not occur, Scripture indicates that "because of your stubbornness and your unrepentant heart, you are storing up wrath against yourself for the day of God's wrath, when his righteous judgment will be revealed" (Rom 2:5). This "storing up of wrath" by God for the unrepentant is essentially the same as "heaping burning coals of fire" by Christians. Jesus also says that the rejection of his call to repent and the failure to acknowledge his mighty deeds exacerbated the guilt of his hearers and made them all the more liable to judgment (Matt 11:20–22; cf. 18:23–25). With this certainty of the justice of God, the Christian is called to love his enemy and is freed from the tendency to keep account of wrongs (1 Cor 13:5) in the name of justice. Christians are to be like Christ who, "when he suffered, he made no threats. Instead, he entrusted himself to him who judges justly" (1 Pet 2:23).[44]

Christians should make their ethical decisions from this eternal perspective. Their ethical decisions are also based on God's example and what he has done for them. Matthew 5 urges Christians to love their enemies by appealing to the example of God's providential love. However, in Romans the appeal to love enemies is based on God's plan of redemption: "While we were still sinners, Christ died for us" (Rom 5:8).[45] (Although he died to offer salvation and relationship to all humanity, he actually establishes relationship only with those who repent and believe.) The ethical exhortations of Rom 12 all stand under the introductory exhortation in verses 1–2: "Therefore, I urge you, brothers and sisters, in view of God's mercy . . ." In verse 1, the word "therefore" and the phrase "in view of God's mercy" refer to Rom 1–11, referencing God's entire plan of redemption. In other words, "in view of" what God has done for them—extend mercy—Christians should follow his example. Like Rom 12, 1 Pet 1, in instructing Christians to love others (v. 22), gives as motivation the fact that God loved them. In a burst of praise Peter says, "Praise be to the

44. Piper, *Love Your Enemies*, 118–19.
45. Carson, *Love in Hard Places*, 48.

God and Father of our Lord Jesus Christ! In his great mercy he has given us new birth" (v. 3). It is because of God's great mercy toward them that Christians are to "bless" others.

1 Thessalonians 5:15

> Make sure that nobody pays back wrong for wrong, but always
> strive to do what is good for each other and for everyone else.

First Thessalonians 5:15 is the second of the three NT passages concerning enemy love outside of the Gospels. This passage tells Christians not to pay back wrongs and to be kind to everyone both in the church and outside of the church. The first responsibility is to behave properly toward those within the church. If this were always easy, it would not need to be said. Paul, then, realistically recognizes that problems occur among Christians, and personal attacks can come from within the church. Paul's realism is apparent in the phrase "as far as it depends on you" (Rom 12:18), which recognizes that peace and reconciliation cannot always be achieved. Neither is God at peace with or reconciled to all people. The call to bless and not curse may be hard, but it is not naive; and it is even applicable close to home.[46]

1 Peter 3:9

> Do not repay evil with evil or insult with insult. On the contrary,
> repay evil with blessing, because to this you were called so that
> you may inherit a blessing.

First Peter 3:9 is the third passage that speaks of enemy love outside of the Gospels. The context concerns trials that prove one's faith (1 Pet 1:6). One such trial is persecution from enemies. This faith, which is being proven, is to be demonstrated by the distinctively Christian response of blessing rather than cursing. Jesus says, "Blessed are those who are persecuted because of righteousness, for theirs is the kingdom of heaven. Blessed are you when people insult you, persecute you and falsely say all kinds of evil against you because of me. Rejoice and be glad, because great is your reward in heaven, for in the same way they persecuted the prophets

---

46. Carson, *Love in Hard Places*, 52.

who were before you" (Matt 5:10–12). Persecution does not have to be violence, ending in prison or the grave; insults and slander are specifically mentioned as persecution that the prophets suffered. Jesus says that his followers should expect to experience persecution and opposition because that was his experience (John 15:18; 16:1–4).[47] In response, Christians are to bless. How tender it is that in this extremely hard command Christians are assured that their actions will not go unnoticed or unrewarded. Both passages (Matt 5:10–12 and 1 Pet 3:9) emphasize that those who bless will, by so doing, "inherit a blessing" (1 Pet 3:9), and no meager one at that, for "great is [their] reward in heaven" (Matt 5:12).

In no way does this love of enemy include forgiveness apart from repentance, although it certainly would include following God's example of *offering* forgiveness on the condition of repentance. Kindness and the prospect of forgiveness is what is to be given to enemies, not approval of wrongdoing or reconciliation, which amounts to condonation of wrongdoing. It is "God's kindness [that] leads . . . to repentance," not God's forgiveness (Rom 2:4). If these actions do not lead an enemy to repentance, he will become the object of wrath and the receiver of "burning coals." But, the wrath will be God's wrath, and the coals will be from God.[48]

God's love, in the sense of his "will to embrace" (to use Volf's phrase), is unconditional and indiscriminate. Like the sun it shines on the evil and on the good; like the rain it falls on the righteous and on the unrighteous. The Christian will to embrace does not necessarily overcome another's enmity, just as God's love does not always overcome enmity. Those who are the children of the "Father in heaven" (Matt 5:45) offer kindness nonetheless, for this is what following Christ means.[49] God desires good—repentance, faith, and transformation—for all, and so should Christians.

SUMMARY: LOVE OF ENEMIES

Part II is titled, "When Are God's People to Forgive?" The overriding question is, Does the NT instruct Christians to forgive in the absence of repentance? Chapter 8 discusses the scriptural directives concerning how believers are to treat enemies, which can be summarized in six points.

47. Carson, *Love in Hard Places*, 51, 65, 67.

48. Carson, *Love in Hard Places*, 50.

49. Volf, *Exclusion and Embrace*, 215.

The first is that the teachings of the OT and the NT are exactly the same concerning love of enemies. This is seen by examining the OT texts, by observing that these OT texts are repeated in the NT, and by noting that no NT text carries the meaning of enemy love beyond that of the OT. This is not to deny that ultimately God will reject those who reject his love, for they remain unforgiven and will be condemned for their actions.

The second point concerns the meaning of enemy love in the OT and the NT. Love is defined by the examples given and is essentially goodwill and kindness. Jesus speaks of the need to practice this love with both personal and national enemies, but the rest of the NT only speaks of love for personal enemies. Jesus corrects the common misunderstanding of the OT concerning national enemies by correcting the understanding of the meaning of "neighbor." The NT authors repeat the OT directives concerning personal enemies by quoting the OT itself. However, the meaning of enemy love, which is goodwill and simple human kindness, should not be pushed beyond its scriptural meaning.

The third point is that hatred is reserved for evil. Hatred in its judicial sense is the only hatred that is to be emulated by God's people.

The fourth point is that vengeance (judgment/justice) is reserved for God. God's people are not to try to emulate God's judgment in their personal relationships. Rather, they are to show kindness with the assurance that not only will justice ultimately be done, but also that their actions will be both vindicated and rewarded. If their deeds of kindness do not lead to the reform of their enemies, then their kindnesses will multiply the guilt of their enemies.

The fifth point is that there is no indication in Scripture that the concept of enemy love includes the forgiveness of enemies or reconciliation with them, much less forgiveness or reconciliation in the absence of repentance. Not forgiving is not the same thing as not loving. Part III will argue that to wipe out unrepented sin is, in fact, a failure to love.

Sixth, Scripture gives several reasons for commanding God's people to love their enemies: (1) because God loved them when they were sinners/enemies (alienated from him), (2) because Christians are to follow God's example; refusing to do so will affect their own ongoing experience of God's forgiveness, (3) because God will ultimately judge all unrepented sin, and (4) because they will be vindicated and rewarded for their obedience.

Scripture does not indicate that loving enemies will result in a positive response by offenders. Certainly, all people do not respond positively to God's offer of love and forgiveness. Jesus himself was treated brutally and crucified. His disciples and later followers often suffered persecution and death. For a follower of Jesus, the call to love enemies is to be obeyed regardless of response.[50]

CHRIST DYING FOR ENEMIES

> You see, at just the right time, when we were still powerless, Christ died for the ungodly. Very rarely will anyone die for a righteous person, though for a good person someone might possibly dare to die. But God demonstrates his own love for us in this: While we were still sinners, Christ died for us. Since we have now been justified by his blood, how much more shall we be saved from God's wrath through him! For if, while we were God's enemies, we were reconciled to him through the death of his Son, how much more, having been reconciled, shall we be saved through his life! Not only is this so, but we also boast in God through our Lord Jesus Christ, through whom we have now received reconciliation. (Rom 5:6–11)

These verses refer to the eschatological reconciliation that was accomplished when Christ redeemed the world through his death. The "reconciliation" (v. 11) refers to a historical event, the atonement, through which the world was redeemed from the forces of darkness. This reconciliation takes place before humankind responds to God's actions, while humans are still sinners/enemies. "Reconciliation is viewed as something accomplished once for all in the death of the Son of God."[51] As John Murray says in his commentary *The Epistle of Romans*, "the term reconciliation [in verses 10 and 11] refers not to actual justification by faith but to the objective ground established by the death of Christ."[52] Individual persons must receive this reconciliation as a gift of God for it to be effective for personal salvation.

Romans 5:10 says, "For if, while we were God's enemies, we were reconciled to him through the death of his Son . . ." The phrase "while we were God's enemies" refers to the time of alienation between God and

---

50. Davis, *Lex Talionis*, 168.

51. Murray, *Romans*, 173.

52. Murray, *Romans*, 170.

humankind that resulted from the fall.[53] Humankind was in the enemy camp, but the word enemy is not used in an active, hostile sense.[54] The word enemy is used in the sense of alienation in Rom 11:28 to denote Israel's alienation from the favor of God; it is contrasted with "the beloved" of God. So, an enemy is one who is alienated from God by God's action.[55]

Jesus died for enemies, for those who are alienated from him and in the enemy camp, but this is not the specific behavior that Christians are expected to emulate. His sacrificial death was an eschatological event in which the ransom was paid and the world was redeemed. In other words, Christians are not asked to sacrifice their lives for enemies. Scripture is specific about how they are to love enemies. They are to show kindness rather than exact vengeance, to bless (wish for/pray for good—for their repentance and reformation) and not curse (wish for evil), and *that is all* that Scripture specifies. Christians are not told to forgive and be reconciled with the unrepentant. Neither are Christians told to pour out their lives for enemies/abusers. The command to love one's enemy should not be pushed beyond its scriptural boundaries and made into something different. Scripture explains the concept of enemy love clearly, simply, and consistently throughout the OT and the NT. In no case does love of enemies demand forgiveness of enemies apart from repentance, or reconciliation with enemies in the absence of repentance.

Another verse that refers to the historical objective work of Christ is 2 Cor 5:18.

> All this is from God, who reconciled us to himself through Christ and gave us the ministry of reconciliation: that God was reconciling the world to himself in Christ, not counting people's sins against them. And he has committed to us the message of reconciliation. (2 Cor 5:18–19)

As stated earlier, this verse (like Rom 5:10, "while we were God's enemies, we were reconciled") refers to a finished work of reconciliation/ atonement that takes place apart from any human response. This is made clear by the rest of the sentence, for if reconciliation is complete there is no need for the "ministry of reconciliation." This verse also speaks of "not counting people's sins against them." This "not counting" occurs at the same time as "reconciling." Can these words be saying that God forgives

53. Murray, *Romans*, 172.

54. Murray, *Romans*, 172.

55. Murray, *Romans*, 172.

the world when he reconciles the world? If this is the case, there is no need for further forgiveness following or dependent upon repentance. This verse would then contradict countless other Scripture verses that have been examined. This is not the case, however, for the word forgive is not used. Rather, the words "not counting" should be taken in the sense of not holding their sins against them. In other words, in spite of their sins and the fact that they were still "sinners" and "enemies" (Rom 5:8, 10), God intervened in history to reconcile/atone/rescue/redeem humankind. This redemption, this purchase from the enemy camp—the powers of sin, Satan, and death (John 8:36; 12:31; Rom 7:14; 1 Cor 7:22; 1 Tim 2:6; 2 Tim 1:10; Heb 2:14–15; 1 John 3:8b; Rev 1:5)—takes place apart from any human action such as repentance. Humankind has not repented and is not crying out to God for deliverance from the powers of darkness (Col 2:15; 1 John 3:8b) that enslave. God delivers humans anyway, not holding their sins against them, not letting their choices prevent him from intervening on their behalf, not deciding that they are only getting what they deserve. Rather, he delivers them on the chance of, and in hopes of, their choosing to repent and believe and become his children in the kingdom of light.

OBEYING THE LOVE COMMAND

Having defined enemy love according to its scriptural usage, the question becomes, How does one obey this hard command? It is a most difficult practice even when one understands that this love does not include forgiving the unrepentant. Two concepts must be embraced.

First, one should recognize that Scripture states that some things are only possible with God (Mark 10:27). Surely this is one such thing. A new birth is necessary, a new life within. God's life must be called upon to practice God's ways. One must first will to obey, and then depend on God's Spirit to enable the obedience (see the author's book *Victorious Substitution: A Theory of the Atonement*, 225–30).

Second, after committing to obey the love command and depending on God's strength, one must seek God's guidance as to *how* to obey. Each situation and each relationship is different, just as each example Jesus gives in Matt 5 is different. In advocating turning the other cheek Jesus is not literally suggesting submitting to the power of evil and unjust violence. He rather shows a new way to respond other than violence or rebellion. Turning the other cheek denies the oppressor the intended humiliation. Giving a garment in court would mean stripping off all clothing other than the loin cloth. Nakedness was taboo in Israel and shame would fall on the person who caused it. Disrobing would expose the cruelty and injustice of the oppressor and challenge the action—an act of courage, confronting injustice with truth. In other words, the victim should choose his response to evil actions thoughtfully, not paying back evil for evil.[56] *Lex talionis* (an eye for an eye) is like divorce, allowed because of the hardness of human hearts (Deut 32:35; Matt 19:8; Rom 12:19). Lex talionis is meant to curb ever-escalating violence and revenge by creating a system of justice. But in personal matters a Christian is to leave justice to God and not retaliate in kind. A Christian must resist evil as his obligation, but he must choose his tool wisely.

What is Jesus saying in suggesting going a second mile? Roman soldiers had the right to impose forced labor on subjected peoples, requiring them to carry a burden up to a mile. If they required more they were subject to punishment. Taking a soldier's burden a second mile would get him in trouble and expose the injustice of the system. It could even be interpreted as insulting to the soldier's strength. Perhaps Jesus is not saying to go the second mile as a show of kindness, but as a way to protest this practice of forced labor. As Andrew Sung Park, in his book *From Hurt to Healing*, says:

> Jesus counseled neither flight (submission, passivity, withdrawal, or surrender) nor fight (armed revolt, violent rebellion, direct retaliation, and revenge). Instead Jesus taught a third way: Find a creative alternative to violence, assert your own humanity and dignity, meet force with ridicule or humor, break the cycle of humiliation, refuse to accept the inferior position, expose the injustice of the system, shame oppressors into repentance, stand your ground, recognize your own power, force the oppressor to see you in a new light, deprive the oppressor of a situation where a show of force is effective, be willing to undergo the penalty of breaking unjust laws, seek the oppressor's transformation, and so on.[57]

God's wisdom is promised to those who ask (Jas 1:5), and this applies to the need for direction concerning the love command. His guidance should be sought in each and every situation. One should expect

56. Park, *Hurt to Healing*, 65.
57. Park, *Hurt to Healing*, 65.

God's guidance to vary according to the circumstances. Confrontation, possibly resulting in exclusion, was seen to be the biblical method of handling sin within the Christian community. The words spoken in Matt 5, however, address a non-Christian setting and involve unequal persons.[58] The context and application of the two ideas must be distinguished; each personal situation must likewise be recognized as unique.

EATING WITH TAX COLLECTORS AND "SINNERS"

> As Jesus went on from there, he saw a man named Matthew sitting at the tax collector's booth. "Follow me," he told him, and Matthew got up and followed him. While Jesus was having dinner at Matthew's house, many tax collectors and sinners came and ate with him and his disciples. When the Pharisees saw this, they asked his disciples, "Why does your teacher eat with tax collectors and sinners?" On hearing this, Jesus said, "It is not the healthy who need a doctor, but the sick. But go and learn what this means: 'I desire mercy, not sacrifice.' For I have not come to call the righteous, but sinners." (Matt 9:9–13)

Sometimes these verses are interpreted to mean that Christians should have fellowship with all people regardless of their behavior. The context of these verses is important in determining if this conclusion is warranted. These verses follow Jesus' call to Matthew, a tax collector who then becomes a follower of Jesus. Later, Jesus dines at Matthew's house with a wider group of undesirables (from the Pharisees' point of view) referred to as "tax collectors and sinners." The Pharisees then criticize Jesus for associating with them (vv. 11–13).[59] Note that the question asked in verse 11 comes from the Pharisees and not, as is often supposed, from ordinary people wondering why Jesus associates with undesirables.

Tax collectors were hated because they worked for an unpopular government (the tetrarchy of Herod Antipas) sanctioned by Rome, as well as the fact that they often took more than was necessary.[60] The fact that Jesus ate a meal at Matthew's house should not be separated from its context, a celebration of Matthew's decision to repent and follow Jesus. The mercy to which Jesus refers (Matt 9:13) in defending himself against

---

58. Park, *Hurt to Healing*, 70.

59. France, *Matthew*, 350.

60. France, *Matthew*, 351.

the criticisms of the Pharisees cannot be thought of as acceptance in fellowship of sinners (in this case, those who steal from and oppress the poor). Jesus himself defines this mercy as a call to sinners (Matt 9:13), that is, a call to repent and be forgiven.

The term *sinner* (Matt 9:11, 13; 11:19; cf. Mark 2:14–17; Luke 5:27–32) could refer to evildoers or criminals (Matt 26:45), but from the viewpoint of the Pharisees included those who did not observe the laws concerning ritual purity, food, and the Sabbath.[61] The term also referred to those who practiced despised trades (herders, tax collectors, publicans) as well as Gentiles and Samaritans. Some workers were despised because of the unclean or ill-smelling nature of their job (e.g., butchers, tanners, and coppersmiths). Those who practiced these lowly jobs were alienated and could not participate in worship. Likewise, those who could not fulfill the duties of the law because of poverty were also labeled sinners in the eyes of the Pharisees. In addition, the blind, lepers, the mentally disturbed, and the hemorrhagic were considered sinners due to the belief that sickness was a result of sin.[62] The most desperate and rejected of society, such as prostitutes, were also considered sinners. Because of the difference in meaning, the term sinner is put in quotation marks in the NIV translation (1984) where this is appropriate (e.g., Matt 9:11 but not 26:45; also Mark 2:16). In summary, two kinds of "sinners" existed in Jewish society in the days of Jesus: publicly recognized criminals who had broken civil laws, and persons in lowly and socially unacceptable occupations or of low social status.[63]

The terms tax collector and sinner are often paired (Matt 9:10; 11:19; Luke 15:1; 18:9–14) and generally refer to these social outcasts (Matt 5:46; 18:17; 21:31–32) rather than to evildoing.[64] Jesus' table fellowship with them has nothing to do with tolerance of evil, but rather with reaching out with grace to society's despised and rejected. His presence with them is an offer of acceptance and forgiveness—metaphorically, the healing of the sick (Matt 9:9–13).[65] It is clearly not the same thing as fellowshipping with those who practice evil.

61. Turner, *Matthew*, 252.
62. Park, *Hurt to Healing*, 23.
63. Park, *Hurt to Healing*, 22–23.
64. Volf, *Exclusion and Embrace*, 72.
65. Piper, *Love Your Enemies*, 81.

The following quotation from *Exclusion and Embrace* sums up the meaning of "sinner" this way:

> In the Palestine of Jesus' day, "sinners" were not simply "the wicked" who were therefore religiously bankrupt, but also social outcasts, people who practiced despised trades, Gentiles and Samaritans, those who failed to keep the law as interpreted by a particular sect. A "righteous" person had to separate herself from the latter; their presence defiled because they were defiled. Jesus' table fellowship with "tax collectors and sinners" (Mark 2:15–17), a fellowship that indisputably belonged to the central features of his ministry, offset this conception of sin. Since he who was innocent, sinless, and fully within God's camp transgressed social boundaries that excluded the outcasts, these boundaries themselves were evil, sinful, and outside God's will. By embracing the "outcast," Jesus underscored the "sinfulness" of the persons and systems that cast them out.
>
> It would be a mistake, however, to conclude from Jesus' compassion toward those who transgressed social boundaries that his mission was merely to demask the mechanisms that created "sinners" by falsely ascribing sinfulness to those who were considered socially unacceptable. He was no prophet of "inclusion," for whom the chief virtue was acceptance and the cardinal vice intolerance. Instead, he was the bringer of "grace," who not only scandalously included "anyone" in the fellowship of "open commensality," but made the "intolerant" demand of repentance and the "condescending" offer of forgiveness (Mark 1:15).[66]

One thing this passage mentions that Jesus does not do is embrace real sinners by acting as if their sin is not there. If this were the case, justice and truth would be suspended and instead condonation would reign.[67]

THE EARLY CHURCH

The early church did not interpret Jesus' table fellowship with "sinners" as fellowship with evildoers or the immoral. In 1 Cor 5:1–13 Paul addresses the situation of gross sexual immorality within the church and counsels the Corinthians not to "associate with anyone who claims to be a brother

66. Volf, *Exclusion and Embrace*, 72.

67. Volf, *Exclusion and Embrace*, 294.

or sister but is sexually immoral or greedy, an idolater or a slanderer, a drunkard or a swindler." He goes on to say, "Do not even eat with such people" (v. 11). Otherwise, they would be accepting (condoning) within their community the immoral and intolerable behavior. Separation from unbelievers (2 Cor 6:14–18; Eph 5:7; 2 Tim 3:2–5; 2 John 10) and from disobedient believers (Rom 16:17; 2 Thess 3:6; Titus 3:10) is taught in the early church. But the separation is based on immoral or divisive behavior, never on social status or nationality.[68]

> Do not be yoked together with unbelievers. For what do righteousness and wickedness have in common? Or what fellowship can light have with darkness? What harmony is there between Christ and Belial? Or what does a believer have in common with an unbeliever? Or what agreement is there between the temple of God and idols? For we are the temple of the living God. As God has said:
>
> > "I will live with them
> > > and walk among them,
> > and I will be their God,
> > > and they will be my people."
>
> Therefore,
>
> > "Come out from them
> > > and be separate,
> > > > says the Lord.
> > Touch no unclean thing,
> > > and I will receive you."
>
> And,
>
> > "I will be a Father to you,
> > > and you will be my sons and daughters,
> > > > says the Lord Almighty." (2 Cor 6:14–18)
>
> (As is so often the case in the NT, 2 Cor 6:14–18 cites the OT to support the argument. The OT quotation also shows that immoral behavior is the reason for separation in the OT as well as in the NT.)
>
> Therefore do not be partners with [those who are disobedient]. (Eph 5:7)

---

68. Piper, *Love Your Enemies*, 42.

> People will be lovers of themselves . . . , having a form of godliness but denying its power. Have nothing to do with such people. (2 Tim 3:2–5)

> If anyone comes to you and does not bring this teaching, do not take them into your house or welcome them. (2 John 10)

> I urge you, brothers and sisters, to watch out for those who cause divisions and put obstacles in your way that are contrary to the teaching you have learned. Keep away from them. (Rom 16:17)

> In the name of the Lord Jesus Christ, we command you, brothers and sisters, to keep away from every believer who is idle and disruptive and does not live according to the teaching you received from us. (2 Thess 3:6)

> Warn a divisive person once, and then warn them a second time. After that, have nothing to do with them. (Titus 3:10)

Paul, an apostle charged with protecting the flock of God, displays a passion for justice as well as moral outrage. He labels certain people "false apostles" and compares them to Satan, who "masquerades as an angel of light" (2 Cor 11:13–15). He also advises the church to expel anyone involved in moral debauchery (1 Cor 5:13) and insists that Hymenaeus and Alexander be "handed over to Satan" so that they might learn not to blaspheme (1 Tim 1:20). This may be the same Alexander whom Paul is confident the Lord will repay for all the harm he has done (2 Tim 4:14). In addition, Jude calls down "woe" for certain people (Jude 11), as did Jesus (Matt 23). These examples suggest that a lack of indignation or moral outrage may, in certain circumstances, be evidence not of love, but of a failure of love and/or moral integrity.[69]

CONCLUDING STATEMENT: PART II

Having completed an examination of every NT text concerning forgiveness, D. A. Carson's words are appropriate. He says, "The biblical passages [about love and forgiveness] are subtle and wise. . . . They warn against an easy proof-texting that makes one passage or theme [the dominant idea], without adequate reflection on the context or on complementary or even competing mandates."[70] "Theological reflection [is required] for

69. Carson, *Love in Hard Places*, 85.

70. Carson, *Love in Hard Places*, 71.

any serious attempt to relate some of the Bible's complex interlocking themes to some of today's complex, interlocking problems."[71] Part III of this book will provide a theological and ethical reflection on the subject of forgiveness and its place in a moral context.

71. Carson, *Love in Hard Places*, 145.

CHAPTER 8 STUDY QUESTIONS

Resisting Evil

1. With what OT principle does Jesus contrast his teaching on resisting evil in Matt 5:38–42?

2. According to Jesus and the OT, why does *lex talionis* not apply in personal situations?

3. What does "do not resist evil" mean? What six illustrations does Jesus use to make his point?

4. What understanding of God's character enables one to submit to injustice and mistreatment?

Love and Hate

1. What assumption is often made based on the NT injunction to love one's enemies?

2. In the Bible, the meaning of the words love and hate may vary according to what?

3. What kind of hatred is authorized in the Bible? Is personal hatred authorized?

4. Why are Christians told to love their enemies in Matt 5:45?

Enemies

1. Summarize the OT teaching concerning personal enemies.

2. Summarize the OT teaching concerning national enemies.

3. What is the basis for Jesus' command to love enemies?

Context

1. How does the eschatological context of Jesus' teaching redefine the Jewish expectation of the kingdom of God and therefore expand the love command?

Reasons for Loving Enemies

1. What are two reasons given in Matt 5:46–48 for loving enemies?

2. How is Jesus' love command balanced by his words to the Pharisees in Matt 23?

The Teaching of the Early Church on Enemy Love

1. What is the essence of the teaching on loving enemies in Rom 12, 1 Thess 5, and 1 Pet 3? Does the teaching in these passages differ from that of the OT?

2. What kind of enemies do these passages address?

Romans 12:17–20

1. Why does Paul quote the OT so often in this passage?

2. What does the love command involve doing in Rom 12:17–20?

3. What do the phrases "heap burning coals" and "leave room for God's wrath" mean here?

4. What characteristic and promise of God is helpful in comforting those who carry out God's love command with no apparent positive results?

5. In Rom 12:1–2 the appeal to love enemies is based on what?

1 Thessalonians 5:15

1. What truth does the phrase "as far as it depends on you" acknowledge?

1 Peter 3:9

1. What is promised to those who follow the love command in 1 Pet 3:9?

2. Does the command to love one's enemies suggest that they are to be forgiven apart from repentance? What should enemies be offered?

Christ Dying for Enemies

1. In what sense did reconciliation take place between God and humans "while we were still sinners"? How is the term "enemy" used in this passage?

2. What does the phrase "not counting people's sins against them" in 2 Cor 5:18 mean?

Obeying the Love Command

1. What two steps need to be taken in order to obey the difficult love command of Scripture?

Eating with Tax Collectors and "Sinners"

1. What does the term "sinner" mean in its Jewish social context?

2. What does Jesus' action of eating with tax collectors and "sinners" demonstrate?

The Early Church

1. In the early church, the decision to separate from someone was based on what?

PART III

Forgiveness in an Ethical Context

THE BRIEF CONCLUDING STATEMENT to Part II states that theological reflection is required to make proper application of the Bible's words concerning repentance, forgiveness, reconciliation, and justice. Part III engages in such theological reflection. The discussion will be theological in that the biblical foundations are laid, and no conclusion will be drawn that violates any biblical principle. The discussion will be reflection in that analysis and contemplation are needed to discern the ethical basis for biblical injunctions, as well as to make proper application. In other words, forgiveness must be understood in a moral context; there must be a reason for forgiving.

In examining the moral issues surrounding the practice of forgiveness, Part III draws heavily on the reflections of philosophers and is thus a study in the ethics of forgiveness. In applying those reflections, the reader can draw his own conclusions and will certainly have personal experiences that will no doubt readily come to mind. Be aware that "philosophical ideas are deeply sensitive to one's own life experiences."[1] However, personal perspective is advantageous, for, as Jeffrie Murphy in his book *Forgiveness and Mercy* says, "Without some personal perspective, it would be unclear why one is bothering to think and write about certain topics [such as forgiveness] at all and why one is commending them to others for their reflection."[2]

---

1. Murphy and Hampton, *Forgiveness and Mercy*, 185.
2. Murphy and Hampton, *Forgiveness and Mercy*, 185–86.

9

Therapeutic Forgiveness versus Biblical Forgiveness

IN CITING THE WORK of philosophers, once again the problem of definitions arises. In order to determine when forgiveness is ethical, one must define what exactly is meant by forgiveness.

CONTEMPORARY DEFINITIONS OF FORGIVENESS

In stating the thesis of his book *Before Forgiveness*, David Konstan says that "the modern concept of forgiveness . . . did not exist in classical antiquity, that is, in ancient Greece and Rome, [and] . . . that it played no role whatever in the ethical thinking of those societies. What is more, [the modern concept] is not fully present in the Hebrew Bible, nor again in the New Testament or in the early Jewish and Christian commentaries on the Holy Scriptures."[1] Konstan also says that the absence of the modern definition of forgiveness in the pre-modern Western world may not point to a deficiency in past ethical or psychological understanding, but rather to a problem in the modern definition of forgiveness.[2]

What is this modern concept of forgiveness that Konstan says is ethically problematic and not found in ancient definitions, whether philosophical, ethical, or theological? And if this concept did not originate in

1. Konstan, *Before Forgiveness*, 9.
2. Konstan, *Before Forgiveness*, 11.

the philosophical or theological discussions of the ancient world, where did it originate? Bash says, "The most significant contribution to recent understanding of forgiveness has come, not from Christian theologians, but from philosophers and psychologists who have generally sought to work from a nonreligious standpoint."[3] The result is a new, modern definition of the act of forgiveness that is a departure from the ancient or biblical meaning. Even more problematic, there are many variations in the modern definition of what it means to forgive. Because of these variations, in order to discuss or reflect on forgiveness ethically or theologically, a working definition of the term forgiveness must be established. Two persons cannot come to any agreement about the ethics of forgiveness (if, when, and how it is to be practiced) if they have different definitions of the term and different ideas of what the practice involves. Thus, this section will examine modern definitions of forgiveness so that they may be distinguished from each other as well as from the biblical concept. The author contends that modern variations in the definition of forgiveness have influenced (or infiltrated) Christian teaching and preaching and have thus distorted its true Christian meaning, resulting in teaching that is both unbiblical and ethically unsound.

THERAPEUTIC FORGIVENESS

Nigel Biggar, in his article "Forgiveness in the Twentieth Century," reviews the history of literature on the subject of forgiveness. He maintains that forgiveness in modern times has been redefined as an attitude that has to do with overcoming resentment, and this alteration can be traced to philosophers of the latter decades of the twentieth century.[4] Psychologists have embraced this new understanding, and forgiveness is thus conceived "as a process internal to the psyche of the victim."[5] According to this modern understanding, forgiveness is about overcoming negative emotions. It happens within an individual and not between individuals. Reconciliation is what occurs between individuals, but is a separate process. Forgiveness is unconditional and therefore not dependent on the repentance of the offender. Neither does it necessarily lead to reconciliation, which is dependent on the guilty party's response to

---

3. A. Bash, *Forgiveness and Christian Ethics*, 174–75.

4. Biggar, "Forgiveness," 188–89.

5. Biggar, "Forgiveness," 213.

the victim's forgiveness.[6] This understanding of forgiveness as internal and unilateral will be referred to as *therapeutic forgiveness*, because the purpose of this forgiveness is the therapeutic overcoming of the negative personal emotions of the victim. This definition is primarily negative in that forgiveness is an *absence* of negative emotion and not an action with the positive result of reconciliation. There is no way to distinguish forgiveness from the absence of negative emotion that may result, not from forgiveness, but from condonation, forgetfulness, or disengagement. It focuses on what has been removed (negative feelings) rather than on what has been given (relief from guilt feelings) or produced (reconciliation).[7] Neither does therapeutic forgiveness require any moral stance or confrontation.[8] According to the meaning of therapeutic forgiveness, the minimal "essential condition for 'genuine' forgiveness to take place [is] the eradication of resentment, or some other negative attitude."[9] In other words, if the victim still feels resentment and hostility, he has not forgiven. Every definition put forward in the philosophical literature in the last three decades includes this emotional change on the part of the forgiver.[10]

The scientific study of forgiveness began only recently. According to Everett Worthington in *Dimensions of Forgiveness*, before 1985 only five such studies existed.[11] Célesten Musekura in *An Assessment of Contemporary Models of Forgiveness* states that psychologists working in the area of forgiveness are generating a plethora of definitions with a psychological emphasis.[12] She notes a lack of agreement on a common definition.[13] Since there is no consensus in the new model for forgiveness, any discussions of therapeutic forgiveness need to begin by defining forgiveness. Some have suggested that forgiveness be defined as overcoming negative feelings. Another definition is abandoning one's right to resentment toward one who unjustly injured us, while fostering compassion, generosity,

6. Biggar, "Forgiveness," 213.

7. MacLachlan, "Forgiveness," 43.

8. MacLachlan, "Forgiveness," 43.

9. MacLachlan, "Forgiveness," 78.

10. MacLachlan, "Forgiveness," 79.

11. Biggar, "Forgiveness," 212.

12. Musekura, *Models of Forgiveness*, 15.

13. Musekura, *Models of Forgiveness*, 17.

and even love toward him or her.[14] Psychologists also debate whether forgiveness is a process or an event in which the injured party utters words of pardon to the offender. Most view forgiveness as a psychological process rather than an event. According to this process model, one cannot forgive by making the decision to do so or by simply saying the words but must labor at overcoming negative emotions.[15] In therapeutic forgiveness, no concern exists for the dimensions of guilt and justice or for the harm done to the guilty offender by granting him forgiveness apart from his repentance. In the biblical model the wrongdoer/sinner is held accountable, demonstrating concern for his well-being as well as for justice and morality.[16]

Therapeutic forgiveness thus internalizes and privatizes forgiveness by making it primarily an act that occurs in people's hearts and minds. Little need then exists for specific action. It ignores the issues of culpability and repentance, thus separating forgiveness from the reality of sin. Forgiveness simply becomes a way for the victim to heal himself. But biblical forgiveness is about being healed by God and others through the specific practices of repentance, forgiveness, and reconciliation.[17] The stress in Scripture is on being right with God and others, not on the psychological benefits of the absence of negative emotion.[18]

Therapeutic forgiveness encourages the forgiver to see others as weak, needy, and fallible—therefore the objects of compassion. This view has an element of truth, but it trivializes sin and abrogates human responsibility, effectively degrading others. The suggestion is that people are doing the best they are able when in fact they often are not.[19] The biblical view is that wrongdoers should be urged to repent of their wrongdoing and encouraged to do what is right, thus expressing concern for the wrongdoer as one who is worthy of care and higher expectations. Therapeutic forgiveness is not concerned for the offender and does not involve an act of grace and mercy toward him that relieves his guilt. The objective of therapeutic forgiveness is rather to relieve *oneself* of the burden of negative feelings. As Volf says, "In much of popular culture,

---

14. Musekura, *Models of Forgiveness*, 18.

15. Musekura, *Models of Forgiveness*, 18.

16. Biggar, "Forgiveness," 214.

17. L. Jones, *Embodying Forgiveness*, 49–50.

18. Carson, *Love in Hard Places*, 80.

19. L. Jones, *Embodying Forgiveness*, 51–52.

to forgive means to overcome feelings of anger and resentment. . . . By forgiving they hope to do themselves a favor, to be freed from negative emotions in which the offense they've suffered entangles them."[20] This motive is vastly different from the biblical model in which a gracious gift is given to the wrongdoer.

One reason therapeutic conceptions of forgiveness have caught on in the Christian churches is that they overlap with Christian forgiveness just enough to distort a proper understanding of their differences.[21] From a Christian perspective many negative emotions do indeed need to be overcome for a person to be pure in heart and *willing* to forgive *if* the offender repents. If a wrongdoer truly repents, he should be viewed differently by the victim, although some negative emotions may still need to be overcome during the process of reconciliation. Overcoming negative feelings is the right and appropriate thing to do even if difficult. To attempt to overcome negative emotions toward one who has not changed in heart or behavior, however, is most difficult because it can be argued that it is *not* the right or appropriate thing to do. This question of when and how to overcome negative emotion involves a subtle distinction between the therapeutic and biblical models of forgiveness and will be discussed more fully later.

Of course, vindictive emotions and emotions such as personal hatred always need to be overcome; this may indeed be a process, but it is the Christian way, regardless of whether forgiveness is tendered or not. In order to be *willing* to forgive (to be merciful) one must forgo malicious and vindictive emotions. In the biblical model, one must be *willing* to forgive regardless of whether the offender actually ever repents or whether forgiveness is ever enacted. Being willing to forgive is not overcoming or eliminating *all* negative emotions. Indignation and righteous anger at wrongdoing and injustice are feelings that should not be rejected. The emotions that must be rejected and overcome in the biblical model are those that prevent one from forgiving a repentant offender, in other words, feelings that would prevent one from being merciful and having a pure heart.

20. Volf, *Free of Charge*, 168–69.
21. L. Jones, *Embodying Forgiveness*, 68.

CHRISTIAN REACTION TO THERAPEUTIC FORGIVENESS

As the definition of forgiveness changed, Christian writers betrayed a lack of understanding of the true biblical model and began to embrace this new therapeutic concept of unconditional forgiveness that does not insist on repentance or reconciliation. Thankfully, not all Christian writers and thinkers have done so. Gregory Jones in his book *Embodying Forgiveness* seeks to "rescue forgiveness from the privatized world of interior spirituality."[22] Jones says that many Christians have accepted a "cheap therapeutic forgiveness" in place of biblical forgiveness.[23] He calls this change in the Christian understanding the "trivialization of forgiveness,"[24] and says this process of trivialization actually began as Christians distanced themselves from their OT roots.[25] Today the therapeutic emphasis has increasingly distorted true Christian forgiveness, which insists that if people do not confess and repent, the sin is retained and forgiveness and reconciliation should be temporarily suspended in the hope that the offender himself will be "saved on the day of the Lord" (1 Cor 5:5).[26]

Another book that has resisted the new definition of forgiveness is Gestrich's *The Return of Splendor in the World*. Gestrich (as does Jones) "follows Bonhoeffer in attributing the decline of the Christian church in Western Europe in large part to the preaching of forgiveness without discipleship."[27] A weakened concept of interpersonal forgiveness naturally follows a weakened concept of the gospel.

WRONGFUL GUILT

Accepting the therapeutic forgiveness model as "Christian" has caused many to experience wrongful guilt. Liz Gulliford points out in "Intrapersonal Forgiveness" that it is not uncommon for people to feel guilt

---

22. Biggar, "Forgiveness," 204.

23. L. Jones, *Embodying Forgiveness*, 36.

24. L. Jones, *Embodying Forgiveness*, 36.

25. L. Jones, *Embodying Forgiveness*, 38.

26. L. Jones, *Embodying Forgiveness*, 20.

27. Biggar, "Forgiveness," 204.

and unworthiness because they cannot forgive grievous wrongs.[28] This is particularly true of Christians who, under the influence of the therapeutic model, believe that they must forgive unconditionally and overcome their negative emotions, lest they remain somehow unclean and displeasing to God. They are made to feel guilty and unchristian, and if they embrace this false guilt, they will often say they have forgiven when in fact they know they have not. Making the claim to have forgiven may also become a matter of pride and self-righteousness. They then feel hypocritical as well as guilty and unchristian, not to mention lonely because they cannot express their true feelings in intimate friendship with others. These victims become victimized a second time by those who are ignorant of the true character of biblical forgiveness. Overcoming resentment is difficult, even following the repentance of the wrongdoer, but overcoming resentment in the absence of repentance and/or when the harmful behavior continues is extremely difficult and in reality probably impossible. Forgiving in the biblical sense of pardon leading to reconciliation is even more difficult under circumstances in which the guilty party has not repented. Thus many Christians have found forgiveness in the biblical sense of pardon leading to reconciliation to be impossible, and they struggle with wrongful guilt because of what they perceive to be an inability to forgive. They deserve for the biblical injunction to forgive *as God does* to be clarified.

Those who define forgiveness as the internal act of overcoming resentment often say that forgiveness does not insist upon reconciliation. This of course makes the prospect of "forgiving" less objectionable to one who does not want to be reconciled with an unrepentant or habitual offender. But the view that reconciliation does not necessarily follow forgiveness ignores the biblical pattern. The true focus of biblical forgiveness is the gaining of a brother, not the healing of oneself. As Gulliford says (quoting David Augsburger), "It is easy to get caught up in the cultural values of individualism, self-actualization, self-emancipation, etc. But this is a distortion of the Christian understanding of forgiveness with the primary motive of making one feel better about oneself."[29]

28. Gulliford, "Intrapersonal Forgiveness," 84; A. Bash, *Forgiveness and Christian Ethics*, 2.

29. Gulliford, "Healing of Relationships," 106.

CHAPTER 9 STUDY QUESTIONS

Contemporary Definitions of Forgiveness

1. Where did modern definitions of forgiveness originate?

Therapeutic Forgiveness

1. What is therapeutic forgiveness? How does it differ from the biblical model?

2. What is the relationship between biblical forgiveness and personal healing?

3. Does the practice of therapeutic forgiveness involve concern for the wrongdoer?

4. Where do biblical forgiveness and therapeutic forgiveness overlap?

Christian Reaction to Therapeutic Forgiveness

1. What has been suggested as the cause of Christian acceptance of therapeutic forgiveness?

Wrongful Guilt

1. Why do Christians, under the influence of the therapeutic model of forgiveness, often feel wrongful guilt? Why do advocates of therapeutic forgiveness often omit reconciliation?

10

Resentment and Anger

THE MORAL SIGNIFICANCE OF RESENTMENT

IN ORDER TO DISCUSS the primary modern definition of forgiveness as the overcoming of resentment, resentment itself must be examined. Whether resentment should even be overcome must be addressed from a moral perspective. What is the moral significance of resentment, anger, and hatred? Cannot anger and frustration be emotions of a deep longing for justice or for the consummation of the kingdom of God?[1] It should be repeated at the beginning of this discussion that the Bible forbids vengeance. Scripture also often warns against anger and counsels giving it up (Eph 4:26). Yet, to feel no anger or resentment at injustice (whether it is directed at another or oneself) is to lack moral judgment. Therefore the anger that the Bible so often forbids is unrighteous, malicious anger. In the Bible, God is often depicted as angry. His anger is, of course, justified and proceeds from his righteousness. Should his people, created in his image and desiring to emulate him, not also feel anger at injustice? Indeed they should. In the absence of repentance by the wrongdoer, feelings of anger or resentment express a refusal to condone or accept wrongdoing, injustice, or evil. One must, of course, distinguish between moral anger and malicious anger. One should not abandon moral anger that expresses a commitment to what is good and just. Jesus condemns malicious hatred (Matt 5:22), but he encourages his disciples to oppose moral adversaries and not to reconcile with them, even when they are

1. L. Jones, *Embodying Forgiveness*, 231.

members of one's own family, so long as they remain committed to their evil cause. "Do not suppose that I have come to bring peace to the earth. I did not come to bring peace, but a sword. For I have come to turn 'a man against his father, a daughter against her mother, a daughter-in-law against her mother-in-law—a man's enemies will be the members of his own household'" (Matt 10:34–36, partially quoting Mic 7:6).

RESENTMENT, INDIGNATION, AND SELF-WORTH

Anger or resentment can express a sense of one's self-worth. Hence a refusal to be passive or be pacified in the face of injustice or suffering may be a moral protest that Christians should practice (as opposed to irrational, unreasonable, or overly sensitive feelings of anger).[2] Resentment is the response not to general wrongs, but to wrongs committed against oneself as opposed to indignation at wrongs committed against another person. Resentment functions as a defense, not of all moral issues, but rather of the value of oneself. It is personal and demonstrates self-respect. In his book *Forgiveness and Mercy*, Jeffrie Murphy, speaking of resentment as a proper moral response, says, "The primary value defended by the emotion of resentment is self-respect. A person who does not resent moral injuries done to himself is almost necessarily a person lacking in self-respect."[3] This statement does not deny that resentment may also have a very unattractive and unhealthy form. According to this analysis resentment is not instinctive anger following an injury, but a logical cognitive response. When a person deliberately wrongs another he treats the other in a demeaning and disrespectful manner, degrading the other in the process.[4] People do not resent harm done by hurricanes or tornados, but rather injuries that are deliberately inflicted by someone who should respect them as persons. Resentment is a feeling expressing a person's judgment that the harmful treatment he experienced is unjustified and inappropriate given his value as a human being. The ability to feel resentment following an injury depends upon one having a sufficient sense of his own self-worth and therefore believing the actions to be inappropriate and worthy of protest.[5] The wronged one defends himself, but that is

---

2. L. Jones, *Embodying Forgiveness*, 246.

3. Murphy and Hampton, *Forgiveness and Mercy*, 16.

4. Murphy and Hampton, *Forgiveness and Mercy*, 52.

5. Murphy and Hampton, *Forgiveness and Mercy*, 55.

not the point of the protest. The protest is a cognitive moral protest.[6] This proper form of resentment is not sudden instinctual anger,[7] but anger that focuses on the moral mistake of the offender. It does not focus on insecurities about what the actions may show about one's true value. Moral resentment is not personal anger, and the protest made is not a personal defense;[8] it is a reflective and warranted emotion based on the belief that the injury received should not have been inflicted.[9] Anthony Bash calls this type of resentment "a principled response to wrongdoing."[10]

Resentment presupposes that one has self-respect and a proper sense of one's value. One who feels unworthy of dignified treatment may not resent abusive treatment.[11] Acquiescing to repeated degrading behavior may destroy self-respect, especially in children. It may take some time to reestablish self-respect if the harmful treatment caused a person to doubt his own value—experiencing feelings of failure and inadequacy when, for example, he or she is abused, abandoned, or betrayed.

RESENTMENT VERSUS ANIMOSITY, HATRED, AND VINDICTIVENESS

Resentment that is a principled response to wrongdoing must be distinguished from resentment characterized by ill will and animosity, or vindictiveness.[12] It is not necessarily true that a victim who has not forgiven the offender and who resents the harm done to him feels ill will and animosity toward the offender. Resentment or anger may be a correct moral response that does not necessarily have to be accompanied by personal animosity or ill will toward the offender. If resentment or anger is a correct moral response based on justice and self-respect, then it stands to reason that it should be maintained in this sense.[13] Conversely, animosity as an incorrect response to an offense should be overcome. If one is morally resentful or angry at a particular time because of a wrong done,

6. Murphy and Hampton, *Forgiveness and Mercy*, 56.

7. Haber, *Forgiveness*, 35.

8. Murphy and Hampton, *Forgiveness and Mercy*, 56.

9. Haber, *Forgiveness*, 38.

10. A. Bash, *Forgiveness: A Theology*, 37.

11. Haber, *Forgiveness*, 38.

12. A. Bash, *Forgiveness: A Theology*, 37.

13. A. Bash, *Forgiveness and Christian Ethics*, 49.

then (in the absence of repentance) he should still have the same feelings at a later date (although the intensity of the feelings may be dulled by time).

Resentment and anger, then, may be appropriate, but animosity and vindictiveness should be overcome. Certainly resentment should not be allowed to turn into hatred or lead to acts of vengeance. Vindictiveness, by definition, involves the desire to get even.[14] In other words, moral hatred must be distinguished from personal hatred. Personal hatred involves spite and/or malice toward the person who brought harm (where the harm may or may not be a moral wrong). It often results from feelings of personal devaluation. If this analysis is correct, then the less secure a person is, the more he will succumb to personal hatred and the harder it will be for him to overcome it. Persons who have a transcendent source of self-respect—the view that they are a beloved child of God—are less likely to succumb to personal hatred.[15] Persons who do experience this kind of hatred may try to regain their desired value by securing the opinion of others (because they take the opinions of others to be significant evidence of their own worth). They often misrepresent the situation by rigging the evidence to put others in their favor. But as Jean Hampton says in her book *Forgiveness and Mercy*, "Unscrupulous recognition-seekers are engaging in a self-defeating strategy; that is, their method of achieving a secure sense of their high worth will actually prevent them from achieving that goal." Because they know they have rigged the evidence, they feel like frauds and impostors.[16]

Malicious resentment or hatred toward perceived enemies will often lead to vengeful actions that are controlling, harmful, or mastering. By winning in this way, one desires to diminish the enemy and thus indirectly to elevate himself. The story of David and King Saul is a good example (1 Sam 17–18). King Saul hates David and seeks to have him killed because of his skill as a warrior. In Saul's eyes this skill and success in battle elevates David above himself. David does nothing wrong, and yet Saul hates him and wishes to do him harm. So resentment can be an unjustified emotional reaction that protests what one considers to be a diminishing action. Malicious resentment attacks the one who performed the action as a way of defying the diminishing message and elevating

14. Haber, *Forgiveness*, 72.

15. Murphy, *Getting Even*, 78.

16. Murphy and Hampton, *Forgiveness and Mercy*, 63–64.

himself. One can experience this kind of hatred only if one believes that human beings can differ in rank. Malice therefore demonstrates that a person has accepted the idea that persons are not of equal worth. If one thinks that some people are worth more than others, then one may fear that he is lower in rank than another. This belief may lead to the desire to degrade another in order to elevate oneself.[17] Clearly this kind of malicious resentment can be avoided with a proper biblical view of one's value and the understanding that all people are of equal worth in God's eyes. People with strong self-concepts are not malicious haters.

Spite is similar to malice. A malicious hater wants to lower another in order to elevate himself, whereas a spiteful person simply loves company at the bottom and desires to bring others down. Thus, both malice and spite are irrational as well as morally wrong. Both emotions are also harmful to the one who experiences them. So, Scripture encourages Christians to lay aside (work to eliminate) these irrational and harmful emotions. "Put off all these: anger, wrath, malice, blasphemy, filthy communication out of your mouth" (Col 3:8 KJV; cf. Eph 4:31). This is not an unreasonable ask, but a call to be realistic, sensible, and to recognize and live in God's love and approval. Matthew 11:28–30 says, "Come to me, all you who are weary and burdened, and I will give you rest. Take my yoke upon you and learn from me, for I am gentle and humble in heart, and you will find rest for your souls. For my yoke is easy and my burden is light." Verse 25 begins, "At that time Jesus said . . . ," indicating the time or context in which Jesus spoke these words to his disciples.[18] The context is the judgment he pronounces on the cities that have rejected him (vv. 20–24). There will be a judgment of those who refuse to receive the message of the twelve who are sent out (Matt 10:5, 11–15), but the disciples are not to be burdened with this rejection.[19]

Another reason that malice and spite are morally wrong is that they involve feelings one chooses, not emotions that one feels involuntarily. Christians are called to give up malice and spite (Eph 4:31; Col 3:8), indicating that these are voluntary emotions and therefore emotions for which one can be held responsible.[20] In order to work through (let go of) an emotion that is morally wrong as well as harmful to oneself, one must

---

17. Murphy and Hampton, *Forgiveness and Mercy*, 79.

18. France, *Matthew*, 443.

19. Murphy and Hampton, *Forgiveness and Mercy*, 79.

20. Murphy and Hampton, *Forgiveness and Mercy*, 79.

first acknowledge that he does indeed feel the emotion. A person cannot work through or let go of animosity that he will not admit he feels. The imprecatory psalms are filled with the expression of such emotion. As in the psalms, the emotion should be admitted and properly vented (to God). One should be careful not to bury these destructive emotions, but rather do what Scripture advocates—voice them to God. These emotions certainly cause one to be "weary and burdened"; therefore, they are to be brought to God and abandoned to him so that "one may find rest for [his] soul." It is neither impossible nor unreasonable to turn over harmful emotions to the One who is all-caring and all-powerful, knowing that he has promised to judge evil and right all wrongs.

This letting go, abandoning the heavy burden of harmful emotions, does not mean that one should abandon moral anger. Letting go of animosity, malicious hatred, and spite is emotional preparation for coming to a place of mercy, a place of willingness to forgive a repentant offender and be reconciled to him. Obviously, true forgiveness cannot be given if one harbors malice or spite. However, one need not, and indeed should not, let go of moral anger. These two very different emotions must be distinguished for one to correctly understand the proper actions of forgiveness and reconciliation. Moral hatred is what one feels toward an evil dictator, a mass murderer, or a person who has harmed one's child.[21] The aversion is not to the person as much as it is to the immoral cause with which he is associated. No personal animosity exists that desires to hurt the other person, but there is a willingness for the offender to be hurt in the pursuit of victory over his immoral cause. Whereas, in the case of malicious hatred, one desires to diminish or hurt the other as a way to get even with or gain advantage over him and his status.[22] People who appear to be without any goodness and well beyond repentance should be morally hated. With such people there can be no reconciliation. This kind of moral hatred accepts the reality of evil and evil people. A moral hater may properly rejoice in the defeat of an evil enemy as a victory for morality. The rejoicing is not personal but righteous. Vindication (truth) is both proper and good. As Hampton says, moral haters may properly enjoy bringing the bully down a notch or two by wanting "the opponent's false sense of self-worth and rank to be exposed and defeated."[23]

---

21. Murphy and Hampton, *Forgiveness and Mercy*, 80.
22. Murphy and Hampton, *Forgiveness and Mercy*, 88.
23. Murphy and Hampton, *Forgiveness and Mercy*, 82.

Understanding the difference between moral anger and malicious anger is important for drawing proper conclusions concerning the definition of forgiveness and for determining when forgiveness should be offered or granted. To determine the moral correctness of forgiveness, one must distinguish between the change of heart that takes place for the forgiver and the preparations for it that involve working through malice and/or spite. According to Bash "the challenge of getting ready to forgive is to move from resentment that is unhelpful to resentment that is appropriately focused and continues to hold [the offender] to account without bitterness and vengeful feelings."[24] This process that makes forgiveness and reconciliation possible for a victim is the emotional *preparation* for the change of heart that takes place in genuine forgiveness. One also must regain confidence in one's worth (if it has been shaken) despite the hurtful action that challenged it. (Understandably, this may take time. One may need to say, to admit, that he is not yet ready or able to forgive.) After the malicious or spiteful feelings are overcome, then the victim may be in a psychological position to truly forgive a repentant offender. If the wrongdoer repents he shows himself to also be someone who morally hates his own actions. He has become someone with whom the forgiver can be reconciled without condoning immoral behavior.[25] If a wrongdoer has not repudiated his actions through confession and repentance, then the victim still should be *willing* to forgive should the offender choose to change, but in this case, forgiveness itself cannot be granted without harming morality.

Forgiveness in the therapeutic sense cannot be willed if one does not believe a change has taken place in the wrongdoer. To make the claim that one has forgiven in the sense of overcoming all negative emotion when in fact one knows he has not is fiction and hypocrisy. Forgiveness, if defined as overcoming negative emotion, is not an act of the will. It can only be a process—saying it is done does not make it so. However, if one defines forgiveness in the biblical sense of granting pardon based on repentance for the purpose of reconciliation, it may be an act of the will that does not involve a process. One can be forgiven, pardoned, even if the offended one still has to sometimes deal with recurring negative emotions. Forgiveness involves an action that takes place at a specific time

---

24. A. Bash, *Forgiveness: A Theology*, 37.
25. Murphy and Hampton, *Forgiveness and Mercy*, 83.

and cannot be undone. It is simply a fact. The forgiveness is granted: the sin is removed.

Of course, if forgiveness is *defined* as overcoming malice and spite rather than *all* negative emotion, including resentment, then one should forgive regardless of whether the offender has repented or not. But this would not be forgiveness according to the biblical definition, or even many therapeutic definitions.

Any suggestion that a person should not forgive must make clear what is meant by forgiveness. Refusing to forgive from a biblical perspective is ethically correct if it involves unrepented sin, because according to the biblical definition, forgiveness involves the removal of the sin. Refusing to forgive from a therapeutic perspective, which insists on abandoning *all* negative emotion, is also ethically correct in the absence of repentance, because it involves maintaining correct moral anger. Therefore, as previously stated, meaningful discussion of the practice of forgiveness requires that the term first be defined clearly.

SERVANT VERSUS SERVILE

If eliminating negative feelings of malice or spite prior to becoming willing to forgive a repentant offender does not involve eliminating justified resentment, we must clarify justified and unjustified resentment. This distinction is found in the difference between servanthood and servility. Christians are called to follow Christ's example of servanthood. They are not called to be servile; a servile person is one without self-respect. He acts as if he has no inherent rights or significance. This attitude fails to comprehend being created in God's image and being loved and valued by him. Christians may attempt to humble themselves (Matt 23:12) and forswear any resentment at how they are treated by others, but this is actually not being humble; it is being servile. Such action fails to comprehend that one's life has value, meaning, and dignity even in (especially in) servanthood. Christians have often confused servility and servanthood, resulting in a moral failure to protest degrading treatment properly. One may protest when he sees another person being treated in an unjust or demeaning manner because he respects the dignity of the other person and has a sense of justice. Yet when receiving such treatment himself, he may incorrectly feel that, in the name of humility, he must endure it without protest. But morality that includes human dignity and justice should not be forfeited in the name of misguided humility. Christ himself pointed out the demeaning inhospitality of Simon the Pharisee (albeit in love, see Luke 7:44–46). Christians often believe they have no right to be treated with dignity and thus incorrectly link their refusal to mention demeaning treatment with Jesus' willingness to become a servant to humankind (Phil 2:7). This attitude fails to recognize Jesus' pronouncements of woe and judgment on those who reject him and his mission (Matt 11:20–24), as well as on those who are unjust (Matt 23:33–35), immoral (Herod, Mark 8:15), or who distort the law for their own benefit (Matt 15:3–6). Refusing to accept unjust treatment is to take a moral stand against it just as Jesus did.

A proper Christian view is that all people are equally valuable irrespective of their abilities, because all people are loved and valued by God. To have a servant's heart is to be willing to serve or minister to one another, recognizing the equal value of all persons. Servants do the good works that God has ordained for them (Eph 2:10), but they may say no to the good works that *others* have ordained for them (usually for their own personal benefit). God's servants are givers, but they should give in the way that God leads and refuse to be used by the takers of this world. Selfish people take the lives of others for their own benefit. If Christians give in to them, they are actually unable to accomplish what God would have them do and thus fail to live in God's will. This failure can be avoided with a proper understanding of humility and Christian servanthood.

MAINTAINING INDIGNATION/RESENTMENT: THE PROPER RESPONSE TO INJUSTICE

If indignation/resentment is the proper moral response to personal injury, and a failure to resent is therefore indicative of an improper attitude of servility or of a moral defect (such as approving of injustice or not caring), then why does resentment have such a bad name? This is the case because resentment is often not a legitimate moral response, but is directed at trivial affronts and sometimes results in excessive negative behavior. However, as Bishop Joseph Butler points out, "It would be a mistake to condemn resentment just because it admits of irrational extensions—so does love for that matter."[26] Resentment itself is not the problem, but its

---

26. Haber, *Forgiveness*, 70.

tendency to overreact and cause people to respond in immoral ways.[27] A simple definition of resentment is anger that one *properly* feels when personally injured. Therefore, if someone wants to make a case against resentment, he must make a case against *justified* anger or indignation rather than petty, irrational, or excessive anger, which are feelings that are clearly morally wrong. As Haber says, "In addition to informing us how to behave in certain situations, morality is concerned with informing us how to feel at various times and what attitudes to take under relevant conditions."[28] Scripture also gives such instruction; examples include the counsel against gloating at the misfortune of others (Prov 24:17), the encouragement to weep with those who weep and rejoice with those who rejoice (Rom 12:15), and the instruction to resist anxiety and cultivate thankfulness (Phil 4:6). Psychologists sometimes say that feelings are neutral in the sense that they are neither right nor wrong; however, that is not the view of Scripture. Feelings may be justified or unjustified, moral or immoral, based on truth or falsehood. Therefore, feelings may need to change accordingly. Resentment may be a justified emotion based on truth and a proper sense of self-worth. To be able to distinguish what is and is not justified in one's own emotional response to personal injury, a person needs to reflect morally as well as pray for God's light and perspective.

Because of the connection between resentment and self-respect, reconciliation at any cost—apart from apology and repentance—may come at the expense of one's very dignity as a human being. Such action can hardly be virtuous or morally correct. If feeling indignation is proper when one sees others harmed, it should be equally proper when the moral wrong is done to oneself. Murphy therefore argues that "forgiveness [in the sense of overcoming all resentment] is acceptable only in cases where it is consistent with self-respect, respect for others as responsible moral agents, and allegiance to the rules of morality (i.e., forgiveness must not involve complicity or acquiescence in wrongdoing)."[29] *So, even philosophers who define forgiveness as overcoming all resentment do not recommend it unconditionally, that is, without proper moral reason.* Haber, for instance, says that repentance is the lone moral reason for

27. Haber, *Forgiveness*, 70.
28. Haber, *Forgiveness*, 78.
29. Murphy and Hampton, *Forgiveness and Mercy*, 19.

forgiveness.[30] Overcoming resentment following repentance, however, is both reasonable and righteous. It is reasonable because the wrongdoer has changed, and it is righteous because it enables reconciliation to take place. In contrast, overcoming resentment in the absence of repentance is unreasonable and unrighteous. It is unreasonable because the resentment is justified, and it is unrighteous because it denies the self-respect of the victim and ignores the well-being of the wrongdoer.

EXPRESSING RESENTMENT/INDIGNATION

Just as one should reflect and pray about proper feelings, one should also reflect and pray about proper actions in response to personal injury. According to Haber, if it makes sense that a context exists in which feeling resentment/indignation is proper, it follows that certain actions have moral value as expressions of resentment/indignation. Certainly there must be a connection between how one feels and how one behaves, for feelings are expressed through actions.[31] There may be times when a relationship may be severed appropriately or other times in which one refuses to do an offender a favor. Whatever the appropriate reaction may be, the important point is that it has *moral value* as an expression of resentment/indignation. The purpose of the action or its expression is to make a statement of morality. No formula exists for deciding which expressions of resentment/indignation are appropriate and which are not; it depends on the nature of the relationship and the severity of the offense.[32] As is so often the case for a Christian, the principle that feeling resentment/indignation can be morally correct may be understood, but he still must seek the Lord for guidance as to the proper way to express feelings in response to injury. As previously stated, one form of expressing resentment that is morally prohibited is revenge.

If in certain situations resentment/indignation is the morally correct response to harmful actions and expression of that resentment is appropriate, then a failure to (in some way) express that resentment is a moral deficiency. When a victim expresses resentment he not only shows self-respect, but respect for the offender as a moral agent. If there is no respect, then one need not bother to respond, demonstrating that the

30. Haber, *Forgiveness*, 7.

31. Haber, *Forgiveness*, 79.

32. Haber, *Forgiveness*, 80.

offender is not cared for or taken seriously. If the victim protests the injury, the offender may well recognize the offense and refrain from repeating it, thus moral good has resulted. On the other hand, if one forgives unconditionally in a word or gesture of absolution, one signifies that all is once again well. This may prevent the moral reformation of the offender.[33] So, resentment/indignation may or may not need to be expressed. It may be properly (morally) expressed as an action (exposing wrongdoing) that promotes truth and human dignity. It also may be properly expressed as an act of care for the moral well-being of the wrongdoer, who is thereby given an opportunity to change his behavior.

Proper actions or reactions vary depending on the severity of the harmful treatment. A person can be injured most by those with whom he is closest. They are the ones to whom vulnerabilities have been exposed and who are counted on for support. Therefore, when one is harmed by another person with whom he or she is intimate, the moral injury is not just an injustice, but a betrayal.[34] Betrayal is painful and personal, and the victim's reaction is therefore stronger because the wound is much deeper. Forgiveness may be given, but trust is rarely fully reestablished in such situations. Full reconciliation cannot be accomplished unless the victim becomes convinced that the offender has truly become a different person from the one who betrayed him.

The preceding discussion demonstrates that any analysis of forgiveness must begin by defining what is meant by the term. If by forgiveness one means the act or utterance of pardoning an offender, the discussion will proceed along certain lines. Whereas, if one means simply the internal act of overcoming resentment (as most philosophers and psychologists do), then the discussion will proceed along different lines. Depending on the situation, forgiveness may or may not be praiseworthy, and even may not be a virtue.[35] To forgive is not a virtue if in doing so one denies his own self-worth; it is a virtue only when given for moral reasons.

33. A. Bash, *Forgiveness and Christian Ethics*, 49; Murphy and Hampton, *Forgiveness and Mercy*, 16; Kolnai, "Forgiveness," 96.

34. Murphy and Hampton, *Forgiveness and Mercy*, 17.

35. Haber, *Forgiveness*, 6.

THERAPEUTIC FORGIVENESS: PROBLEMATIC IN PRACTICE

Therapeutic forgiveness is not only problematic from an ethical point of view, but also from a practical point of view. The therapeutic definition of forgiveness implies that even if one sincerely says the words "I forgive you," forgiveness has not truly taken place until all resentment is gone (the view of Butler, Downie, Murphy, and others).[36] This definition becomes problematic in real life when one desires to forgive as a virtue and cannot, feeling guilty for the inability to forgive. Another problematic situation exists when the victim states that he has forgiven when in fact he knows that resentment is still present, leading to feelings of hypocrisy and guilt. On the other hand, if a victim refuses to be hypocritical by refusing to claim internal forgiveness that has not actually taken place, he is left in the uncomfortable position of being seen as bitter and unforgiving. Thus the therapeutic definition creates multiple practical problems for the victim: he may want to forgive, thinking it is the right thing to do, but be unable to rid himself of all resentment and therefore feel guilt for his inability to forgive. If he is open and honest, admitting his inability or unwillingness to forgive, he risks being criticized and considered a bitter and unforgiving person. But if he says he has forgiven when he knows that all resentment is not gone, he feels hypocritical *and* guilty. Based on these practical problems, Haber would modify the requirement of overcoming all resentment by saying that when a speaker states forgiveness, he need not have overcome *all* resentment. Rather, he would be stating that he is willing to *try* to overcome it.[37] Instead of redefining the practice of forgiveness, however, would it not be better to take the difficulties as a clue that something is amiss? What is amiss is that ridding oneself of negative emotion is to deny this sense of justice and self-worth. A modification of the therapeutic forgiveness concept based on the reality of the difficulty (or perhaps the impossibility) of ridding oneself of all negative emotion is comparable to saying that forgiveness is good, but because it is so difficult to practice, the meaning of forgiveness should be changed so it becomes not so difficult.

In contrast, biblical forgiveness is clearly defined and is a willful choice—less related to feelings, positive or negative. It is a moral choice, based on repentance, to remove the offense that prevents reconciliation.

36. Haber, *Forgiveness*, 6–7.

37. Haber, *Forgiveness*, 7.

It is a commitment to overcome resentment (which may be a process) and be reconciled. If feelings of resentment reemerge as the relationship is being restored, the victim does not have to feel hypocritical or unforgiving. It does not change the fact that forgiveness has been given.

DEALING WITH ANGER AND PAIN

A victim should certainly work to let go (rid himself) of destructive, malicious, or vindictive feelings, but not let go of accurate moral judgments. Letting go may bring some relief from the personal suffering caused by these unpleasant feelings. More important, though, one should resist these destructive feelings so that, from a Christian perspective, one may have a pure heart and "be holy as the Lord is holy" (Lev 19:2). People may not be wholly responsible for or in control of their emotional reactions in all situations, but Christians are responsible for seeking to cultivate certain habits and feelings over time.[38] A first step is often to express the feelings to God in prayer. As Volf and many others have observed, "In the imprecatory psalms torrents of rage have been allowed to flow freely. . . . The main message is that rage belongs before God—not in the . . . form of a confession, but as a pre-reflective outburst from the depths of the soul."[39] In the presence of God, hate may begin to recede and the seed is planted for the possibility of forgiveness.[40] Forgiveness is possible only when the sinned-against becomes *willing* to forgive, if the one who has harmed him repents. Rage must be allowed to express itself and then to subside in the light of God's care and ultimate justice. Only then can a *willingness* to forgive (should the offender repent) be cultivated.

Resentment and anger are unpleasant emotions. They are burdensome in that they weigh people down, making life harder instead of light, joyful, and free. Unfortunately, the sinned-against (especially those who are abused, abandoned, or betrayed by a loved one) often carry a heavy burden in spite of a desire for a pure heart, a commitment to non-retaliation, and even praying for the offender. Although resentment is unpleasant and burdensome, that does not mean it is morally right to do away with it altogether. If one no longer resents the harmful action, it may be an indication not of healing, but that he no longer cares. Sometimes it

---

38. MacLachlan, "Forgiveness," 160.

39. Volf, *Exclusion and Embrace*, 124.

40. Volf, *Exclusion and Embrace*, 124.

may be difficult to distinguish between the two. Perhaps the ideal is to continue to feel the anger at the wrong done, that is, to continue to care, yet not feel the personal hurt. But is this possible? To say, "I am healed of the hurt" may in reality mean "I do not care anymore." The Bible indicates that God is grieved when rejected (Jer 3:19–20; Hos 1–2; 11:8–9; Ps 78:40; Luke 19:41; Eph 4:30). Should his people not hurt also? Nowhere does Scripture indicate that all tears are wiped away before the consummation of this present age and the beginning of the new age (Rev 21). The fact that others inflict pain is a part of life that must be recognized and accepted. Therefore, striving to eliminate personal pain may in reality be striving to reach the place of disconnection. It may be incorrect, then, for one to say that since he no longer cares about the wrong done to him, he is healed of the hurt. To say that not caring is morally righteous is also incorrect. Doing away with the burden and being yoked to the Lord so that he carries the load are two different things. One should recognize that in the Christian worldview the world is filled with evildoers, and if one stands up for what is right he will have broken relationships and enemies. Tribulation, including opposition and broken relationships, is an inescapable part of living in a fallen world (John 16:33). The good news is that Christians are promised that when God's kingdom is fully established in eternity, God "will wipe every tear from their eyes. There will be no more death or mourning or crying or pain, for the old order of things [will pass] away" (Rev 21:4). Not all people suffer physical disabilities in this life and not all people are abused, abandoned, or betrayed. Many different kinds of burdens exist, but the promise is that in eternity they will all be lifted. Just as one should seek the Lord's comfort and sustaining presence in physical difficulties, he must seek the Lord's comfort and sustaining presence in emotional pain. The sinned-against is one who suffers. He suffers not only the violation but also the emotional pain associated with being wronged. In addition, removing the burden or pain may be impossible. Therefore, Christians should not strive to eliminate their pain through not caring, but should instead remember that happiness or freedom from pain is not the goal of this life: faithfulness is. Perhaps the time of complete healing comes only when memory is somehow dealt with in the age to come (this idea will be examined in chapter 19). In the meantime, "The LORD is close to the brokenhearted and saves those who are crushed in spirit" (Ps 34:18).

In conclusion, to have a pure heart and be holy, having been abused, abandoned, or betrayed, one must take the proper steps. To purify one's heart, a person must first recognize and express his rage before God. This is the first step toward eliminating any vindictiveness or malicious hatred. But one should retain moral resentment (which usually happens involuntarily) and need not feel guilty because of this moral anger. He should pray and reflect about any actions that need to be taken to protest harmful treatment. Pain, which will diminish with time but probably not be eliminated altogether, should be accepted. In time he should come to the place where he is willing to forgive should the offender repent. Finally, if the offender does repent, he must forgive him and work to eliminate all negative feelings. He should be willing to be reconciled and willing to begin to reestablish trust. These steps are all biblically based and, unlike so-called therapeutic forgiveness, represent a therapeutic healing that is realistic and does not violate any moral principle.

RESENTMENT, BLAME, AND GUILT

Being guilty or blameworthy does not depend on being resented. A person may be blameworthy even if he is not resented by the one harmed. However, before repentance, the injured party *should* blame and properly resent the offender for moral reasons. After repentance and forgiveness, the wrongdoer is still guilty of the wrongful act, even if he is forgiven and no longer resented. Forgiveness, therefore, is not directed toward blame, nor does it remove blame. Then what is forgiveness directed toward?[41] From the biblical perspective, it is directed toward the sin. Pardon removes the sin, which is the moral barrier to reconciliation. It does not eliminate guilt; the offender is still guilty and therefore blameworthy. But, because an offender acknowledges his guilt in repentance, he agrees with the victim and accepts the blame. Because he changes as a person, a new present reality emerges that is different from the past reality. Forgiveness removes the sin as an ongoing and present reality. Reconciliation takes place because the moral barrier is gone. The past does not change; it simply is no longer relevant to the victim. Neither should it be relevant to the offender, because his repentance and forgiveness has entitled him to cast off his burden of guilt feelings. The fact of his past guilt does not change, but the burden of carrying it is removed.

Similarly, reconciliation does not eliminate guilt or blame. If the offender repents and is forgiven, he is relieved of the burden of guilt

41. Haber, *Forgiveness*, 37–39.

feelings (perhaps through his choice of repentance even more than the forgiveness he is granted), but the fact of guilt never changes. Therefore the one who forgives, in forgiving, is not eliminating blame or guilt (if he were, it would be harder to forgive), but is becoming willing to treat the offender *as if* he were not guilty. The sin is symbolically removed, but the facts never change. However, the facts do not have to ever be "mentioned" (KJV) or "remembered" (NIV) again because they have lost their significance (Ezek 18:22; 33:16).

GUILT AND SHAME

Any study of repentance, forgiveness, and reconciliation must address the role of guilt and shame. Both wrongdoers and the wronged experience shame. When one is abused, abandoned, or betrayed by someone greatly loved he feels nervous and experiences shame even though he has done nothing of which to be ashamed. Eventually this false shame will depart, but it is a present reality for many who suffer from the deeds of others. The shame of the wronged one stems from humiliation and is undeserved, as opposed to the shame of the guilty one, which comes from deserved disgrace.[42]

Wrongdoers feel (or should feel) regret and guilt. Jeremiah indicts the Israelites of his generation, saying, "Are they ashamed of their detestable conduct? No, they have no shame at all; they do not even know how to blush" (Jer 6:15; 8:12). There are, of course, qualified differences in guilt that are determined by the nature and severity of the offense, the intent of the offender, the relationship to the wronged one, and the duration of the offense. Guilt is a stain on one's soul that requires repentance to eradicate. It initially lies on the surface, but if accepted and lived with, it becomes embedded deep in the soul.[43] Guilt is serious business, and one should not try to absolve another's guilt apart from his repentance. If God has not absolved someone's guilt, why do humans think they can? Guilt is a powerful force to bring someone to repentance and should not be prevented from doing its work.[44] Healthy guilt that leads to reformation causes one to empathize with his victim. Therefore, for the guilt and

---

42. Park, *Hurt to Healing*, 38.

43. Swinburne, *Responsibility and Atonement*, 75.

44. Swinburne, *Responsibility and Atonement*, 80.

stain on his soul to be removed, he needs absolution from the one he has harmed. Third-party forgiveness is not sufficient.[45]

When one speaks of removing guilt, he should recognize that the word guilt is a metonym for guilty feelings. Objective guilt, the historical fact that one committed a certain act, cannot be removed without tampering with truth. However, subjective guilt, the feelings associated with the act, can and should be removed by repentance and forgiveness. The sinner then is justified, meaning he is restored to right standing (reconciled). He is made righteous (made right—put in right standing) in that the stain of his guilt is gone. He is cleansed (1 Cor 6:11) and restored just as if he had never sinned. This is not the same as being declared not guilty. In justification, one is made righteous, put in right standing, in spite of being guilty: this is forgiveness. He is never declared not guilty— that is legal fiction. The debt metaphor helps make this distinction clear. The sin is removed in the same way that a debt is wiped out through being pardoned. The debt no longer exists because it is forgiven, but that does not mean that the debt was never incurred. Someone who has never sinned has a clean slate. Someone who has sinned, repented, and been forgiven also has a clean slate. He has the same standing as the one who never sinned, who never incurred a debt. Once a debt is removed and the ledger is wiped clean, one does not need to carry the burden of being in debt because the debt no longer exists. Zephaniah 3:11 says, "On that day you, Jerusalem, will not be put to shame for all the wrongs you have done to me." The reason that there need be no shame, because the transgressions occur no more (repentance), is explained in the clauses that follow (vv. 12–13).

A forgiving victim may be very helpful to a truly repentant offender, who may hate himself for what he has done and may have trouble believing in his own new status as a changed person. The gift of forgiveness helps him recognize that he still has worth. It may even prevent self-loathing or self-destruction, creating instead the hope that he is indeed worth saving. This forgiveness is, of course, what God offers to humankind.[46] It is powerful and transformative and motivates a repentant person not to let down the one who has so graciously believed in his worth. When seen from this perspective, to forgive "*as God forgives*" is indeed a privilege.

---

45. Haber, *Forgiveness*, 44, 49.
46. Murphy and Hampton, *Forgiveness and Mercy*, 86–87.

CHAPTER 10 STUDY QUESTIONS

The Moral Significance of Resentment

1. What do feelings of anger/resentment express?

2. What is the difference between malicious hatred and moral hatred?

Resentment, Indignation, and Self-Worth

1. What is the difference between resentment and indignation?

2. Describe the relationship between resentment and self-worth.

Resentment versus Animosity, Hatred, and Vindictiveness

1. Does resentment necessarily produce ill will, animosity, or vindictiveness?

2. What is the root cause of personal (as distinguished from moral) hatred?

3. Why are malice and spite morally wrong?

4. What is the first step toward letting go of personal hatred? To whom should hatred be vented?

5. Could it be appropriate to say that one is not yet ready or able to forgive a repentant offender?

6. What does it mean that, if the wrongdoer has not repented, "forgiveness cannot be granted without harming morality"?

7. Can therapeutic forgiveness be willed in the absence of repentance by the wrongdoer?

Servant versus Servile

1. How do the concepts of servanthood and servility differ?

2. How does being able to distinguish these two concepts guide a Christian's behavior?

Maintaining Indignation/Resentment: The Proper Response to Injustice

1. What is the difference between legitimate, moral resentment and resentment that is immoral?

2. Why is reconciliation at any cost, apart from apology or repentance, not morally correct?

3. Why is overcoming resentment following repentance both reasonable and righteous?

Expressing Resentment/Indignation

1. Why should victims sometimes take action to express resentment/indignation?

2. What form of resentment is morally forbidden for Christians?

3. How does expressing resentment show concern for the offender?

Therapeutic Forgiveness: Problematic in Practice

1. What practical problems does therapeutic forgiveness create for the victim?

2. How does biblical forgiveness avoid these problems?

Dealing with Anger and Pain

1. Why should Christians seek to eliminate destructive, malicious, or vindictive feelings?

2. How is one to handle legitimate feelings of resentment that are nevertheless unpleasant and burdensome?

3. Summarize the steps toward purifying one's heart after being abandoned or betrayed.

Resentment, Blame, and Guilt

1. Does receiving forgiveness make the offender no longer guilty?

Guilt and Shame

1. Why and in what sense do both the wronged and wrongdoers experience shame?

2. Apart from repentance, why should one not attempt to absolve another's guilt?

3. How does the debt metaphor illustrate that a person is still guilty even if the sin (debt) is removed?

4. How does the gift of forgiveness help a repentant offender?

11

Hate the Sin and Love the Sinner

REGARDING ETHICAL ISSUES INVOLVED in damaged human relationships, consider the popular maxim "hate the sin but love the sinner." The inference is that God does this, but is this the case? Some models of forgiveness are built on this idea, which is not stated in Scripture, but is based on Augustine's statement in Letter 211, paragraph 11. In contrast, Scripture indicates that a person is defined by his actions and not by his words, as the parable of the two sons illustrates (Matt 21:28–32). Suggesting that a person can be separated from his actions is not only unbiblical, but also nonsensical. One "cannot know with any degree of certainty who is a virtuous person apart from his behavior."[1] Sin and sinner simply cannot be separated, because a person cannot be separated from his actions.[2] One who loves justice will condemn the doer of the wrong as well as the wrong itself. Sin cannot occur without the doer; therefore the doer of the sin should indeed be condemned.[3]

To morally hate a person is to hate not just his actions, but who he has become as a result of his actions. One then hates who the evildoer is; one hates the evil person.[4] God himself is spoken of as hating evil persons because he hates evil and loves justice: "The LORD examines the righteous, but the wicked, those who love violence, he hates with a passion.

1. Haber, *Forgiveness*, 13.
2. Haber, *Forgiveness*, 98.
3. Volf, *Free of Charge*, 141.
4. Murphy and Hampton, *Forgiveness and Mercy*, 24–25, 146.

. . . For the LORD is righteous, he loves justice" (Ps 11:5, 7); "The LORD detests all the proud of heart. Be sure of this: They will not go unpunished" (Prov 16:5). If a person's actions are arrogant, he is arrogant. If a person's actions are evil, he is evil (though perhaps not beyond reform). Jean Hampton, in *Forgiveness and Mercy*, maintains that moral hatred blocks forgiveness and reconciliation because moral hatred "involves the belief that [the evildoer] is (to some degree) a bad [person] and an enemy whom one must not welcome back."[5] Scripture is filled with such examples.

Hating evil and evil persons does not preclude loving them in the sense of desiring the evildoer's reformation and salvation. In other words, a distinction may logically be made between (1) moral love (desire for good) and (2) moral hatred (hatred of what is evil), but that distinction is not logical when made between sin and sinner (a person and his deeds). Evil and the one who does evil both fall into the second category—that which is evil. One cannot both hate and love the same thing at the same time in the *ordinary* sense of the words love and hate. However, God can hate evil (and therefore persons who have become evil) and still love such persons in the sense of desiring their reform. This love proceeds from who he is and not from the object of his love. This is a subtle but important distinction. Love for a sinner, which means hope for his reformation, precludes forgiving apart from his repentance.

A distinction can thus be made between moral hatred and moral love, and both feelings can be held simultaneously. But a distinction cannot be made between persons and their actions, and therefore one cannot love an evil person while simultaneously hating his evil deeds. This is important to understand for the following reason: If a person wants to be obedient and pleasing to God, and knows that he hates the evil person and not just that person's evil deed, he may feel false guilt because of this hatred. However, he should not experience guilt because this hatred is moral hatred directed against that which is evil, both action and person. He may attempt to talk himself into loving the person in order to be like what he thinks God would have him be—one who has a pure heart and is holy. God desires that his people be like him in that he hates evil (evil deeds and persons who have become evil), yet is pure in heart, desiring the repentance, salvation, and restoration of the evil person. When a Christian understands that he can dislike another person and maintain

---

5. Murphy and Hampton, *Forgiveness and Mercy*, 147.

a pure heart as long as he still desires that person's reform and salvation, he can be freed of false guilt and fruitless attempts to feel love for someone he in fact abhors. He may also be freed of the hypocrisy, if he has engaged in it, of saying that he loves someone he knows he does not. "Unfortunately," as Jones points out, "we too often have difficulty in loving our enemies precisely because we are afraid they *might* repent. Such was Jonah's problem."[6]

However, when a wrongdoer repents, it is logical to differentiate the person and his former actions. He has rejected and condemned his own actions and committed himself to forsake those actions in the future. Then, and only then, can a *legitimate logical* distinction be made between the sin and the sinner, for he has become a person who will not commit that offense. Forgiveness can only be a response to a change of heart; only then can the deed be separated from the agent.[7] Otherwise, separation between sin and sinner is simply fictitious.[8] In other words, a person cannot be dissociated from his actions until he dissociates himself from them. When that happens, the offended is free to follow Augustine's advice and love the sinner by forgiving him without condoning the sin. Forgiveness in this case clearly does not condone the sin.[9] In contrast, if prior to repentance one *says* that he is forgiving the sinner but not the sin, his action of forgiving indicates otherwise. The offender knows he has gotten away with his deeds. Actions (accepting and reconciling) always speak louder than words (condemning the sin). As Hampton contends, Christianity does not require that one maintain faith in everyone's decency, and clearly includes the idea that some people are beyond redemption.[10] What Christianity does require is that one forsake malicious hatred (Matt 5:23), both desiring and being willing to respond to repentance. People cannot *will* a favorable belief about someone who does not deserve it without being dishonest and without forsaking their own integrity.[11]

Forgiveness based on love of sinner and hate of sin is only pretend forgiveness, for the moral hatred will resurface. A genuine change of heart on the part of the victim depends on a genuine change of heart

---

6. L. Jones, *Embodying Forgiveness*, 265.

7. Benn, "Forgiveness and Loyalty," 372.

8. Kolnai, "Forgiveness," 97.

9. Murphy and Hampton, *Forgiveness and Mercy*, 24–25.

10. Murphy and Hampton, *Forgiveness and Mercy*, 153.

11. Murphy and Hampton, *Forgiveness and Mercy*, 154.

from the sinner.[12] After the repentance of the offender, the sinned-against may have a real change of heart, because there is a genuine reason for it. In such a situation, forgiveness is both *reasonable* and *desirable* as a moral good.

Another criticism of Augustine's dictum is that separating the offender from his act, artificially distinguishing the two, minimizes the power of forgiveness. When a person is forgiven *as a wrongdoer* he is still guilty, still blameworthy, and still a wrongdoer even after he repents. This is why forgiveness is so powerful. It is an undeserved gift that removes the sin along with its stain and its burden. Forgiveness also honors the sinner in that he is recognized as a responsible person and believed to be capable of better. (Small children and those who are not wholly rational due to mental illness are not in need of forgiveness because they are not fully culpable.)[13] A person may be the sum of his actions, but after being forgiven, some actions (sins) are removed and the forgiven one is therefore a different person. What an amazing and transformative gift is forgiveness!

In summary, Scripture maintains that God can simultaneously love and hate in a certain sense. He judicially and morally hates evil, and if a person *is* evil by virtue of his evil actions, he is hated by God (Prov 6:16, 19; Hos 9:15; Mal 1:3). Yet one who is hated in this sense can also be loved in the biblical sense of desiring that the evil one repent and be transformed by the power of God. The alternative would be for God to desire, as people sometimes do, that an evil person not repent and therefore be consigned to the fires of hell, but Scripture tells us that he desires that all men be saved (1 Tim 2:4). This simultaneous love and hate is not the Augustinian concept of hating the sin and loving the sinner, which dissociates a person from his sin. God does not dissociate people from their sins. That simply cannot be done, for in reality a person is responsible for his sin, and a person's actions indicate what kind of a person he has chosen to be. Augustine's dictum involves a subtle change from the biblical position of simultaneous love and hate. The result of this subtle change is that people think they are emulating God when they act loving and accept a person in spite of evil actions. This acceptance, rather than confrontation or rejection, fails to make a godly stand on behalf of righteousness, and even encourages continued sin; therefore, *it is not loving.* Separation from

---

12. Murphy and Hampton, *Forgiveness and Mercy*, 154.

13. MacLachlan, "Forgiveness," 21.

persons (unbelievers in 2 Cor 6:14–18; Eph 5:6–7; 2 John 10; and disobedient believers in Rom 16:17; 2 Thess 3:6; Titus 3:10–11) in the early church follows God's example of rejecting evildoers. As Jer 6:29–30 says in reference to some of the people of Israel, "The bellows blow fiercely to burn away the lead with fire, but the refining goes on in vain; the wicked are not purged out. They are called rejected silver, because the LORD has rejected them." Later, Jeremiah is instructed by God no less than three times not to even pray for those whom God has rejected (Jer 7:16; 11:14; 14:11).

It has sometimes been suggested that loving the sinner but hating the sin should lead to distinguishing between forgiving the wrongdoer and forgiving the deed. However, this too is nonsensical. Scripture speaks of forgiveness in both ways, and they are interchangeable (Gen 50:17; Exod 34:7; Mark 3:29; Luke 6:37; Eph 1:7). As stated in chapter 3, if the direct object of the verb forgive is sins, then the reference is to the removal of sin. If the direct object is the sinner, then the reference is to setting the sinner free from sin—its power or its consequences.

CHAPTER 11 STUDY QUESTIONS

1. Where did the maxim "hate the sin but love the sinner" originate?

2. What biblical parable indicates that a person is defined by his actions?

3. If one hates evil and evil persons, in what sense can they still love them?

4. Simultaneously held moral hatred and moral love frees one from what two emotions?

5. When is it logical to draw a distinction between a person and his actions?

6. Why does artificially distinguishing between sin and sinner minimize the power of forgiveness? How can Augustine's maxim lead to non-loving behavior?

12

Retribution and Discipline

ANOTHER TOPIC THAT MUST be addressed from an ethical perspective concerns the proper practice of retribution, or vengeance, in human relationships. Like forgiveness, abandoning retribution must, in a moral context, address the question of justice. "To argue that [people] have a duty to forgive all wrongdoers unconditionally would be, in a sense, to deny the legitimacy of retributive justice altogether."[1] Retribution is not morally wrong, as shown by the fact that in the Bible (both the OT and NT: Deut 32:35; Rom 12:19) God says, "Vengeance is mine." However, God instructs his people not to exact vengeance themselves; it is better left to the One who knows all and loves perfectly.[2] Justice as it relates to repentance and forgiveness was addressed in Part I, which argues that forgiveness in response to repentance does not deny justice. The justice of God refers to fair treatment for all. Within this biblical concept of God's justice, however, is the certainty that God "will by no means clear the guilty" (meaning the unrepentant guilty, Exod 34:6–7; Num 14:18; Deut 5:11; Nah 1:2–3) and the certainty that the gift of forgiveness is available to all who choose to repent. When forgiveness is granted, the demands of *retributive* justice must remain unsatisfied,[3] but God's justice (fair play) is not violated. As stated in Part I concerning justice, Christians sometimes say that they want God's mercy and not his justice as if the two are

1. MacLachlan, "Forgiveness," 175.
2. Murphy and Hampton, *Forgiveness and Mercy*, 163.
3. Volf, *Exclusion and Embrace*, 224.

opposites. But mercy and justice are not at odds. The opposite of justice is injustice, not mercy. In other words, justice does not *require* retribution. This section will reflect on the ethical relationships between forgiveness, retribution, and justice. It will be argued that retribution is a legitimate, if optional, part of justice and in some cases may be necessary even following repentance and forgiveness.

The desire for retribution—to punish or bring an offender down—may be motivated either by ill will and malicious hatred or by a deep sense of justice. In either case, from a Christian perspective, it should not be acted out (Deut 32:35; Rom 12:19). Its righteous dimension may come from the feeling that "another person's level of well-being is undeserved or ill-gotten (perhaps at one's own expense), and that a reduction in that well-being is simply a matter of justice."[4] This righteous dimension is illustrated when crime victims whose lives have been ruined call for harsh sentences. They express their desires publicly and without shame. These desires are natural, understandable, and deserving of respect, because they are neither immoral nor irrational.[5] Because they are based on a sense of justice they should not be dismissed with self-righteous moral or religious clichés. Murphy says that to label victims spiteful or malicious is "indecently insensitive and presumptuous."[6] Victims should certainly not be charged with the so-called vice of being unforgiving; such charges only add to the victim's pain. If the victim has not been able to think through his feelings ethically or morally, then, in the face of such charges, he may become laden with false guilt.[7] Such a victim may be wounded by the crime, wounded again by labels of self-righteous and presumptuous people, and wounded yet again by his own false sense of guilt, when, in fact, the desire for retributive justice comes "from the thoroughly unmodern view that there is such a thing as evil in the world," as well as a strong sense of justice and justified feelings.[8]

Forgiveness forgoes punishment as a means of retribution, but it may not always forgo such consequences as a form of discipline. Some

4. Murphy and Hampton, *Forgiveness and Mercy*, 89.
5. Murphy and Hampton, *Forgiveness and Mercy*, 90.
6. Murphy and Hampton, *Forgiveness and Mercy*, 91, 92.
7. Murphy and Hampton, *Forgiveness and Mercy*, 92.
8. Murphy and Hampton, *Forgiveness and Mercy*, 92.

discipline or consequence is desirable if it is in the best interest of the offender. This is especially true for children.[9]

In Scripture, the concept of judgment denotes both God's retributive justice (also called vengeance, Deut 32:35; Rom 12:19; Heb 10:30; see also Ps 94:1–2; Rom 11:22; 1 Thess 4:6; Rev 6:10) and his disciplinary actions (Prov 3:11–12; Heb 12:5–6) on behalf of his people. Do not confuse retribution with discipline, and take care to distinguish which is meant within a narrative. Consequences as discipline are not precluded by forgiveness. Consider the story of the Israelites' refusal to enter the Promised Land (Deut 1:41–45). After the judgment against that generation is announced, the people decide to enter the land and fight. Moses warns them that God will not be with them and that they will be defeated; they need to accept the consequences of their initial failure—anything else would be disobedience. When punishment as discipline is needed for the good of the offender or for the upholding of the moral good (which is the responsibility of the state and other organizations such as the church), one must not forgo punishment in the name of forgiveness. *This is a difficult concept because forgiveness does indeed forgo punishment as retribution in the name of justice.* To punish as well as forgive is the exception to the rule and is done only to uphold the moral good or for the necessary discipline of the offender. In general, this homage to righteousness is not necessary when contrition and repentance are complete.

Hampton argues that retribution differs from revenge. She says, "A commitment [to retribution] may be a commitment to asserting moral truth in the face of its denial."[10] If one person has value equal to that of their assailant, then that moral truth is asserted by punishing the offender. In victimizing another, the wrongdoer declares himself to be elevated over the other. He has acted as a superior who deems it appropriate to use or abuse another for his own purposes—a false moral claim. Punishment asserts the victim's value, thereby correcting the false claim. Moral truth is spoken whether or not the abuser listens or embraces it. Retribution is not, in the words of Moberly, "a process to effect future reformation; it is the suffering which has been deserved by past sin. To make it anything else than this is to destroy its essential character." The punishment is "a

9. Volf, *Free of Charge*, 170.

10. Murphy and Hampton, *Forgiveness and Mercy*, 125.

public declaration or manifestation on behalf of righteousness. . . . It exhibits righteousness to all those who stand by and look on."[11]

Repentance acknowledges guilt and with it accepts the deserved punishment. When criminals press vehemently and publicly for their release (or preachers for their reinstatement) based on repentance and faith, this behavior indicates that they have not truly repented. The truly penitent would accept that he is getting the punishment he deserves. Asking for forgiveness is not the same thing as expecting no consequences for one's wrongdoing. True repentance and humility exclude these self-seeking expectations.[12] Repentance that "would shrink back from shame and suffering" is incomplete.[13] True repentance is seen in the parable of the prodigal son, who did not expect to be restored to sonship (Luke 15:18–19).[14]

A desire for retribution (justice) as a principle, then, is permissible (if not mandatory) as the response of a victim to wrongdoing (e.g., Jer 11:20; 20:12)[15]. That does not mean it is morally permissible for a person to act on that desire. The state must make and enforce the law. A victim certainly has a responsibility to judge evil, speak out against it, and seek justice through the law. Not doing so is apathy or cowardice rather than generosity; it condones or excuses. Morally reflective persons should take the time to consider their feelings and the courses of action upon which these feelings tempt or lead them.[16] They should also remember that only God knows all the facts and judges perfectly.

Another argument for legal retribution is that it deters crime and protects others from crime.[17] This is sometimes true in individual relationships as well. If a husband yells harshly at his wife telling her to do something for him and apologizes when she objects to his treatment, she may do well to forgive him, but she also might be wise not to do the thing demanded as a deterrent to future abuse. She has asserted her value, correcting his misconception of it. *Apology and repentance may be sufficient for forgiveness and restoration to good favor, but may not necessitate a*

---

11. Moberly, *Atonement and Personality*, 3–4.

12. A. Bash, *Forgiveness and Christian Ethics*, 17.

13. Moberly, *Atonement and Personality*, 38.

14. A. Bash, *Forgiveness and Christian Ethics*, 21.

15. Murphy and Hampton, *Forgiveness and Mercy*, 95.

16. Murphy and Hampton, *Forgiveness and Mercy*, 103.

17. Murphy and Hampton, *Forgiveness and Mercy*, 139.

return to the former state of affairs. It is in this sense that an offender may have to bear the consequences of his actions in spite of being granted forgiveness.

The desire for retribution may come from multiple sources. It may come from the desire to protect oneself from future abuse, as in the previous example.[18] It may come from malicious hatred, or from concern to help the offender change, or from the desire to protect others.[19] Sometimes the desire for retribution may not involve emotion at all. It may be based on aversion to the wrongdoing and come from a simple desire for justice, which asserts that better treatment of the victim is required.[20] In this case, the attention is primarily on the crime and the victim's value rather than on the offender.[21] "In the case of the state any disciplinary purpose is subsidiary. The primary purpose is retributive as justice. The primary effect is intended for society."[22]

In summary, retribution is just, and justice requires it in the absence of repentance. Justice does not, however, require retribution following repentance, but permits forgiveness that forgoes retribution. This forgoing of retribution is logical, because inflicting punishment upon true and full repentance would be pointless.[23] Forgiveness and retribution are not mutually exclusive, for retribution may be necessary, even following forgiveness, to uphold the moral good or for the beneficial discipline of the offender, who needs to bear some consequences for his behavior. "The more ideally complete his penitence, the more [the offender] accepts the penalty."[24]

ULTIMATE JUSTICE

Despite the fact that it is not always attainable, the desire for justice is deeply embedded in humans. The hunger for vindication remains even after many years. A victim's sense of justice may be deeply offended when

18. Murphy and Hampton, *Forgiveness and Mercy*, 139.

19. Murphy and Hampton, *Forgiveness and Mercy*, 139.

20. Murphy and Hampton, *Forgiveness and Mercy*, 132.

21. Murphy and Hampton, *Forgiveness and Mercy*, 143.

22. Moberly, *Atonement and Personality*, 8.

23. Moberly, *Atonement and Personality*, 40.

24. Moberly, *Atonement and Personality*, 21.

instructed to forgive in the absence of repentance. It may even be repugnant and is usually impossible. As Bash says:

> There are . . . genuine psychological difficulties that prevent many victims from reaching a point where they may "forgive" an unrepentant offender. In such cases, a person who has been wronged may try to suggest to themselves that the wrongdoing was not so severe as it had seemed, that it would be "Christian" to "forgive and forget" and that others are in worse plights and "therefore" it would be wrong to continue to reflect on one's own situation. This may be especially so if the victim is being told to "move on" and "get on with life." What the victim may lose in such a scenario is truth (that the victim has been wronged), psychological integrity (that the victim is deeply hurt or injured), and the victim may experience guilt at being unable both to achieve the goals for which the victim longs and to heed the well-meaning (but foolish) advice the victim has been receiving. At best, the supposed "forgiveness" is a sleight of hand, a self-administered therapeutic tool to recover peace of mind that in the long term will not promote or effect psychological health and well-being.[25]

A scriptural example of this desire for vindication and justice is seen as Paul discusses Alexander. "Alexander the metalworker did me a great deal of harm. The Lord will repay him for what he has done. You too should be on your guard against him, because he strongly opposed our message" (2 Tim 4:14–15). The Christian perspective is that God shares a victim's desire for justice (the biblical word used is vengeance, Deut 32:35, 41, 43; Ps 94:1; Isa 34:8; 35:4; 47:3; 59:17; 61:2; Jer 46:10; 50:15, 28; 51:6, 11, 36; Ezek 25:14, 17; Mic 5:15; Luke 21:22; Rom 12:19; 2 Thess 1:8). One day God will bring all to judgment (Rom 14:12; 2 Cor 5:10; Rev 20:11–12) and justice (Exod 34:7 KJV, "[God] will by no means clear the guilty"). His retributive judgment stems from a commitment to justice, but also from his love. In this case it is "the love of the victim which includes a deep-seated commitment to the victim's value."[26] His foremost desire, however, is that he not have to inflict retributive justice, but that each would repent and receive his forgiveness. God "wants all people to be saved and come to a knowledge of the truth" (1 Tim 2:4). Those who have been severely harmed by the acts of another may not be able to

---

25. A. Bash, *Forgiveness and Christian Ethics*, 61.
26. Murphy and Hampton, *Forgiveness and Mercy*, 161.

emulate God in this respect, but they should at least aspire to cultivate God's viewpoint.

A person who desires retribution remains unsatisfied if that desire is not fulfilled. A Christian, however, should be able to abandon that dissatisfaction to a large degree in the knowledge that God is just. He should be content to leave justice to God. Volf argues that non-violence or a refusal to exact vengeance does not come from the belief that a loving God does not judge, but rather from the opposite.

> My thesis that the practice of non-violence requires a belief in divine vengeance will be unpopular with many . . . in the West. . . . [But] it takes the quiet of a suburban home for the birth of the thesis that human non-violence [results from the belief in] God's refusal to judge. In a scorched land, soaked in the blood of the innocent, it will invariably die.[27]

In other words, Volf argues that the lack of belief in a God of vengeance "nourishes violence."[28] The best resource for resisting the temptation to act on one's desire for vengeance is belief in divine justice.[29] Timothy Keller agrees: referencing Volf in his book *The Reason for God*, "If I don't believe that there is a God who will eventually put all things right, I *will* take up the sword and will be sucked into the endless vortex of retaliation. Only if I am sure that there's a God who will right all wrongs and settle all accounts perfectly do I have the power to refrain."[30] An essential part of the ability to refuse retaliation is to entrust oneself to the God who judges justly. As Volf says, "The certainty of God's just judgment at the end of history is the presupposition for the renunciation of violence in the middle of it."[31]

Numerous biblical passages make it clear that God will bring final and irrevocable judgment at the end of the age. In Rev 6:10 the martyrs cry out to God, "How long, Sovereign Lord, holy and true, until you judge the inhabitants of the earth and avenge our blood?" The martyrs are not asking for forgiveness for their murderers. They know that final judgment is God's prerogative and will be just. Their prayer is that justice

27. Volf, *Exclusion and Embrace*, 303.
28. Volf, *Exclusion and Embrace*, 303.
29. Volf, *Exclusion and Embrace*, 303.
30. Keller, *Reason for God*, 77.
31. Volf, *Exclusion and Embrace*, 302.

would come sooner rather than later. None is rebuked for this prayer, and each is given a white robe and told they must wait a little longer.[32]

For smaller matters than the blood of the innocent, one may even the score without inflicting retributive hurt. To decline to do something helpful for someone who has been mean may be an appropriate response, whereas being mean to him in return is not morally appropriate. Similarly, avoiding the wrongdoer may be reasonable in the absence of his repentance in order to avoid the appearance of condonation as well as to protect oneself from further hurt. In everyday life there are endless ways to even the score, make a protest, or maintain self-respect, but when serious harm has been done, such ways rarely exist. It may be impossible or much too costly to get even.[33] Knowing how to handle small interpersonal problems is a matter of wisdom, and from the Christian perspective wisdom is promised to those who ask. "If any of you lacks wisdom, you should ask God, who gives generously to all without finding fault, and it will be given to you" (Jas 1:5).

It should be recognized, however, that punishment does not always satisfy justice. Retribution is compelling as an appropriate justice for only some offenses—like stealing a car or robbing a bank. As Volf points out, "Magnify the crime sufficiently, and punishment leaves us unsatisfied."[34] For great crimes punishment cannot create the sense that justice has been done. For example, what would be a sufficient punishment for Joseph Stalin, who murdered twenty million people? Retribution fails justice before the enormity of such crimes[35] and reveals that in this world justice is often illusory. Moberly also acknowledges this truth, saying, "No conceivable equality between wrong done and pain suffered, could in itself so compensate as to cancel, or atone for, wrong."[36]

LEGAL JUSTICE AND THE STATE

In the pursuit of retributive justice one must distinguish between personal relationships and the authority of the state. Romans 13:4 declares that civil magistrates "are God's servants, agents of wrath to bring punishment

32. Carson, *Love in Hard Places*, 83.
33. Murphy and Hampton, *Forgiveness and Mercy*, 104.
34. Volf, *Free of Charge*, 135.
35. Volf, *Free of Charge*, 135.
36. Moberly, *Atonement and Personality*, 18.

on the wrongdoer." There is no suggestion that the state is to forgive or pardon the wrongdoer, even though these verses immediately follow the insistence that Christians are to leave vengeance to the Lord (Rom 12:19). The state is to pursue justice, and, by implication, if the state's representative is a Christian, he should recognize that in his position of authority as a servant of the state (and therefore of God), retributive justice takes precedence.[37] Without a system of retributive justice there would be little way to struggle against oppression and injustice.[38] As Volf says, "The attempt to transcend judgment . . . does not eliminate but enthrones violence."[39] N. T. Wright agrees: "God wants the world to be governed because he wants people to live in peace and justice, and if you don't have structures of justice, then the bullies, the extortionists, and the rest will always win."[40]

Forgiveness involves a personal reaction to wrongdoing, but impersonal mechanisms fulfill the demands of justice in criminal cases. A wrongdoer may repent and a victim may forgive, yet let the mechanisms proceed as they ought.[41] Objections to forgiveness may not be relevant because retributive justice proceeds anyway. "An individual's forgiveness and the state's punishment are compatible."[42] The state does not mete out the grace of God, although there are sometimes provisions for pardon. As Volf says, "Is wrath against injustice appropriate? Yes! Must the perpetrators be restrained? By all means! Is punishment for the violation necessary? Probably. But all these indispensable actions against injustice must be situated in the framework of the will to embrace the unjust."[43] What Volf calls the "will to embrace" is the personal willingness, even desire, to forgive in response to repentance.

Although the state insists upon justice, it is rarely, if ever, perfect. Only God knows the way things really were, and one day he will proclaim it (Rom 2:2, 5). Human beings know only partially and therefore can judge and punish only inadequately. God, however, makes infallible

37. Carson, *Love in Hard Places*, 82.

38. Volf, *Exclusion and Embrace*, 290.

39. Volf, *Exclusion and Embrace*, 290.

40. N. T. Wright, *Acts for Everyone*, 168.

41. MacLachlan, "Forgiveness," 134, 136.

42. Volf, *Free of Charge*, 171.

43. Volf, *Exclusion and Embrace*, 224.

judgments.[44] To reconstruct the past as it actually occurred, independent of a particular standpoint, is impossible for humans. Only God can do this,[45] and one day he will.

MERCY AND PARDON

In addition to the place of retribution, any discussion of the ethics of forgiveness must analyze the place of mercy and its relationship to justice and forgiveness. First, let us clarify the concept of mercy. What does it mean to be merciful?

It is tempting to argue that if mercy is a tempering of justice, then mercy requires a departure from justice. Thus, to be merciful is possibly to be unjust. However, to be unjust is a vice, not a virtue; therefore, by this argument mercy is also a vice—a product of dangerous sentimentality.[46] (This line of reasoning lies behind the penal substitution theory of the atonement, which claims that God had to punish someone for sin or he would be guilty of injustice. Therefore, he punished innocent Jesus as a substitute for guilty humankind, as if that could be just.)[47] But showing mercy is not a departure from justice. It would only be a denial of justice if, under the exact same circumstances, one offender was arbitrarily shown mercy and another was not. Justice is fair play, and arbitrarily dispensing mercy to one and not to another is not fair.

Murphy says, "To be merciful is to treat a person less harshly than, given certain rules, one has a right to treat that person."[48] Mercy means that the wrongdoer is punished less than he *deserves*. If a defendant convicted of vehicular homicide had killed his own child, and another defendant is convicted of murder in cold blood, the parent would surely receive a lesser sentence or none at all. He is not being shown mercy, but is rather being treated appropriately under the circumstances. The basic demand of justice is that like cases be treated alike; a hardened criminal may be given a harsher sentence than a first-time offender. The persons and/or circumstances are different, therefore making the demands of justice different. Other circumstances may also require the tempering

44. Volf, *Exclusion and Embrace*, 243.
45. Volf, *Exclusion and Embrace*, 244.
46. Murphy and Hampton, *Forgiveness and Mercy*, 167.
47. Chandler, *Victorious Substitution*, 23.
48. Murphy and Hampton, *Forgiveness and Mercy*, 20.

of retributive justice, which is not really showing mercy, but just acting appropriately under the circumstances. For example, a mother may be given a suspended sentence because if she is imprisoned, her children would have no one to care for them.[49]

If morality is to be maintained when God or anyone else shows mercy, the mercy must be morally relevant and based on good reason, repentance being the most obvious. As previously stated, repentance as a moral reason for showing mercy is applicable in interpersonal relationships, but not always in an institutional role where the one in authority is expected and/or required to carry out retributive justice.[50]

God is said to be merciful, willing to punish less than deserved or not at all. But that does not mean that he always shows mercy. Exodus 33:19 (KJV) says, "[I] will be gracious to whom I will be gracious, and will show mercy on whom I will show mercy." This verse does not mean that God is capricious like the pagan gods, but that mercy is his prerogative. He will not be criticized for showing mercy, for not exacting punishment. Neither is he obligated to show mercy. What determines his will in extending mercy or not doing so? It is the repentance or lack thereof on the part of the offender, as explained in Part I. In other words, God chooses to show mercy when it is the right (righteous) thing to do. His acts of mercy proceed from his love and his righteousness. Forgiveness following repentance is therefore right, just, moral, and merciful. Forgiveness is always an act of mercy, because the forgiver is not obligated to forgive, and the offender does not *deserve* forgiveness. But, as previously discussed, it might not always be right to be merciful in the sense of doing away with all retribution.

Forgiveness, then, is always an act of mercy, but extending mercy is not always an act of forgiveness. Forgiveness must be distinguished from the related concepts of mercy and pardon. Pardon, as an act of mercy, may be granted by one in authority who may not have any personal relation to the offense. In that case it is only an act of pardon and not an act of forgiveness. As R. S. Downie says in his article "Forgiveness," "The crucial difference between pardoning and forgiving is that we pardon as officials in social roles but forgive as persons."[51] If the one who pardons is also the one who has been harmed, then pardon is an act of mercy and

49. Murphy and Hampton, *Forgiveness and Mercy*, 170–71.

50. Haber, *Forgiveness*, 64.

51. Downie, "Forgiveness," 132.

forgiveness. But the two, pardon and forgiveness, are not automatically equivalent. The ability to be merciful in the sense of reducing a punishment (and not in the sense of a change in attitude) is related to one's authority to punish. One is merciful if he gives lenient treatment or no retribution at all when it is deserved and could be justly enforced. Anyone who could legitimately treat an offense harshly is in a position to show mercy. He need not have been personally involved, as is the case with forgiveness. Therefore, pardon and forgiveness are distinguishable even though forgiveness may sometimes include pardon. Pardon is possible because of one's authority, and forgiveness is possible because of one's personal involvement.[52] If a person (or God) is described as merciful or forgiving, this means that *under the morally appropriate circumstances* he is willing to forgo his own right to reject the offender and is willing to show mercy by forgiving and being reconciled.

From an ethical point of view, if one refrains from exacting retribution from someone who has done him harm, he has already been merciful. This mercy should only be extended, however, if the one harmed does not have a duty to retributive justice.[53] In this way, by not exacting vengeance, one is merciful prior to forgiveness or reconciliation. In other words, even if a victim has not yet forgiven the one who did him harm, he is still being merciful if he does not exact retribution to which he is entitled by justice.

If one accepts a therapeutic definition of forgiveness, then forgiveness is not about mercy. It is instead primarily an internal matter involving how one feels about the one who has wronged him. If forgiveness involves a pardon and the removal of the sin, as in the biblical definition, then forgiveness involves extending mercy and is complete when it is granted, regardless of whether the victim still sometimes struggles with resentment. In this case, the mercy that has been shown in forgiveness involves an action that has been completed.[54] Forgiveness in this biblical sense is clearly an act of mercy (even if retribution is enacted by the state or by God), because the offender does not get what he deserves. He deserves the stain and guilt associated with his sin, and he deserves alienation from the one he has harmed. But when forgiven, he is free from the stain and guilt and can be restored to relationship (in some sense) with

---

52. MacLachlan, "Forgiveness," 37–39.

53. Swinburne, *Responsibility and Atonement*, 99.

54. Murphy and Hampton, *Forgiveness and Mercy*, 21.

the one he wronged. He therefore receives less punishment than he deserves, even if he does bear some form of retribution, punishment, and/or consequences. Therapeutic forgiveness, however, might not involve mercy, because the sin is not removed and the parties are not necessarily reconciled. Biblical forgiveness is *always* merciful, because the sin is wiped out and the victim is willing to reconcile.

Pardon eliminates the punishment associated with an offense, whereas forgiveness eliminates the sin itself.[55] Forgiveness involves cleansing and healing and is therefore much more significant than pardon, which only deals with the outward consequences of the sin. Forgiveness deals with the inward consequences/effects of the sin, the "stain," to use the biblical term, on the wrongdoer. As an allegory, consider a tattoo. If a child gets a tattoo, he may be pardoned from the punishment promised by his parents for doing so, but the stain is still there as a part of the child. Forgiveness, however, wipes out the stain too.

To forgive is always merciful, and to pardon is always merciful, but this does not always make it right to forgive or pardon. Why is this? It is because it is always right to be merciful in the sense of desiring the repentance of the offender and being willing to forgive should he repent, but it is not always right to be merciful in the sense of always granting pardon or forgiveness. This is a subtle but crucial distinction concerning the concept of mercy.

Just as pardon is not the same thing as forgiveness (though it is included in biblical forgiveness), so amnesty is also not the same thing as forgiveness. Amnesty is the decision of a government not to prosecute certain crimes. It does not necessarily follow repentance or demonstrate compassion for the wrongdoer. It is offered because the offenders no longer pose a threat to the peace or good of the society based on a change in political circumstances.[56] In the case of South Africa, amnesty was granted for the greater good—the avoidance of civil war and much bloodshed. But it was only granted after confession of wrongs was made. The Commission for Truth and Reconciliation was in practice more about truth and amnesty than repentance and forgiveness.

Contrary to much so-called Christian teaching, mercy is not a contradiction of justice. It is true that when mercy is shown, retribution may be forgone, but showing mercy as well as exacting retribution is the right

---

55. Haber, *Forgiveness*, 14–15.
56. Biggar, "Forgiveness," 210–211.

of the victim (philosophically, morally, and ethically). God may justly do either according to the circumstances and the heart of the sinner. In other words, mercy can have ethical merit only if retribution is a prerogative and not a duty. Retribution is clearly righteous because it is what God promises to do fully at the end of the age. Showing mercy is also clearly righteous because it is also what God often does. Exacting retribution and extending mercy are both God's prerogatives. However, at the end of the age, in order to eliminate all evil in his new world, one could argue that God has the duty to banish those who have not repented and would thus continue in sin and rebellion, thereby extending evil into the renewed creation.

CHAPTER 12 STUDY QUESTIONS

1. In a biblical context, what is the opposite of justice? Does justice require retribution?

2. Is the desire for retribution unrighteous? How are victims with this desire sometimes viewed?

3. In what situation might one who forgives not forgo punishment or retribution?

4. In Scripture, what two actions are both referred to as God's judgment?

5. How can retribution be considered "a commitment to asserting moral truth"?

6. Why would one who has truly repented not shrink from punishment?

7. In what sense does retribution serve as a deterrent for future offenses?

8. Summarize the relationship between retribution, justice, and repentance.

Ultimate Justice

1. What is God's foremost desire regarding retributive justice? Should we emulate this desire?

2. Why should Christians be able to live with the dissatisfaction that comes with injustice?

3. Does retribution, in the sense of evening the score, have a place in everyday Christian life?

4. Can retribution always satisfy justice?

Legal Justice and the State

1. Should retributive justice be abandoned by the state when an offender has repented?

Mercy and Pardon

1. What does it mean to be merciful?

2. How is forgiveness distinguished from mercy and pardon?

3. Why does therapeutic forgiveness not involve showing mercy?

4. How is forgiveness in the biblical sense an act of mercy?

5. Why is it not always right to forgive or pardon?

6. What is amnesty and why is it generally offered?

13

Forbearance, Tolerance, and Condonation

FORBEARANCE

IN REFLECTING ETHICALLY ABOUT the morality of forgiveness, we must distinguish it from forbearance. Scripture instructs Christians to practice forbearance toward one another.

> Therefore, as God's chosen people, holy and dearly loved, clothe yourselves with compassion, kindness, humility, gentleness and patience. *Bear with each other* and forgive one another if any of you has a grievance against someone. Forgive as the Lord forgave you. And over all these virtues put on love, which binds them all together in perfect unity. (Col 3:12–14; emphasis added)

> Be completely humble and gentle; be patient, *bearing with one another* in love. Make every effort to keep the unity of the Spirit through the bond of peace. (Eph 4:2–3; emphasis added)

Colossians instructs God's people not only to forgive as God forgives, but also to "bear with each other" ("forbearing one another" KJV). In much of life, what is needed is not so much forgiveness, but simply what Scripture calls forbearance.[1] Colossians says this forbearance is based on "compassion, kindness, humility, gentleness and patience"— virtues that all proceed from love. Forbearance proceeds from humility, because a humble person recognizes his own weaknesses and failings,

1. Carson, *Love in Hard Places*, 54.

and he also recognizes that only God knows and understands fully the reasons that underlie one's failings. As Cornelius Plantinga says:

> None of us knows the degree to which other human beings bear responsibility for their behavior, the degree to which they "could have helped it." That is one important difference between us and God. So even if, for the purposes of discussion, we call an addict's immoral acts sin, we do so provisionally. Perhaps, if we had all the facts, we might downgrade some of these acts. . . . Indeed, when one observes the rifts and scars of children . . . who have lived in the shadow of their bereft childhood, and who attempt with one addictor after another to relieve their distress and to fill those empty places where love should have settled, only to discover that their addictor keeps enlarging the very void it was meant to fill . . . one hesitates to call all this chaos sin.[2]

Christians may sometimes need to "bear with one another," recognizing the provisional nature of their judgments about sin and righteousness. Often one cannot know the degree to which another could have helped their harmful deeds.[3]

Forbearance is also based on the knowledge of the other person as imperfect, yet decent and worth having relationship with. Sometimes the harm done by another may be small, hardly noticeable, and the best policy is simply to ignore it. In everyday language the word forgive might be used to describe this forbearance, but it is not actually forgiveness. The problem is not eradicated, the sin is not removed; rather, it is overlooked in tolerance for the other person. The behavior is condoned in the sense that it is accepted, without confrontation, as a part of the relationship. It is acceptable, or tolerated, because it involves a small offense, perhaps one of which the offender may not even be aware. Or it may be accepted because the relationship is only casual and nothing more is expected. The offense does not break the relationship, and therefore the relationship is not in need of restoration.

Scripture says that "all have sinned" (Rom 3:23), but it does not follow that all sins are equal. "The rapist's violation and the woman's hatred are equally sins but they are manifestly *not* equal sins."[4] Sometimes people sin in small ways that call for patience and forbearance. These little failings should not be allowed to break fellowship. In Col 3:12–14

2. Hunsinger, "Forgiving Abusive Parents," 72–73.

3. Hunsinger, "Forgiving Abusive Parents," 73.

4. Volf, *Exclusion and Embrace*, 82.

the concern is the unity of believers (3:11). As Volf says, "We must treat many low-grade offenses by disregarding them . . . for life would have to stop if we did not."[5] So forbearance means putting up with the failings and weaknesses of others, as well as with the irritations they may cause. Forbearance is encouraged as a virtue in Scripture—a virtue that comes from humility and compassion and seeks to preserve unity among persons. The arena of forbearance is everyday life, whereas the arena of forgiveness involves serious hurts and harm done. The two concepts should not be confused with each other.

TOLERANCE

Likewise, we must not confuse tolerance with forgiveness. Tolerance, like forbearance, seeks to preserve unity despite a difference of ideas. Unity should be maintained through respect for persons whose ideas differ from one's own. Note that there has been a radical change in the meaning of tolerance in the Western world in the last couple of decades. Previously, a person was tolerant if he insisted that those who disagreed with him had rights no less than his own right to speak his positions freely. Tolerance was respect for people but not necessarily for their ideas. The idea of tolerance actually presupposes disagreement, for one does not have to tolerate someone with whom they are in complete agreement. The new idea of tolerance, however, insists that calling any worldview, religion, or philosophy deficient or untrue is intolerant and disrespectful. As Carson says, "Postmodernism does not call for a broader tolerance; rather, it removes the need for any tolerance."[6] In contrast, the NT condemns false apostles, commands that the man who is sleeping with his stepmother be expelled, declares that it would have been better for Judas Iscariot if he had never been born, assures readers that the evil of Alexander the metalworker will be required of him, and solemnly warns of judgment to come.[7]

---

5. Volf, *Free of Charge*, 168.

6. Carson, *Love in Hard Places*, 147.

7. Carson, *Love in Hard Places*, 149.

CONDONATION

In discussing the ethics of forgiveness, which means examining what makes forgiveness morally right or wrong, we must also separate the concepts of condonation and forgiveness. Condonation means that one deliberately refrains from responding to what he knows to be offensive, wrong, or evil, thereby implicitly accepting the action.[8] He does not confront or make any expression of displeasure. This failure to respond may be due to fear or indifference, or it may be done in the name of tolerance; but by failing to confront and condemn, the wrong *is* condoned. Condonation is not a mere overlooking of small offenses as is the case with forbearance; condonation acquiesces to serious wrongdoing and is therefore complicit and morally offensive. In his article "Forgiveness" Aurel Kolnai says, "Just as it is highly undesirable to live at peace with our own misdeeds and vices, it is, generally speaking, also undesirable to condone those of others."[9] Refusal to condone wrongdoing is also an act of love, for "love cannot help but manifest itself as displeasure."[10]

Condonation often occurs in contractual relationships. If one party's actions break the contractual understanding of the relationship, the other party can restore the contract either by insisting on satisfaction (payback) or punishment (withholding the benefits due the other). If he insists on neither, then he has condoned the behavior, thus establishing new terms in the relationship, or effectively creating a new contract.

Condonation should not be practiced in relationships of love and fellowship in which concern for the well-being of the other person is paramount. God does not condone. How can one avoid condonation if, after confrontation, the other refuses to change his behavior? This is a difficult question. Foremost, disapproval must be made known. If there is no response to disapproval, the relationship becomes damaged and the depth and quality of the love will deteriorate, even if the relationship persists. Unacceptable behavior is accepted in that change cannot be forced; nevertheless, it does not become acceptable. The relationship cannot continue unchanged, for some level of alienation has occurred. If unacceptable behavior persists or expands, the relationship may die a slow death. Acceptance of the inability to change another's behavior may result in acquiescence, because there is simply no choice. *But this*

8. Kolnai, "Forgiveness," 95.

9. Kolnai, "Forgiveness," 96.

10. Moberly, *Atonement and Personality*, 64.

acquiescence is not the same thing as condonation, because displeasure and disapproval have been expressed and the relationship has changed. Sometimes relationships must be continued for some greater good, even as they deteriorate. Deciding when this is the case may be difficult, and persons will often differ in their opinions. Sometimes, however, relationships of love must be broken off if the behavior or betrayal is sufficiently heinous. Approval simply cannot be given because of self-respect or concern for moral integrity.

In order to get along with each other, human beings must put up with much imperfect behavior. As previously discussed, forbearance involves overlooking, patience, and grace, and it is practiced in response to trivial offenses and human frailties. However, forbearance is different from condonation, which is practiced in response to serious offenses and moral wrongs. Both differ sharply from forgiveness.[11] But condonation often masquerades as forgiveness when, in fact, it is "spineless accompliceship . . . plainly at variance with the condemnation of wrong which is implicit in forgiveness."[12] Condemnation and exposure of wrong is always involved in forgiveness, because it is necessarily for an injury that a person is forgiven. To disguise the fact that a moral wrong has been committed is not morally appropriate and certainly is not what God does. Forgiveness does not disguise the wrong but, having exposed and condemned it, chooses to remove the barrier that the injury has caused.[13]

A refusal to condone another's behavior in a relationship of love and fellowship may result in loss of the relationship. Often, the one whose behavior is condemned refuses to continue to have a relationship with the one who expresses disapproval. The choice to express disapproval is especially difficult and painful for the one who refuses to condone, because he risks losing a relationship that is his life. This choice is a decision to suffer rather than sin (1 Pet 3:16–17; 4:1) for to condone would be to sin.

11. Kolnai, "Forgiveness," 96.

12. Kolnai, "Forgiveness," 97.

13. Downie, "Forgiveness," 132.

CHAPTER 13 STUDY QUESTIONS

Forbearance

1. How is forbearance related to humility?

Tolerance

1. How has the meaning of the word tolerance changed in modern times?

2. Does the NT command tolerance or intolerance, according to each definition?

Condonation

1. What is condonation?

2. What is the relationship between condonation and morality? Between condonation and love?

3. What is the difference between forbearance and condonation?

4. How is biblical forgiveness different from forbearance? From condonation?

14

Ethical and Psychological Reasons against Unconditional Forgiveness

THUS FAR, THIS BOOK has established the biblical definition and model of forgiveness and has distinguished it from the modern concept of therapeutic forgiveness, as well as from the related concepts of mercy, pardon, forbearance, tolerance, and condonation. In the biblical model, forgiveness is tendered only after repentance and results in reconciliation. If one thinks ethically about this model and the biblical injunction to forgive as God forgives, one deciphers moral reasons for these biblical guidelines. Chapters 14–17 reflect on why the biblical model is both ethically right and morally righteous.

NO RIGHT TO BE FORGIVEN

In considering the ethical reasons to forgive or not forgive, it must first be understood that the offender does not deserve forgiveness and therefore has no right to it. As Bash says, "The Christian view of forgiveness is that forgiveness is an act of undeserved favour, imitative of the love that God has shown human beings (Eph 4:32; Col 2:13; 3:13) and offered in the confidence that to forgive is a moral good."[1] He also says, "This approach to forgiveness is a development of what is in the Hebrew Scriptures where God, through grace, forgave . . . in response to repentance. . . . Repentance

---

1. A. Bash, *Forgiveness and Christian Ethics*, 24.

preceded forgiveness. There was no guarantee that God would necessarily forgive if a person repented. Forgiveness was a gift of grace, and God did not have to forgive except by God's own choice."[2] Repentance itself does not satisfy the debt nor does it substitute for satisfaction of the debt. The debt is remitted (wiped out) by forgiveness and therefore is never satisfied (paid back). The fact that the debt is not satisfied when the wrongdoer repents is obvious, because if the debt were satisfied, forgiveness would be unnecessary.[3] In other words, forgiveness is neither deserved nor earned because of repentance, but is rather the gift of the forgiver given in the belief that to forgive is morally virtuous.[4]

Philosophy makes a distinction between moral duties and moral virtues.[5] From the philosopher's view, forgiving is not a moral duty for three reasons. First, forgiving is not always morally right, for apart from repentance it becomes condonation of wrongdoing and is therefore also harmful to the wrongdoer. Second, sometimes one finds it impossible to forgive, and a moral duty cannot be impossible because one would be condemned for failing to do the impossible. Third, giving a gift is never a moral duty.[6] However, in biblical teaching (in contrast to secular ethical morality), forgiving when it is morally right (following repentance) is obligatory. If a Christian finds it impossible, he should seek God's promised help. Christians are instructed to forgive as God forgives (Col 3:13). God does not forgive because the repentant offender has a right to forgiveness, but because this is what he chooses to do. Christian choices should follow God's choices. In addition to emulating God's behavior, a Christian should also forgive others because God forgives him. One could say Christians have an obligation to forgive for these reasons, but the obligation is not due to any right of the offender.[7] Forgiveness is always a voluntary act.[8] As Kolnai maintains, there is no right to be forgiven, and there is no obligation to forgive,[9] but one who has received God's forgiveness acts in kind. From a Christian perspective, then, forgiving

2. A. Bash, *Forgiveness and Christian Ethics*, 24.

3. Haber, *Forgiveness*, 11, 101.

4. A. Bash, *Forgiveness and Christian Ethics*, 89.

5. A. Bash, *Forgiveness and Christian Ethics*, 101.

6. A. Bash, *Forgiveness and Christian Ethics*, 102.

7. Swinburne, *Responsibility and Atonement*, 88.

8. Konstan, *Before Forgiveness*, 12; Kolnai, "Forgiveness," 101–2.

9. Biggar, "Forgiveness," 192.

a repentant offender is not just a virtue, but also a duty. Nevertheless, forgiveness is still a gift, but for a Christian it is "a gift [a Christian] would be wrong not to give."[10]

Logically, if forgiveness is a virtue, then, in the right circumstances, one ought to forgive even though no obligation exists.[11] Yet it would be presumptuous for a wrongdoer to judge his victim for not forgiving. Perhaps the debt metaphor illustrates this point more clearly than any other. In that case it would certainly be presumptuous for the debtor to assume that his creditor is obligated to waive his debt because he is sorry he incurred it; the creditor may choose to suffer the loss, but he has no obligation to do so. Therefore, forgiveness should never be taken for granted, and the forgiver should always be recognized for his sacrifice, especially by the one whose debt is remitted. The debt metaphor emphasizes that the victim absorbs rather than exacts the cost. It is surely easier for a debtor to ask that his creditor waive what he owes than for the creditor to give up what he is rightfully owed.[12] To repent is less costly and therefore easier than to forgive. The one who forgives is the one who makes the sacrifice in order for reconciliation to take place. Even if one believes that a person is morally obligated to forgive following repentance, "forgiveness is still never someone's due."[13]

ETHICAL REASONS AGAINST UNCONDITIONAL FORGIVENESS

The earlier study of repentance demonstrates that the biblical pattern of forgiveness is conditional. Repentance is the condition; only then can reconciliation occur. This pattern holds in God's relationship with people, and Scripture instructs God's people to emulate him ("Be ye holy; for I am holy" 1 Pet 1:16 KJV; "forgive as" he forgives). Scripture does not, however, elaborate on why this pattern is holy and righteous. The following section analyzes this pattern and suggests reasons that it is moral as well as psychologically healthy.

Good ethical reasons exist to withhold forgiveness in the absence of repentance. From a moral perspective these reasons fall into two main

---

10. A. Bash, *Forgiveness and Christian Ethics*, 103.

11. Murphy and Hampton, *Forgiveness and Mercy*, 30.

12. MacLachlan, "Forgiveness," 132.

13. Benn, "Forgiveness and Loyalty," 370.

categories: (1) unconditional forgiveness condones the wrongdoing, and (2) unconditional forgiveness harms the wrongdoer.

Concerning the first objection to unconditional forgiveness, Anthony Bash, in his book *Forgiveness and Christian Ethics*, says:

> Wrongdoing is often an expression of oppression or the abuse or misuse of power. Sometimes if a victim forgives a wrongdoer, the victim will, in effect, be colluding with the abuse of power and those who urge a victim to forgive may be colluding with and reinforcing not only the particular abuse of power but also structures that sustain that abuse of power. In other words, it would be immoral not to resist the abuse of power. Some might even say that to forgive in such circumstances would be to acquiesce in the abuse, to surrender to it and to discharge the wrongdoers from moral accountability to the victims.[14]

Similarly, Steven Burns, in his article "Forgiveness in Challenging Circumstances," strongly maintains that, "any views of forgiveness that put victims at risk of further victimization and abuse, that collude with oppression or accommodate legacies of wrongdoing might themselves be regarded as pathological."[15] In contrast, refusing to condone harmful actions demonstrates self-respect as well as moral strength.

The second ethical objection to unconditional forgiveness is that it harms the wrongdoer. Forgiving unconditionally cannot be a virtue, because forgiving apart from repentance undercuts the redemption of abusers by preventing them from being held accountable for their behavior. Famously, for example, the battered wife's forgiveness may be enabling. In such situations, forgiveness should wait on genuine repentance.[16] In Alistair McFadyen's book *Forgiveness and Truth*, Deborah van Deusen Hunsinger quotes a pertinent story:

> A group of incest offenders in a treatment program made a powerful plea: "Don't forgive so easily." All were Christians [or claimed to be] and had gone to their pastors as soon as they were arrested, asking to be forgiven. Each had been prayed over, forgiven and sent home. They said that this pastoral response had been the least helpful to them because it enabled them to continue to avoid accountability for their offenses.[17]

14. A. Bash, *Forgiveness and Christian Ethics*, 71.

15. Burns, "Forgiveness," 159.

16. Hunsinger, "Forgiving Abusive Parents," 95.

17. Hunsinger, "Forgiving Abusive Parents," 95.

The pastors' granting of forgiveness also involves third-party forgiveness, which is discussed in chapter 18. Similarly, Bash says that in the absence of repentance, the morally appropriate response within a community or family is to insist that the wrongdoer bear consequences for his actions. *This decision may mean that one should no longer engage the wrongdoer in a trusting relationship.*[18]

PSYCHOLOGICAL REASONS AGAINST UNCONDITIONAL FORGIVENESS

Reasons against unconditional forgiveness also exist from a psychological perspective. Forgiving unconditionally may be an excuse by the victim to repress unpleasant anger or avoid confrontation.[19] As has been discussed, moral anger is justified and therefore a righteous emotion, even if unpleasant. To fail to feel this anger, to brush it aside, or to deny its existence may be moral cowardice.

It is also contradictory for a victim to say that he has overcome anger while at the same time insisting that the wrongdoing is wrong. Why is this problematic? Because there is something wrong with having no anger over wrongdoing. Having anger, however, does not mean that the victim must allow the anger to define himself (i.e., cause him to become a bitter person) or control his life. Time may soften one's sense of anger and injustice about a particular harmful act as the memory fades, but if one reimagines the wrong and how it felt, the resentment will likely return. If anger does not return, it may be because the wrong is condoned or because the victim blames himself (as is typical in cases of child abuse or domestic violence).[20]

Some support unconditional forgiveness because it "denies an unrepentant wrongdoer power over the victim."[21] This reasoning sounds appealing from a psychological perspective, but nevertheless has serious problems. The forgiveness is often more pretend than real, and denying that the wrongdoer affects one emotionally is probably disingenuous. As previously stated, this practice may deny the real feelings of anger or involve hypocrisy about one's true feelings, neither of which is

18. A. Bash, *Forgiveness and Christian Ethics*, 70.
19. A. Bash, *Forgiveness and Christian Ethics*, 71.
20. A. Bash, *Forgiveness and Christian Ethics*, 161.
21. A. Bash, *Forgiveness and Christian Ethics*, 71.

psychologically healthy. By way of example, Bash says, "Urging women who have been physically and psychologically abused to forgive may not be in their psychological and moral best interests."[22] Truth is important, and being honest about one's feelings honors truth and is a healthy practice.

Another analytical reason to reject unconditional forgiveness is truth. If internal forgiveness is a "'decision to see a wrongdoer in a new, more favorable light,' it is reasonable to ask how a person can *decide* to see another person as other than what he is without engaging in self-deception."[23] Truth acknowledges who a person is, and love calls him to rise above his current choices and become a better person. Choosing to see him in a different light does neither. Truth is important, and what the offender is really like as a person is a part of truth that should not be denied. So, internal unconditional forgiveness denies truth concerning the victim's real feelings and truth concerning the character of the wrongdoer.

Bash summarizes the case against unconditional forgiveness: "It is difficult to make a cogent case for unconditional forgiveness. With very few exceptions, examples of unconditional forgiveness are rare and usually ambivalent."[24] Forgiveness means that the wrongdoer is released from his moral debt; therefore the effects of forgiving unconditionally are a sentence of injustice for the victim and an escape route from moral accountability and responsibility for the wrongdoer. It denies the wrongdoer the opportunity to understand the effects of the wrongdoing from the victim's point of view. Unconditional forgiveness also fails to engage the relational aspect that should be a part of forgiveness. Sometimes unconditional forgiveness simply expresses the powerlessness felt by the victim.[25]

When a wrongdoer repents, however, the ethical and psychological barriers to forgiveness disappear. The victim senses the moral correctness of his action and therefore finds it easier to forgive and to overcome negative feelings, for he forgives a repentant wrongdoer. The wrongdoer is in a sense no longer the same person, for he has repudiated his actions.[26]

---

22. A. Bash, *Forgiveness and Christian Ethics*, 71.

23. Haber, *Forgiveness*, 14.

24. A. Bash, *Forgiveness and Christian Ethics*, 72.

25. A. Bash, *Forgiveness and Christian Ethics*, 72.

26. Haber, *Forgiveness*, 95–96.

If sin "affects and perverts the essential self," repentance is another alteration in the essential self.[27] Also, following repentance, the victim's sense of justice does not rise up and protest forgiveness, because the one forgiven is someone who repudiates the wrong and has had a change of heart.[28] Forgiveness of one who has changed does not condone the sin. In fact, forgiveness becomes both reasonable and sensible. Forgiving a person who has changed, for an act of wrongdoing that he now repudiates as wrong, is not so difficult because it is logical, morally upright, and psychologically healthy. In addition, reconciliation can be *real* because there is *real* agreement, and morality and truth are honored instead of compromised.

A good example of reconciliation that honored both morality and truth can be seen in recent events in South Africa. The Commission for Truth and Reconciliation worked for justice and healing. Truth was critical to what the commission sought to accomplish. The offense had to be truthfully acknowledged, admitted, and agreed upon. Then the offer of amnesty opened up the possibility of a peaceful solution without condoning the offense. As Scripture says, "In mercy and truth atonement is provided for iniquity" (Prov 16:6 NKJV).

Another variation also attempts to justify unconditional forgiveness. Christians sometimes say that forgiveness is a choice one makes even if he does not feel differently about the wrongdoer. The idea that forgiveness is a choice is correct. If a victim chooses to forgive an unrepentant offender but admits that he does not want to have a relationship with him, his forgiveness is little more than a charade and a mere shadow of biblical forgiveness. Imagine God saying, "I forgive you, but I still do not like you and I do not want anything to do with you." Clearly, such so-called forgiveness is not forgiving as God forgives—it is not biblical forgiveness.

Perhaps philosophers and psychologists (and many Christians) have redefined forgiveness away from its historical and biblical meaning due to the inherent problems with unconditional forgiveness. In other words, because they believe unconditional forgiveness to be virtuous, and yet recognize the moral problems with unconditional forgiveness, they redefine forgiveness to something that can be unconditional *and* avoid these problems. If forgiveness is something that only takes place within the

27. Moberly, *Atonement and Personality*, 32.
28. A. Bash, *Forgiveness and Christian Ethics*, 160–61.

victim (according to the modern therapeutic definition, see chapter 9), then it does not necessarily lead to or have as its purpose reconciliation. Refusing to reconcile can be claimed as evidence of refusing to condone the sin. In this way, those who propose unconditional forgiveness, having redefined it as only an internal act, maintain that they avoid the problem of condoning the wrongdoing. However, the problem still exists. If forgiveness means that the victim overcomes feelings of resentment and therefore has a change of heart about the wrongdoer, it means the victim puts aside the wrong and disregards it when it comes to how he views and responds to the wrongdoer. In other words, this therapeutic internal forgiveness, *if it were real*, would lead to reconciliation. If a victim is reconciled with the wrongdoer without any change in the wrongdoer's actions, then the actions have been condoned as an accepted part of the relationship. He may say he does not condone, and in his mind he may not approve, but the absence of any consequences is what the offender experiences as condonation.

In preparation for true forgiveness, the victim must overcome malicious anger and desire the reformation of the wrongdoer. He should be prepared to reconcile with the offender (in an appropriate way) as well as continue the process of overcoming any residual negative feelings. If the wrongdoer repents, the victim *should* feel differently about him and some form of reconciliation should take place.

In summary, strong reasons exist against unconditional forgiveness from both an ethical and psychological point of view. (1) Forgiveness granted in the absence of repentance condones the wrongdoing and sometimes even supports it. This condonation may be due to moral cowardice that is unwilling to confront the wrong. (2) Unconditional forgiveness fails to consider the well-being of the wrongdoer. Truly caring holds an offender accountable for his actions. Consequences, including even a potential break in relationship, are necessary to help the wrongdoer take responsibility for his actions and change his future behavior. (3) It is psychologically unhealthy to expect a victim (in the absence of repentance) to abandon justified resentment and anger over the harm done to him or his life. For both moral and psychological reasons he should not be asked to abandon either the truth about the offense or the truth about his feelings.

CHAPTER 14 STUDY QUESTIONS

No Right to Be Forgiven

1. Does an offender who repents have a right to be forgiven?

2. Why is forgiving not a moral duty? When does it become a moral duty for Christians?

3. Which is easier, to repent or to forgive? Why?

Ethical Reasons against Unconditional Forgiveness

1. From a moral point of view, what are the reasons against unconditional forgiveness?

2. Why is forgiving unconditionally harmful to a wrongdoer? What response is appropriate?

Psychological Reasons against Unconditional Forgiveness

1. Is justified moral anger a righteous and healthy emotion? Is it a pleasant emotion?

2. In what ways is internal unconditional forgiveness a denial of truth?

3. Why is unconditional forgiveness so hard (if not impossible) to put into practice?

4. Why is forgiveness following repentance morally correct?

5. Biblical forgiveness is a choice, but why is it not a choice in spite of one's personal feelings?

6. How does therapeutic forgiveness appear to avoid the moral problems with unconditional forgiveness? Why does it ultimately fail to do so?

7. Summarize the ethical and psychological reasons against unconditional forgiveness.

15

Overcoming Destructive Resentment
The Prelude to Forgiveness

"LETTING GO" AND "MOVING ON"

ANOTHER ETHICAL CONSIDERATION RELATED to the practice of forgiveness is the need to overcome destructive resentment—to let go and move on. From an ethical and psychological perspective, what one actually needs to do is overcome resentment as a feeling that would *preclude* one from forgiving *if* the wrongdoer repents. This should take place prior to forgiveness and as soon as possible, though the process itself requires time. What, specifically, does the victim need to let go? He needs to overcome feelings of resentment and anger that are destructive (as opposed to moral)[1]—emotions that may prevent him from being able to think or talk about anything else, work effectively, or have fun. This effort is not forgiveness itself, but is psychologically desirable so that unpleasant emotions do not control one's life. One should be able to say "I have let it go" without forgiveness being granted, meaning he no longer dwells on or obsesses over the wrong.

The process by which one lets go of and eventually moves on from harmful emotions has many parallels with the stages of grief—pain, depression, anger, and eventual acceptance that leads to hope and

---

1. A. Bash, *Forgiveness and Christian Ethics*, 161–62.

involvement in new things. But sometimes people get stuck and are unable to accept, let go, and move on. Why is this so? Often, it is because of a preoccupation with justice or vindication. A wronged person longs for justice and vindication, or even just an acknowledgment of the wrong. Such longing for what is right lies deep within human beings. For some, this may only be possible after meditating on the fact that God will ultimately ensure justice and hold wrongdoers accountable. The words "Vengeance is mine, I will repay" (NRSV), quoted from the OT in Rom 12:19, are also quoted in Heb 10:30, this time in reference to eschatological judgment. This knowledge of accountability and judgment in an eschatological sense can make it possible for victims to let go and move on, even when they believe the offender will never acknowledge his wrongdoing.[2]

The inability to let go may cause a spiritual crisis in that one thinks he is not able to practice what he believes.[3] In this situation one can be helped greatly by distinguishing between destructive resentment and moral resentment, as well as distinguishing between forgiveness and letting go. Letting go is a process that one must work through and may include the same anger and the same seemingly unbearable loss as does grief. The feelings are so much like grief because they actually are grief. Add to that suffering a strong need for vindication. The wounded one must go through the process of absorbing the pain, the depression, and the anger. Being wounded is hard and healing is not easy, and those who move on have done well. They are scarred, but from a Christian perspective they are scarred as the Lord is scarred and have become privileged ones who know something of the "fellowship of His sufferings" (Phil 3:10 NKJV).

The psychological preparation for forgiveness involves more than just letting go of destructive resentment and moving past the grief of a broken heart. It also involves "regaining of one's confidence in one's own worth despite the immoral action challenging it."[4] This may take years and involve consecrating one's will to appeal to God on behalf of their offender.[5]

However, letting go *entirely* may not be possible or morally right. Righteous indignation (moral resentment) should be maintained against

2. Bash and Bash, "Early Christian Thinking," 46.

3. Gulliford, "Intrapersonal Forgiveness," 84.

4. Murphy and Hampton, *Forgiveness and Mercy*, 83.

5. Moberly, *Atonement and Personality*, 69.

sin. Letting go entirely is especially morally incorrect if it involves unconditional reconciliation. In this case, no matter how much the victim may
claim he has not condoned or accommodated the sin against him, he has.
The sin has become a part of the relationship that no longer harms the
relationship. As Deborah van Deusen Hunsinger says in her article "Forgiving Abusive Parents," "Forgiveness before repentance is 'cheap grace'
and cannot contribute to authentic psychological/emotional healing and
restoration of wholeness for the victim or for the offender. It cuts the
healing process short."[6]

Concerning forgiveness and reconciliation, there are three stages in
the effort made by the victim to "be holy" as God is holy. The first stage
is to overcome and let go of malicious resentment, anger, and hatred that
desire the offender's destruction rather than his repentance and restoration to relationship. The victim must abandon this destructive resentment or anger while retaining righteous indignation or anger against the
offender for the harm done to himself. This righteous anger or resentment demonstrates self-respect and holds the offender accountable. *If*
the offender repents, the victim may proceed to stage two: forgive and
be reconciled. Forgiving wipes the sin away; therefore no reason exists
to hold on to righteous anger or resentment. Giving up all anger and
resentment should be natural and not so difficult at this point, because
the offender has admitted his offense and repudiated the wrong. Just as
there is "rejoicing in heaven over one sinner who repents" (Luke 15:7),
the victim should feel happy that the one who wronged him has changed.
In stage three, the victim develops trust, as the wrongdoer continues to
behave in a trustworthy manner. The victim also needs to eliminate any
residual anger or resentment. One needs to realize that forgiveness and a
degree of justified resentment may coexist as the victim learns to respect
and trust again. Many victims who forgive acknowledge this truth.[7]

---

6. Hunsinger, "Forgiving Abusive Parents," 94.

7. A. Bash, *Forgiveness and Christian Ethics*, 161.

CHAPTER 15 STUDY QUESTIONS

"Letting Go" and "Moving On"

1. What healthy psychological process must take place before a Christian can forgive?

2. What are the stages of grief, which parallel the process of letting go harmful emotions?

3. What is the reason people sometimes get stuck and are unable to move on?

4. What steps should the victim take in an effort to "be holy" as God is holy?

16

Ethical Reasons to Forgive the Repentant Offender

EVEN PHILOSOPHERS WHO DEFINE forgiveness in a therapeutic sense recognize that ceasing to resent does not constitute forgiveness, unless it is done for moral reasons. Murphy points out that forgiveness must be more than overcoming resentment, because not all cases of overcoming resentment involve forgiveness. If situations involve offenses that are not deeply hurtful and damaging, people sometimes simply forget or become too busy to be bothered by their resentments. This may happen involuntarily, which does not involve making a choice. On the other hand, one's resentment may eat away at his peace of mind. He loses sleep, becomes irritable, is less effective in his work, etc. Because he is miserable, he may go to a therapist who will try to help eliminate the resentment (assuming this can even be done). The motivation is to promote one's own mental health. It is self-serving and not a choice made for moral reasons.[1]

The earlier discussion touched upon the reasons to forgive a repentant offender. (1) No condonation of the wrongdoing is involved, because the offender acknowledges the wrongfulness of his actions. (2) Repentance means the victim no longer has reason to resent, because no need exists to protest on moral grounds.[2] The repentance of the offender means that the victim may forgive *and* maintain his self-respect. With the

1. Murphy and Hampton, *Forgiveness and Mercy*, 23.
2. Haber, *Forgiveness*, 99.

danger of condonation removed and respect for the victim established, the victim may now give the gift of forgiveness to the offender without violating a moral principle. (3) This gift relieves the offender's burden of guilt feelings, and therefore is a good gift that benefits another. The gift of forgiveness is given not because the offender deserves it or has a right to it, but because of the goodwill of the victim who has chosen to benefit another—clearly a moral good. (4) Reconciliation, the restoration of harmonious relationship, is also a moral good. Thus, forgiving the repentant offender is a choice based in morality, and for this reason is generally accepted as a virtue.

If forgiveness (whether biblical or therapeutic) includes forswearing resentment based on moral grounds, what makes it moral and, therefore, the right thing to do? Murphy points out several reasons that are commonly given to justify forgiveness of an offender: (1) he has repented or has had a change of heart; (2) he meant well—that is, his motives were good despite the results; (3) he has suffered enough; or (4) he has been a good, loyal friend in the past.[3] Do any of these reasons, other than repentance, constitute moral grounds for forgiveness?

Murphy says, "Acceptable grounds for forgiveness must be compatible with self-respect, respect for others . . . , and respect for the rules of morality."[4] What does it mean to say that to be a virtue, forgiveness must be compatible with self-respect? As Murphy says, persons deeply resent moral injuries not simply because of the harm done, but also because "such injuries are . . . symbolic communications. They are ways a wrong-doer says, 'I count but you do not,' or 'I can use you for my purposes,' or 'I am up high and you are there down below.'"[5] Intentional wrongdoing is insulting and attempts to degrade. It involves injustice and is thus a moral injury. When people are treated with contempt, it attacks them in profound and deeply threatening ways. Perhaps this is why Scripture uses such strong words against insulting others: "Whosoever shall say, Thou fool, shall be in danger of hell fire" (Matt 5:22 KJV). Persons naturally resent those who belittle them, and therefore they want to separate themselves from their presence. Their feelings may be strong enough that they desire to get even, or at least "banish them from the realm of those

---

3. Murphy and Hampton, *Forgiveness and Mercy*, 26–29.

4. Murphy and Hampton, *Forgiveness and Mercy*, 24.

5. Murphy and Hampton, *Forgiveness and Mercy*, 25.

whose well-being [is] their concern."[6] If offenders, by repentance, separate themselves from their message, then the way is clear for a forgiveness that does not compromise self-respect.[7] An offender can thus be forgiven without fear that the victim acquiesces to the offender's former judgment that he lacks worth.[8] Scripture says, "Do not be deceived: God cannot be mocked. A man reaps what he sows" (Gal 6:7). God cannot be presumed upon; he will stand up for himself and for what is right. Neither should humans allow themselves to be "mocked" (presumed upon), and they should also stand up for what is right.

The degree to which the other three items on Murphy's list represent ways that separate a wrongdoer from his actions is the degree to which they represent moral grounds for forgiveness that are compatible with self-respect. The following discussion examines each of the three remaining reasons to ascertain if they separate the offender from his actions, or if they are basis for forgiveness that does not compromise morality or self-respect.

Some say forgiveness is justified if an offender's motives are well-meaning. The offender does not hold the other in contempt or think of him as less valuable than himself. A good example is paternalism. A person who interferes with another's liberty for reasons he thinks are good may be acting wrongly. For example, it is hard to view the person who locks another's liquor cabinet because he thinks he drinks too much in the same way one views someone who steals. Both, however, violate one's personal rights. The case for forgiving the well-meaning offender is reasonable, at least the first time.[9] However, an ongoing pattern requires communication and a request that the offensive behavior change. Without communication one lowers his own value, and by not communicating one removes the offender's chance to amend his ways.

Another reason for forgiving is that the wrongdoer has suffered enough. This reason is questionable, since it does not separate the offender from his actions. Pardon, rather than forgiveness, is a more appropriate action based on this reasoning, treating the offender with mercy in that he is not required to suffer the full consequences of his actions. One can be pardoned without being forgiven. There may be some merit in the

6. Murphy and Hampton, *Forgiveness and Mercy*, 25.

7. Murphy and Hampton, *Forgiveness and Mercy*, 25.

8. Murphy and Hampton, *Forgiveness and Mercy*, 26.

9. Murphy and Hampton, *Forgiveness and Mercy*, 26.

view that one should forgive because, if the offender has suffered greatly and been brought low in the process, he may not be the same person who committed the offense.[10] Without full knowledge of the offender's internal thoughts and motives, this reason remains dubious.

Murphy's final reason is forgiving for prior loyalty. When one forgives a repentant offender, he does so because of who the offender is now. When one forgives for old times' sake, he forgives because of who the offender once was. Much forgiveness of old friends and family is based on this line of thought,[11] but it is not a matter of thought so much as a matter of emotion. In this case the offender has not separated himself from his actions. Perhaps the lasting emotions of love and concern for family or old friends should prevent the breaking of relationships, even though forgiveness is not given because the moral requirements have not been met. Therefore, these relationships may require boundaries or adjustments rather than total alienation.

In addition to the reasons Murphy suggests, there are other justifications for forgiveness that may be proposed. A common one, especially among Christians, is the suggestion that forgiveness provokes repentance, the idea being that repentance is a lot easier if forgiveness is given first. This could be considered compatible with self-respect, but it is not so compatible with respect for the wrongdoer or for the rules of morality. Should not the wrongdoer feel sorrow for what he has done, and should not that sorrow lead him to repentance? Indeed it should, according to Scripture, which says, "Godly sorrow brings repentance that leads to salvation" (2 Cor 7:10). Sincere repentance should come from deep within the soul of the wrongdoer. A prominent biblical example of an attempt to provoke repentance is the prophet Nathan's confrontation of King David to expose his sins of adultery and murder. Nathan, however, does not grant forgiveness, but rather gives strong condemnation (2 Sam 12:7–10). Nathan's action results in David's confession and expression of deep sorrow (Ps 51). In contrast, stories are often told in which victims go to prisons to tell their offenders that they have forgiven them. Sometimes, according to the accounts, repentance appears to be the result, but in general this is not the case. If a victim is deeply concerned about his offender it would be more effective to let the offender know that, *if* he repents, forgiveness awaits. His offense can be wiped out and he can be cleansed,

10. Murphy and Hampton, *Forgiveness and Mercy*, 26–27.
11. Murphy and Hampton, *Forgiveness and Mercy*, 29.

according to the biblical pattern. To forgive apart from repentance and then tell the offender of one's forgiveness is not morally sound and may instead have a negative impact. Telling an offender that he is forgiven prior to repentance can be self-righteous and arrogant, and if rejected by the wrongdoer, may have the effect of making it more difficult for the offender to confess at a later time.[12]

Another reason people sometimes think they should forgive is that the wrongdoer is or has become pathetic. Sustaining opposition to wrongdoers when they are seen as weak and vulnerable is difficult. Compassion or benevolence may (or may not) be more appropriate than anger or resentment. Compassion may help the victim overcome malicious hatred and resentment and be more concerned with the well-being of his offender.[13] However, what the offender needs is not forgiveness apart from repentance (which condones and enables), but tough love that does not condone his actions and that facilitates his reformation. Whether the offender is pitiful is not an issue when making the moral choice of whether or not to forgive, unless his pathetic circumstances have changed him as a person.

Sometimes reasons are presented on behalf of forgiveness that are irrelevant from a moral point of view. For example, one may argue that family harmony should be promoted. But even if good consequences result, "consequentialist reasons for tendering forgiveness are essentially practical rather than moral. . . . Thus if the 'ought' of forgiveness is to be anything more than a counsel of prudence, it must be directed at repentant wrongdoers. Otherwise, forgiving behavior is essentially no different from condonation of wrongdoing. This is true regardless of the positive utilities that result."[14]

Another misguided reason for forgiving appears at first glance to be a good reason and a reason based on Scripture: one should forgive because he, too, is in need of forgiveness. However, as Haber points out, our own need to be forgiven does not constitute an ethical reason to forgive someone else. Our own moral history in *this* situation is not the issue.[15] MacLachlan agrees, saying that there are serious dangers in grounding a duty to forgive universally in an argument from common frailty. Not all

12. Murphy and Hampton, *Forgiveness and Mercy*, 30.

13. Murphy and Hampton, *Forgiveness and Mercy*, 150.

14. Haber, *Forgiveness*, 108.

15. Haber, *Forgiveness*, 109.

wrongs are equal.[16] One may be guilty of some wrongdoing, but he should still judge serious crimes. In other words, one does not insist on forgiving evil because he is sometimes inconsiderate.[17] (Once a moral reason *does* exist for forgiving, then the fact that one is also sometimes in need of forgiveness should make him compassionate and ready to forgive.)[18]

A related reason proposed for unconditional forgiveness is based on the belief that some good can be found in everyone. But as Piers Benn says in his article "Forgiveness and Loyalty," "The argument that forgiveness should be given because the offender may not be wholly rotten—there is some decency in him—is irrelevant."[19]

In summary, whether using a biblical or a therapeutic definition, if morality is not to be compromised, then no situation requires forgiveness except that of repentance. Those who use a biblical definition arrive at this conclusion by discerning the biblical pattern. Philosophers who use a therapeutic definition arrive at the same conclusion by discerning ethical rules of morality. Only those who follow neither the biblical pattern nor the rules of morality advocate automatic, unconditional forgiveness.

The situations in the preceding discussion involve serious and harmful wrongdoing and not petty disagreements or small offenses, which simply require forbearance. Many situations are complicated and require wisdom, but as one seeks to be wise he should think through his actions ethically and base his actions on morality. Forgiveness, then, is a virtue practiced for moral reasons following the repentance of the offender. It is also logical, for why should the victim resent the offender for holding him in contempt when the offender no longer does so? Such resentment is now misplaced.[20] In his book *Forgiveness*, Joram Haber offers a good summary: "An appropriate reason for forgiveness is one that negates the justifiability of the injured party's resentment. The only reason that would serve this function is that the wrongdoer has repented the wrong he has done."[21] This is true regardless of whether one is speaking of biblical forgiveness or therapeutic forgiveness.

---

16. MacLachlan, "Forgiveness," 178.

17. MacLachlan, "Forgiveness," 177.

18. Biggar, "Forgiveness," 201.

19. Benn, "Forgiveness and Loyalty," 379–80.

20. Murphy and Hampton, *Forgiveness and Mercy*, 29.

21. Haber, *Forgiveness*, 90.

As stated earlier, forgiveness must only be granted for moral reasons, and forgiving for moral reasons is virtuous. In her dissertation, entitled "The Nature and Limits of Forgiveness," Alice MacLachlan summarizes the reasons that forgiveness is a moral good. From an individual perspective, forgiveness has value (1) for personal healing (removal of anger for the victim and removal of guilt feelings for the wrongdoer), (2) for expressing respect for persons, and (3) for promoting harmony between persons (reconciliation). Forgiveness also develops character in the victim in that his forgiveness is an act of self-sacrifice.[22] From a social perspective, forgiveness is also a moral good because, as Volf says, it "makes the spiral of vengeance grind to a halt."[23]

22. MacLachlan, "Forgiveness," 119.
23. Volf, *Exclusion and Embrace,* 121.

CHAPTER 16 STUDY QUESTIONS

1. What moral/ethical reasons does Murphy say are often suggested for forgiving an offender?

2. Why, in order to be a virtue, must forgiveness be compatible with self-respect?

3. What principle determines whether the reasons suggested for forgiveness, other than repentance, constitute moral reasons?

4. Is forgiveness justified if an offender's motives are good?

5. Is forgiveness justified if one believes that the wrongdoer has suffered enough?

6. Should one forgive for old times' sake?

7. Christians may claim that forgiveness provokes repentance. Is this true? Is this scriptural?

8. Should forgiveness be granted because the wrongdoer is pathetic?

9. Should forgiveness be given because the victim also sometimes needs forgiveness?

10. What reasons does MacLachlan give for forgiveness being a moral good?

17

Vindication for Victims

JUSTICE FOR THE OPPRESSED VERSUS JUSTIFICATION FOR OPPRESSORS

THE BOOK OF HABAKKUK speaks of the faith of the just. Habakkuk lived at a time when evil prospered. He questions God as to why he is "silent while the wicked swallow up those more righteous than themselves" (1:13). God answers him, saying:

> Write the vision; make it plain on tablets, so that a runner may read it. For there is still a vision for the appointed time; it speaks of the end, and does not lie. If it seems to tarry, *wait* for it; it will surely come, it will not delay. Look at the proud! Their spirit is not right in them, but the *righteous live by their faith.* (2:2–4 NRSV; emphasis added)

By "living by faith" Habakkuk means waiting for God's judgment against the wicked and vindication of the wronged. Faith is connected to justice rather than justification, and faith applies to the sinned-against rather than the sinner.[1] In his book *Hurt to Healing*, Andrew Sung Park explains that in the Bible two different ways exist of expressing faith in God. The faith of sinners is in God's mercy, for God has revealed himself to be merciful (Exod 34:6). If sinners have faith, God will respond and justify (forgive) them. The faith of the sinned-against is in God's justice, for God has revealed himself to be One who "will by no means clear the [unrepentant] guilty" (Exod 34:6 KJV; also Rev 6:10, "How long,

---

1. Park, *Hurt to Healing*, 105.

265

Sovereign Lord, . . . until you judge the inhabitants of the earth and avenge our blood?"). The faith of the sinner is aimed at God's acceptance, and the faith of the sinned-against is aimed at vindication and God's verdict against the guilty. Park says, "In receiving prayers God has to listen to [both] sides. The sinned-against, placing his trust in God's justice, prays for that justice to be made manifest. The sinner prays for his justification [forgiveness and restoration to right standing], having faith in God's grace. God wants to restore both groups, but . . . the Bible shows us that he is more concerned about the victim than the victimizer."[2]

This concern of God for victims is seen throughout the Bible. The emphasis on justice for the oppressed rather than justification of oppressors is evident in Jesus' explanation of his mission. Quoting from Isaiah, Jesus says he came to bring good news to the poor, to proclaim release to the captives and recovery of sight to the blind, to let the oppressed go free, and to proclaim the year of jubilee (Luke 4:18–19). It would require spiritualization of these categories (and would still be a stretch) to claim that he says his mission is to forgive oppressors. The poor, the captives, the blind, the oppressed, and the slaves freed at the jubilee are clearly the sinned-against, or marginalized. In the Sermon on the Mount Jesus does not say, "Blessed are sinners for they shall be forgiven." Rather, he says, "Blessed are those who hunger and thirst for righteousness [literally, justice], for they will be filled. Blessed are those who are persecuted because of justice [righteousness], for theirs is the kingdom of heaven" (Matt 5:6, 10). The translation "justice" for "righteousness" emphasizes the social aspect of the gospel and links these words with the OT expectations of the Messiah.[3] Jesus says those who long for justice and who have been persecuted will be satisfied through the kingdom he brings. He comes into the world to "take up our infirmities" and "to bear our diseases" (Matt 8:17). He shows compassion for the crowds "because they are harassed and helpless" (Matt 9:36). He proclaims "good news" for those who are "heavy laden" and promises to "give [them] rest" (Matt 11:28 KJV).

It is in this regard that Jesus teaches that one cannot expect to interact with God at the altar if he has not made amends with everyone he has wronged. Matthew 5:23–24 says, "Therefore, if you are offering your gift at the altar and there remember that your brother or sister has something against you, leave your gift there in front of the altar. First go and

2. Park, *Hurt to Healing*, 103.

3. Park, *Hurt to Healing*, 109.

be reconciled to them [which involves admission of guilt, apology, and reparations when possible]; then come and offer your gift." The victim is the priority, not the wrongdoer. God stands by the victim, and before the wrongdoer can interact with God he is required to go and restore his victim's right. If God loyally stands by victims in this way, certainly his people should do the same. Justice and justification occur not when God lets wrongdoers off the hook, but when God's forgiveness concurs with the offender's restoration of his victim's rights, goods, and/or respect. In other words, justification by faith does not mean that sinners are reconciled to God without repentance or without making amends for their past wrongs (e.g., Zacchaeus). If this were not true, then justification by faith, which exonerates the guilty, is not good news but rather an act of injustice.[4] But God does not justify or pardon oppressors apart from their repentance; justification only occurs with God's grace convicting sinners to make right their wrongs.[5] For, after all, when a wrong is done both the victim *and* God are wronged.[6] God is wronged in the same way that a parent is wronged when his child is harmed.[7] God is concerned for both the sinner and the sinned-against, but the victim is primary. The church needs to cultivate God's compassion for victims, and forgiveness of victimizers should fit into this context.[8]

God has compassion for victims and passion for justice, but also grace and pardon for the repentant. The Messiah brings in the kingdom that will ultimately result in justice for the downtrodden, but he also offers grace to the offenders.[9] Offering the grace of God to the world should not eclipse working for justice and equality, which is the heart of what Jesus came to accomplish. The verses quoted from Isaiah concerning the mission of the Messiah indicate that justice for the oppressed is not secondary in God's agenda. Reaching out to broken and brokenhearted victims with healing is the mission and ministry of the church. Reaching victimizers with the call to repentance is also the mission of the church. The church needs to emphasize the good news for victims (theirs is the kingdom, they shall be filled, they shall see God, they shall inherit the

---

4. Park, *Hurt to Healing*, 106.

5. Park, *Hurt to Healing*, 107.

6. Park, *Hurt to Healing*, 107.

7. Biggar, "Forgiveness," 209.

8. Park, *Hurt to Healing*, 114.

9. Park, *Hurt to Healing*, 110.

earth), which promotes their healing through faith in God's promises for them and from God's presence with them.

JUSTICE, VICTIMS, AND THE MINISTRY OF THE CHURCH

How does the church help victims who have been abused or who need healing for brokenheartedness after being abandoned or betrayed by someone who was loved more than life? According to Isaiah, the One to come will "bind up the brokenhearted" (61:1b) and "comfort all who mourn" (61:2b). Although Jesus did not quote this part of the passage (Luke 4:16–20), should not the church, the body of Christ, be committed to this ministry? Second Corinthians 1:3–5 refers to this ministry, saying that Christians are blessed by "the God of all consolation, who consoles us in all our affliction, so that we may be able to console those who are in any affliction with the consolation with which we ourselves are consoled by God. For just as the sufferings of Christ are abundant for us, so also our consolation is abundant through Christ" (NRSV). Clearly, the people of God are to engage (that means spending time) in the ministry of consolation to those who are hurting. This verse also states that the consolation believers have to offer is "abundant." Those who have suffered in like ways can bring great truth to those in pain. Consoling others may be a daily and time-consuming ministry, for healing from severe hurts always requires time.

Perhaps there is a reason Jesus did not quote Isaiah's words "bind up the brokenhearted," just as he did not quote the phrase saying the Messiah would proclaim "the day of vengeance of our God."[10] The church gives consolation—even "abundant" consolation—but complete healing may not be possible in many circumstances until Jesus returns. Then he will indeed proclaim "the day of vengeance of our God" and "bind up the brokenhearted." There will be a new world, a new heaven and a new earth (Rev 21:1) with "no more . . . mourning or crying or pain" (Rev 21:4). God will "wipe every tear from their eyes" (Rev 21:4), and the brokenhearted will be healed. In the meantime, "the just shall live by faith," and there is indeed consolation abundant. Perhaps, for those who know their broken

---

10. Vaughan, *Bible from 26 Translations*, 2002. The words "heal the brokenhearted" are used in the KJV Luke 4:18b but omitted in others, because they "are now recognized as not adequately supported by original manuscripts."

hearts are not yet healed, applying the "already but not yet" can help them overcome feelings that God has not fully come through for them or that their relationship with God is somehow deficient. The title of Solomon Schimmel's book *Wounds Not Healed by Time* is a recognition of this "not yet" aspect and of the faith that knows there is a future worth waiting for.

The kingdom of God has been inaugurated, but it is still a fallen world, therefore suffering and loss are "common to mankind" (1 Cor 10:13). The loss of a loved one through abandonment or betrayal is similar to grief following a death. Loss involves pain, and mourning involves not just the initial, intense pain, but also the states of depressive broken-heartedness, anger, and, eventually, acceptance. *Even acceptance is not without pain, for the knowledge that one's world is not right and not likely to become right again remains ever-present.* At each stage of the process, feelings need to be acknowledged and expressed (perhaps sometimes only to God)—anger, hatred, shame, failure, etc. If feelings are denied because one feels guilty for having such feelings, a person can get stuck in the process of healing. The church can counter this, for true feelings can be expressed more easily to another who has been through similar circumstances and had similar emotions, and who therefore understands and does not condemn.

Mary Anne Coate says in *The Capacity for Forgiveness*, "During the *normal* developmental process some degree of repression of hatred is necessary as a defense against destructiveness, but if hate is to play a positive role in the process of healing, it needs to *become conscious* and then *got over*" (emphasis added).[11] There will be a time to move on beyond feelings of hatred, anger, and maybe even hurt, but one must recognize that one cannot will it to be so. The process must be experienced and lived through and cannot be hurried. Each situation of abandonment or betrayal is different, therefore no proper timeline for healing exists. In this regard Jones says, "We can only adequately understand how people are dealing with anger and resentment by examining their progress (or lack thereof) over an extended period of time."[12] How long this process takes depends on a variety of factors, such as the relationship of the parties, the culpability of the wrongdoer (i.e., if it was on purpose), the magnitude of the injury, and whether the wrongdoing is ongoing. For example, intentional betrayal by a close family member, of great magnitude

---

11. Coate, "Capacity for Forgiveness," 135.

12. L. Jones, *Embodying Forgiveness*, 233.

[such as harming one's child], especially ongoing, makes it quite difficult to manage the resentment and anger.[13]

Bash makes an extremely astute observation concerning victimhood that only those who have been victims of abandonment or betrayal by close loved ones can understand. He says that one of the greatest damages of a betrayal, sometimes greater than the offense itself, is that "it destroys [one's] freedom to be [himself], for [he] will find [himself] involuntarily dominated by the inner rage and resentment—a type of spiritual prison which permeates throughout all [his] being—which will be a subconscious but very powerful influence in [his] life."[14] In addition, after abandonment or betrayal, one often finds it difficult to trust and give to others. One is now different and not by his own choice. He now has to overcome his new inclination to distrust and to refuse to give of himself. This soul damage alone is grounds for deep resentment. The victim may like the person he was more than the person he has become, although he may not want to go back to the former state of innocence and ignorance.

A proper understanding of victimhood and a proper compassion for victims should therefore ensure that ministry to wrongdoers includes counsel to make things right with those whom they have harmed; otherwise, the ministry fails both the victim and the wrongdoer. The wrongdoer's repentance is incomplete, and ministry to those who need to be forgiven is impotent and unhelpful if they do not see the need for change. Insistence on apology and restitution also motivates future change, for if sinners always need to ask for forgiveness and make restitution in order to interact with God (Matt 5:23–24), one has strong personal motivation not to sin against another. The church often fails here, perhaps because of its emphasis on God's grace and forgiveness. Alcoholics Anonymous does not fail in this way, for one of the twelve steps of recovery is to go to every person one has wronged, admit the wrong, and apologize. This step toward healing the alcoholic is foremost a recognition that people who have been wronged deserve better: they deserve an apology and personal vindication.

Even when appropriate compassion and empathy exist for a victim, asking for his forgiveness is still a delicate matter. The offender must consider the feelings of the victim and anticipate the possibility of rejection. If the offender is motivated to make himself feel better or to just check an

13. L. Jones, *Embodying Forgiveness*, 235.
14. A. Bash, *Forgiveness and Christian Ethics*, 70–71.

item off his list, then expecting and even asking for forgiveness and absolution is inappropriate, because the motive is personal gain. However, if
motivated for the sake of the victim, asking for forgiveness is appropriate.
The one who asks forgiveness recognizes that forgiveness is a conscious
decision and action by the forgiver that benefits the offender. The forgiver should be given credit for making a sacrificial decision. In cases of
extreme hurt the decision to forgive requires "a generosity of spirit and a
self-transcendence that is close to divine."[15] The offender should recognize this and be fully appreciative of the gift he has been given. Victimizers too often take for granted being forgiven by those whom they have
harmed. The ministry of the church must counter this attitude.

Because forgiveness is a conscious decision and action that involves
self-sacrifice, it may take time for the hurt one to reach the place of being
able to choose it. The wrongdoer, as well as others (including the church),
must recognize this. Those who have been wounded deeply must pray
for God to empower them to forgive. This involves a prayerful process of
entering into God's presence and perspective.[16] The question, "Have you
forgiven him?" is rarely appropriate from outsiders and usually carries
self-righteousness, a lack of wisdom, and a lack of empathy. As Jones says,
"One of the most offensive things Christians all too often do is proclaim
a general and abstract forgiveness without any regard for the complexities of a specific situation or a particular person's life. In this there is a
tendency to trivialize the suffering endured and thereby trivialize the
sufferer. . . . Simply exhorting people to forgive is often most unhelpful."[17]

The psalms are full of expressions of the kind of faith Habakkuk
describes, faith in the righteousness of God, who will be faithful to his
people and his covenant, and who will make things right. He will vindicate the righteous who look to him and wait for him to act on their
behalf. Living by faith in the sense of having faith in God's justice is also
found in the NT. Second Corinthians 5:7 says, "For we live by faith, not
by sight"—the context is future expectation. In the parable of the unrighteous judge, in which a widow comes to a judge to ask for "justice against
[her] adversary," the lesson is clearly stated: one "should always pray and
not give up" (Luke 18:1). In other words, victims should not quit praying
and waiting. They should not give up, but should pray for justice and

---

15. Biggar, "Forgiveness," 193.
16. Gulliford, "Intrapersonal Forgiveness," 84–85.
17. L. Jones, *Embodying Forgiveness*, 228–29.

vindication, having faith that God will act. Prayer is an expression of this *faith* that *waits* and *expects* God to act in righteousness and justice.

In summary, how should the church minister to victims who suffer at the hands of loved ones or others? By showing the understanding, comfort, and compassion needed for healing, as well as patience when the process is slow. Conversely, how should the church minister to wrongdoers? The answer is also with understanding, comfort, and compassion, but with the essential element of justice in mind. The offer of justification should not be made by disregarding justice. It must insist that the wrongdoer confess and make right his wrongs. In this way justice is honored rather than violated.

CHAPTER 17 STUDY QUESTIONS

Justice for the Oppressed versus Justification for Oppressors

1. God's instruction to Habakkuk to "live by faith" meant what in his circumstance?

2. The Bible instructs sinners to have faith in what? In what should the sinned-against have faith?

3. How is God's concern for victims, as opposed to victimizers, revealed in the Bible?

4. How, according to Scripture, is one's relationship with God hindered if he wrongs another?

5. In what sense is God also wronged when a victim is wronged?

Justice, Victims, and the Ministry of the Church

1. What is the mission of the church in relation to the brokenhearted and oppressed? How is the church to carry out this mission?

2. Why might Jesus have chosen to omit "to bind up the brokenhearted" when quoting Isaiah?

3. How is losing a loved one through abandonment or betrayal similar to experiencing the stages of grief following a death? How is it worse?

4. What factors may determine how long it takes a victim to deal with anger and resentment?

5. In what sense have those who have been abandoned or betrayed lost the freedom to be themselves? Specifically, what character traits are often damaged?

6. How does the biblical injunction to go to the person one has wronged and make things right show proper compassion for the victim?

7. What should be the motivation for a wrongdoer to make things right with his victim?

8. Why might it take some time for a victim to be able to forgive?

9. What is the lesson of the parable of the unrighteous judge? What is the context of this parable?

18

Additional Questions

THIS CHAPTER CONSIDERS ADDITIONAL questions on the subject of forgiveness. Who can rightfully forgive? Are there limits to forgiveness? What is the role of loyalty for friends of the victim? Must words of apology and forgiveness be spoken? How does one discern the time to embrace and the time to refrain from embracing (Eccl 3:5b)?

FORGIVING INJURIES TO OTHERS: WHO CAN RIGHTFULLY FORGIVE?

Anthony Bash, in *Forgiveness and Christian Ethics*, says, "It is regarded as axiomatic that only victims can forgive wrongs against them. . . . Forgiveness is the gift of the person who has been wronged and not of any other person."[1] Most philosophers, when considering who is in a position to grant forgiveness, have concluded that only the victim has the right to forgive. Certainly, all would consider it presumptuous if someone assaulted another and a passerby offered the wrongdoer forgiveness.[2] Alice MacLachlan, in her dissertation, "The Nature and Limits of Forgiveness," says, "Indeed it is common, almost universal, among philosophers writing on the subject of forgiveness to claim that only the victim of a wrong can forgive it. . . . The power to forgive is only held legitimately by one agent and to speak of third-party forgiveness is seriously and wrongfully

1. A. Bash, *Forgiveness and Christian Ethics*, 134.
2. Scheiber, "Truth and Reconciliation," 173.

to disrespect the victim of harm."[3] Others agree. Murphy says one does not have the standing to resent or to forgive a wrongdoer unless he himself is the victim.[4] And Haber says there is an intuitive objection to those who proclaim forgiveness when they are not the ones who have been injured, for people consider the harm less serious when they are not the ones wronged.[5]

Sometimes others become involved through their connection with the victim. Surely they, too, are in a position to forgive *in some sense* by virtue of their own resentment, but the emotional involvement of a third party is never the same as that of the victim himself. Of course, the degree of involvement depends on the relationship. It is often harder for a parent to forgive harm done to his child than for the child himself to forgive.[6] Dowie Ackermann, whose wife was murdered in South Africa, argues that he can forgive for the hurt caused to himself, but not for the sin of murder. He says only his wife and God can forgive that.[7] In other words, one who commits murder cannot be forgiven comprehensively in this life, because his victim is no longer here.[8]

The question then is, Can God comprehensively forgive sins that are committed against persons?[9] One might even ask, Is God even in a position to forgive? At first glance, God's right to forgive might be thought to rest on the fact that he is the cosmic judge. But if an assault case is brought to court, the judge is not able to forgive just because he is judge. As a judge, his task is to assess the crime and assign the punishment according to the law and circumstances. A judge may offer mercy based on circumstances, but not based on his personal feelings. In addition, the one assaulted may forgive the offender regardless of how the judge decides the case. Given this, why is God in a position to forgive as well as a victim? He is in a position to forgive, not because he is judge, but because he loves. He, too, is hurt because of his love—his love for the

---

3. MacLachlan, "Forgiveness," 194–95.

4. Murphy and Hampton, *Forgiveness and Mercy*, 16.

5. Haber, *Forgiveness*, 48.

6. MacLachlan, "Forgiveness," 197, 202, 206, 213, 218.

7. Biggar, "Forgiveness," 209. This scene is recorded in "Getting Away with Murder," a BBC TV documentary about the Truth and Reconciliation Commission, presented by Michael Ignatieff and originally broadcast on 1 November 1997 as part of the *Correspondent* series.

8. Biggar, "Forgiveness," 210.

9. Biggar, "Forgiveness," 209.

victim, his love for his world created good, and even his love for victim-izers. Thus, every offender needs the forgiveness of his victim and also of God.[10] Anyone else who claims to forgive is presumptuous.

Since seeking forgiveness is aimed at restoring a relationship, asking forgiveness only makes sense if one asks it of the person he has harmed. For a believer, all sin is an affront to goodness and the will of God and as such mars his relationship with God. For this reason he asks God's forgiveness for all his sins, whereas he can only ask a person for forgive-ness for the injury done *to that person*. A believer should ask forgiveness both from the person he has wronged and from God; only then can sin be blotted out completely.[11]

The expectation of a prayer of repentance directed to God is, how-ever, different from the expectation of an expression of repentance to-ward one's victim. Forgiveness depends on the freewill decision of the victim. Since forgiveness is not guaranteed, a repentant offender cannot count on it. Because he is human, a victim may find it impossible to over-come his resentment for the suffering. But because God is perfect in love, he never fails to forgive those who are truly repentant. "If we confess our sins, he is faithful and just to forgive us our sins, and to cleanse us from all unrighteousness" (1 John 1:9 KJV). This promise of forgiveness does not mean that forgiveness is necessitated by repentance. It is simply what God chooses to do.

The expression of repentance directed toward God is also different from that directed toward a person in that one does not express to God something he does not already know. But this confession of wrongdoing is a necessary condition for restoring personal fellowship with God. In confessing to God, a person expresses the fact that he is in relationship with him and that he is willing to humble himself. Concealment and pre-tense come to an end,[12] and health is restored to the relationship.

ARE THERE LIMITS TO FORGIVENESS?

A couple of Scripture passages need to be considered, indeed recovered, to complete any understanding about forgiveness in a context of evil.[13]

---

10. Scheiber, "Truth and Reconciliation," 175, 178–80.
11. Brümmer, *When We Pray*, 103–4.
12. Brümmer, *When We Pray*, 101–2.
13. Burns, "Forgiveness," 148.

These include the sin of blasphemy against the Holy Spirit, which is stated to be unforgivable (Matt 12:32; Mark 3:28–29; Luke 12:10); and the claim in the Letter to the Hebrews that excludes the possibility of repentance, and therefore restoration, of apostates (Heb 6:4–8). As Burns says, "These . . . do not always feature widely in contemporary theological construction about forgiveness but they may play a meaningful role in the consideration of forgiveness in the context of acute suffering."[14]

The Unforgivable Sin

> Truly I tell you, people can be forgiven all their sins and every slander they utter, but whoever blasphemes against the Holy Spirit will never be forgiven; they are guilty of an eternal sin. (Mark 3:28–29)

Although these verses were considered previously, we must understand that, in the words of MacLachlan, "To call something unforgivable . . . suggests that there are limits to forgiveness, certain acts which or agents who cannot be forgiven."[15] Paul calls himself a "blasphemer" (1 Tim 1:13a), but he is clearly forgiven in that he spoke ignorantly and repented (1 Tim 1:13b). Therefore, one may logically conclude that blasphemy against the Holy Spirit is committed in spite of a knowledge of the truth; in other words, deliberately and knowingly.

Those Who Fall Away Cannot Be Brought Back to Repentance

> It is impossible for those who have once been enlightened, who have tasted the heavenly gift, who have shared in the Holy Spirit, who have tasted the goodness of the word of God and the pow-ers of the coming age and who have fallen away, to be brought back to repentance. To their loss they are crucifying the Son of God all over again and subjecting him to public disgrace. Land that drinks in the rain often falling on it and that produces a crop useful to those for whom it is farmed receives the blessing of God. But land that produces thorns and thistles is worthless and is in danger of being cursed. In the end it will be burned. (Heb 6:4–8)

14. Burns, "Forgiveness," 148.
15. MacLachlan, "Forgiveness," 181.

These verses clearly state that there can be a falling away from which it is impossible to return. It applies to those who have known ("been enlightened") and experienced ("have tasted") the truth of the gospel ("the heavenly gift"), the Holy Spirit, and the "powers of the coming age." If such persons reject the truth and reject Jesus, they mock him and figuratively crucify him again (in themselves). These verses do not state that this apostasy is unforgivable, but that any who turn from truth and discard the Son of God *will* not return to repentance. Moberly maintains that this statement is based on the fact that the more one sins the "feebler one's capacity for contrition," therefore repentance becomes progressively more difficult and eventually impossible.[16]

Many have tried to compromise these verses. Some suggest that this is a hypothetical situation that cannot occur. But why would the author of Hebrews warn his readers in such strong words about something that does not happen? Others have said that if someone turns away from the Lord it shows that he was never a true believer. However, the author heaps on his subjects phrase upon phrase describing them as those who have indeed been converted.

To say that they cannot or will not repent means that they cannot or will not be forgiven. It is unthinkable that those who would again crucify (even if figuratively) the Son of God and do not repent could then be welcomed into the age to come. The actions are unforgivable because they are by choice, indicating that their character is settled: they are hardened, to use the biblical word (Ps 95:8; Prov 28:14; Acts 19:9; Heb 3:13), to the point of no return. As humans with limited knowledge and discernment it is wise not to judge others to be in this category, but it is also wise to accept that there is such a category.

Do these Scriptures suggest that unforgivable wrongs exist? Only one such wrong is named in Scripture. If there can be one, could there not be more within the unforgivable category (Deut 29:18–20)? Christians, however, are reluctant to put even the most atrocious sins in this category. This reluctance is surely wise, but it may derive from a misguided notion of God's power to change an evil person or redeem a situation created by evil. This reasoning is misguided because the issue is not God's power or even his sovereignty. The issue involves the question, *Should* every evil act be forgiven if its perpetrator repents? Is it morally right? Philosophers are not as reluctant to discuss the possibility that certain evil acts *should*

---

16. Moberly, *Atonement and Personality*, 43–44.

remain unforgiven. They argue that, even according to the Christian tradition, there is a limit to what should be forgiven. That truth is biblically established by the unforgivable sin. These philosophers maintain that some acts are so reprehensible that they are unforgivable (Arendt, Golding, Lang, North, Shachnow, Goulden, Telshkin, Langer, and Ozick). Others argue that all people, no matter how reprehensible their behavior, can change and therefore can be forgiven.[17] The philosophical question is not really whether it is *possible* to forgive in all situations, but whether it is morally right to forgive. MacLachlan makes the following comment:

> Philosophical discussions of what is unforgivable often occur in conjunction with discussions of what is *evil*. . . . There are acts for which it does not make sense even to ask whether or not we should forgive because the option is ruled out from the outset. . . . To speak of forgiveness, in these cases, is to make a moral mistake.[18]

For many horrifying acts there are examples of people who forgive.[19] But that does not make it morally right to do so.[20] We should not assume that they are righteous or holy.

Making a distinction between sin and evil enlightens the discussion.[21] All evil is sin but not all sin is evil. Failing to do a kindness may be a sin, but it is not evil. Advocating the forgiveness of evil raises profound problems, for evil is to be discerned and defeated.[22] Evil may be hard to define exactly, but it certainly includes the conscious pursuit of harmful actions that are enjoyed for their own sake.[23]

Judas, the betrayer of Jesus, is an interesting study (Matt 26:14–16). Many Christian teachers insist that Judas did not truly repent: in defense of this belief they point out that Matthew uses a different verb for "repent" than the usual one (*metamelomai* rather than *metanoeo* in Matt 27:3, translated "remorse" in NIV). They also point out that Judas did not emend his life but destroyed it (Matt 27:5). However, Bash's argument that Judas *did* repent has some merit. Judas recognized that his actions

---

17. A. Bash, *Forgiveness and Christian Ethics*, 11.

18. MacLachlan, "Forgiveness," 229–31.

19. MacLachlan, "Forgiveness," 231–32.

20. Haber, *Forgiveness*, 107–8.

21. Sedgwick, "Forgiveness and Awareness," 121, 124.

22. Sedgwick, "Forgiveness and Awareness," 121.

23. Sedgwick, "Forgiveness and Awareness," 124.

were morally wrong and returned the blood money (Matt 27:3). Apparently he did not feel that he *could* be forgiven, a belief supported by Matt 26:24 ("But woe to that man who betrays the Son of Man! It would be better for him if he had not been born"), which implies that Jesus' betrayer would face damnation.[24] Is it not worth considering that this sin of Judas was unforgivable?

Jesus himself was prepared, based on their behavior, to judge some people as hell bound (Matt 23:33). His injunction to love does not apply to cases of pure evil.[25] One is not called to love evil. Many evil acts cannot be repaired in any sense and destroy the possibility of hope. Perhaps crimes exist that are pure evil and too horrific for either the victim to forgive or for the guilt feelings of the perpetrator to be removed.

In the parable of the unmerciful servant (Matt 18:23–35), the master takes severe actions against the servant who does not forgive. Note, however, that the debt owed to the unforgiving servant is very small. The parable does not indicate that the master is angry because the servant (whom he has forgiven) refuses to forgive, for example, someone who has tortured and murdered his daughter.

In summary, perhaps the least that can be said in considering the limits of forgiveness is that the answer is not obvious.[26] No consensus exists among Christian theologians or among philosophers concerning the limits of forgiveness. Theologians acknowledge that there is at least one sin that is said to be unforgivable. This could mean either that no forgiveness is available in spite of repentance or that no possibility of repentance exists due to the nature and degree of evil involved. Or, perhaps this sin indicates rejection of God, which makes forgiveness and reconciliation impossible. Among philosophers, the majority appear to support Leroy Howe's view that, from a moral standpoint, some harm outweighs any apologies or amends-making, and that some wrongs are so atrocious that repentance itself is not only insufficient, it is simply irrelevant.[27] Burns points out that many have failed to recognize the lifelong impact of some acts perpetrated against others. They may speak casually of the joy of forgiveness or of abundant life. However, one should speak of forgiveness

---

24. A. Bash, *Forgiveness and Christian Ethics*, 82.

25. Biggar, "Forgiveness," 199.

26. Burns, "Forgiveness," 147.

27. Howe, *Guilt*, 91.

only from experience.[28] A theology of forgiveness should be formed within the experience of having been abused, abandoned, or betrayed. In line with what has been said about who has the right to forgive, if forgiveness is to be considered appropriate in Holocaust-like circumstances, it should be considered so by those who know rather than inappropriately proposed by those who do not know.[29] Perhaps the conclusion should be that the last word belongs to the victim and to God. Others may only speculate and certainly should not be dogmatic or judgmental toward those who have not yet or will not forgive because their lives have been shattered by evil.

WHAT IS THE ROLE OF LOYALTY FOR FRIENDS OF THE VICTIM?

We must also address how others should relate to the guilty party of a broken relationship. Piers Benn, in his article "Forgiveness and Loyalty," says, "Loyalty means that one stands by one's friends and loved ones and tries to represent their interests. To be loyal to someone is to give them your support, typically in circumstances in which it would be easier simply to detach oneself from them."[30] Loyalty is a virtue that affirms the value of another and the correctness of their moral position. Outsiders may have no need to feel indignation at a wrongdoer's actions and can justifiably continue normal dealings. However, there is something morally defective in a person who does not react with indignation when directly confronted with the grave and malicious harming of a friend or loved one. Such indignation can be expressed by terminating the relationship with the wrongdoer, thereby protesting the moral wrong and harm done as well as affirming the victim's worth.[31] Failure to protest tacitly approves of the wrongdoer and condones the wrong done. As previously noted, Kolnai says, "Condonation is spineless accomplissment."[32] "It is an intrinsically bad thing and plainly at variance with the condemnation of wrong which appears to be implicit in the genuine concept of forgiveness."[33] It is well

28. Burns, "Forgiveness," 146–47.

29. Burns, "Forgiveness," 155.

30. Benn, "Forgiveness and Loyalty," 379.

31. Benn, "Forgiveness and Loyalty," 381.

32. Kolnai, "Forgiveness," 97.

33. Kolnai, "Forgiveness," 97.

known that those who practice "submissive meekness before evil" often speak of it as forgiveness.[34]

MUST WORDS OF APOLOGY AND FORGIVENESS BE SPOKEN?

An obligation exists on the part of the wrongdoer to seek forgiveness from the one he has wronged (Matt 5:23–24). Bash states this necessity with strong words, saying, "It is repulsive to suppose that God offers a route to forgiveness that spares the wrongdoer from engaging with the person wronged."[35]

What is involved in genuine apology? In answering, Haber says:

> We are all familiar with the difference between a friend or lover who simply says, "I am sorry you were hurt," and the one who says, "What I did was wrong; you have every right to be hurt and I am sorry." The former personality somehow manages to place the entire burden of forgiveness [the restoration of relationship] on the one who has already been hurt. The former is not an apology that expresses repentance.[36]

A genuine apology establishes common truth between the wrongdoer's narrative of what took place and the victim's.[37]

An apology is only acceptable if it is sincerely penitent. There are several indicators of sincerity. One is that the apology acknowledges wrongdoing with a clear statement that the offender's actions are morally wrong. A second indicator is that the apology recognizes the harm done to the victim as well as the victim's innocence in the matter. A third indicator of sincerity is an effort to right the wrong. A guilty person should not only apologize, admitting the wrong, but also do something to demonstrate the sincerity of the confession—something costly in money, effort, or time that recognizes the harm done.[38] The apologizer directly benefits from the actions of the forgiver by having his guilt feelings relieved; therefore, he should try to find some way for the forgiver to benefit as well. This does not negate the fact that the forgiver's gift is

---

34. Kolnai, "Forgiveness," 96.

35. A. Bash, *Forgiveness and Christian Ethics*, 106.

36. Haber, *Forgiveness*, 98.

37. MacLachlan, "Forgiveness," 192.

38. Swinburne, *Responsibility and Atonement*, 84.

free. This action is also helpful in convincing the victim of the sincerity of the confession. If a victim is not convinced, then forgiveness is tentative and true reconciliation cannot take place. A cordial relationship may be established, but not a trusting one. Sincere apology is difficult because it is humbling, but the apologizer must remember that forgiving, which is what he is asking the other to do, is likewise difficult.

A spoken apology merits spoken forgiveness.[39] MacLachlan says that speaking forgiveness involves the acceptance of an apology which is a minimal condition for forgiving.[40] The apology should be accepted in such a way as "to acknowledge the wrongfulness of the act (as opposed to using phrases like, 'Don't worry about it' or 'It was nothing')."[41] To state "I forgive you" acknowledges wrongdoing and makes a commitment to future behavior such as non-retaliation, forswearing hostility, and some appropriate commitment to the well-being of the wrongdoer.[42]

A model of forgiveness that involves *spoken* forgiveness in response to *spoken* apology recognizes just how important words of absolution are to a contrite wrongdoer, as well as how important words of confession and regret are to a victim. *Words* of forgiveness help the wrongdoer release the burden of guilt feelings and thus they have a moral dimension.[43] Equally, *words* of apology have the moral dimension of helping the victim to forgive. So both apology and forgiveness are morally good performative actions expressing the changes that have occurred within the apologizer and forgiver and involving a commitment to appropriate future behavior. The foundation is thus laid for reconciliation.

HOW DOES ONE DISCERN THE TIME TO EMBRACE AND THE TIME TO REFRAIN FROM EMBRACING?

Relationships and people are complex, and the victim must discern how to react appropriately and morally to abandonment or betrayal. As Scripture says, "There is a time for everything" (Eccl 3:1). For a victim there is a time for silence and a time for speaking truth; a time for waiting and a time for confrontation; a time for vigorous protest and a time for gentle

39. MacLachlan, "Forgiveness," 105.
40. MacLachlan, "Forgiveness," 107.
41. MacLachlan, "Forgiveness," 107.
42. MacLachlan, "Forgiveness," 106–7.
43. MacLachlan, "Forgiveness," 108.

protest; a time for setting boundaries and a time for breaking off relation-ships; a time for grieving and a time to let go and move on; a time for consequences and a time for pardon; a time to keep distance and a time to come close; and a time for anger and a time for forgiveness. How does one discern the times? The answer is carefully, slowly, and prayerfully. Wisdom is essential, and those who seek God's guidance should fully ap-propriate God's beautiful promise of wisdom for those who ask (Jas 1:5). As MacLachlan says, we need practical wisdom and discernment to be able to respond correctly for moral reasons "to situations that are subtle, context-dependent and difficult to articulate."[44]

From the offender's point of view, the matter is much less complex: the time to repent is present; the time to confess is present; the time to apologize is present; and the time to make reparations is present. Wis-dom is not needed; rather, humility, truth, determination, and courage are required. Of course, the guilty one can ask God for *strength* to do the right thing. An offender who repents and a victim who forgives are both to be lauded, but the praise should primarily go toward the victim who forgives, because he is the one who has absorbed the pain.

44. MacLachlan, "Forgiveness," 168.

CHAPTER 18 STUDY QUESTIONS

Forgiving Injuries to Others: Who Can Rightfully Forgive?

1. What is third-party forgiveness, and why is it not legitimate?

2. Why might non-victims sometimes be in a position to grant forgiveness?

3. Why is God in a position to forgive wrongs done to others?

4. To be comprehensively forgiven, from what two parties does a wrongdoer need forgiveness?

5. How is the expected response of a prayer directed to God for forgiveness different from the expected response of seeking forgiveness from the victim?

6. If God knows a person's heart, why does that person still need to confess his sin?

Are There Limits to Forgiveness?

1. What two rarely emphasized passages of Scripture consider the limits of forgiveness?

The Unforgivable Sin

1. What do Scriptures regarding an unforgivable sin reveal about the limits of forgiveness?

Those Who Fall Away Cannot Be Brought Back to Repentance

1. Does Scripture indicate that it is never too late to repent?

2. According to Scripture, do unforgivable wrongs exist? How many?

3. Is it possible that certain evil acts should not be forgiven? What is the majority view of philosophers on this subject? What is the Christian view? How does Judas fit into this discussion?

4. Does maintaining that a sin is unforgivable mean that no forgiveness is available in spite of repentance, or that no repentance is possible because of the nature and degree of evil involved?

What Is the Role of Loyalty for Friends of the Victim?

1. Why is loyalty a virtue? In other words, what does it affirm? What does it protest?

Must Words of Apology and Forgiveness Be Spoken?

1. What are some indicators of the sincerity of an apology (and therefore of the repentance)?

2. Why should a guilty party try to do something to demonstrate the sincerity of his apology?

3. Why is apology so hard?

4. What are the advantages of a model of forgiveness that includes spoken apology and spoken forgiveness?

How Does One Discern the Time to Embrace and the Time to Refrain from Embracing?

1. How does a victim "discern the times" to act wisely concerning a broken relationship?

2. How does an offender "discern the times" regarding repentance and reconciliation?

19

Memory and Reconciliation

THE TITLE OF THE introductory chapter, "Reconciliation, a Worthy if Illusory Goal," acknowledges the difficulty of achieving reconciliation between an offender and an innocent victim. In light of this difficulty, this final chapter introduces some thoughts and speculations about remembering wrongs suffered and reconciliation in the world to come. What role does remembering or non-remembering play in reconciliation between persons both in this life and in the life to come? As the footnotes indicate, the following discussion is adapted almost entirely from the book *The End of Memory* by Miroslav Volf, and it considers the positive use of memory of wrongs done, as well as the misuse of memory.

Remembering wrongs suffered—especially from the hands of loved ones—is painful. Evil is truly insidious, with a life that extends well beyond the deed itself. If the evil is returned it has had a double victory;[1] and when it lingers on in the mind of the victim, darkening his world, it also has a double victory. How does a victim resist giving evil this victory? He may be able to resist returning evil for evil and thus overcome evil with good (Rom 12:21), but how does he prevent the second type of victory for evil? How does he erase the memory that can color all his days? Can it be erased? Should it be erased?

The victim often desperately wants to cease to remember. When he remembers, he relives the pain, causing the past to break into the present.[2]

---

1. Volf, *End of Memory*, 9.
2. Volf, *End of Memory*, 21.

One of the most devastating aspects of abandonment or betrayal is that one is even deprived of the memory of what was once good. One can no longer delight in the memories of happy times together and love shared because the abandonment or betrayal has caused what was formerly good to become a source of pain. Thinking of past joy only causes pain when the relationship is lost and the love is gone. How unfair for evil to be able to destroy not only the present and future, but also the past. The past should not change; and yet it does. So we try to forget, but should we? Can we?

Volf says that "memory of wrongs suffered is from a moral point of view *dangerously undetermined*."[3] Remembering may have a positive use, and yet it often has a negative outcome. In Bosnia, for example, "It is memory that is a problem. It is because they remember what happened to their parents, or their sister, or their grandparents that they hate each other."[4] Volf says of the negative use of memory:

> Instead of generating solidarity with victims it may breed in-difference and reinforce cycles of violence. Instead of truthfully acknowledging wrongdoing, it may bolster a victim's false self-perceptions and unjust demands. Instead of healing wounds, it may simply re-injure. Remembering wrongs will forge an identity, but the identity may be that of a person imprisoned in his own past and condemned to repeat it. Notice the word "may" in the previous sentences—the memory of wrongs *may* wound, *may* breed indifference, *may* reinforce false self-perceptions, *may* re-injure. I am not arguing that remembering wrongs *must* produce all these results, or even that as a rule it does produce them. . . . If this is true it is essential to explore ways of *redeeming* memories of wrongs suffered. . . .[5]
>
> By remembering we pay a debt of honor to those who have been wronged and have suffered.[6] . . . To uphold the impor-tance of wrongs responsibly, we need to filter out the poison from the medicine of memory. But how? How can we remember rightly?[7] . . . What we have suffered weighs down on us like a heavy load we long to have lifted; like an indefatigable enemy.[8]

3. Volf, *End of Memory*, 34.

4. Volf, *End of Memory*, 34.

5. Volf, *End of Memory*, 33–34.

6. Volf, *End of Memory*, 40.

7. Volf, *End of Memory*, 41.

8. Volf, *End of Memory*, 42.

. . . Will the ordeal be rendered somehow meaningful or will it remain a random intrusion of fruitless suffering that casts a shadow of malaise over the whole of my life?[9]

Memory, then, can be a destructive force for many reasons, not the least of which is that it may create endless personal suffering.

If the negative use of memory is obvious, its positive use must be found, for it is not so easily determined. Yet, there are many positive reasons to remember.

REMEMBERING

Justice May Be Served

The pursuit of justice for victims requires remembering. In many societal situations, remembering is a part of the fight against political oppression. This public remembering honors those who have suffered and refuses to forget their suffering. A wrong that is not remembered or ever mentioned is unseen. To the outside observer, a victim is not a victim, and an offender has done nothing wrong. Both are therefore perceived incorrectly. A double injustice is done—the first when the deed is done and the second when it is allowed to disappear. The injustice of hiding sins motivates victims to make known what they have suffered. The public remembering of wrongs acknowledges them and is therefore an act of justice. The same is true in private lives.[10] Concerning the work of the South African Truth and Reconciliation Commission, Andre' du Toit writes:

> The victims of political killings cannot be brought back to life, nor can the harm and trauma of torture and abuse somehow be negated. What can be done, though, is publicly to restore the civic and human dignity of those victims precisely by acknowledging the truth of what was done to them. This was the function and purpose of the victim's hearings where people were enabled to tell their own stories, and to have them publicly acknowledged in non-adversarial procedures.[11]

9. Volf, *End of Memory*, 43.

10. Volf, *End of Memory*, 29.

11. Volf, *End of Memory*, 29.

The commission was then supposed to recognize "the *truth* of what was done to them."[12] The important word is "truth." Untruthful memories do not serve justice, but truthful memories do.[13] Truthful remembering is a way to treat victims justly. "Such remembering is an indispensable precondition of reconciliation between parties estranged by the transgression of one against another. For peace can be honest and lasting only if it rests on the foundation of truth and justice."[14] Wrongs should not be forgotten until after justice has been done,[15] for "love includes a concern for justice."[16] As Volf says, "Memory *is* judgment in the absence of more public judgment, including the Last Judgment."[17]

Christian tradition has long claimed that to forgive fully and be reconciled means that one is willing to let go of the memory of wrongs suffered.[18] This is certainly true. However, in the biblical model, forgiveness occurs after repentance. Scripture does not suggest that one abandon the memory of wrongs before the wrongdoer's repentance. In fact, as argued previously, such forgetting would encourage non-repentance and would therefore not be an act of love. As Katongole and Rice say, "One insufficient version of Christian mission is reconciliation without memory, jumping over the past too quickly by offering cheap grace to those who have done wrong and never repented."[19] As long as evildoers remain evildoers, the wrongs they commit should be remembered and not hidden.[20]

What, then, does 1 Pet 4:8 (quoting Prov 10:12b) mean: "Love covers over a multitude of sins"? It cannot mean that love hides sin and pretends that it does not exist. This is certainly not the way of God, who does not obscure the truth and who loves perfectly. Psalm 32:1 says, "Blessed is the one whose transgressions are forgiven, whose sins are covered" (quoted in Rom 4:7). The parallelism is obvious: sins covered are sins forgiven. As seen in chapter 2, one of the Hebrew words (*kipper*) and one of the Greek words (*aphiemi*, in Rom 4:7) rendered "forgive" translate literally "to cover." In other words, part of what one is willing to do *when*

12. Volf, *End of Memory*, 29.

13. Volf, *End of Memory*, 30.

14. Volf, *End of Memory*, 56.

15. Volf, *End of Memory*, 108.

16. Volf, *End of Memory*, 174.

17. Volf, *End of Memory*, 204.

18. Volf, *End of Memory*, 132.

19. Katongole and Rice, *Reconciling All Things*, 33.

20. Volf, *End of Memory*, 204.

he forgives someone who has wronged him is to wipe out (the root idea of *kipper*; see chapter 2), or cover his sin. Although its truth is never denied, the sin is no longer relevant because it has been repudiated by repentance and blotted out (another meaning of the Hebrew term) by forgiveness. Therefore, it is covered, or hidden, by love; love being the motivation for forgiveness. To say that love covers sin is simply a way of saying that love forgives sin (repentance being presupposed). Love cannot hide sin in a way that hinders repentance, confession, and amends-making, for if it does it is not love. In fact, as James says, the wrongs should not only be re-membered but addressed: "My brothers and sisters, if one of you should wander from the truth and someone should bring that person back, re-member this: Whoever turns a sinner from the error of their way will save them from death and cover over a multitude of sins" (Jas 5:19–20).

Empathy May Be Given

A second reason to remember wrongs is that victims can continue to empathize with others.[21] To fully empathize with a person in pain, one must understand his suffering, and that understanding only comes from having similarly suffered. A person can empathize to some degree from hearing the victim's stories, but generally such feelings are only surface feelings and not deep and painful. However, if he has known and con-tinues to know through memory the same pain as the victim, they can share a bond and communion that truly ministers to the pain of both (2 Cor 1:4). The call in Scripture to the children of Israel to remember the exodus (Exod 13:3) is not only a call to remember their deliverance and thus maintain their attitude of thanksgiving to God; it is also a call to remember their suffering so that in later years they might empathize with aliens in their land and thus treat them justly (Deut 16:11–12; 24:17–22). The imperative to remember enables those who have been wounded to help those with fresh wounds. The call to memory is also a call to trust that God will ultimately vindicate the afflicted and judge the oppressors.[22]

21. Volf, *End of Memory*, 31.

22. Volf, *End of Memory*, 108.

The Wrongdoer May Come to Repentance

The highest aim of remembering truthfully is that it may bring about the repentance, forgiveness, and salvation of wrongdoers, as well as reconciliation between wrongdoers and their victims. This goal, which involves enemy love, requires remembering.[23] Volf says:

> It takes knowing the truth to be set free from the psychic injury caused by wrongdoing. Christian tradition has always insisted on this tenant in relation to guilt—objective guilt, that is, not the mere feeling of guilt, appropriate or not. Freedom from guilt requires that the light of truth shine upon the dark corners of our lives, whether in this life through uncoerced confession, private or public, or at the doorway to eternity during God's final judgment.[24]

When the wrongdoer has recognized his transgression and has been transformed, memory can be let go without compromising principle.[25] Memory can then be called back into service when empathy is needed in ministry to others. As Volf says, "As long as reconciliation has not taken place, the obligation to remember stands."[26] This is because lasting reconciliation must be based on truth as well as the wrongdoer's reformation.

The Victim May Be Healed

A fourth reason for correct remembering concerns the victim's personal healing. Truthful remembering is in the best interests of the wrongdoer who needs to see truth and repent, but it is also necessary for the victim's healing. Volf says:

> The same is true in regard to the wounds caused by wrongdoing. We must name the troubling past truthfully—we must come to clarity about what happened, how we reacted to it, and how we are reacting now—to be freed from its destructive hold on our lives. Granted, truthful [remembering] will not by itself heal memories of wrongs suffered; but without truthful naming, all

23. Volf, *End of Memory*, 65.
24. Volf, *End of Memory*, 75.
25. Volf, *End of Memory*, 65.
26. Volf, *End of Memory*, 205.

measures we might undertake to heal such memories will remain incomplete.[27]

We can learn how to remember well . . . Remember truthfully! . . . Remember so as to heal![28]

The victim must accept his suffering and its ongoing nature. Through the violation he may have gained some understanding that otherwise would have remained unknown. He may recognize this positive aspect of his pain and therefore conclude that his suffering has meaning.[29] This is not to say that he must regard the pain as being a worthy price for the understanding.

Horrendous wrongs, however, rarely lend themselves to this sort of integration and healing. Some things are too horrendous to be integrated, and some healing must wait until the life to come, when God will wipe away every tear (Rev 21:4). Just as some physical wholeness must wait, so must some psychological healing wait for the world to come. Truth and reality are served when one labels horrendous suffering as senseless segments of his life story.[30] Too often Christians believe that everything that happens to them comes from God and therefore must have meaning (against such a view see *Satan and the Problem of Evil* by Gregory Boyd). Consider Jesus' practice of healing and casting out demons—two central aspects of his ministry that demonstrate the will of God and the power of the new age he inaugurates. Jesus never attempts to give meaning to illness or evil. He simply heals and casts out.[31] As Volf says, no effort to give meaning to deeply wounding experiences ultimately satisfies.[32]

Suffering May Be Properly Integrated into One's Life

A fifth reason for remembering suffering is to properly integrate painful experiences into one's identity. Meaning may be denied to painful experiences, but the experiences themselves cannot be repressed without denying one's identity. Memory is a fundamental human function, and

---

27. Volf, *End of Memory*, 75.
28. Volf, *End of Memory*, 85.
29. Volf, *End of Memory*, 76.
30. Volf, *End of Memory*, 77.
31. Volf, *End of Memory*, 187.
32. Volf, *End of Memory*, 186.

memories are a part of identity.[33] If suffering is a part of one's past or present life, then pain is a part of one's identity. Things happen to people after which they are never the same. "Their old way of being in the world won't work anymore."[34] People whose identity includes pain are different from people whose identity does not. Sometimes one who has experienced abandonment or betrayal wishes to be the person he was before the experience, not because he was a better or wiser person, but because he was happier and more carefree. But this identity as one abandoned or betrayed has become part of his essential self and cannot and should not be denied. Maintaining memory prevents him from living a lie as one who has not suffered.[35] However, the experience of pain should not *define* a person. One should not see himself primarily as a person who has suffered, but as a person who has been delivered and sustained by God. For example, the ancient Israelites saw themselves not as those who suffered in Egypt, but as those delivered to freedom by God. One can maintain justified anger while also giving thanks for God's deliverance and sustaining presence.

As Volf says, "To be sure, not all experiences of pain will be sidelined so easily. Some will stubbornly insist at being at the heart of our identity; the memory of them will define us without our having much to say in the matter. But clearly these are exceptions and not the rule."[36] In general, what one does with his memories is a choice.

HOW TO INTEGRATE THE MEMORY OF WRONGS

The experience and memory of abuse, abandonment, or betrayal by a loved one challenges basic assumptions about the character of the world and the outcome of loving and living righteously. Suffering a serious wrong often shatters these assumptions in one blow, leaving the victim disoriented.[37] This disorientation may last for some time while the victim grieves and attempts to heal and make sense of what has happened (see *The Message of the Psalms* by Walter Brueggemann).

---

33. Volf, *End of Memory*, 147.

34. Katongole and Rice, *Reconciling All Things*, 88.

35. Volf, *End of Memory*, 24.

36. Volf, *End of Memory*, 26.

37. Volf, *End of Memory*, 86.

A Judeo-Christian framework helps this healing process. If abandonment and betrayal are seen as symptoms of a good world temporarily gone wrong rather than as the expected ongoing state of affairs, one may more easily emerge from the pain of his experience. Those with a Judeo-Christian worldview experience the same grief and pain as others, but they see the world as something worth fighting for and evil as something to fight against. They embrace the difficult task of healing as well as the need to fight evil with good (Rom 12:21), not giving into despair and cynicism.[38] A Judeo-Christian outlook defines a person not merely in terms of his life experiences (abandonment and betrayal, successes and failures, joys and pains), but primarily as one loved by God.[39] *This* identity, even in the midst of ruin, helps heal a wounded and broken heart.[40]

But the wounded soul must choose to integrate his suffering properly. Making this a choice requires effort and discipline; a victim first needs to be aware that he has a choice, and then he must work toward making that choice. He must balance pain or truthful memory of pain with an outlook that sees goodness in life and hope for the future. He must cultivate joy that comes from delighting in something or someone. Joy is the most effective way to resolve brokenheartedness.[41] If a victim is to live truthfully yet not become defined by his suffering, he must engage in a mental and spiritual battle to seek and maintain this balance. Volf speaks of this balance, saying that memories must be integrated into one's life story "either by labeling them as patches of absent meaning in the quilt of our life or by coming to see how they fit into its whole and contribute to some good. With a new identity in the center of that quilt, wrongdoings suffered are relegated to its periphery."[42]

A person is more than his memories; his identity is also determined by his hopes for the future. Although the past can crush some dreams for the future, one who is healing is open to new possibilities. He will eventually leave behind his disorientation and formulate new dreams, allowing them to draw him out of the past and into the future.[43]

---

38. Volf, *End of Memory*, 13.

39. Volf, *End of Memory*, 79.

40. Volf, *End of Memory*, 80.

41. Park, *Hurt to Healing*, 147–48.

42. Volf, *End of Memory*, 81.

43. Volf, *End of Memory*, 25.

Many reasons exist and have been discussed to hold the memory of wrongs in spite of the painfulness of doing so. Memory serves the moral good in the cause of justice; it serves the need for empathy for others who suffer similarly; it serves the need of the wrongdoer to repent; and it serves the need of the victim for healing.

FORGETTING

If remembering serves such varied purposes, should sins ever be forgotten? As previously stated, forgetting sin must come from repentance and forgiveness; otherwise, wrongs should be remembered. But the situation is reversed when the wrongdoer repents and the victim forgives. If the wrongdoer has genuinely repented, then *not* to remember the offense every time one thinks of him makes forgetting the apex of forgiveness.[44] *Consigning forgiven wrongdoings to oblivion, done at the right time and in the right way, denies evil its very existence.*[45]

The close association of forgiving and forgetting is not just a NT concept. It appears first in the OT, where it is even better attested than in the NT.[46] Forgiveness is first associated with forgetting, because Scripture says that God blots out sins and does not remember them (Isa 43:25). In the book of Jeremiah God announces a new covenant, saying, "I will forgive their wickedness and will remember their sins no more" (Jer 31:34). Forgetting sin is logical following repentance and forgiveness because the sin no longer has relevance; the reasons for remembering no longer exist. Yet, as Volf says:

> The gift [of forgetting] can be given *irrevocably* only in God's new world, where the wronged are secure, wrongdoers transformed, and both *unalterably* reconciled. [For example, in the parable of the unmerciful steward God revokes the unmerciful servant's forgiveness.] Here and now if we give the gift of non-remembrance at all, we give it only tentatively, haltingly, provisionally, and often with a great deal of pain[47] (emphasis and brackets added).

44. Volf, *Free of Charge*, 175.

45. Volf, *Free of Charge*, 176.

46. Volf, *End of Memory*, 134.

47. Volf, *End of Memory*, 143.

According to Scripture, then, forgiven sin is to be wiped out in non-remembrance. Forgetting is the ideal goal. The advantage of this is obvious for the offender in lifting guilt feelings, but it is equally powerful for the victim in lifting pain. However, forgiveness is rarely completed in non-remembrance in this life.[48] Can one, whether sinner or sinned-against, truly forget? Can he make a choice to remember no more? No. People cannot selectively delete memories. But, if this is true now, is it also true in the world to come?

MEMORY AND THE WORLD TO COME

In spite of all efforts to heal and to properly integrate wrongs suffered into the fabric of one's life without them destroying joy and hope, a person is still "bound in a perverse bond with wrongdoers by having suffered at their hands."[49] Only when wrongdoers genuinely repent and reconciliation takes place are victims fully liberated and healed from the wounds of wrongdoing, but even then, memory persists.[50] If this is true then one must recognize that he may not be fully liberated or healed in this world. But what about the world to come? To remember painful experiences is to keep one's wounds open. The larger the wound and the more vivid the recollection, the more past and present merge and past suffering becomes present pain.[51] If the new world is a perfect world where sorrow has ceased (Rev 21:4), then logically the painful memory of wrongs must be erased. God says through Isaiah, "See, I will create new heavens and a new earth. The former things will not be remembered, nor will they come to mind" (65:17), but what exactly does this mean?

Christian tradition has not had much to say about the future life and non-remembering. Augustine, though, speculates that in the world to come people will have "no sensible recollection of past evils."[52] Augustine does not attempt to explain how such erasure will be effected, but his conclusion is plausible because if memory revives bad experiences, then the effects of evil are not fully gone until those memories are eliminated.[53]

48. Volf, *Free of Charge*, 176.
49. Volf, *End of Memory*, 119.
50. Volf, *End of Memory*, 119.
51. Volf, *End of Memory*, 22.
52. Volf, *End of Memory*, 22.
53. Volf, *End of Memory*, 22.

Augustine also speculates that people will also forget even how evil felt.[54] Volf argues that in God's new world "non-remembrance of wrongs suffered is the gift God will give to those who have been wronged,"[55] but he is not convinced that non-remembrance is erasure. Rather, wrongs simply will not come to mind because everyone will be fully immersed in the love and presence of God and love of others.[56] He says, "[In the new world] I propose that memories of wrongs, rather than being deleted, will simply fail to surface in one's consciousness—they will *not come to mind*."[57] Volf acknowledges that this is his *hope*.[58]

What is the relationship between this hope of non-remembrance and the final judgment? Most Christians think of final judgment as an event in which God will pronounce eternal condemnation and eternal salvation. However, considering the need for reconciliation of "all things" (Col 1:20) and what must occur for reconciliation to take place, it stands to reason that the final judgment will be much more involved. Volf comments:

> The Last Judgment is a *social* event; it happens not simply to individuals but between people. Human beings are linked by so many ties to neighbors near and far, both in space and in time. We wrong each other and rightfully have cases against each other. At the last judgment God will settle all these "cases" which all involve offenses against God too, since any wrongdoing against a neighbor is also an offense against God. Ultimately God will right all wrongs. . . .
>
> If the last judgment, understood as a social event, is to succeed as a transition to the world of love, each person will joyfully *appropriate* the results of the judgment. The Last Judgment will reach its goal when all the wronged standing at the threshold of the world to come receive their rightful vindication, and when wrongdoers eschew attempts at misplaced self-justification, acknowledge their wrongdoing, and are freed from the hold of evil on their lives.[59]

---

54. Volf, *End of Memory*, 23.

55. Volf, *End of Memory*, 142.

56. Volf, *End of Memory*, 141–42.

57. Volf, *End of Memory*, 145, 177.

58. Volf, *End of Memory*, 181.

59. Volf, *End of Memory*, 180.

If sinner and sinned-against are both to enjoy the world to come, they must be reconciled and know the goodness of being there together. They cannot go their separate ways, pretending that all is well. In this case all would not be well in the world to come, for they would not love each other. They must name the wrongdoings, agree about their nature, forgive, and receive forgiveness, affirming that they are glad to be there together.[60]

God then exposes all wrongs (Rom 2:5–6), condemns every evil deed (Rom 2:8), redeems every repentant perpetrator, and vindicates and heals every innocent victim, thus reconciling them to himself and to each other. Therefore, past evil, although unchangeable, is not allowed to have the final word.[61] In the final judgment, reconciliation and healing are complete for guilty and innocent alike. A sinner's actions are both condemned and forgiven. Through the gift of non-remembrance he may live without the stain and awareness of his guilt to mar his joy. For the innocent victim, truth is told and he is vindicated. Through the gift of non-remembrance he may live without pain. Sinner and sinned-against rejoice in their new relationship. "In the here and now this rarely happens, . . . for reconciliation is mostly incomplete in this world,"[62] but in the world to come the unalterable sequence will be: remembrance, forgiveness, and non-remembrance.[63] Following final judgment, the need for justice no longer creates a need to remember wrongs. Nor does anyone have a need to protect himself from future harm. The question of justice is settled, and there are no dangers lurking in the dark,[64] whereas, in the here and now, justice is hardly ever attained and threats persist; therefore, wrongs must be remembered.[65]

If non-remembrance will be part of the outcome of final judgment/redemption, will non-remembrance compromise one's sense of identity?[66] "Experiences, especially painful ones, inevitably . . . change people."[67] However, one's sense of identity comprises both remembering

60. Volf, *End of Memory*, 181.

61. Volf, *End of Memory*, 44.

62. Volf, *End of Memory*, 149.

63. Volf, *End of Memory*, 204.

64. Volf, *End of Memory*, 149.

65. Volf, *End of Memory*, 151.

66. Volf, *End of Memory*, 192–93.

67. Volf, *End of Memory*, 193.

and forgetting.[68] Events of early childhood are not remembered, yet are said to be among the most formative.[69] One forgets much of what happens throughout life, but one does not lose the sense of his identity because of this forgetting. He still feels like himself.[70] In this life, however, one cannot choose what to forget and what to remember. Many people want desperately to forget certain parts of their lives, but are unable to do so. To be able to forget (in the sense of not coming to mind, rather than deletion) in the life to come can therefore be considered a beautiful gift from God. The memory is not deleted, which would compromise one's identity, but it simply does not come to mind, perhaps by choice and perhaps because there is no necessity for it to do so. This non-remembrance is the result of full, final, truthful, and powerful reconciliation, taking away the double victory of evil when memory sustains it.

Thus when Scripture says "the former things will not be remembered" (Isa 65:17), perhaps it does not mean that memory is deleted, but only that former things simply do not come to mind. The new world cannot be marred by the memory of evil, for "the eternal memory of wrongs suffered implies the eternality of evil in the midst of God's new world"—this cannot be.[71] Jesus told his disciples of the contrast between the present and the future using a powerful image that can be applied to the question of memory.

> A woman giving birth to a child has pain because her time has come; but when her baby is born she forgets the anguish because of her joy that a child is born into the world. So with you: Now is your time of grief, but I will see you again and you will rejoice, and no one will take away your joy. (John 16:21–22)

It was true for the disciples following the resurrection. How much more will these words be true for eternity? "No one" means no one and includes anyone who harmed a person during his lifetime, regardless of whether or not reconciliation took place. Just as in God's new world, a person's resurrection body cannot be harmed by the powers of disease, decay, or death; their souls cannot be harmed. Their joy cannot be

---

68. Volf, *End of Memory*, 194.
69. Volf, *End of Memory*, 196.
70. Volf, *End of Memory*, 196.
71. Volf, *End of Memory*, 213.

compromised by another. As N. T. Wright in *Evil and the Justice of God* says, this is the "outreaching of the promise of resurrection itself."[72]

72. N. T. Wright, *Evil and Justice of God*, 142.

CHAPTER 19 STUDY QUESTIONS

1. In what ways may evil sometimes have a double victory? In other words, what is the negative use of memory?

Remembering

1. What are five ways in which the memory of evil can become positive (even if painful)?

2. What is the meaning of the statement "Love covers a multitude of sins"?

How to Integrate the Memory of Wrongs

1. How does a Judeo-Christian framework help one integrate the memory of wrongs suffered?

2. What steps must a person take to prevent the memory of wrongs suffered from defining his identity?

Forgetting

1. Why can the gift of forgetting wrongs be given irrevocably only in God's new world?

2. How is the forgetting of wrongs helpful to the offender? To the victim?

Memory and the World to Come

1. Why is it logical to think that, in the world to come, past evils will not be recalled?

2. What does Isaiah say concerning memory and the world to come?

3. How does Miroslav Volf picture the final judgment in terms of "the reconciliation of all things"?

Conclusion and Final Comments

CONCLUSION

ACCORDING TO MURPHY, TWO basic questions concerning forgiveness warrant detailed consideration: "(1) What is forgiveness; that is, how is the concept to be analyzed and distinguished from other concepts with which it may be confused? and (2) When, if at all, is forgiveness justified?"[1] I agree that understanding forgiveness depends on these two questions, but in writing from a biblical perspective I approach these questions from a Christian viewpoint. The questions thus become: (1) What is the biblical definition of forgiveness? and (2) When should it be practiced according to the biblical mandate and model?

Nigel Biggar, in his chapter "Forgiveness in the Twentieth Century" (*Forgiveness and Truth*, edited by McFadyen), gives a summary of his view, which I will quote at length because of its excellence:

> Forgiveness, as I see it, comes in two parts. The first comprises the victim's overcoming of vindictive resentment, the growth of his compassion, and the formation of his intention to restore some kind of "friendship" with the wrongdoer. This part of forgiveness precedes the wrongdoer's expression of repentance, and is unilateral and unconditional. However, because what it intends has yet to be realized, it remains incomplete. Its completion waits upon the declaration, verbal or otherwise, of "absolution"; that is, the moment when the victim declares that he will no longer view the wrongdoer in the light of his misdeed and that their relationship may proceed as before. The second part of forgiveness *is* conditional. It depends upon the wrongdoer's demonstration of sincere repentance, precisely because it takes seriously both the wrongdoer and his relationship with the victim.

1. Murphy, *Getting Even*, 19–20.

The initial part of forgiveness, then, does not involve forgetting the injury. On the contrary, out of care both for the wrongdoer and for the integrity of any future "friendship" with him, that should be remembered; and it should be remembered with the resentment appropriate to the deliberate [wrongful] act. Nevertheless, qualified by compassion and a desire for restored "friendship" such resentment will not be vindictive. It will be the anger without sin, of which Paul wrote to the Ephesians (4:26).

The final part of forgiveness, however, does involve a commitment on the part of the victim to "forget" the injury. Since memory is often beyond the will's command, this cannot be a promise never to remember. It can, however, be a resolve at least not to allow the memory of past injury to jaundice future relations with resentment. Insofar as it is based on the assumption that the offender's repentance is sincere, this commitment is conditional: if there is a further offense of a similar kind, it should be withdrawn. Still, this conditionality does not mean that the wrongdoer is robbed of all assurance of forgiveness; only that he is withheld assurance of unconditional absolution.

I have said that the first part of forgiveness involves the victim's intention to restore some kind of "friendship" with the wrongdoer. Exactly which kind will depend partly on the nature of the antecedent relationship, and partly on what degree of restoration is possible in the time available and circumstances attendant. Former intimates might aim at "reconciliation," whereas fellow-citizens need aspire to nothing more than "accommodation," and strangers to a mere cessation of hostilities and a "peaceful" parting of the ways. Sometimes, of course, the end of warfare is as much as even intimates can realistically hope for, given the gravity of the injury involved.

Are some injuries unforgivable? Yes—but only comprehensively, by surviving human beings, and in this life. If there is a God, and if the dead will be raised, and if there is life beyond history, then intractable resentment may yet be tamed by love, stubborn impenitence yet wooed by it, and murderers may yet receive absolution from their victims. Note that this *provisional* kind of unforgivableness grants victims no license to ossify into bitterness and hatred.

So, victims then are not obliged to forgive their oppressors? The answer to this is, "Yes and No." Humble and honest awareness of the fact of their *own* fatedness and frailty, and of their *own* need of forgiveness, does oblige victims to foster compassion for their fellow-sinners; but it does not oblige them to grant absolution in the absence of repentance. Are victims obliged to grant absolution to sincere penitents? Yes, they are, but this does not mean that penitents deserve absolution; for what obliges the victim is not the morally admirable repentance of the wrongdoer, but the truth about himself and the duty to will what is good.[2]

According to its biblical definition, forgiveness means the sin is wiped out, and because a sin cannot be wiped out in two parts, I would not divide forgiveness into separate parts. I would call Biggar's first part (overcoming resentment) the *preparation* for forgiveness—the emotional work the victim must do in preparation for giving the gift of forgiveness. This preparation is necessary so that the victim becomes willing and able to forgive should his offender repent. Cleansing oneself of all vindictive or malicious resentment or hatred is part of maintaining a pure heart before God and man, and it puts one in a position to "forgive as God forgives." It actually goes beyond personal cleansing to the biblical mandate to love one's enemies in the sense of desiring their well-being and reformation.

The forgiveness model in this book includes all the biblical metaphors and is multidimensional, with cognitive, emotional, performative, and relational components. Forgiveness is cognitive in that it involves a change of mind on the part of the forgiver in response to the change of mind (repentance) on the part of the sinner. The forgiver must decide to acknowledge the change in the wrongdoer. Forgiveness is emotional in that the forgiver must absorb the pain, relinquishing his justified resentment to begin the relationship anew. Forgiveness is performative in that when the offender confesses, apologizes, and makes restitution, the victim should speak the words of absolution to lift the wrongdoer's burden of guilt. He gives the gift of forgiveness and the wrongdoer accepts it. Forgiveness is relational in that it marks the beginning of a new relationship in which the offender and forgiver are reconciled in an appropriate way. None of these elements, which include all of the biblical metaphors, should be omitted if forgiveness is to be practiced to its fullest.

FINAL COMMENTS

To suffer abandonment and betrayal may be life's primary opportunity to know "the fellowship of his sufferings" (Phil 3:10 KJV). It is certainly helpful in establishing intimacy and dependence on God and in that sense is a blessing and privilege. Also, to forgive one who has betrayed

2. Biggar, "Forgiveness," 215–16.

or abandoned you may be life's primary opportunity to live in a way that emulates God and witnesses to others. Forgiveness is a powerful and transformative act. It is an act of love, an act of sacrifice, and an act of righteousness. What better way to be like our Father in Heaven and like our Lord Jesus.

While writing this book, many times I thought, "How rare is true repentance!" and therefore how rare the opportunity to give the powerful gift of forgiveness—to absorb the pain, cast away the sin, and love freshly, fully, and freely. This book has been written for those abandoned and betrayed by those they loved deeply and intimately. My hope is that, in addition to helping the abandoned and betrayed, it will also lead those who have wrongfully wounded others who loved them to repentance, apology, and reconciliation. In a very real way the ball is in their court: it takes the actions of two to be reconciled, but the offender must make an essential, if not the first, move.

There is little in this book that has not been said before. However, during my research I was unable to find a single book that combined an ethical study of forgiveness with sufficient scriptural exegesis. I hope that many will benefit from this blend of ethics and biblical insight and that Bible teachers and Christian counselors will use this work to teach and help others. By embracing the method of philosophers—by defining terms and drawing distinctions—I have come to think more clearly about ethical issues involved in the practice of forgiveness.[3] This book attempts to present biblical doctrine and then put it to ethical scrutiny. One should not fear this process. I am aware that no one person gets it all right—that others will disagree with some of my conclusions—and that is okay.

I have broken relationships, and as a result, I live, as perhaps most people do, aware that my world is not right. But I also live with longing for and expectation of a world certain to be made right by its Creator. This is the Christian perspective: the truth of present reality (broken relationships) balanced by the truth of future expectation ("reconciliation of all things"). That is not to say that it is easy.

For nearly every page of this book I can think of an example that would enlighten the teaching or discussion. However, examples have been omitted to avoid a five-hundred-page book. I hope each teacher shares his or her own examples as appropriate.

---

3. Murphy, *Getting Even*, 7, 9.

As Jones says, people continuing in the craft of forgiveness "develop a deeper and wider range of discernment about what the appropriate response ought to be to this or that situation or circumstance."[4] Such learning never stops because there are always new situations and circumstances. May my learning never stop, and through that learning may I be corrected in any error.

A phrase from a song grabbed my heart some years ago: "blameless till he come." It expresses my heart's desire, so my prayer and quest toward that end is to be one who repents when I need to repent and forgives when I need to forgive. "We are looking forward to a new heaven and a new earth, where righteousness dwells. So then, dear friends, since you are looking forward to this, make every effort to be found spotless, blameless and at peace with him" (2 Pet 3:13b–14).[5]

---

4. L. Jones, *Embodying Forgiveness*, 227.

5. Final Note: Having quoted Miroslav Volf extensively throughout this book I would like to clarify one point of disagreement between his view and my view of forgiveness. My respect for his views and work are unbounded in spite of this disagreement. Volf says:

> Forgivers forego the punishment of persons who deserve it and release them from the bonds of their guilt. Of course to obtain this forgiveness wrongdoers must receive forgiveness of their misdeeds as just that—*forgiveness*—just as any person must accept a gift to be given, not simply offered. Wrongdoers must acknowledge their actions as wrongdoing, distance themselves from their misdeeds, and where possible restore to their victims what the original violation took away. Failure to do so would not result in the withdrawal of forgiveness; that gift is unconditional. But it would result in the suspension of forgiveness between its generous giver and the intended but untaking recipient. (*End of Memory*, 121)

This quotation reveals the point of disagreement. Volf defines forgiveness as an internal unconditional act, not based on repentance, not removing the offense, and not resulting in reconciliation. The act of forgiveness is complete but reconciliation cannot take place until the wrongdoer repents and "receives" his forgiveness. In my opinion this represents a reversal of the biblical order. If I understand him correctly, Volf bases his view on the Scripture verses that in my opinion refer to eschatological forgiveness. He believes that all sin is forgiven in Christ's death (*End of Memory*, 123). This belief represents a fundamentally different view of the atonement from mine (see my book *Victorious Substitution: A Theory of the Atonement*). In *The End of Memory* he uses the words "atoned for" and "forgiven" as parallel (123). In my view the atonement does not represent the forgiving of all individual sin but the redemption of the world from the powers of evil—Satan, sin, and death. Individual forgiveness awaits repentance.

In *Free of Charge* Volf argues that God forgives a person before he repents, but that person does not receive the forgiveness until he repents. He says it is as if forgiveness has left the forgiver but is stuck somewhere in the middle if the wrongdoer does not acknowledge guilt, therefore God forgives but the wrongdoer is not forgiven (182). In my opinion this is an awkward and incorrect distinction. It ignores the biblical meaning of the term forgive, which involves the removal of sin. It is like saying God has removed the sin but the sin is not removed. I believe the Scripture indicates that God makes known to sinners his willingness to forgive them should they repent (his grace), and in this sense offers his forgiveness. But forgiveness only takes place when that conditional offer is accepted through confession and repentance.

In *The End of Memory*, in reference to his prison experiences at the hands of his interrogator, Volf says, "I must admit that I do resist the idea that in the death of Christ God forgave this wrongdoing against me. I even rebel against it. The cross is a scandal for me too—an affront to my sense of justice" (123). Forgiving the unrepentant requires us to compromise our sense of justice. I truly believe that our sense of justice need not be called into question by the death of Christ.

Appendix A

Luke 23:34a

Most biblical commentaries seek to help the reader understand the meaning of the text, paying close attention to the context of the passage. However, there is another question that often needs to be addressed first: What *is* the original text? The reason such a question must be asked is because none of the original documents of the Bible exist today and the copies that do exist differ from one another.[1] In the case of Luke 23:34a the earliest known manuscripts do not have this sentence. Therefore, it becomes the task of textual critics to try to determine the original, based on the manuscript evidence and the evidence within the biblical text itself. In the case of Luke 23:34a critics must try to determine whether the sentence was added to the original text or deleted from it.

THE HISTORY OF THE TRANSMISSION OF THE NT TEXT

In order to understand the need to determine the original text, let us examine the history of the transmission of the NT. In the earliest days of the spread of Christianity, handwritten copies of an apostolic letter or a Gospel had to be made and circulated. In this process differences from the original emerged. Most of the discrepancies arose from accidental mistakes. Such accidental errors might occur because a scribe was fatigued, had defective eyesight, or was less attentive than he should have

---

1. Metzger, *Commentary on Greek NT*, viii.

been.[2] Other differences arose from deliberate attempts to improve the text by smoothing out grammatical or stylistic harshness or attempting to clarify a passage. In this way, during the years following the composition of the documents that eventually became the NT, hundreds, if not thousands, of variant readings evolved.[3]

As more and more copies were made, several distinctive types of NT text emerged in different localities. Today the type of text can be determined by comparing its distinctive readings with the writings of the Church Fathers in a particular location.

One of the most important of the distinctive types of NT text is the Alexandrian text (original location, Alexandria, Egypt), which is considered to be the most faithful in preserving the original text. This text is characterized by brevity and austerity. It is generally shorter than other texts and does not exhibit the degree of grammatical and stylistic polishing that characterizes texts arising in other locations.[4] Until recently the two chief Alexandrian manuscripts were Codex Vaticanus (B) and Codex Sinaiticus (א). These are parchment manuscripts that date back to about the middle of the fourth century. However, after the discovery of the Bodmer Papyri (especially P[66] and P[75], which date back to the end of the second or the beginning of the third century) scholars have concluded that the Alexandrian text-type must go back to an archetype dated early in the second century.[5]

Another text-type is referred to as the Western text. It existed in Italy, Gaul, North Africa (including Egypt), and elsewhere, and can also be traced back to the second century. The most important of the Western text-type are Codex Bezae (D[ea]), which dates to the fifth century; Codex Claromontanus (D[p]), which dates to the sixth century; and the Old Latin versions. The Western text is not as true to the original and is characterized by its fondness for paraphrase. Sometimes words, phrases, or even whole sentences are changed, inserted, or omitted.[6] For example, in the Western text the book of Acts is nearly ten percent longer than that which is generally regarded as original.[7]

2. Metzger, *Commentary on Greek NT*, xv.

3. Metzger, *Commentary on Greek NT*, xvi.

4. Metzger, *Commentary on Greek NT*, xvii.

5. Metzger, *Commentary on Greek NT*, xviii.

6. Metzger, *Commentary on Greek NT*, xviii.

7. Metzger, *Commentary on Greek NT*, xviii.

A third text-type is the Caesarean text. It is thought to have originated in Egypt and later been brought to Caesarea. It was then taken to Jerusalem and carried by Armenian missionaries to Georgia. It dates from the third century and is characterized by a distinctive mix of Western and Alexandrian readings.[8]

A fourth text-type is called the Byzantine text (sometimes called the Syrian text, the Koine text, the Ecclesiastical text, or the Antiochian text). It is the latest of the distinctive NT text-types and is characterized by clarity and completeness. The writers of this text tried to smooth out any harshness of language, combine any two or more divergent readings into an expanded reading (called conflation), and harmonize divergent passages. This conflated text, thought to have been composed in Syria, was taken to Constantinople where it was distributed widely throughout the Byzantine Empire. From the sixth or seventh century until the time of the printing press (1450–56) the Byzantine text-type was generally considered the authoritative text and was therefore the most widely distributed and accepted.[9] Unfortunately, after Gutenberg's press, it was this debased and corrupted text that became the standard text to be printed and distributed.[10]

The Greek NT was first published in 1516 by the Dutch scholar Desiderius Erasmus. In subsequent years many other editions reproduced this text. He relied on two inferior texts from the twelfth century, comparing them with several others and adding corrections in the margins. There are several readings from this procedure that have never been found in any other text but which are perpetuated today in the Greek NT text called the Textus Receptus. The second edition of Erasmus' text was used by Martin Luther and William Tyndale as the basis for their translations into German (1522) and English (1525), respectively. Editors sometimes had access to older manuscripts, but because they differed so much, they were rarely used. Between 1565 and 1604 nine editions of the Greek NT were issued by Theodore Beza, and it was these editions that popularized what came to be called the Textus Receptus, on which the King James Bible (1611) was based. The term *Textus Receptus* originated from printers who prefaced their edition with the words, "Therefore you, dear reader, now have the text received by all, in which nothing has

8. Metzger, *Commentary on Greek NT*, xix.

9. Metzger, *Commentary on Greek NT*, xx.

10. Metzger, *Commentary on Greek NT*, xxi.

been changed or corrupted." These words are ironic because it was this Byzantine text-type that was the most disfigured by the accumulation of myriad scribal alterations over the centuries. This form of text provided the basis for almost all translations of the NT into modern languages until the nineteenth century.[11]

This situation changed in 1831 when Karl Lachmann, a German scholar, applied to the NT the methods he had used in editing texts of the classics. Then other editions that used this same method appeared, including that of Constantin von Tischendorf, whose 1869–72 edition contains "a monumental thesaurus of variant readings." Two Cambridge scholars, B. F. Westcott and F. J. A. Hort, also put out an edition in 1881. The present United Bible Societies' edition is based on the work of Westcott and Hort. The twentieth century has seen the discovery of manuscripts older than any others, resulting in editions of the NT that are ever more close to the original manuscripts.[12]

CRITERIA USED IN CHOOSING AMONG CONFLICTING READINGS IN NT WITNESSES

As can be seen by the preceding discussion, after fourteen centuries of transmission by handwritten copying, many thousands of variant readings exist in the approximately five thousand Greek manuscripts that are known today. In publishing and translating the Bible, editors and translators must decide which variants to include and which to relegate to what is called the apparatus. The apparatus is a listing of variants that are not considered original. Although determining what is original would at first appear to be an impossible task, textual scholars have developed sound criteria of evaluation. However, considerations based on probabilities must sometimes be weighed against one another. The main criteria and considerations that help textual critics evaluate variant readings are (1) external evidence having to do with the entire manuscript and (2) internal evidence having to do with two types of probabilities: transcriptional (i.e., relating to the habits of scribes) and intrinsic (i.e., relating to the style of the author).[13]

---

11. Metzger, *Commentary on Greek NT*, xxii–xxiii.

12. Metzger, *Commentary on Greek NT*, xxiii.

13. Metzger, *Commentary on Greek NT*, xxiv–xxv.

Outline of Criteria

I. External Evidence

A. The Date and Character of the Manuscript: In general, the earlier the manuscript the more error free it is likely to be. However, of even greater importance is the character of the manuscript—the text-type of the manuscript and the care of the individual copyist who produced the manuscript.

B. The Geographical Distribution of the Manuscripts That Support a Variant: The agreement of manuscripts from a variety of regions is, all else being equal, more important than the reading of a manuscript from a single locality.

C. The Genealogical Relationship of Texts and Families of Manuscripts: The number of manuscripts supporting a variant reading does not necessarily prove the superiority of that reading. This is because multiple manuscripts may have been copied from one source. It is that original source manuscript that must be compared to the manuscript containing a different reading. Therefore, witnesses are to be "weighed rather than counted." In other words, those manuscripts that are generally trustworthy in clear-cut cases of variant readings should be given more weight in cases in which the textual problems are more ambiguous and therefore more difficult.[14]

II. Internal Evidence

A. Transcriptional Probabilities: Errors that may be a result of the copying process are evaluated by taking into account the habits of scribes.

   1. In general, the more difficult reading is to be preferred because a scribe was more likely to simplify rather than make a reading more difficult. This is especially true when a reading at first appears to be difficult but careful consideration renders it correct. Occasionally, however, a reading may be so difficult that it is thought to have arisen through scribal error.

   2. In general, the shorter reading is considered preferable because "intentional changes are far more likely to involve additions than

---

14. Metzger, *Commentary on Greek NT*, xxv–xxvi.

omissions."[15] The shorter reading is not considered more likely to be correct when it appears that the eye of the copyist may have passed from one word to another having a similar sequence of letters, causing him to repeat a phrase or sentence.

3. Neither is the shorter reading considered more likely to be correct when it appears that a scribe chose to omit a troublesome word or phrase in order to simplify a text's style or meaning.[16] The shorter reading also may not be correct when it appears that the scribe may have omitted material that he could have judged to be superfluous, harsh, or contrary to pious belief or to church use or practice.[17]

Thus, the study of scribal habits reveals that they "tended to add and to simplify more than they tended to omit and to complicate."[18]

B. Intrinsic Probabilities: Intrinsic probabilities consider what the author is more likely to have written. In making this decision textual critics take into account several criteria.
   1. In general:

      a. the author's style and vocabulary as revealed throughout the book

      b. the immediate context

      c. harmony with the author's other work

   2. In the Gospels:

      a. the Aramaic background of the teaching of Jesus

      b. the priority of the Gospel according to Mark

      c. the possible influence of the church upon the passage[19]

---

15. Edwards, "Using the Textual Apparatus," 128.
16. Edwards, "Using the Textual Apparatus," 128.
17. Metzger, *Commentary on Greek NT*, xxvii–xxviii.
18. Edwards, "Using the Textual Apparatus," 129.
19. Metzger, *Commentary on Greek NT*, xxvii-xxviii.

THE TEXTUAL APPARATUS OF THE UBS (UNITED BIBLE SOCIETIES) GREEK NT

The committee of textual critics that produces the United Bible Societies' editions of the Greek NT must weigh all these considerations, although it is obvious that they may not all apply in each case. In difficult cases, where there is a divergence of evidence, it is inevitable that scholars may have different opinions as to the significance of the evidence.

The textual apparatus of the Greek NT published by the United Bible Societies exists to help offer what it considers to be the best translations of NT variants. The belief of the United Bible Societies is that the translator should have some involvement in the decisions concerning biblical variants. The *UBS/GNT* (*United Bible Societies Greek NT*) gives the manuscript evidence for only 1,400 passages, which is about one percent of the total text. The translator, by using the commentary on these 1,400 passages and based on a general knowledge of the principles of textual criticism, is free to make his own decision regarding the text. In order to show the degree of certainty (doc) in the mind of the committee for the reading chosen for the text, an identifying letter is included within brackets at the beginning of each set of textual variants. The letter {A} indicates that the text is certain, while {B} indicates that there is some doubt concerning the reading selected for the text. The letter {C} indicates that there is a considerable degree of doubt whether the text chosen or the variant relegated to the apparatus is the better reading. The letter {D} means that there is a very high degree of doubt concerning the reading selected.[20] These letters are intended to either encourage or discourage a translator from making his own decision. For example, a translator would be more apt to consider the translation for himself if the passage has a {C} or {D}.[21] The *UBS/GNT* includes commentary on the more difficult passages to indicate how the committee made their decisions.

A translator can also refer to *A Textual Commentary on the Greek NT* written by Bruce M. Metzger (1971), who was one of the five *UBS/GNT* editors. His book gives a lengthy introduction and then lists some of the commentary on some of the passages in the *UBS/GNT*.

20. Metzger, *Commentary on Greek NT*, xxvii–xxviii.
21. Edwards, "Using the Textual Apparatus," 121.

LUKE 23:34a

External Arguments

Elizabeth Edwards, an interregional Translations Research Associate of the United Bible Societies, writes concerning the work of these editors that is found in the apparatus of the *UBS/GNT*, "This passage [Luke 23:34a] witnesses to the attitude of the editors, their openness to new insights, and the open-endedness of their decisions, because of a change from the first edition to the third edition."[22] In the first edition, Luke 23:34a was given within the text (rather than relegated to the apparatus), but it is bracketed and given a {C} doc indicating the committee's opinion that it is a gloss (not original). However, in the third edition, although the sentence is still in the text, it is given in double brackets, thereby indicating the committee's certainty that it does *not* belong in the text.[23] In Metzger's commentary he says:

> The absence of these words from such early and diverse manuscripts as P[75] B D* W Θ it[a, d] syr[s] cop[sa, bo mss] is most impressive and can scarcely be explained as a deliberate excision by copyists, who considering the fall of Jerusalem to be proof that God had not forgiven the Jews, could not allow it to appear that the prayer of Jesus had remained unanswered. At the same time, the logion [translation], though probably not a part of the original Greek of Luke, bears self-evident tokens of its dominical origin, and was retained, within double square brackets, in its traditional place where it had been incorporated by unknown copyists relatively early in the transmission of the Third Gospel.[24]

What this means is that, although the saying is found in early and diverse manuscripts, because it is not found in the earliest manuscripts, the UBS has concluded *with certainty* that it is a gloss. In other words, the external evidence drives the conclusion. However, it is included in the text rather than relegated to the apparatus because it was an early addition to the text.

In the fourth edition of the *UBS Greek NT*, published in 2007, the passage is still in double brackets with no letter (doc) indicating *degree* of certainty, because it is regarded with *certainty* to be an addition to

---

22. Edwards, "Using the Textual Apparatus," 137.
23. Edwards, "Using the Textual Apparatus," 137.
24. Metzger, *Commentary on Greek NT*, 180.

the text. If the editors had regarded its presence as disputed, the passage would have been placed in single brackets. It is included within the body of the text because of its antiquity.[25] (Double brackets are also used for the ending of Mark's Gospel, 16:9–20.)

Another external reason (based on manuscript evidence) for concluding that Luke 23:34a is a gloss is put forward by Whitlark and Parsons, who have argued that the evidence for inclusion is restricted to the Western text prior to the fourth century. The recognized tendency of the Western text to introduce new material increases the probability that Luke 23:34a was not original.[26]

Internal Arguments

Transcriptional probabilities indicate that Luke 23:34a is spurious both because the shorter reading is preferred and because scribes are more likely to add than delete. One internal argument for considering the saying an addition is that the saying interrupts the narrative flow of Luke 23:33 and 23:34b. Without the logion the passage reads: "When they came to the place called the Skull, they crucified him there, along with the criminals—one on his right, the other on his left. And they divided up his clothes by casting lots." If the saying is included the text reads: "When they came to the place called the Skull, they crucified him there, along with the criminals—one on his right, the other on his left. Jesus said, 'Father, forgive them, for they do not know what they are doing.' And they divided up his clothes by casting lots." This argument is only marginally relevant, however, because Luke himself could have been using several documents and made the insertion himself.[27]

Most of the arguments for the inclusion of Luke 23:34a are related to intrinsic probabilities.[28] (However, they are generally countered by other intrinsic probabilities.) The vocabulary is typically Lucan, meaning that all the words used are commonly found in Luke–Acts. However, the vocabulary is not *distinctively* Lucan. The passage is also similar to the account of Stephen's death in Acts.[29] However, it could be argued that

---

25. Aland et al., *UBS Greek NT*, 11, 243.
26. Whitlark and Parsons, "Seven Last Words," 191.
27. Whitlark and Parsons, "Seven Last Words," 193.
28. Whitlark and Parsons, "Seven Last Words," 191.
29. Whitlark and Parsons, "Seven Last Words," 191.

Stephen's words provided the motivation for giving Jesus similar words so that Stephen would not appear more holy than Jesus.

In considering the intrinsic evidence, the most important aspect involves answering the question, Why delete? or, Why add? It has been suggested that it could have been deleted because of a scribe's conclusion that Jesus' prayer was not answered, as evidenced by the fall of Jerusalem. It has also been suggested that, reflecting the anti-Jewish sentiment of the early church, a scribe was unhappy with Jesus' forgiving attitude toward the Jews. However, in agreement with Metzger and the UBS committee, Edwards says that these proposals "rest on very shaky grounds."[30] In other words, based on a knowledge of scribal habits, they are not convincing. The opposite view, put forward by David Flusser, is that the words were inserted by a Jewish Christian in the context of an ongoing mission to the Jews.[31]

Others have pointed out that it is not clear that Jesus is even referring to the Jews. Many commentators have thought the reference is to the Roman soldiers, which the text mentions immediately after the saying and of whom it could more readily be said that they did not know what they were doing.[32]

Many have questioned that a scribe would choose to omit words of Jesus that were original—especially such important words. As Edwards points out, "It is difficult enough for editors today to omit them; one can hardly imagine their willful omission sixteen and one half centuries ago."[33] In fact, since the time of Westcott and Hort many scholars have argued that no Christian could have willfully omitted some of Jesus' dying words.[34] Hort says, "Its omission on the hypothesis of its genuineness, cannot be explained in any reasonable manner. Willful excision on account of the love and forgiveness shown to the Lord's own murderers, is absolutely incredible."[35] Hort also says that "even among the numerous unquestionably spurious readings of the NT, there are no signs of deliberate falsification for dogmatic purposes."[36]

---

30. Edwards, "Using the Textual Apparatus," 138.

31. Whitlark and Parsons, "Seven Last Words," 193.

32. Whitlark and Parsons, "Seven Last Words," 194.

33. Edwards, "Using the Textual Apparatus," 139.

34. Eubank, "A Disconcerting Prayer," 526.

35. Eubank, "A Disconcerting Prayer," 527.

36. Harris, "Textual Criticism," 317.

The suggestions put forward as motivation for a scribe to purpose-fully add the saying include seeing it as a gloss on another manuscript, seeing it written down elsewhere, or knowing of it orally. These reasons are not convincing.[37] Others have suggested that the prayer was added so that Stephen (Acts 7:60b) does not look more compassionate than Jesus.[38] Still others have pointed out that there is an ignorance motif in Luke–Acts that would argue for the saying's originality.[39] Just as the suggested reasons for omission are not convincing, neither are the arguments for addition very convincing. However, a more substantial argument for addition has been presented by Jason A. Whitlark and Mikeal C. Parsons, as the following section will detail.

The "Seven" Last Words: A Numerical Motivation for the Insertion of Luke 23:34a

In their article "The 'Seven' Last Words: A Numerical Motivation for the Insertion of Luke 23:34a," Whitlark and Parsons present the theory that the words were originally added into the early four-Gospel tradition in order to make seven total sayings from the cross. These authors first cite Martin Hengel and Graham Stanton, who argue that the four-Gospel tradition was established well before the end of the second century.[40] This early acceptance of four Gospels is indicated by Irenaeus in the West and by the papyri of Egypt in the East. The fact that there were four accepted Gospels stimulated several attempts to harmonize the four into one account. The most famous Gospel harmony was written by Tatian around 170 in the East and was called *The Diatessaron*.[41]

If Luke 23:34a is not original, based on the textual evidence, then when the four Gospel accounts were first read as a harmony and all of Jesus' words from the cross are taken together, there are six sayings. This presents a serious problem symbolically. First, the number six had negative connotations. For example, the number of the beast from the earth is the number of humanity: namely 666 (Rev 13:18). Jesus is crucified at the sixth hour (John 19:14), and darkness covers the land during the

---

37. Edwards, "Using the Textual Apparatus," 138.

38. Eubank, "A Disconcerting Prayer," 525–26.

39. Eubank, "A Disconcerting Prayer," 526.

40. Whitlark and Parsons, "Seven Last Words," 195.

41. Whitlark and Parsons, "Seven Last Words," 196.

crucifixion at the sixth hour (Luke 23:44). But the main problem with six is simply that it is not the number seven, which symbolizes perfection or completeness in Scripture. The number seven occurs eighty-eight times in the NT. It is especially evident in the numerical symbolism of Revelation. There are seven disciples listed in John 21:2, seven deacons in Acts 6:3, seven afflictions in Rom 8:35, seven gifts in Rom 12:6–8, seven qualities of wisdom in Jas 3:17, seven virtues in 2 Pet 1:5–8, seven affirmations in the doxology of Rom 11:33–36, seven petitions in the Lord's prayer in Matt 6, and seven loaves used by Jesus to feed the four thousand with seven baskets collected afterward in Mark 8:1–10.[42]

Seven is also used in the structure of many texts. In Rev 2 and 3 there are seven letters to the seven churches. In Rev 4:1—22:5 there are seven visions of the future times. In John's Gospel, the beginning (1:19—2:11) and the end (chapters 12–20) are organized around seven days. John 2:13—11:57 contains seven events demonstrating that Jesus both fulfills and supersedes Jewish practice. In Matt 1 the genealogy is structured into three sets of fourteen (two times seven). There are other collections of seven in the NT as well. In Matthew, there are seven fulfillments of Scripture by Jesus. In Matt 13, there are seven parables, and in Matt 23, seven woes.[43] Based on the scriptural use of seven for completeness, it can be argued that the saying was added to Tatian's harmony so that there would be seven sayings of Jesus from the cross rather than six.

The most compelling evidence that the saying "Father, forgive them . . ." originated in Tatian's *Diatesseron* and was later added to the Gospel of Luke is the order of the sayings in later Diatesseronic witnesses. In Tatian's *Diatesseron*, which is the earliest extant witness (ca. 170) to the sayings of Jesus from the cross collected within a single narrative, Luke 23:34a is given as the sixth saying. This place is significant because in Tatian's order the sayings from John and the two undisputed sayings from Luke maintain their original canonical narrative order. Only Luke 23:34a is out of order.[44]

By contrast, the later Gospel harmonies, such as the Pepysian Gospel Harmony (written in Middle English) and the Persian Diatessaron have Luke 23:34a first. [Middle-English Pepys has: (1) Luke 23:34a, (2) John 19:26–27, (3) Luke 23:43, (4) Mark 15:34, (5) John 19:28, (6) John

---

42. Whitlark and Parsons, "Seven Last Words," 198.

43. Whitlark and Parsons, "Seven Last Words," 199.

44. Whitlark and Parsons, "Seven Last Words," 201–2.

19:30, and (7) Luke 23:46a; the Persian Diatessaron gives the sayings in
the following order: (1) Luke 23:34a, (2) John 19:26–27, (3) John 19:28,
(4) John 19:30, (5) Luke 23:43, (6) Mark 15:34, (7) Luke 23:46a.] It would
make sense that if the saying had been added to Luke by the time of these
later Gospel harmonies, then in all these later examples, the saying "Father, forgive them . . ." would be the first saying, even though the order of
the others vary. This would maintain the narrative integrity of the sayings
from the Gospel of Luke. Putting Luke 23:34a first would also maintain
the logical chronological sequence (if the saying had by then been added
to Luke) when all the Gospels are read together, since this saying occurs
in the Gospel of Luke immediately after the Roman soldiers nail Jesus to
the cross.[45]

The Syriac Diatessaronic versions c and s also indicate that the saying was added to Luke. These manuscripts are thought to be from the
fourth to fifth century, but their texts are thought to go back to the second
or third century; syr[s] is thought to be pre-Tatian, and it does not contain
Luke 23:34a, whereas syr[c], which is post-Tatian, has the saying. Therefore, in these two Syriac versions the transition from the saying's absence
from Luke in the early second century to its appearance in Luke in the
early third century can clearly be seen.[46]

All of this indicates that at the time Tatian wrote his *Diatesseron* this
saying had not yet been added to the text of Luke. It would make sense
that this saying was added to a Gospel harmony to make a seventh saying
and was then later added to the Gospel of Luke.[47] If, from these early
Gospel harmonies, the saying then made its way into Scripture, why was
it added to Luke? Unlike Matthew and Mark, Luke's crucifixion narrative
already had two sayings. By adding a third to Luke, canonical balance was
achieved: three sayings in Luke, three in John, and one in Matthew and
Mark (the same saying). Furthermore, the saying was probably modeled
after the saying of Stephen in Acts 7:60. Why would it have been inserted
at the particular location where it is found? One theory, according to J.
H. Petzer, is that it was added there (Luke 23:34) out of anti-Jewish bias,
the prayer being directed toward the Romans who crucified Jesus, not the
Jewish leaders who rejected him.[48]

45. Whitlark and Parsons, "Seven Last Words," 203.
46. Whitlark and Parsons, "Seven Last Words," 202.
47. Whitlark and Parsons, "Seven Last Words," 203.
48. Whitlark and Parsons, "Seven Last Words," 204.

SUMMARY

The saying in Luke 23:34a, "Father, forgive them, for they do not know what they are doing," was either added to, or deleted from, the original text of Luke's Gospel. (This much is certain because there are early manuscripts that have the saying, in which case it was deleted in others, and there are early manuscripts that do not have the saying, in which case it was added to others.) This appendix has attempted to make clear the issues involved in determining what was original. This determination is primarily the task of textual critics who base their conclusions on the manuscript evidence (external evidence) and evidence within the biblical text itself (internal evidence).

The history of the transmission of the NT text was examined in order to explain the necessity of determining the original text. In the case of Luke 23:34a, the words "Father, forgive them, for they do not know what they are doing" are not found in the *earliest* manuscripts but *are* found in other *early* manuscripts. The *UBS/GNT*, the work of textual critics, concludes that Luke 23:34a is a gloss, or not original. Although Bible translations include Luke 23:34a in the text, all versions indicate in some manner that the words are not found in the earliest manuscripts. This would seem to be conclusive, but it is not, as some biblical scholars believe that the verse could have been original and was later deleted for various reasons. Most Bible readers are not even aware of the controversy.

In addition to relating the external textual evidence that has led textual critics to reject the verse as original, this appendix has explained the most common internal reasons for this verse's addition or deletion. The author has found the internal reasons suggested for inclusion, as well as those suggested for deletion, unconvincing with one exception—the numerical motivation for insertion. This theory, put forth by Whitlark and Parsons, argues that the words were originally added to the early four-Gospel harmony of Tatian to make a seventh saying from the cross. After this, the words were at some point added to the Gospel of Luke. This possibility is advanced by the fact that in the earliest Gospel harmony (Tatian, ca.170) Luke 23:34a is out of order (in other words, not based on the order we now have in Luke). However, in later Gospel harmonies (presumably after the saying was added to Luke), the saying is always put first. This would indicate that authors of later Gospel harmonies based their order on the placement they *then* found in Luke.

Appendix B

Answers to Study Questions

CHAPTER 1—RECONCILIATION: A WORTHY, IF ILLUSORY, GOAL

Introductory Comments

1. reconciliation; repentance

2. the offense

3. betrayal has occurred

Lamentation

1. lament

2. grief, protest, and pain; Psalms

The Biblical Model

1. (i) forswear retaliation; (ii) acknowledge anger; (iii) pray and lament; (iv) state wrongdoing; (v) offer forgiveness if repentance; (vi) accept outcome and move on

2. angry at injustice; refusing to condone; hurting because of rejection; desiring vindication; desiring the salvation of the one loved; calling for repentance; expressing willingness to forgive; helping the wrongdoer

3. (i) recognize wrongdoing; (ii) admit guilt; (iii) regret; (iv) decide to change

4. accept, forgive, show compassion, and begin to trust (Ezek 18:21–22; 33:16)

Full Restoration

1. Hosea; the parable of the prodigal son (Hos 1:2b; 11:8; Luke 15:11–32)

2. victims: wounded and reconciled; wrongdoers: guilty and forgiven

Amends-Making

1. make right (restitution); shows genuineness of repentance, begins to restore trust

2. apparent repentance may not be sincere

3. endures pain; forswears retaliation; gives up anger; forgives; becomes vulnerable

Reconciliation and Consequences

1. no

2. not necessarily: the reconciled relationship may include consequences appropriate to the situation

Is Reconciliation Always Possible?

1. reconciliation requires both parties; one must choose to be reconciled to God

2. it removes pressure to do something not even God is always able to do

3. being realistic holds out hope, even if painful; being cynical is refusing to hope, may lead to bitterness

4. the loss of the situation prior to the offense

Truth and Reconciliation

1. if parties cannot agree on the truth, then forgiveness, amends, and reconciliation cannot occur

2. reconciliation will occur in the new creation

3. be truthful and refrain from offering forgiveness, but do not rule out future forgiveness

Reasons Reconciliation May Not Occur

1. one party has died; too much pain; unwilling/unable to reconcile; reconciliation is inappropriate; time runs out

2. the victim may only be able to offer a sort of forgiveness without reconciliation

Third Parties

1. third parties are not fully informed, advice may be presumptuous

2. (i) inconvenience of broken relationships; (ii) the hurts are not their own

CHAPTER 2—REPENTANCE: THE CALL OF LOVE

The Term Repentance

1. repentance

2. to change one's mind; a decision

3. remorse: present feeling related to past behavior; repentance: present decision related to future behavior

4. his change of mind concerning intended punishment

The Biblical Call to Repentance

1. repentance precedes and therefore prepares the way for forgiveness (Mark 11:1–4, 15)

2. repent and believe

3. repentance for the forgiveness of sins (Luke 24:46–47)

4. repent and be baptized for the forgiveness of sins (Acts 2:38; 8:22)

5. turn to God in repentance and have faith in the Lord Jesus Christ (Acts 26:18; 20:21; 2 Tim 2:19b; Acts 26:20; 17:30; Luke 13:3; Isa 30:15b)

6. sinners misled to empty professions of faith; misrepresents the gospel message

Regret versus Repentance

1. repentance as a change of mind now thought of as grief over sin

2. no; Pharaoh, Saul (Exod 9:27–28)

3. no; Judas (Matt 27:3–5)

4. sorrow for sin should lead to repentance; repentance should lead to salvation

Repentance Is the Condition of God's Favor and Forgiveness

1. no

2. judgment shows that God cares; sinners cannot presume upon his love

3. *if* one repents *then* God forgives

The Ministry of a Prophet

1. prophet; yes, Christians should also call for repentance

2. indifference to wrongdoer's well-being (Amos 4:11–12)

Repentance and Forgiveness Lead to Reconciliation

1. God chooses to forgive based on his love

2. removal of sin

Demonstration of Repentance

1. trespass offering (restitution plus 20 percent; Lev 6:1–7)

2. demonstration of repentance (Matt 3:5–8; Acts 26:20)

3. restitution (four times what was owed), giving to the poor (Luke 19:1–9)

Repentance, Forgiveness, and Judgment: A Case Study

1. whether the wrongdoer chooses to repent

The Biblical Model

1. a duty to obey and emulate God

2. no

Moral and Ethical Considerations Related to Repentance

Repentance Does not Earn Forgiveness

1. the offender asks for forgiveness on his own behalf; the victim grants the gift of forgiveness

Regret: Remorse

1. other-oriented regret and true remorse produce repentance

Guilt

1. concern for the victim

Confession, Apology, and Reparations

1. if guilt is buried, it may not lead to repentance

2. if apology is easy, it is generally insincere

The Limits of Amends-Making

    1. no, the harm done cannot always be fixed

The Logic and Morality of Unforgiveness

    1. it encourages sin to persist

    2. not when refusing to face sin

    3. prior: wrath and love; after: love and joy

    4. it does not want the best for the loved one

    5. no, God does not forgive the unrepentant

CHAPTER 3—THE BIBLICAL MEANING OF FORGIVENESS

    1. resentment

    2. the biblical concept includes both parties, is an external act, and ends in reconciliation

The Old Testament Concept of Forgiveness

    1. atonement

    2. it now refers to compensation by the wrongdoer

    3. sin and wrath

    4. to send away or let go

    5. to lift up, take away, or carry away; also to bear someone's sin

    6. to wipe, wipe out, erase, blot out, exterminate, or obliterate from the memory

The New Testament Concept of Forgiveness

    1. (i) *aphiemi*: to send away or remove sin; (ii) *aphesis*: freedom or liberation (from sin); (iii) *charizomai*: to pardon or graciously remit (sin); (iv) *apoluo*: to release, let go, send away, or set free (from sin)

2. sin; reconciliation

3. it is the same: forgiveness removes sin as the barrier to reconciliation

Biblical Metaphors for Forgiveness

1. (i) carrying away a burden; (ii) covering up or blotting out a stain; (iii) canceling a debt; (iv) giving a gift

2. wrongdoer: release from the burden of sin and remission of debt; forgiver: elimination of offense as a barrier to reconciliation; community: erasure of the stain of sin

Lifting a Burden and Bearing It Away

1. if guilt were not burdensome, then lifting the burden would mean nothing

Blotting Out Sin

1. the victim no longer sees the offense when looking at the wrongdoer; it is no longer part of the relationship

2. the repentance of the wrongdoer means he has changed as a person

Remission of Debt

1. the one sinned against waives the right to retribution/satisfaction

2. acknowledge the sin debt and ask for its cancellation

Giving a Gift

1. there is no obligation for a victim to forgive; it is not just negative (remission of debt), but positive (receiving forgiveness)

2. the good of the wrongdoer

The Meaning of Sacrifice

1. sacrifice (typically involving blood)
2. (i) laying hands on the animal—identification; (ii) animal slain—surrender of life to God; (iii) blood taken to the Holy Place—acceptance by God; (iv) animal burned on the altar—offerer giving himself to God; (v) meal—peace and fellowship with God restored

Appointed by God

1. God instituted the means of forgiveness (sacrifice) before man was able to appropriate it

The Meaning of Blood

1. blood symbolizes life
2. heals broken lives, provides a means of reconciliation

The Message of the Prophets

1. when moral offenses continue without repentance (Isa 1:11–15)

The Message of the Scapegoat: The Removal of Sin

1. (i) the sins of the people were confessed over the scapegoat; (ii) the scapegoat was completely removed from their midst (Lev 23:29)

High-Handed Sin

1. presumptuous, willful, or defiant sin that is not repented; lack of repentance renders sacrifice ineffective

CHAPTER 4—ESCHATOLOGICAL FORGIVENESS—"THE FORGIVENESS OF SINS"

1. victory over sin and death; prior repentance was not involved

2. no, it represents the defeat of evil that separates people from God

3. the complete removal of all sin at the end of the age

4. (i) proclaiming the kingdom of God (Col 1:13–14); (ii) healing the sick; (iii) forgiving sin (Matt 9:5)

5. God promised Abraham he would be a blessing to the world and a light to the Gentiles;

6. jubilee was also a time of corporate forgiveness of all debts (Luke 4:18–21)

7. one could misinterpret this forgiveness to mean all people are forgiven of individual sins without repentance

8. no, reconciliation in this sense refers to Christ's finished work prior to individual repentance and salvation

CHAPTER 5—THE JUSTICE OF GOD

The Concept of Justice

1. God must punish sin; that is, he is not free to forgive apart from punishment

2. discipline (Ps 62:12)

3. God gives fair play to every person (Gen 18:25)

4. his own right to punish

5. no

6. injustice; mercy

God Is Free to Remit Sins

1. he forgives apart from satisfaction/payback (Neh 9:16–17, 26–28; Ps 32:1–2, 5; Jer 18:7–8; Ezek 33:14)

Repentance: The Determining Factor

1. the state of the sinner's heart; forgiveness requires repentance/change of heart (Ezek 33:11)

2. God "takes no pleasure in the death of the wicked"

3. no, the condition is repentance; thus it does not undermine morality (2 Pet 3:7–9)

Mercy

1. sinners are not entitled to forgiveness, nor can they demand it; forgiveness depends on a free decision, and so is an act of mercy on God's part (Isa 55:7)

The Wrath of God

1. God's personal reaction to sin, resulting in estrangement and judgment; if his children's sinful behavior did not bother him, it would reveal a lack of love

2. disciplinary (restorative) and retributive (justice)

3. he gives ample time and opportunity for the sinner to repent (Matt 3:2, 8)

Forbearance

1. if God never pursued justice, he would be open to criticism and mockery; God will judge, so he cannot be mocked by failing to do so (Jer 3:19; Rev 6:10–11)

Judgment

1. put an end to evil, violence, and all refusal to accept his love (Ps 14:5)

2. wrath caused by sin leads to estrangement between God and man; wrath is removed by repentance and God's forgiveness

CHAPTER 6—RESTORATION OF RELATIONSHIP

The Hebrew Original

1. the goal of forgiveness is reconciliation, and atonement is another way to speak of reconciliation

Models of Relationship

1. (i) controlling: one dominates another; asymmetric and impersonal; (ii) contractual: parties relate in terms of a social agreement; each seeks to benefit from the terms; value is determined by usefulness; (iii) fellowship (love): persons are inherently valuable regardless of utility and are irreplaceable

Breaking and Restoring Relationships

1. by the controlling partner, who receives all the credit

2. (i) the offending party can make satisfaction (payback); (ii) the offended party can punish the offender or withhold services; (iii) the offended party can condone the wrong

3. the wronged party must be willing to forgive and the offending party must repent and seek forgiveness

Reconciliation with God

1. God would unilaterally deliver sinners from the consequences of sin

2. God would punish humans for wrongdoing or require humans to make satisfaction by good works (condonation of sin is not an option for God)

3. God and humans freely choose to make the other's interests their own (God being concerned with salvation and humans with obeying God's will)

Applications for Models of Relationship

1. the wrong means of reconciliation may be employed: e.g., apology, when satisfaction/punishment is needed; attempted restoration of fellowship where none existed

CHAPTER 7—WHEN AND WHY DOES SCRIPTURE INSTRUCT GOD'S PEOPLE TO FORGIVE?

Interpersonal Forgiveness in the OT

1. (i) love your neighbor (Lev 19:17–18); (ii) confront wrongdoing, but do not take revenge; (iii) encourage confession, sacrifice, and restitution

Judaism versus Christianity

1. Judaism appears more concerned with justice, while Christianity seems concerned primarily with forgiveness, even if inappropriate; due to misunderstanding the NT to teach forgiveness in the absence of repentance

Interpersonal Forgiveness in the NT

1. the forgiveness of God offered in Christ

Confrontation

1. no, personal matters may not require confrontation
2. it shows that a high standard is not expected of them
3. (i) admonish privately; (ii) involve witnesses; (iii) bring it before the church; the motivation is care for the offender and desire for reconciliation
4. loosing refers to forgiveness (being loosed from sin), while binding refers to retention of sin; repentance leads to loosing, while lack of repentance leads to binding

5. God is present with any size group of his people; this passage is related to church discipline and is not needed to support the promise of God's presence (Gal 2:11–14)

Seventy Times Seven

1. a disciple has harmed another disciple (deals with forgiveness within the community); "seventy-seven" is a figure of speech indicating no limit exists for forgiveness following repentance

2. Matthew: the parable of the unmerciful servant; Luke: explicitly stated ("if they repent, forgive them")

The Parable of the Unforgiving Servant

1. the teaching of unlimited forgiveness following repentance; "shouldn't you have mercy on your fellow servant just as I had on you?"

2. sin that needs forgiveness; he humbly acknowledges the debt and asks for forgiveness

3. (i) fear of punishment; (ii) gratitude/imitation of God's grace

4. the master revoking the servant's debt relief illustrates that forgiveness is provisional and may also be revoked

The Lord's Prayer

1. asking forgiveness in the Lord's Prayer shows acknowledgment of sin and repentance

2. disciples are to ask God for forgiveness in the same way they have already forgiven others; they are not to ask God to do something for them that they would not do for others

Verses in Which Repentance Is Presupposed

Forgive as God Forgives

1. freely, following forgiveness; because the Lord has already forgiven them

Forgive and You Will Be Forgiven

1. the link between the Lord's forgiveness and interpersonal forgiveness would not be parallel unless repentance is presupposed

The Woman Who Anoints Jesus' Feet

1. related teachings like Luke 17:3–4 and the emphasis on repentance in the rest of Scripture

Prayer and Forgiveness

1. neither Titus 3:7 nor 1 Cor 6:11 mention faith in connection to salvation, but it is clearly presupposed based on the totality of Scripture

Confession of Sin

1. *if* we confess our sins, *then* God will forgive our sins
2. healing

The Unforgivable Sin

1. no, blasphemy against the Holy Spirit is refusing God's message and thus refusing the forgiveness of sins

Forgive versus Retain

1. Jesus is commissioning his disciples to take the Gospel to the world, proclaiming the forgiveness of sin for all who believe
2. because one may reject the Gospel message; those who accept have their sin forgiven ("loosed"), while those who refuse remain in their sin ("bound")

"*Father Forgive Them . . .*"

1. he asks God to forgive those crucifying him, out of their ignorance; repentance is not explicit, but implied based on other Scripture related to sins of ignorance, as well as the fact that Jesus did not himself forgive them

2. no, Jesus does not forgive them, but prays that God will forgive them (i.e., in his normal way, contingent upon repentance); we should not do what Jesus refused to do—automatically forgive

3. the earliest manuscripts lack this verse, and there is evidence that it is an interpolation; thus, it should not be used to support a doctrine of automatic forgiveness

4. it is the only verse that can be interpreted (incorrectly) in that way

The Healing of the Paralytic

1. both are negative elements that will be removed in the coming kingdom of God

2. the authority to forgive sins; nonvisible forgiveness is verified by visible healing

The Woman Caught in Adultery

1. there is disagreement among manuscripts containing this story, and it does not fit well into the context

2. Jesus is not passing judgment in a legal sense, but still calls for the woman's repentance

The Prodigal Son

1. words about repentance in Luke 15:10: "There is rejoicing in the presence of the angels of God over one sinner who repents"

2. the prodigal son confesses to his father, "Father, I have sinned against heaven and against you"; he refuses to be presumptuous by asking to be reinstated as a servant instead of a son

3. the father (both in the story and God the Father) loves the son and is willing to forgive

CHAPTER 8—WHAT DOES SCRIPTURE SAY ABOUT HOW CHRISTIANS ARE TO RELATE TO EVIL PERSONS AND ENEMIES?

Resisting Evil

1. the principle of *lex talionis*, which the scribes and Pharisees seem to have applied in personal matters

2. retaliation and vengeance are God's prerogatives

3. disciples are not to resist evil persons (but should resist evil in general and Satan); (i) slap on the cheek (personal insult); (ii) loss of shirt (unjust lawsuit); (iii) conscription (forced labor); (iv) giving to the poor (generosity); (v) lending to those who ask (righteousness); (vi) loving enemies (mercy)

4. knowing that God will provide for one's needs and ultimately deal with injustice

Love and Hate

1. it is often (incorrectly) assumed that loving one's enemies means unconditional forgiveness

2. context

3. judicial hatred of those who oppose God's people (2 Chron 19:2; Ps 139:21–22; Matt 23:29, 33); personal hatred is not authorized in Scripture

4. to imitate the Father (Matt 5:45, "that you may be children of your Father in heaven")

Enemies

1. (i) show them kindness (Exod 23:4–5); (ii) do not gloat over their misfortune (Prov 24:17–18); (iii) do not take vengeance (Prov 24:29)

2. Israel's national enemies were set against God and were not to be joined, but destroyed, if God commanded (Neh 3:19b; Rev 18:20)

3. the OT—Israelites are to be a light and to love personal enemies (Prov 25:21)

Context

1. the kingdom of God is not based on overthrowing world authorities (i.e., Rome), but on God bringing Jews and Gentiles to him; therefore, Israelites are to love all people, not just fellow Israelites

Reasons for Loving Enemies

1. (i) emulates God (Matt 5:48, "Be perfect, as your heavenly Father is perfect"); (ii) reward by God

2. Jesus both loved his enemies and confronted and rebuked evil

The Teaching of the Early Church on Enemy Love

1. don't take vengeance—instead, bless; same as OT teaching, often quoting directly from OT passages on enemy love

2. personal enemies (as opposed to national enemies)

Romans 12:17–20

1. Paul seeks to verify his teaching—to lend weight to this hardest of commands and to deflect criticism (Rom 3:31)

2. Romans 12:17–20 repeats the OT: (i) do not take vengeance; (ii) bless those who curse you; (iii) seek peace; (iv) meet physical needs should the situation arise; (v) desire spiritual well-being of enemies

3. burning coals: a symbol of God's divine eschatological judgment; leave room: allow God's wrath to work its purpose, perhaps even leading to repentance (Rom 2:4–5)

4. God will ultimately take care of justice; this should comfort Christians who follow Christ's lead in loving enemies

5. God's plan of redemption; in view of God's mercy already extended to humanity, we should likewise love our enemies

1 Thessalonians 5:15

1. peace and reconciliation cannot always be achieved, even between God and all people

1 Peter 3:9

1. they will receive a reward in heaven

2. no passage teaches forgiveness in the absence of repentance; instead, what should be offered to enemies is the prospect of forgiveness on the condition of repentance

Christ Dying for Enemies

1. in an eschatological sense, when Christ redeemed (reconciled) the world in the atonement; enemy means one alienated from God

2. human sin did not prevent God from acting; does not mean that sins were automatically forgiven, but that God was willing to intervene on their behalf in spite of their sinfulness

Obeying the Love Command

1. (i) believe God and depend on his Spirit to enable obedience; (ii) seek God's wisdom and guidance, as every situation is different

Eating with Tax Collectors and "Sinners"

1. a publicly recognized criminal or one with low social status or an unacceptable occupation

2. Jesus is not condoning evil behavior, but is extending grace to society's outcasts in hopes they will repent and be forgiven

The Early Church

1. immoral or divisive behavior (not social status or nationality)

CHAPTER 9—THERAPEUTIC FORGIVENESS VERSUS BIBLICAL FORGIVENESS

Contemporary Definitions of Forgiveness

1. secular philosophers and psychologists

Therapeutic Forgiveness

1. the internal and unilateral overcoming of negative emotions/resentment by a victim of wrongdoing; biblical model is external (involving both parties), bilateral (involving repentance by the wrongdoer and willingness of the victim to forgive), and has the goal of reconciliation

2. biblical forgiveness involves being healed by God and others, not healing oneself

3. no

4. both involve overcoming negative emotions—in the biblical model, it precedes willingness to forgive; in the therapeutic model, it is an end in itself

Christian Reaction to Therapeutic Forgiveness

1. distance from OT roots; preaching of forgiveness without discipleship (repentance and obedience)

Wrongful Guilt

1. they believe that if they do not (or cannot) forgive unconditionally, they are disobedient (and therefore displeasing) to God; hypocrisy may result if forgiveness is falsely claimed, adding to guilt; reconciliation is difficult if not impossible between a victim and an unrepentant offender—if not required, one may easily claim to have forgiven

CHAPTER 10—RESENTMENT AND ANGER

The Moral Significance of Resentment

1. a desire for justice and the coming of the kingdom of God
2. malicious hatred is condemned by Jesus and should be abandoned; moral hatred should be maintained as long as the evil persists

Resentment, Indignation, and Self-Worth

1. resentment is the reaction to personal injury, while indignation is the reaction to the injury to another person
2. resentment or anger can be an expression of self-worth; one who does not resent moral injury may be lacking in self-respect

Resentment versus Animosity, Hatred, and Vindication

1. no, animosity and ill will are different from resentment and moral anger (Col 3:8)
2. personal devaluation/insecurity
3. malice degrades others in order to elevate oneself, while spite brings others down to the level of the hater; both are emotions one chooses and may lead to vengeful actions
4. the emotion must first be admitted (to oneself), then vented to God
5. yes, the victim must be emotionally prepared to forgive
6. if the wrongdoer has not confessed and repented, then forgiveness would result in condonation, not reconciliation
7. no, the lack of repentance will cause negative emotions and resentment to remain; simply claiming forgiveness in this situation does not make it so

Servant versus Servile

1. servanthood is the calling of all Christians to be willing to minister to one another, recognizing the equal value of all persons; servility comes from a lack of self-respect and is contrary to Jesus' teachings

2. servanthood allows a Christian to be humble, yet still oppose injustice and evil; servility leads to not protesting moral evil but unjustly submitting to it

Maintaining Indignation/Resentment: The Proper Response to Injustice

1. legitimate resentment is justified anger at a personal injury; immoral resentment is anger in response to a petty insult, which may result in excessive negative behavior

2. it may come at the expense of one's human dignity

3. it is reasonable because the wrongdoer has changed, and righteous because it permits reconciliation

Expressing Resentment/Indignation

1. it is an outward statement of morality

2. revenge is a forbidden way to express resentment for Christians

3. it respects the offender as a moral agent who has the ability to repent and seek forgiveness

Therapeutic Forgiveness: Problematic in Practice

1. (i) guilt feelings from being unable to forgive (according to the therapeutic definition); (ii) accusations of bitterness if the victim admits an inability to forgive; (iii) feelings of hypocrisy (and guilt) if the victim claims to have forgiven but still has resentment

2. biblical forgiveness is a moral choice, not based on feelings and emotion but on repentance

Dealing with Anger and Pain

1. Christians are called to have pure hearts and be holy

2. one should try to overcome personal hurt, but not necessarily the moral anger at the injustice, as this shows one still cares; rely on the fact that God will ultimately set things right

3. (i) recognize and express rage before God; (ii) retain moral resentment without feelings of guilt; (iii) accept the pain, which diminishes with time (Ps 34:18); (iv) be willing to forgive and work toward reconciliation if the offender repents

Resentment, Blame, and Guilt

1. forgiveness does not erase guilt and blame, but makes the sin irrelevant, removing the moral barrier to reconciliation

Guilt and Shame

1. the wronged experience a false shame from humiliation, while wrongdoers experience deserved shame from guilt

2. guilt is a stain that may be deeply embedded in the soul; if God has not absolved it, we should not attempt to do so; guilt needs time to motivate repentance

3. when a debt is forgiven, it does not change the reality of the debt being incurred; likewise, sin can be forgiven and the record wiped clean, yet the sin still occurred

4. forgiveness shows the repentant offender he still has worth (Zeph 3:11)

CHAPTER 11—HATE THE SIN AND LOVE THE SINNER

1. Saint Augustine, in his Letter 211, paragraph 11

2. the parable of the two sons in Matt 2:28–32

3. evil persons can still be loved in the sense of desiring their reformation and salvation

4. false guilt for being unable to feel love for the wrongdoer; hypocrisy if love has been falsely proclaimed (Ps 11:5, 7; Prov 16:5)

5. when a wrongdoer repents, it is logical to distinguish the person from his actions, for he has condemned and forsaken his former self

6. forgiveness is minimized (pretend) because the one "forgiven" is still guilty and blameworthy; accepting Augustine's maxim fails to stand for righteousness by not confronting the sinner with his actions and may even encourage sin; this is neither loving nor moral

CHAPTER 12—RETRIBUTION AND DISCIPLINE

1. the opposite of justice is injustice; justice does not require retribution

2. not if based on a sense of justice; victims may be labeled (falsely) as spiteful or malicious

3. one may choose not to forgo punishment if it is in the best interest of the offender

4. (i) God's retributive actions; (ii) God's disciplinary actions

5. retribution asserts the value of the victim, countering the wrong-doer's false moral claim of superiority

6. true repentance acknowledges guilt and accepts punishment as justly deserved

7. retribution shows such actions will not be tolerated or ignored

8. (i) retribution is just and is required in the absence of repentance; (ii) justice does not require retribution if there is repentance; (iii) forgiveness and retribution are not mutually exclusive—retribution may be needed to uphold moral good and to benefit the offender

Ultimate Justice

1. God desires to not inflict retribution, but to forgive repentant offenders; emulating this desire is the goal, but not all victims will be able to do this

2. God is just, and he will deliver vengeance

3. yes, if done without taking vengeance or violating morality; not for more serious offenses

4. no, some crimes are so extreme that retribution directed at the offender feels insufficient

Legal Justice and the State

1. not at all—repentance and forgiveness is personal, while the justice of the state is impersonal; retributive justice is in place to punish and deter crime

Mercy and Pardon

1. punishing an offender less than he deserves; it is not arbitrary, and it is not being unjust

2. forgiveness is a personal response to repentance, while mercy may or may not be personal—mercy is only extended by one having authority to punish; pardon is even less personal—often the one who pardons has no personal involvement, unlike the one who forgives

3. therapeutic forgiveness is directed inward at the feelings of the victim; mercy requires action on the part of the victim directed toward the offender

4. the repentant offender does not get what he deserves; namely, the stain and guilt of his sin and estrangement from the victim; forgiveness wipes away the sin

5. forgiving or pardoning a repentant offender in cases without repentance would be unjust

6. amnesty is the decision of a government not to prosecute certain crimes; it is extended without regard to repentance or as an act of mercy, but because the offenders are no longer a threat

CHAPTER 13—FORBEARANCE, TOLERANCE, AND CONDONATION

Forbearance

1. forbearance proceeds from a humble heart, because one realizes his own failings and understands that only God knows the reasons for another's feelings

Tolerance

1. tolerance has changed from respect for another person with whom one disagrees to a prohibition against calling any idea deficient or untrue

2. the NT commands tolerance in the sense of preserving peace amid disagreement, but rejects the modern definition of moral relativism

Condonation

1. condonation is the implicit acceptance of a serious offense by not responding to it

2. condonation is morally wrong and demonstrates a lack of love for the offender

3. forbearance is appropriate for trivial offenses and is done for the good of the relationship; condonation overlooks serious wrongs and gives implicit acceptance to those acts

4. forgiveness removes the barrier to reconciliation, while forbearance simply overlooks a wrong; forgiveness is in many ways the opposite of condonation: where forgiveness identifies, condemns, and removes the barrier, condonation minimizes, accepts, and leaves the barrier in place

CHAPTER 14—ETHICAL AND PSYCHOLOGICAL REASONS AGAINST UNCONDITIONAL FORGIVENESS

No Right to Be Forgiven

1. no, because forgiveness is undeserved

2. (i) it may not always be morally right (without repentance it is condonation); (ii) it may be impossible (moral duties cannot be impossible); (iii) giving a gift is never a moral duty; forgiveness becomes a duty when it is morally right, that is, following repentance

3. repentance is easier because the one repenting is in the wrong; the one forgiving is the one who suffers loss

Ethical Reasons against Unconditional Forgiveness

1. (i) it condones the wrongdoing; (ii) it is harmful to the wrongdoer

2. it prevents the wrongdoer from being held accountable; one should wait for genuine repentance

Psychological Reasons against Unconditional Forgiveness

1. it is righteous and healthy, but it is not pleasant

2. (i) it denies the true feelings of the victim, who ignores the barrier that still exists; (ii) it denies the truth about the character of the wrongdoer

3. it requires an injustice for the victim and a means of escape for the wrongdoer

4. the offender realizes and rejects his former self, while the victim sees the moral benefit to forgiving the offender

5. granting forgiveness in spite of one's feelings is not biblical forgiveness because God does not forgive in that way; he desires reconciliation

6. therapeutic forgiveness claims that refusing to reconcile is evidence of not condoning the offense; it fails because the problem still exists and neither the wrongdoer's actions nor the victim's true feelings are recognized

7. (i) it condones and may support wrongdoing; (ii) it does not consider the well-being of the wrongdoer; (iii) it forces a victim to abandon justified resentment

CHAPTER 15—OVERCOMING DESTRUCTIVE RESENTMENT: THE PRELUDE TO FORGIVENESS

"Letting Go" and "Moving On"

1. letting go of destructive anger and resentment that would preclude forgiveness

2. (i) intense pain (due to initial brokenheartedness); (ii) depression (due to feelings of hopelessness and possibly loss of self-worth); (iii) anger at the offender (for damage to one's soul and life); (iv)

acceptance (knowing that vengeance and vindication belong to God)

3. the victim may become preoccupied with justice or vindication

4. (i) overcome malicious resentment, anger, and hatred; (ii) forgive and reconcile (if the offender repents); (iii) develop trust and eliminate residual anger and resentment

CHAPTER 16—ETHICAL REASONS TO FORGIVE THE REPENTANT OFFENDER

1. (i) the offender has repented or has had a change of heart; (ii) the offender meant well (his motives were good); (iii) the offender has suffered enough; (iv) the offender has been a loyal friend

2. the initial offense degrades the victim and lowers self-respect; for forgiveness to be virtuous, it must not maintain the loss of self-respect, but seek its restoration

3. whether the reasons separate the offender from his actions and do not compromise morality or self-respect

4. perhaps the first time, but an ongoing pattern requires one confront the offender

5. suffering does not separate the offender from his actions; therefore, it is a questionable basis for forgiveness

6. forgiving for old times' sake is based on who the offender once was, not who he is now; it overlooks the lack of repentance and instead appeals to emotion

7. forgiveness does not typically provoke repentance—true repentance should arise within the offender, not be prompted externally; forgiveness provoking repentance is not the model in Scripture

8. a pitiful status is not grounds for forgiveness, unless the offender's situation has led to repentance; compassion and tough love may be appropriate

9. the victim's own moral failings are irrelevant to whether the offender should be forgiven; likewise, other morally good behavior on the offender's part is irrelevant

10. (i) it leads to personal healing (both of the victim's anger and of the wrongdoer's guilt); (ii) it creates respect for others; (iii) it promotes harmony (reconciliation); (iv) it develops character in the one willing to forgive; (v) it stops the cycle of vengeance

CHAPTER 17—VINDICATION FOR VICTIMS

Justice for the Oppressed versus Justification for Oppressors

1. to trust that God would judge the wicked and vindicate the wronged

2. God's mercy; God's justice

3. Jesus explains his mission in terms of bringing freedom to the oppressed by satisfying justice through his reign

4. a wrongdoer cannot interact with God until he has repented and made amends with the victim; God stands with the victim

5. God is wronged as the compassionate parent is wronged when his child suffers harm

Justice, Victims, and the Ministry of the Church

1. minister to the oppressed and bring healing to the brokenhearted; the church's mission is engaging and consoling them—a time-consuming but necessary effort

2. Jesus may have been communicating that complete healing is not likely until he returns

3. abandonment and betrayal cause pain, mourning, depression, anger, and, finally, acceptance; the knowledge that one's world is not right and not likely to become right is ever-present

4. (i) the relationship of the parties; (ii) the culpability (or intentionality) of the wrongdoer; (iii) the magnitude of the injury; (iv) whether the wrongdoing is ongoing

5. they are involuntarily burdened by justified resentment against the wrongdoer; the inclination to trust and give of oneself is often damaged as a result

6. it recognizes that victims deserve better; they deserve an apology and personal vindication

7. the benefit of the victim

8. forgiveness is a choice that involves self-sacrifice

9. victims should not quit praying and should not give up; the context of the parable is justice for the wronged

CHAPTER 18—ADDITIONAL QUESTIONS RELATED TO THE PRACTICE OF FORGIVENESS

Forgiving Injuries to Others: Who Can Rightfully Forgive?

1. forgiveness granted to the wrongdoer by someone other than the victim; it is illegitimate because the third party was not wronged, and it tends to minimize the harm done

2. one in a close relationship with the victim can grant forgiveness in a sense, based on their own resentment of the wrongdoer

3. God can forgive because of his love, both for the victim and for the wrongdoer

4. from his victim and from God

5. God will always forgive a truly repentant wrongdoer because his love is perfect; a human victim may not be able to forgive

6. confession shows humility and a desire to restore relationship with God

Are There Limits to Forgiveness?

1. (i) Matt 12:32 (also Mark 3:28–29; Luke 12:10)—blasphemy against the Holy Spirit; (ii) Heb 6:4–8—apostasy

The Unforgivable Sin

1. the fact that there is a sin called an "unforgivable sin" suggests that there are, in fact, limits on forgiveness

Those Who Fall Away Cannot Be Brought Back to Repentance

1. no, this is never stated in Scripture

2. only one such wrong is named (blasphemy), but this does not preclude there being more

3. yes, some reprehensible acts should not be forgiven; the majority of philosophers concur with this; no consensus exists concerning the limits of forgiveness among Christian theologians; in the case of Judas there is debate whether he repented, and whether he could be forgiven

4. this issue has not been fully resolved, yet it seems that the evil nature of certain acts would preclude genuine repentance; it is best that Christians not be dogmatic here

What is the Role of Loyalty for Friends of the Victim?

1. loyalty affirms another's value and the correctness of their moral position; it protests the moral wrong by distancing from the wrongdoer

Must Words of Apology and Forgiveness Be Spoken?

1. (i) acknowledgement that the offender's action was morally wrong; (ii) recognition of the harm done and of the victim's innocence; (iii) an effort to right the wrong

2. the guilty party benefits from forgiveness; therefore, it is reasonable that he in turn attempt to benefit the one offering forgiveness

3. it is humbling

4. a spoken apology is a moral action that acknowledges wrongdoing and helps the victim forgive; spoken forgiveness is a moral action that helps the wrongdoer release his feelings of guilt

How Does One Discern the Time to Embrace and the Time to Refrain from Embracing?

1. the victim should seek the fullness of God's wisdom carefully, slowly, and prayerfully, as such situations can be complex and potentially volatile

2. for the offender, the time to repent is always "now"; strength and humility, rather than wisdom, are needed for the one seeking forgiveness

CHAPTER 19—MEMORY AND RECONCILIATION

1. evil may gain a double victory if the victim returns the wrong, or if the wrong lingers in the mind of the victim; the memory of wrongs can steal the joy of positive memories and continually re-injure the victim

Remembering

1. (i) justice may be served—exposing the truth of the wrongdoing paves the way for justice and reconciliation; (ii) empathy may be given—memory allows victims to collectively grieve and minister to each other; (iii) the wrongdoer may come to repentance—truthful remembrance aims to bring repentance, forgiveness, and salvation to the wrongdoer and reconciliation to both wrongdoer and victim; (iv) the victim may be healed—accepting and naming suffering is needed for healing, though one may not be able to give meaning to horrendous suffering; (v) suffering may be properly integrated into one's life—memory prevents the denial of pain, but does not need to define one's life

2. love does not hide sin, but removes it (wipes it away) entirely following repentance

How to Integrate the Memory of Wrongs

1. it sees wrongdoing as an evil to be opposed, and healing as a moral good to be pursued; one having this worldview sees himself as loved by God and worth healing

2. (i) choose to integrate suffering into his life (requires effort and discipline); (ii) balance the memory of pain with hope for the future, cultivating joy and continually battling to maintain this balance

Forgetting

1. in God's new world, victim and wrongdoer are unalterably reconciled, meaning there is no need for remembering wrongs; in the current world, our forgetting is tentative and provisional

2. it helps the offender lift his guilt feelings and helps the victim lift his pain

Memory and the World to Come

1. if the new world is perfect, having no suffering, then even the memory of such suffering must be erased, or else it could conceivably cause pain again

2. "former things will not be remembered, nor will they come to mind" (Isa 65:17); how this will happen is not known, but it may be a consequence of God eliminating all traces of evil

3. as God's pronouncement of condemnation and salvation, and as a social event in which all offenders and victims are reconciled to one another; every wrong will be righted and every wound healed; there will be no need to remember wrongs because "all things are reconciled"

Bibliography

Aland, Barbara, Kurt Aland, Johannes Karavidopoulos, Carlo M. Martini, and Bruce M. Metzger, eds. *The UBS Greek New Testament*. 4th rev. ed. Stuttgart: Deutsche Bibelgesellschaft, 2007.

Ashley, Timothy R. *The Book of Numbers*. The New International Commentary on the Old Testament. Grand Rapids, MI: Eerdmans, 1993.

Baillie, D. M. *God Was in Christ*. New York: Charles Scribner's Sons, 1948.

Bash, Anthony. *Forgiveness: A Theology*. Eugene, OR: Cascade, 2015.

———. *Forgiveness and Christian Ethics*. Cambridge: Cambridge University Press, 2007.

———. *Just Forgiveness: Exploring the Bible, Weighing the Issues*. London: Society for Promoting Christian Knowledge, 2011.

Bash, Anthony, and Melanie Bash. "Early Christian Thinking." In *Forgiveness in Context: Theology and Psychology in Creative Dialogue*, edited by Fraser Watts and Liz Gulliford, 29–49. London: T. & T. Clark, 2004.

Beale, G. K., and D. A. Carson, eds., *Commentary on the New Testament Use of the Old Testament*. Grand Rapids, MI: Baker Academic, 2007.

Benn, Piers. "Forgiveness and Loyalty." *Philosophy* 71 (July 1996) 369–83.

Biggar, Nigel. "Forgiveness in the Twentieth Century: A Review of the Literature, 1901–2001." In *Forgiveness and Truth*, edited by Alistair McFadyen and Marcel Sarot, 181–217. Edinburgh: T. & T. Clark, 2001.

Blight, Richard C. *An Exegetical Summary of Luke* 12–24. Exegetical Summary Series. Dallas: SIL International, 2007.

Bock, Darrell L. *Luke*. The NIV Application Commentary. Grand Rapids, MI: Zondervan Academic, 1996.

Bonhoeffer, Dietrich. *The Cost of Discipleship*. Translated by R. H. Fuller. New York: Macmillan, 1963.

Bromiley, Geoffrey W., ed. *The International Standard Bible Encyclopedia*. Vol. 4. Grand Rapids, MI: Eerdmans, 1988.

Brueggemann, Walter. *A Commentary on Jeremiah: Exile and Homecoming*. Grand Rapids, MI: Eerdmans, 1998.

———. *Praying the Psalms*. Winona, MN: Saint Mary's, 1982.

Brümmer, Vincent. *Atonement, Christology, and the Trinity: Making Sense of Christian Doctrine*. Burlington, VT: Ashgate, 2005.

———. "Atonement and Reconciliation." *Religious Studies* 28 (December 1992) 435–52.

———. *What Are We Doing When We Pray? On Prayer and the Nature of Faith*. Burlington, VT: Ashgate, 2008.

Burnaby, John. *Christian Words and Christian Meanings.* New York: Harper & Brothers, 1955.

Burns, Steven. "Forgiveness in Challenging Circumstances." In *Forgiveness in Context: Theology and Psychology in Creative Dialogue*, edited by Fraser Watts and Liz Gulliford, 144–59. London: T. & T. Clark, 2004.

Byrne, Brendan. *Lifting the Burden: Reading Matthew's Gospel in the Church Today.* Collegeville, MN: Liturgical Press, 2004.

Calvin, John. "Articles Concerning Predestination." Pages 178–82 in *Calvin: Theological Treatises.* Edited by J. K. S. Reid. Vol. 22 of Library of Christian Classics. Edited by John Baillie, et al. Philadelphia: Westminster, 1954.

———. *The Institutes of Christian Religion.* Edited by Tony Lane and Hilary Osborne. Translated by Robert Backhouse. London: Hodder & Stoughton, 1986.

Carson, D. A. *Love in Hard Places.* Wheaton, IL: Crossway, 2002.

Carter, Karen S. "Forgiveness Revisited: God's and Ours." *Brethren Life and Thought* 22 (Autumn 1977) 199–208.

Carter, Tim. *The Forgiveness of Sins.* Cambridge: James Clarke & Co., 2016.

Cave, Sydney. *The Doctrine of the Work of Christ.* Nashville, TN: Cokesbury Press, 1937.

Chandler, Vee. *Victorious Substitution: A Theory of the Atonement.* Newburgh, IN: Trinity, 2012.

Cheney, Mary B. *Life and Letters of Horace Bushnell.* New York: Harper, 1880.

Coate, Mary Ann. "The Capacity for Forgiveness." In *Forgiveness in Context: Theology and Psychology in Creative Dialogue*, edited by Fraser Watts and Liz Gulliford, 123–43. London: T. & T. Clark, 2004.

Craddock, Fred B. *Luke.* Interpretation: A Bible Commentary for Teaching and Preaching. Louisville, KY: John Knox, 1990.

Crawford, R. G. "Is the Penal Theory of the Atonement Scriptural?" *Scottish Journal of Theology* 23 (March 1970) 257–72.

Creed, John Martin. *The Gospel according to St. Luke: The Greek Text with Introduction, Notes, and Indices.* London: Macmillan, 1930.

Davies, John Howard. *A Letter to Hebrews.* The Cambridge Bible Commentary on the New English Bible. London: Cambridge University Press, 1967.

Davis, James F. *Lex Talionis in Early Judaism and the Exhortation of Jesus in Matthew 5:38–42.* London: T. & T. Clark, 2005.

Downie, R. S. "Forgiveness." *Philosophical Quarterly* 15 (April 1965) 128–34.

Edwards, Elizabeth G. "On Using the Textual Apparatus of the UBS Greek New Testament." *The Bible Translator* 28 (January 1977) 121–43.

Erickson, Millard J. *Christian Theology.* Grand Rapids, MI: Baker, 1983.

Eubank, Nathan. "A Disconcerting Prayer: On the Originality of Luke 23:34a." *Journal of Biblical Literature* 129 (2010) 521–36.

Fee, Gordon D. *1 and 2 Timothy, Titus.* New International Biblical Commentary. Peabody, MA: Hendrickson, 1988.

Fiddes, Paul S. *Past Event and Present Salvation: The Christian Idea of Atonement.* Louisville, KY: Westminster John Knox, 1989.

Forsyth, P. T. *The Cruciality of the Cross.* London: Independent, 1955.

France, R. T. *The Gospel of Matthew.* The New International Commentary on the New Testament. Edited by Gordon D. Fee. Grand Rapids, MI: Eerdmans, 2007.

Gomes, Alan W. "*De Jesu Christo Servatore*: Faustus Socinus on the Satisfaction of Christ." *Westminster Theological Journal* 55 (February 1993) 209–31.

————. "Faustus Socinus' *De Jesu Christo Servatore*, Part III: Historical Introduction, Translation, and Critical Notes." PhD diss., Fuller Theological Seminary, 1990.

Grudem, Wayne. *Systematic Theology*. Leicester, UK: InterVarsity, 1994.

Gulliford, Liz. "The Healing of Relationships." In *Forgiveness in Context: Theology and Psychology in Creative Dialogue*, edited by Fraser Watts and Liz Gulliford, 106–22. London: T. & T. Clark, 2004.

————. "Intrapersonal Forgiveness." In *Forgiveness in Context: Theology and Psychology in Creative Dialogue*, edited by Fraser Watts and Liz Gulliford, 83–105. London: T. & T. Clark, 2004.

Haber, Joram Graf. *Forgiveness*. Savage, MD: Rowman & Littlefield, 1991.

Hamilton, James M., Jr. *God's Glory in Salvation through Judgment: A Biblical Theology*. Wheaton, IL: Crossway, 2010.

Harris, J. Rendel. "New Points of View in Textual Criticism." *Expositor* 8 (1914) 316–34.

Hodge, Archibald Alexander. *The Atonement*. Grand Rapids, MI: Eerdmans, 1953.

Hodges, H. A. *The Pattern of Atonement*. London: SCM, 1955.

Howe, Leroy T. *Guilt: Helping God's People Find Healing and Forgiveness*. Nashville, TN: Abingdon, 2003.

Hunsinger, Deborah van Deusen. "Forgiving Abusive Parents: Psychological and Theological Considerations." In *Forgiveness and Truth*, edited by Alistair McFadyen and Marcel Sarot, 71–98. Edinburgh: T. & T. Clark, 2001.

Jones, Christopher. "Loosing and Binding: The Liturgical Mediation of Forgiveness." In *Forgiveness and Truth*, edited by Alistair McFadyen and Marcel Sarot, 31–52. Edinburgh: T. & T. Clark, 2001.

Jones, L. Gregory. *Embodying Forgiveness: A Theological Analysis*. Grand Rapids, MI: Eerdmans, 1995.

Katongole, Emmanuel, and Chris Rice. *Reconciling All Things: A Christian Vision for Justice, Peace, and Healing*. Downers Grove, IL: InterVarsity, 2008.

Keller, Timothy. *The Reason for God: Belief in an Age of Skepticism*. New York: Penguin, 2008.

Kleinknecht, Hermann, et al. "Ὀργή, Ὀργίζομαι, Ὀργίλος, Παροργίζω, Παροργισμός." Edited by Gerhard Kittel et al. *Theological Dictionary of the New Testament*. Grand Rapids, MI: Eerdmans, 1964.

Kolnai, Aurel. "Forgiveness." *Proceedings of the Aristotelian Society* 74 (1974) 91–106.

Konstan, David. *Before Forgiveness: The Origins of a Moral Idea*. New York: Cambridge University Press, 2010.

Lewis, C. S. *Letters to Malcolm: Chiefly on Prayer*. New York: Harcourt, Brace & World, 1964.

Lyonnet, Stanislas, and Léopold Sabourin. *Sin, Redemption, and Sacrifice: A Biblical and Patristic Study*. Rome: Biblical Institute, 1970.

MacDonald, George. *Discovering the Character of God*. Edited by Michael R. Phillips. Minneapolis: Bethany House, 1989.

MacLachlan, Alice. "The Nature and Limits of Forgiveness." PhD diss., Boston University, 2008.

Marshall, I. Howard. *The Gospel of Luke*. The New International Greek Testament Commentary. Edited by I. Howard Marshall and W. Ward Gasque. Exeter, UK: Paternoster, 1978.

McFadyen, Alistair. "Introduction." In *Forgiveness and Truth*, edited by Alistair McFadyen and Marcel Sarot, 1–14. Edinburgh: T. & T. Clark, 2001.

McKnight, Scot. *The Letter of James*. The New International Commentary on the New Testament. Edited by Gordon D. Fee. Grand Rapids, MI: Eerdmans, 2011.

Metaxas, Eric. *Bonhoeffer: Pastor, Martyr, Prophet, Spy*. Nashville, TN: Thomas Nelson, 2010.

Metzger, Bruce M. *A Textual Commentary on the Greek New Testament*. London: United Bible Societies, 1971.

Michaels, J. Ramsey. *The Gospel of John*. The New International Commentary on the New Testament. Edited by Gordon D. Fee. Grand Rapids, MI: Eerdmans, 2010.

Moberly, R. C. *Atonement and Personality*. London: Murray, 1932.

Morris, Leon. *The Apostolic Preaching of the Cross*. Grand Rapids, MI: Eerdmans, 1960.

————. *The Gospel according to John*. The New International Commentary on the New Testament. Edited by Gordon D. Fee. Grand Rapids, MI: Eerdmans, 1995.

Murphy, Jeffrie G., and Jean Hampton. *Forgiveness and Mercy*. Cambridge: Cambridge University Press, 1988.

Murphy, Jeffrie G. *Getting Even: Forgiveness and Its Limits*. Oxford: Oxford University Press, 2003.

Murray, John. *The Epistle to the Romans*. The New International Commentary on the New Testament. Grand Rapids, MI: Eerdmans, 1959.

Musekura, Célesten. *An Assessment of Contemporary Models of Forgiveness*. American University Studies. Series 7, Theology and Religion, vol. 302. New York: Peter Lang, 2010.

NIV Quest Study Bible. Edited by Kenneth L. Barker. Grand Rapids, MI: Zondervan, 1994.

Nolland, John. *Luke 9:21–18:34*. Word Biblical Commentary 35b. Dallas, TX: Word, 1989.

Norris, David A. "Forgiving from the Heart." PhD diss., Union Theological Seminary, 1984.

Painter, John. *1, 2, and 3 John*. Sacra Pagina 18. Edited by Daniel J. Harrington. Collegeville, MI: Liturgical Press. 2002.

Park, Andrew Sung. *From Hurt to Healing: A Theology of the Wounded*. Nashville, TN: Abingdon, 2004.

Peters, Ted. "Atonement and the Final Scapegoat." *Perspectives in Religious Studies* 19 (February 1992) 151–81.

Piper, John. *"Love Your Enemies": Jesus' Love Command in the Synoptic Gospels and in the Early Christian Paraenesis*. Cambridge: Cambridge University Press, 1979.

Prince, Derek. *Foundation Series: Repent and Believe*. Ft. Lauderdale, FL: Derek Prince, 1977.

Ridderbos, Herman N. *The Gospel according to John: A Theological Commentary*. Translated by John Vriend. Grand Rapids, MI: Eerdmans, 1997.

Robinson, Norman L. *How Jesus Christ Saves Men: A Study of the Atonement*. London: James Clarke & Co., 1954.

Scheiber, Karen. "Truth and Reconciliation." In *Forgiveness and Truth*, edited by Alistair McFadyen and Marcel Sarot, 173–80. Edinburgh: T. & T. Clark, 2001.

Schimmel, Solomon. "Interpersonal Forgiveness and Repentance in Judaism." In *Forgiveness in Context: Theology and Psychology in Creative Dialogue*, edited by Fraser Watts and Liz Gulliford, 11–28. London: T. & T. Clark, 2004.

————. *Wounds Not Healed by Time: The Power of Repentance and Forgiveness*. Oxford: Oxford University Press, 2002.

Schreurs, Nico. "Truth and Reconciliation: Is Radical Openness a Condition for Reconciliation?" In *Forgiveness and Truth*, edited by Alistair McFadyen and Marcel Sarot, 131–38. Edinburgh: T. & T. Clark, 2001.

Sedgwick, Peter H. "Forgiveness and Our Awareness of Truth." In *Forgiveness and Truth*, edited by Alistair McFadyen and Marcel Sarot, 119–24. Edinburgh: T. & T. Clark, 2001.

Shults, F. LeRon, and Steven J. Sandage. *The Faces of Forgiveness: Searching for Wholeness and Salvation*. Grand Rapids, MI: Baker Academic, 2003.

Smith, David. *The Atonement in the Light of History and the Modern Spirit*. London: Hodder & Stoughton, 1918.

Swinburne, Richard. *Responsibility and Atonement*. Oxford: Clarendon, 1989.

Turner, David L. *Matthew*. Baker Exegetical Commentary on the New Testament. Edited by Robert W. Yarborough and Robert H. Stein. Grand Rapids, MI: Baker Academic, 2008.

Vaughan, Curtis, ed. *The Word: The Bible from 26 Translations*. Moss Point, MS: Mathis, 1988.

Volf, Miroslav. *The End of Memory: Remembering Rightly in a Violent World*. Grand Rapids, MI: Eerdmans, 2006.

———. *Exclusion and Embrace: A Theological Exploration of Identity, Otherness, and Reconciliation*. Nashville, TN: Abingdon, 1996.

———. *Free of Charge: Giving and Forgiving in a Culture Stripped of Grace*. Grand Rapids, MI: Zondervan, 2005.

Watts, Fraser. "Christian Theology." In *Forgiveness in Context: Theology and Psychology in Creative Dialogue*, edited by Fraser Watts and Liz Gulliford, 50–68. London: T. & T. Clark, 2004.

———. "Shame, Sin, and Guilt." In *Forgiveness and Truth*, edited by Alistair McFadyen and Marcel Sarot, 53–70. Edinburgh: T. & T. Clark, 2001.

Watts, Rikk E. "Mark." In *Commentary on the New Testament Use of the Old Testament*, edited by G. K. Beale and D. A. Carson, 111–250. Grand Rapids: Baker Academic, 2007.

Whitlark, Jason A., and Mikeal C. Parsons. "The 'Seven' Last Words: A Numerical Motivation for the Insertion of Luke 23:34a." *New Testament Studies* 52 (2006) 188–204.

Wilson, John. "Why Forgiveness Requires Repentance." *Philosophy* 63 (October 1988) 534–35.

Wright, Christopher J. H. *The God I Don't Understand: Reflections on Tough Questions of Faith*. Grand Rapids, MI: Zondervan, 2008.

———. *The Message of Ezekiel: A New Heart and a New Spirit*. The Bible Speaks Today. Leicester, UK: InterVarsity, 2001.

———. *Salvation Belongs to Our God: Celebrating the Bible's Central Story*. Downers Grove, IL: InterVarsity, 2007.

Wright, N. T. *Acts for Everyone: Part 2, Chapters 13–28*. London: Society for Promoting Christian Knowledge, 2008.

———. *After You Believe: Why Christian Character Matters*. New York: HarperCollins, 2010.

———. *Evil and the Justice of God*. Downers Grove, IL: InterVarsity, 2006.

———. *Following Jesus: Biblical Reflections on Discipleship*. Grand Rapids, MI: Eerdmans, 1994.

————. *Simply Christian: Why Christianity Makes Sense.* New York: HarperCollins, 2006.

————. *Simply Jesus: A New Vision of Who He Was, What He Did, and Why He Matters.* New York: HarperCollins, 2011.

————. *Surprised by Hope: Rethinking Heaven, the Resurrection, and the Mission of the Church.* New York: HarperCollins, 2008.

Young, Frances. *Sacrifice and the Death of Christ.* London: Society for Promoting Christian Knowledge, 1975.

Young, Robert C. *Analytical Concordance to the Bible.* Grand Rapids, MI: Eerdmans, 1972.

Zodhiates, Spiros, ed. *The Complete Word Study Dictionary: New Testament.* Chattanooga, TN: AMG, 1992.

CPSIA information can be obtained
at www.ICGtesting.com
Printed in the USA
FSHW021008291221
87251FS

9 781666 714692